SIXTH EDITION

SOLVING DISCIPLINE AND CLASSROOM MANAGEMENT PROBLEMS

Methods and Models for Today's Teachers

CHARLES H. WOLFGANG

Professor of Education
Florida State University
Tallahassee, Florida

WILEY

JOHN WILEY & SONS, INC.

ACU Library
640 Bay Road
Queensbury, NY 12804

ACQUISITIONS EDITOR   Brad Hanson
SENIOR PRODUCTION EDITOR   Norine M. Pigliucci
SENIOR MARKETING MANAGER   Kate Stewart
SENIOR DESIGNER   Dawn Stanley
NEW MEDIA EDITOR   Lisa Schnettler
EDITORIAL ASSISTANT   Alec Borenstein
PRODUCTION MANAGEMENT SERVICES   Hermitage Publishing Services

This book was set in Times Roman by Hermitage Publishing Services and printed and bound by Malloy, Inc. The cover was printed by Phoenix Color Corp.

This book is printed on acid free paper. ⊗

Copyright © 2005 John Wiley & Sons, Inc. All rights reserved.

No part of this publication may be reproduced, stored in a retrieval system or transmitted in any form or by any means, electronic, mechanical, photocopying, recording, scanning or otherwise, except as permitted under Sections 107 or 108 of the 1976 United States Copyright Act, without either the prior written permission of the Publisher, or authorization through payment of the appropriate per-copy fee to the Copyright Clearance Center, Inc. 222 Rosewood Drive, Danvers, MA 01923, (978)750-8400, fax (978)646-8600. Requests to the Publisher for permission should be addressed to the Permissions Department, John Wiley & Sons, Inc., 111 River Street, Hoboken, NJ 07030-5774, (201)748-6011, fax (201)748-6008.
To order books or for customer service please, call 1-800-CALL WILEY (225-5945).

Library of Congress Cataloging-in-Publication Data

Wolfgang, Charles H.
     Solving discipline and classroom management problems: methods and models for today's
  teachers / by Charles H. Wolfgang. — 6th ed.
     p. cm
     Includes bibliographical references and index.
     ISBN 0-471-65387-X (pbk.)
        1. School discipline. 2. Classroom management. I. Title.
  LB3012.W65 2005
  371.5—dc22   2004042233

ISBN 0-471-65387-X pbk.
WIE ISBN 0-471-66163-5 pbk.

Printed in the United States of America

10 9 8 7 6 5 4 3 2 1

Dedicated to my wife Mary,
thanks, and with love, Chuck

This book is for classroom teachers and the beginning teacher who teaches and works in preschool, elementary, middle, and high schools or others who work with youth in institutional situations. In the first few days of the new school year, we quickly learn that one of the children in the class—Walter—is going to challenge our skills as a teacher and disciplinarian. When fellow teachers see our class roster they quickly state, "Oh, no, you got Walter! Better you than me. Good luck!" He destroys others' property, fights, uses profanity to the extent that parents and classmates complain, and engages in a host of other misbehaviors that require us to deal with him repeatedly, sapping our energy. The bus driver or crossing guards, cafeteria workers, the janitor, and other teachers begin a barrage of complaints about him, and they expect you to do something about Walter. It is as if he deliberately sets "fires" that we are forced to put out, taking up far too much of our teaching time and ruining the pacing and continuity of the school day. Other children are stimulated by his misbehavior as they watch his actions, and they are beginning to attempt similar activities just to see if they can get away with it, in a disruptive game of "monkey see, monkey do." Sending him to the principal's office doesn't seem to help. Although the principal tries to reason with him, three minutes after returning from the office he is up to his old tricks. In fact, he appears to look forward to those "discipline" trips.

We seem to be all alone as a teacher in our classroom. Fellow teachers and school administrators are busy at their own tasks; and we feel locked into our "classroom-cave" with 20 to 35 children who are beginning to challenge us and our authority, with one child leading the charge by throwing "hand grenades" into our daily classroom routine. We also begin to have the feeling that we are no longer in control of our classroom; depression and a sense of "battle fatigue" are quickly setting in, and we are becoming concerned that our professional evaluations might suffer. September isn't even over yet, and we are already thinking about the end of this school year. We have no idea how to regain control of our classroom and deal effectively with Walter.

There are many discipline and classroom management approaches, models, and systems available for the teacher to deal with misbehaving children such as Walter. These models (among them *T.E.T.,* Glasser, Driekurs, *Assertive Discipline,* and many more) have all claimed to know the "right way" to handle difficult students. We have selected these models based on the idea that they offer clear and practical techniques for what to do with our Monday-morning encounters with the "Walters" of the world.

Chapter 1 provides a construct of general teacher behaviors, called a Teacher Behavior Continuum or TBC, that places teacher's actions on a power continuum and gives an understanding of the degree of power being used by a teacher when in conflict with a misbehaving student. The TBC construct will be used in each of the following chapters to display the techniques suggested by each model, thus permitting a comparison of techniques and methods across all models based on inherited power. Also included is a Beliefs About Discipline inventory; when that inventory is taken, you, the teacher, will gain a beginning perspective of your own degree of need for control in classroom settings and how much autonomy you are willing to grant to students. The discipline models have been grouped under three large categories or philosophies, which use similar teacher actions or techniques: Rules and Consequences (Section I), Confronting-Contracting (Section II), and Relationship-Listening (Section III).

Section I begins with Chapter 2 on behavior analysis; Chapter 3 describes Jones's *Tools for Teaching: Instruction, Discipline, and Motivation* (formally Jones's *Cooperative Discipline*); and Chapter 4 presents Canter's *Assertive Discipline.* All of these Rules-Consequences discipline models give the teacher, through the methods suggested, much control for shaping student behavior based on previously established rules, and obtaining compliance to these rules by using both positive and negative consequences.

Section II includes Chapter 5, which describes Albert's *Cooperative Discipline,* merged with Dreikurs's *Discipline Without Tears;* Chapter 6, which presents Curwin/Mendler's *Discipline with Dignity;* and Chapter 7, which introduces Fay and Funk's *Love and Logic.* These models use less power than Rules and Consequences models, but they do challenge or confront the student to stop the misbehavior, and offer a cooperative process of coming to an agreement or contract for more positive change in the student's behavior.

Section III is narrowed to only one model, that contained in Chapter 8, which describes Gordon's *T.E.T.: Teacher Effectiveness Training.* T.E.T. grants maximum power to students to rationally consider their behavior and choose to make behavioral changes based on their problem-solving abilities—punishment and sanctions are not used.

In each of these chapters we have, in very abbreviated form, presented a series of theories, books, or ideas that are nationally known and point out the techniques or methods that might aid teachers.

Section IV involves designing one's own model of discipline. All the techniques and methods in the seven models described in sections I through III can now be compared with a matrix using the TBC as a power continuum. Each of the seven models is a *reactive* model—that is, it provides the teacher with practical actions for dealing with limit setting when a student breaks a rule, disrupts, or acts out. The teacher may decide to pick one of the models, believe in it totally, and implement it daily in his or her classroom. But teachers are often eclectic in their teaching actions, and the matrix display of all techniques in Chapter 9 permits teachers to build their own reactive discipline model that fits their philosophy for limit setting with students and thus determine the degree of power needed to manage or deal with a specific classroom of students.

Section V is entitled Proactive or Preventive Models of Discipline. The reactive discipline models tell us what to do on Monday morning with the Walters who challenge us with their misbehavior and prevent us from teaching. There are other respected proactive models that do not help us on the spot with Walter, but take the position that schools and classroom teachers must establish a process of educating students beforehand as to how to mediate potential conflict that might arise in a school setting, how to develop social skills, and how to treat rule making and consequences in a humanistic manner based on our judicious democratic rights. Thus, Chapter 10, which describes Schrumpf, Crawford, and Bodine's *Peer Mediation: Conflict Resolution in Schools,* is a formal, well-developed proactive mediation program in which students in conflict can bring their problem to a mediation process that would be run by a student facilitator, thus heading off a wide variety of school problems that could result in aggression and disciplinary actions.

Chapter 11, Cathercoal's *Judicious Discipline,* contains another proactive program or model that enlists teachers in accepting the manner in which school and classroom rules are democratically created, and encourages them to view their dealings with students who break rules in a manner congruent with judicious democratic ideals. Rules are built on the Bill of Rights and enforced with regard to due process—the students thus learn to live in a democratic society, and are not managed and controlled through an arbitrary authoritarian manner.

Chapter 12 describes McGinnis and Goldstein's *Skillstreaming—Teaching Prosocial Skills,* another program that takes the position that the reason for many of the disruptive behaviors seen in schools today is because these students have never been taught prosocial skills. Through direct instruction, the model teaches those prosocial skills, drawing from a list of 50 to 60 identified skills. The proactive teaching and training will then have the direct effect of less misbehavior in the classroom and in the wider society.

Section VI deals with today's violent student. Too often the front page in our newspapers or the lead story on the evening news shows a shocking incident involving raw violence in our schools, with fights between students, attacks on teachers, shootings, and negative gang activity. Nationally, teachers are quietly being trained on how to deal with a potentially violent student or situation and how to use methods to keep themselves safe while the acting-out student is restrained or transported to a safe location. Chapter 13 introduces the teacher to these ideas and methods, but hands-on, physically engaging workshops are needed to implement these safety processes.

Section VII, Classroom Management (i.e., the arrangement of furniture in our classrooms, grouping and movement of students, the creation of rules, and a host of other daily management activities), demonstrates that when these management activities are done poorly, they actually are instrumental in causing disruptive behaviors requiring disciplinary actions. In Chapter 14 we summarize the classic research and writings of Kounin, Evertson, and Emmer concerning classroom management for the elementary and secondary levels.

Section VII, Working with Parents, is a response to teachers reading earlier editions of this book who have requested help in dealing with parents. When working with a challenging student who is disruptive, there comes a point when parents or guardians are involved in this process. Sometimes support and help come from these student's parents, but often this is not the case. Some parents become defensive, hostile, or threatening to the teacher and school officials. By their own actions, they may become a part of the problem or perhaps the cause of it. Chapter 15 presents a construct for looking at the behavior of parents, viewing this behavior regarding their or their child's blocked need, evaluating the seriousness of the situation, and then applying human relationship skills (or discipline skills) learned in Chapters 2 to 12 in dealing with these challenging parents. The constructs will give an orderliness to parent behavior, helping us to know how to respond.

At the end of most chapters, the reader will find a list of key concepts for review purposes and a discussion of the strengths and limitations of each model. Following the strengths and limitations sections are quotes from Alfie Kohn. Kohn, with his books *Punishment by Rewards: The Trouble with Gold Stars, Incentive Plans, A's, Praise, and Other*

Bribes; Beyond Discipline: From Compliance to Community, and a host of others, has become today's mother (or actually father) of all discipline critics and is strongly critical of nearly all the models of discipline today. Educational practices, including discipline practices, historically seem to swing much like a pendulum over time from very conservative positions (high-stakes testing, grading of school success based on academics, and the use of rewards and punishment) to that of more open humanistic practices (constructionist learning, developmentally appropriate practices, and the teaching of social problem solving). Kohn's views have filled a void that has existed for many years for an advocate of the humanistic position. Because of his crisp, searing, and insightful criticism, he is quoted at the end of the chapters to encourage reflection by the reader and possibly among students of discipline methods. Also, at the end of the models chapters are four discipline incidents or vignettes, with one chosen to show how that chapter's model would deal with such a child or situation. In the Appendix, another group of real-life discipline incidents are described, permitting still further discussion and application of the practices suggested.

A style note: In order to avoid the awkward writing construction of constantly using "his or her" or "he or she" to refer to the teacher, we often will simply use one gender at a time. Because teaching is a field shared by women and men alike, we will use both genders at various times throughout this text. The use of only one gender at a time, however, should not be taken as an indication that the concepts being presented are more relevant for, or the problems encountered would be more often associated with, one gender rather than the other.

ACKNOWLEDGMENTS

A special thanks to all of our colleagues and the many teachers who read this manuscript and offered their insights and suggestions, and to Pat Carrico for her excellent editing and solid and wise advice.

Charles H. Wolfgang

CONTENTS

SECTION VI
VIOLENCE, GANGS, AND LEGAL ACTIONS

SECTION VII
CLASSROOM MANAGEMENT

CHAPTER 1

DISCIPLINE, TEACHER POWER, AND SYSTEMS OF MANAGEMENT

Mr. Leonard's eleventh-grade government class has 36 students in it, and every desk in the room is occupied—in fact, two students have to sit at a display table at the back of the room. The class is quietly working on an assignment from the textbook, when a commotion erupts in the middle of the room. George, a small, quiet student is frantically looking around and under his desk. Many of the students are watching him and some start to laugh softly. Mr. Leonard moves to George and, speaking softly so others will not be disturbed, asks, "George, what's the matter?" George replies, "Someone swiped my hat!" Kathy, who sits next to George, says, "Mike took it. I saw him!" Mike retorts, "I didn't take it. Check it out; I don't have his stupid hat." Kathy insists, "You do, too!"

Mr. Leonard moves closer to Mike and makes eye contact. He watches to make Mike and George aware that he has seen the difficulty and is providing them with time to resolve this situation themselves. (*Looking.*) The conflict continues! "When you take someone's property and disrupt the class, we lose valuable time. I find that quite annoying." (*Naming.*) Mr. Leonard backs out of Mike's "personal space" and gives him several minutes to respond. Mike takes a baseball hat from inside his desk, places it on his head, throws his feet up onto his desk, and smiles broadly at Mr. Leonard—he is defiant.

"What is the rule regarding personal property?" the teacher asks. "What are you going to do to solve this problem, Mike, so that we may all get back to our work?" (*Questioning.*) Mr. Leonard is still speaking in a soft voice so only the students near George and Mike can hear.

"Mike, put your feet on the floor and return the hat to George," Mr. Leonard states. (*Commanding.*) There is still no action from Mike. "If you cannot quickly put your feet on the floor and return the cap now, I will need to call in Mr. Mack, the assistant principal, and Mr. Baker from across the hall, and we will escort you from the classroom to the principal's office," Mr. Leonard adds. (*Preparatory command.*) "Return George's hat now!" (*Command.*) The four neighboring students turn to look at Mike; slowly he pushes the hat toward George and seats himself with his feet on the floor. If Mike had not responded, Mr. Leonard would have followed through on his stated intent to remove the student. (*Acting.*)

Note: This scenario could apply to an elementary school or even preschool classroom as well.

For purposes of this example, we have successfully ended the incident with George's hat being returned with limited disruption to most of the other students and ongoing classroom activity. However, the experienced teacher realizes that this incident may have degenerated into a situation requiring the teacher's acting to actually remove Mike, restrain

George (who might angrily strike out), or to take some other action to get the students back to their classroom work activity.

When a student acts in an inappropriate manner in our classroom, we ask, "What should be done to stop this behavior?" The natural tendency, especially for a beginning teacher, is to rush toward the student, state in a loud and forceful manner what the student must not do *(high-profile desist)* (Kounin, 1970). If compliance were not obtained, the teacher would begin a search for the hat or physically remove Mike.

TEACHER BEHAVIOR CONTINUUM (TBC)

The confrontation between Mike and Mr. Leonard over the missing hat is an example of those myriad small desist requests—or "teachable moments"—that a classroom teacher faces daily in working with students. The incident is dealt with in a matter of minutes, and we saw the teacher escalate up the continuum of behaviors as he intervened, modifying his approach as he received—or failed to receive—certain responses. With some students, especially physically and verbally aggressive students, these teachable moments may arise five or six times in an hour and occur daily. We may be required over many weeks and months to handle such incidents with one particular student. The many techniques found in the following chapters can be of great help to the teacher.

The general categories of behavior that Mr. Leonard used may be called a Teacher Behavior Continuum or TBC. TBC suggests a power continuum of teacher action, moving from the minimum power of *looking* to the maximum power of *acting* or physical intervention (Figure 1.1). This escalation to more powerful techniques on the TBC also reflects a very real attitudinal and philosophical change on the part of the intervening teacher. This attitude change may be characterized by the three defined philosophies of discipline: *Relationship-Listening, Confronting-Contracting,* and *Rules and Consequences.*

The Relationship-Listening philosophy requires the use of minimum power: *looking* and *naming.* The Confronting-Contracting method of intervention involves *questioning.* The Rules and Consequences "face" requires the use of *commanding, acting,* or *modeling.* The TBC becomes a "clothesline" related to moveable degrees of power, and each of the models presented in the following chapters will use the continuum to display the concrete techniques within that model that are available to the teacher when dealing with a discipline incident.

A CONTINUUM OF DISCIPLINE AND MANAGEMENT MODELS

The three philosophies of discipline may also be placed on a continuum from minimum to maximum use of power with this same TBC. The continuum reflects the level of autonomy

↑ Looking	↑ Naming	↑ Questioning	↑ Commanding	↑ Acting/ modeling/ reinforcement

FIGURE 1.1 Teacher Behavior Continuum

and control given to the student to change his own behavior or the coercive or aversive actions used by the teacher or school officials to get the desired change in student behavior and reestablish order and safety in the educational setting. Figure 1.2 displays the categories, processes, and models that fit this construct. These models *(T.E.T., Peer Mediation, Assertive Discipline, Positive, etc.)* will be described in full detail in the following chapters.

The models—based on psychological theory and, to a lesser extent, research data—serve as the knowledge base of practical techniques and skills needed to handle the wide variety of discipline situations and, to a limited extent, classroom management procedures that the educator will face in today's school setting. Knowing these many models will provide teachers with the widest understanding of today's methods and thus empower them in their classrooms.

To help gain a new perspective on their own philosophical orientation toward discipline, readers are advised to stop at this point and go to the end of this chapter and take the *Beliefs about Discipline Inventory*. Does the inventory suggest that you are a Rules-Consequences teacher, or do you prefer the Confronting-Contracting methods, or, finally, can you grant students as much autonomy and power as that found in the Relationship-Listening model?

	Teacher's Power				
	Maximum		Minimum		
Category	Reactive models			Proactive models	Administrative
	Rules-Consequences	Confronting-Contracting	Relationship-Listening	Creating School Climates	Coercive-Legalistic
Process	Controlling, Rewards, and Punishment	Educational and Counseling	Therapeutic	Judicious, Mediating, and Skill Training	Restraining, Exclusionary, and Legal
Models	Alberto/Troutman's *Applied Behavior Analysis for Teachers* Kauffman, Mostert, Trent, and Hallahan, *Managing Classroom Behavior: A Reflective Case-Based Approach* Jones's *Tools for Teaching: Instruction, Discipline, and Motivation* Canter's *Assertive Discipline*	Dreikurs's *Discipline without Tears* Albert's *Cooperative Discipline* Glasser's *Reality Therapy, Schools without Failure, The Quality School* Fay and Funk's *Love and Logic: Taking Control of the Classroom* Curwin/Mendler's *Discipline with Dignity*	Gordon's *T.E.T.: Teacher Effectiveness Training, Teaching Children Self-Discipline.*	Schrumpf, Crawford, Bodine, *Peer Mediation* Gathercoal, *Judicious Discipline* McGinnis and Goldstein, *Skillstreaming*	CPI—Crisis Prevention Institute

FIGURE 1.2   Today's Discipline Models

DEFINING DISCIPLINE AND CLASSROOM MANAGEMENT

As we display the teacher techniques in the following chapters, we will not only use the TBC, but also the five systems that must be in place in a well-organized classroom:

- Limit setting (stops misbehavior)
- Professional-administrative backup system (isolating a student and enlisting the help of colleagues, parents, and other professionals)
- Incentive system (maintains, increases, and speeds up desired student behaviors)
- Encouragement system (encourages positive behavior focusing on one very difficult student)
- Management/classroom structure (establishing or creating rules and organizing classroom objects, furniture, and the students to support and maintain desired behavior)

Limit Setting

Basic to all discipline is the ability to set effective limits. Limit setting and getting a student to desist (Kounin, 1970) is used in open field supervision (hallways, cafeteria, playground, etc.) and in the classroom when one or more students are failing to follow rules or preventing the teacher from teaching and other students from learning. Stated simply, limit setting is a request to the student that says, "Stop what you are doing, and get back to work" (Jones, 1987). Limit setting will start with the small day-in, day-out off-task behaviors that can potentially escalate into a crisis. Each limit-setting action by the teacher carries with it an inherent degree of power; your crucial skill in limit setting is knowing how much power is appropriate to use in a given situation. Employing too much power would be like using a sledgehammer to drive a tack, whereas too little may communicate to the student that you are afraid or do not mean business (Jones, 1987). Most of the discipline models described in the following chapters focus on limit setting and will give the teacher many alternative actions and viewpoints.

Professional-Administrative Backup System

When you have used all your limit-setting methods and techniques (described in detail in the various models), and the student's behavior is still disrupting the classroom, you may need to declare that this student's actions and behavior are beyond your skills and abilities. You would, through a professional-administrative backup system, use various forms of isolation and seek professional help from others outside your classroom. Such professionals might include other teachers, the school counselor, school psychologist, and various mental health organizations, or—in the most extreme cases—even institutionalized care for the student. The actions of the student could also involve criminal behavior, which could require the intervention of the administration, school board, police, juvenile authorities, and the court system.

Incentive System

While the limit-setting system provides techniques for getting students to stop their misbehavior, the incentive system is a classroom process for motivating students to increase their positive behaviors or to acquire new behaviors not already in their repertoire. Examples would include getting students to do their homework or to care for school property. Incentives suggest that we can understand what motivates students to act in positive ways and can take action based on that knowledge, thus helping students to become self-disciplined and productive. The fascinating aspect for the teacher is that each of the major models will have a very different view of "what motivates students" and, at times, will be openly hostile to other viewpoints. Finally, it will be the teacher's role to decide which of these viewpoints fit their philosophy or personality.

Encouragement System

We may have very difficult students for whom the incentive or rewards system does not work—in fact this student, by his behavior, may actually destroy the incentive system for the other students in the classroom. We view this student as discouraged and wanting to "get even" with his peers, the teachers, school, or life in general. The encouragement system is an individualized, targeted system to deal with the very discouraged and difficult student.

Management/Classroom Structure

Before her, the teacher has a group of 30 high school students in five rows. She walks up and down the aisles, passing out handouts to each student. The waiting students become bored and begin to chatter, which is against the teacher's rules, and finally the class becomes disruptive. Before distributing the handouts, the teacher could have counted them into stacks of five, placed these on the desk of the first child in each row, and told her to pass the papers back. Within seconds, the teacher could be into her lesson, with everyone having the handout. The key to eliminating many discipline problems is understanding and using the elements of classroom management: (1) the design of classroom objects, furniture, and materials; (2) the arrangement of students in large and small groups, including one-to-one interaction; (3) the creation, establishment, and teaching of rules; and (4) the accepted procedures of the schoolwide staff and administration regarding open field management of the total school environment (hallways, cafeteria, playground, and similar areas).

SUMMARY

The many discipline/management models can be understood by answering the following questions: "If Mike was constantly talking and disrupting our lecture, and if, when confronted, he became belligerent to the extreme that he would shout, swear, and become threatening and violent, how would we *set limits* with Mike? If we need a *backup system* that enlists the help of the principal, what are the steps and procedures for getting this help? Can we motivate Mike to be attentive and do his work with a classroom *incentive system,* or does his behavior require us to design an *encouragement system* that fits his unique needs? Finally, could we change our *management system* in the form of a desk arrangement that would permit Mike to talk to his peers when it is desired during group work, then move these desks again when silence is needed?"

REFERENCES

The Reactive Models
Rules-Consequences
Behavior Analysis

Alberto, P. A., and Troutman, A. C. *Applied Behavior Analysis for Teachers,* 3rd ed. New York: Merrill-Macmillan, 1990.

Kauffman, J. M., Mostert, M. P., Trent, S. C., and Hallahan, D. P. *Managing Classroom Behavior: A Reflective Case-Based Approach,* 3rd ed. Boston: Allyn and Bacon, 2002.

Jone's Positive Discipline

Jones, F. *Positive Discipline.* New York: McGraw-Hill, 1987.

Jones, F. *Tools for Teaching: Discipline, Instruction, and Motivation.* Santa Cruz, CA: Fredric H. Jones & Associates, Inc, 2000.

Assertiveness Training

Alberti, R. E., and Emmons, M. L. *Stand Up, Speak Out, Talk Back.* New York: Pocket Books, 1975.

Alberti, R. E. *Your Perfect Right: A Guide to Assertive Living.* San Luis Obispo, CA: Impact Publishing, 1982.

Canter, L., and Canter, M. *Assertive Discipline: A Take Charge Approach for Today's Educator.* Seal Beach, CA: Canter and Associates, 1976.

Love and Discipline Model

Dobson, J. *Hide or Seek.* Old Tappan, NJ: Fleming H. Revell Company, 1974.

Dobson, J. *The Strong Willed Child.* Wheaton, IL: Tyndale House Publishers, 2002.

Dobson, J. *The New Dare to Discipline.* Wheaton, IL: Tyndale House Publishers, 2003.

Confronting-Contracting
Adlerian

Albert, L. *Teacher's Guide to Cooperative Discipline: How to Manage Your Classroom and Promote Self-Esteem.* Circle Pines, MN: American Guidance Service, 1989.

Dinkmeyer, D., and Dreikurs, R. *Encouraging Children to Learn: The Encouragement Process.* Englewood Cliffs, NJ: Prentice-Hall, 1963.

Dreikurs, R. *Children: The Challenge.* New York: E. P. Dutton, 1964.

Dreikurs, R. *Psychology in the Classroom: A Manual for Teachers,* 2nd ed. New York: Harper & Row, 1968.

Dreikurs, R., and Cassel, P. *Discipline without Tears: What to Do with Children Who Misbehave,* rev. ed. New York: Hawthorn Books, 1972.

Dreikurs, R., and Loren, G. *Logical Consequences.* New York: Meredith Press, 1968.

Nelson, J., Duffy, R., Escobar, L., Ortolano, K., and Owen-Sohocki, D. *Positive Discipline: A Teacher's A–Z Guide.* Roseville, CA: Prima Publishing, 1996.

Nelson, J., Lynn, L., and Glenn, H. S. *Positive Discipline in the Classroom: Developing Mutual Respect, Cooperation, and Responsibility in Your Classroom,* rev. 3rd ed. Roseville, CA: Prima Publishing, 2000.

Glasser

Glasser, W. *Schools without Failure.* New York: Peter H. Wyden Publishing, 1969.

Glasser, W. *Reality Therapy: A New Approach to Psychiatry.* New York: Harper & Row, 1975.

Glasser, W. *The Quality School: Managing Students without Coercion,* 2nd ed. expanded. New York: HarperCollins, 1992.

Discipline with Dignity (Curwin/Mendler)

Curwin, R. J., and Mendler. A. *The Discipline Book: A Complete Guide to School and Classroom Management.* Reston, VA: Reston Publishing, 1980.

Curwin, R. J., and Mendler. A. (1984). "High Standards for Effective Discipline." *Educational Leadership, 41,* 8 (1984): 75–76.

Curwin, R. J., and Mendler. A. *Discipline with Dignity.* Alexandria, VA: Association for Supervision and Curriculum Development, 1988.

Relationship-Listening
Rogerian

Gordon, T. *T.E.T.: Teacher Effectiveness Training.* New York: Peter H. Wyden Publishing, 1974.

Gordon, T. *Teaching Children Self-Discipline: At Home and at School.* New York: Times Books, 1988.

Transactional Analysis (TA)

Berne, E. *Games People Play: Psychology of Human Relations.* New York: Grove Press, 1964.

Harris, T. A. *I'm OK—You're OK: A Practical Guide to Transactional Analysis.* New York: Harper & Row, 1969.

The Discipline Critic
Views of Alfie Kohn

Kohn, A. *No Contest: The Case against Competition,* rev. ed. Boston: Houghton Mifflin, 1992.

Kohn, A. *What to Look for in a Classroom and Other Essays.* San Francisco: Jossey-Bass Publishers, 1998.

Kohn, A. *The Schools Our Children Deserve: Moving Beyond Traditional Classrooms and "Tougher Standards."* Boston: Houghton Mifflin, 1999.

Kohn, D. *Punished by Rewards: The Trouble with Gold Stars, Incentive Plans, A's, Praise, and other Bribes.* Boston: Houghton Mifflin, 1993.

THE PROACTIVE MODELS

Skillstreaming

Goldstein, A. P., Sprafkin, R. P., Gershaw, N., and Klein, P. *Skillstreaming the Adolescent: A Structured Learning Approach to Teaching Prosocial Skills.* Champaign, IL: Research Press, 1980.

McGinnis, E., and Goldstein, A. P. *Skillstreaming in Early Childhood: Teaching Prosocial Skills to the Preschool and Kindergarten Child.* Champaign, IL: Research Press, 1990.

McGinnis, E., and Goldstein, A. P. *Skillstreaming the Elementary School Child.* Champaign, IL: Research Press, 1997.

Judicious Discipline

Gathercoal, F. *Judicious Discipline.* Davis, CA: Caddo Gap Press, 1991.

Peer Mediation

Bodine, R. J., Crawford, D. K. and Schrumpf, F. *Creating the Peaceable School: A Comprehensive Program for Teaching Conflict Resolution.* Champaign, IL: Research Press, 1994.

Schrumpf, F., Crawford, D. and Usadel, H. C. *Peer Mediation: Conflict Resolution in Schools.* Champaign, IL: Research Press, 1991.

Dealing with Classroom Violence

Crisis and Violence Management

Nonviolent Crisis Intervention for the Educator: Vol. III, *The Assaultive Student.* Brookfield, WI: National Crisis Prevention Institute, Inc., 2003.

Classroom Management

Emmer, E. E., Evertson, C. M., Sanford, J. P., Clements, B. S., and Worsham, M. E. *Classroom Management for Secondary Teachers.* Englewood Cliffs, NJ: Prentice-Hall, 1984.

Evertson, C., and Anderson, L. "Effective Classroom Management at the Beginning of the School Year," *Elementary School Journal.* Chicago: University of Chicago Press, 1980.

Evertson, C. M., Emmer, E. E., Clements, B. S., Sanford, J. P., and Worsham, M. E. *Classroom Management for Elementary Teachers.* Englewood Cliffs, NJ: Prentice-Hall, 1984.

Kounin, J. *Discipline and Group Management in Classrooms.* New York: Holt, Rinehart, and Winston, 1970.

BELIEFS ABOUT DISCIPLINE INVENTORY

This 12-question inventory will give you insights about yourself and where your personality and the discipline techniques you use would fall under the three philosophies of discipline. In each question, you are asked to choose between two competing value statements. For some questions, you will definitely agree with one statement and disagree with the second, making it easy for you to choose; for others, however, you will agree or disagree with both, and you must choose the one you more closely identify with. There is no "right" or "wrong" answer, merely indicators of your own personal view.

Forced Choices   *Instructions:* Circle A or B to indicate the statement with which you identify the most. You must chose between the two statements for each item.

1. a. Because students' thinking is limited, rules need to be established for them by mature adults.

   b. Each student's emotional needs must be taken into consideration, rather than having some preestablished rule imposed on all.

2. a. During the first class session of the new school year, the teacher needs to assign each student his or her own desk or table space, and the student should be taught routinely to take that space after transitions.

   b. Groups of students can decide through a class meeting what rules they need to govern themselves.

3. a. Students should be given a choice as to which topics for projects they wish to select. Once they choose, they must keep to that decision for most of that grading period.

   b. The materials students must learn and the tasks to be performed must be determined by the teacher, and a specific sequence of instruction to accomplish these goals must be followed.

4. The books and similar classroom equipment are being misused, soiled, and at times destroyed. I will most likely:

a. Hold a class meeting, show the damaged books to the class, and ask them how we may solve this problem, including what action should be taken toward a student found to be misusing books.

b. Physically remove or limit the number of books available, and observe closely to see who was misusing the books; I would then tell that student how such action was affecting other students and how I felt about such loss of books.

5. Two students of equal power and abilities are in a rather loud verbal conflict over a classroom material; I would:

a. Attempt to see that this does not get out of control by approaching the students, telling them of the classroom rule, and demanding that they desist in their actions. I will promise a sanction if they fail to comply.

b. Avoid interfering in something that the students need to resolve themselves.

6. a. A student strongly requests not to work with the group today. I would permit this, feeling that this student has some emotional concerns related to the group experience.

b. One student is being refused entrance into group activities; I would raise this as an issue in a class meeting and ask for a discussion of the reasons and possible solutions from the student and the group.

7. The noise in the classroom is at such a high level that it is bothering me; I would:

a. Flick the classroom lights to get the class' attention, ask the students to become quiet, and later praise those who are talking quietly.

b. Select the two or three students really making most of the noise, take them aside to ask them to reflect (think) about their behavior and how it might affect others, and get an agreement with them to work quietly.

8. During the first few days of class I would:

a. Permit the students to test their ability to get along as a new group and make no predetermined rules until the students feel they are needed.

b. Immediately establish the class rules and the fair sanction I will apply if these rules are broken.

9. My response to swearing by a student is:

a. The student is frustrated by a classmate and has responded by swearing, so I do not reprimand the student but encourage him to talk out what is bothering him.

b. I bring the two students together in a "knee-to-knee" confronting relationship and attempt to get them to work out this conflict while I ask questions and keep the focus on the negotiation.

10. If a student disrupts class while I am trying to lecture, I would:

a. Ignore the disruption if possible and/or move the student to the back of the room as a consequence of his misbehavior.

b. Express my feeling of discomfort to the student about being disrupted from my task.

11. a. Each student must realize that there are some school rules that need to be obeyed, and any student who breaks them will be punished in the same fair manner.

b. Rules are never written in stone and can be renegotiated by the class, and sanctions will vary with each student.

12. If a student refuses to put away his work or materials after using them, I would most likely:

a. Express to the student how not putting his things away will affect future activities in this space, and how frustrating this will be for everyone. I would then leave the materials where they are for the remainder of the day.

b. Confront the student to reflect on his behavior, think about how his non-compliance affects others, and tell him that if he cannot follow the rules he will lose the use of the materials in the future.

Scoring Key and Interpretation Take your responses and circle them on the tables provided:

Table 1		Table 2		Table 3	
4b	1b	2b	4a	2a	1a
6a	5b	3a	6b	3b	5a
9a	8a	7b	9b	7a	8b
12a	10b	11b	12b	11a	10a

Total number of responses in Table 1 ____

Total number of responses in Table 2 ____

Total number of responses in Table 3 ____

The table for which the total number of responses was the highest indicates the school of thought or philosophy in which your values tend to be clustered. Table 1 is Relationship-Listening, Table 2 is Confronting-Contracting, and Table 3 is Rules and Consequences. The table with the next highest score would be your second choice, and the table with the least number may be the philosophy that you associate with the least. If your responses are equally distributed across all three tables, you may be an eclectic teacher who picks and chooses from all philosophies or your philosophy may not have consolidated at this time in your training.

RULES AND CONSEQUENCES

WE **HAVE** described three large categories of philosophies as Relationship-Listening, Confronting-Contracting, and Rules and Consequences. We will begin in Section 1 with Rules and Consequences models. The philosophies of RC models are the most powerful or controlling models, with a methodology that clearly states rules for behavior. The teacher defines and decides what behavior is wanted and assertively takes actions through rewards to get the positive behavior sought. Generally, these methods are based on behavioral theory, while some punishment used would not fit behavioral principles.

CHAPTER 2. The Behavior Analysis Model provides the most complete and true definition of concepts and principles from classical behavioral theory.

CHAPTER 3. Positive Discipline (as defined by Fredric Jones), and now called Tools for Teaching: Discipline, Instruction, and Motivation, is a behavioral model with a fairly precise use of behavioral principles, but adapted into a unique model by Jones for classroom application.

CHAPTER 4. Assertive Discipline appears on the surface to be a behavioral model, but actually it takes its conceptual framework from the assertiveness training movement. We will see praise for good behavior and negative consequences for misbehavior.

CHAPTER 2

THE BEHAVIOR ANALYSIS MODEL

Theorist/Writer: B. F. Skinner
- *Science and Human Behavior*
- *Beyond Freedom and Dignity*

Theorist/Writers for Teachers:

- P. A. Alberto and A. C. Troutman, *Applied Behavior Analysis for Teachers*
- Kauffman, J. M., Mostert, M. P., Trent, S. C., and D. P. Hallahan, *Managing Classroom Behavior: A Reflective Case-Based Approach*
- C. Madsen and C. Madsen, *Teaching/Discipline: A Positive Approach for Educational Development*

OUTLINE OF THE BEHAVIOR ANALYSIS MODEL

Basic Assumptions on Motivation

- Children are not born with self-control; we must help them mold it

- Deal only with outward (external behavior)

- Use scientific techniques to demonstrate effectiveness

- Be concerned with unacceptable behavior and what interventions can be applied to change it

- The cause of the behavior exists outside the child, in the environment

- Motivation reinforcers:
  Positive—something we like
  Negative—something we dislike
  Primary—relating to basic body needs
  Secondary—abstracts, symbols

- The consequences, more than any other factor, determine the behavior

Teacher Behaviors

- Teacher controlling the situation, imitation and shaping, fading, and directive statements for contingency contracting

- Explicit modeling for imitation, forward and backward chaining, saturation, time out, rewards for reinforcement of desired behaviors, commands as directive statements

▨ Using conditioners in the form of material and verbal rewards

▨ Using variable intervals and variable ratios

Guidelines, Planning, or Preparatory Teacher Actions

▨ Reinforcing only the behavior to be increased

▨ Before beginning behavior modification:

    1. Select the behavior to be changed

    2. Collect and record baseline data

    3. Identify appropriate reinforcers

    4. Collect intervention data

▨ Graphing baseline and intervention data to evaluate effectiveness

▨ Changing reinforcers periodically

▨ Reinforcement schedules

OVERVIEW

Before we begin our discussion of behavior analysis techniques, let's look at a teacher in action, without the use of behavioral analysis techniques.

> *Jimmy, a kindergarten student, stands before the paint easel. Using a large, thick paintbrush, he dips the end into the paint pot and begins using it as a "sword" and attempts to "stab" Robert, one of his schoolmates. The peer screams and runs, much to Jimmy's delight. Smiling, Jimmy dips his brush into the paint pot and looks around for a new target.*
>
> *Robert huddles with two friends in the block corner to tell them of Jimmy's antics. The three classmates smile broadly as they move as a group, much like a military squad, tentatively approaching Jimmy. Jimmy dips his paintbrush again and begins stabbing out toward the approaching boys. The three boys scream gleefully and flee, knocking over another student's block building. This creates a loud crash and screams of distress from students using the blocks.*
>
> *The teacher quickly approaches Jimmy and orders, "Jimmy, behave yourself!" Jimmy drops his head before the easel and, placing the brush on the paper, makes circular scribbling actions. After the teacher leaves him alone, Jimmy begins to pump the paintbrush up and down in each of the four vividly colored paints. He continues until the colors in all four pots become a blended mess of muddy brown. The teacher reprimands, "Jimmy, look what you have done. You have mixed all four paints together. You have made them look like mud, and people can't paint with colors like this!" The teacher takes away the ruined paints and replaces them with fresh pots from a nearby easel.*
>
> *The teacher stresses, "Now, Jimmy, do not mix these colors." Once Jimmy is sure that the teacher is involved with another student, he moves so that his back is to the teacher. He dips his brush into the blue paint, then swirls it into the yellow paint. Giggling, Jimmy brings out the brush and inspects it. He reaches over to his neighbor's easel and makes a blue and yellow streak down the student's paper. The student screams, and the teacher once again appears.*

BEHAVIOR ANALYSIS TECHNIQUES

How could this teacher have intervened more successfully by using behavior analysis? The answer is to arrange consequences and measure behavioral change to help the student acquire positive behaviors.

Behavioral Objectives

When dealing with misbehavior, it is imperative to define the behavior that you wish to change in order to be clear about the target behavior. This target behavior may be selected because the current behavior is (1) a behavioral deficit, something lacking in the student's daily activities (using the paintbrush and paints incorrectly; getting to class late, etc.) or (2) a behavior that is correct in form and function but is displayed excessively or at the wrong time (asking so many questions in class that no one else has a chance to ask questions, talking during test taking, etc.).

To decrease an inappropriate target behavior exhibited by a student who fails to respond to your initial efforts and to increase his use of desirable behaviors, you must begin by choosing and defining behavioral objectives for this student and committing these objectives to writing. In order to understand the desired behavioral changes and communicate them to other staff members, you must establish a behavioral objective that identifies the following:

1. The learner
2. The antecedent conditions under which the behavior is to be displayed
3. The target behavior
4. Criteria for acceptable performance

We look again at Jimmy, with his repeated attempts at "stabbing" others, and take the first step in behavioral change by pinpointing—specifying in measurable, observable terms the behavior targeted for change. We do this by establishing a behavioral objective: "Jimmy (1. identify the learner), while at the easel (2. identify the antecedent conditions), will use the brush by marking paint on the paper (3. identify the target behavior) for three of the next four times he uses the easel (4. identify criteria for acceptable performance)." Now that the behaviors are pinpointed, the teacher may move to the next step of behavioral analysis—collecting data to help the student acquire this behavioral objective (see Figure 2.1).

Collecting Data

In the opening scenario, we saw a hard-working, well-meaning teacher attempt to intervene with Jimmy and stop his stabbing with the paintbrush. She reprimands him, physically appears before him, and changes the paint pots, even as other students run or become upset because of his actions. When we begin to understand the concept and operation of positive reinforcement, we discover that the teacher is actually part of the problem. The teacher's reinforcement, in conjunction with the reinforcement for the students and materials themselves, served to reward Jimmy for his misbehavior. This is rather typical when misbehavior is repeated—the teacher unknowingly exacerbates the situation.

Identify the *Learner* (Answers "Who")	Promotes individualization of instruction, requiring the teacher to specify the targeted student or group of students.	*Jimmy* will … (state action).
Identify the *Antecedent* conditions	Description of the preceding activity, condition, or stimuli (antecedent stimulus that sets the occasion for occurrence of the target behavior).	Jimmy, *when using the paint easel,* will place his paintbrush on the paper and paint.
Identify the target *Behavior*	What will the student be doing when desired change is achieved? The words chosen should lead to behavior that is observable, measurable/countable, and repeatable.	*Good verbs:* to mark, to remove, to put on, to label, to place, to say, to cross out, to take, to hand up, to point *Poor verbs:* to apply, to appreciate, to analyze, to understand, to select, to perform, to become competent
Identify *Criteria* for acceptable performance	Sets the standard for evaluation and defines what will be measured to determine completion of the desired behavior; may also include how long the student will perform the desired behavior (duration) or length of time from start signal or cue before the student actually starts (latency).	*Acquisition criteria:* … four days out of five … *Duration criteria:* … stay seated in circle time for 5 minutes … *Latency criteria:* … after waking up, the student will put on her socks and shoes within three minutes…

FIGURE 2.1   Components of a Behavioral Objective: "Learner A-B-C" Criteria

The classroom is a very dynamic environment for teachers, requiring attention to a host of stimuli coming from students, as well as attention to safety concerns with the materials being used. On top of all that, we have students like Jimmy, who are like hand grenades waiting to go off any minute, and who require attention time and again. We must be aware that the student's behavior might be shaping and controlling our own. We will not know for sure until we collect reliable data that can give us a perspective on just what is occurring. Most important, data will tell us if our intervention is working. If it is not, then we can use the data to improve our intervention techniques.

It is the third week of the school year, and Jimmy has made these last three weeks extremely difficult for his teacher, Mrs. Anderson. She realizes that she cannot continue "putting out fires" all year, so she makes a list of the misbehaviors that she can recall from the first two weeks. She finds that:

- Four out of five days a week, Jimmy has a temper tantrum with his parent (usually his mother) when he is dropped off in the morning.
- He has knocked over the block structures of a group of boys on four occasions. The boys involved were Mark, Robert, Walter, and Barry.
- Three out of five days, he was part of a food-throwing activity that turned into aggressive biting during snack time. At the table were Barry, Carol, Robert, and Kevin.
- During one circle time, he began violently kicking those sitting near him, Janet and Robert.

- Nearly every playground period, there is a fight over who can ride on the rickshaw, which carries three students, with Jimmy pulling the rickshaw and hitting other students. Those usually involved were Mark, Steven, and, always, Robert.

From the list, the teacher begins to see the antecedent condition leading to some form of misbehavior: aggression and disruption always involve Robert, whom the teacher considers a generally well-behaved student, and an arrival period when the mother brings Jimmy to school. Mrs. Anderson may decide to collect data on Jimmy's behavior because (1) she wants precise observations and measurements of behavior, which may enable her to determine the best way to change Jimmy's behavior and provide information about Jimmy to other teachers, his parents, school administrators, and, if need be, school counselors or psychologists; and (2) the observation/data collecting will establish a baseline, enabling her to accurately determine whether her particular intervention is working over time.

Almost desperate, Mrs. Anderson decides that Jimmy will be her special project for a one-week period. She believes the time spent on his problem is justified because of the time he is taking away from other students. She begins to focus on him proactively, rather than reactively. On Friday, she meets with her aide, Ms. Walker, and they agree to begin data gathering, using a number of measurements: (1) event recording; (2) an anecdotal report; and (3) time sampling, which indicates stages of play ranging from isolated to cooperative play. The measurements will be conducted by the aide between 10:00 A.M. and 3:30 P.M. for five days.

Event Recording

Mrs. Anderson and Ms. Walker create a cooperative system to count and record Jimmy's disruptive actions (events) over the week. On a centrally located shelf out of reach of the students, they place two plastic cups, one labeled "clips" and containing paper clips, and the second marked "disruption." When Jimmy disrupts his peers or destroys materials, the teacher or aide takes a paper clip from the supply cup and puts it in the "disruption" cup. If they are on the playground out of reach of the cups, they simply move a paper clip from their right pocket to their left pocket, which serves as a temporary "disruption" container. They create a data sheet with the five days listed and divided into four time periods. At the end of each time period, Mrs. Anderson counts the paper clips in the "disruption" cup and records the number on the data sheet (see Figure 2.2).

Graphing

Mrs. Anderson and Ms. Walker graph the total number of disruptive events for each day (see Figure 2.3). Looking at the graph over the week, it is obvious that Monday, Wednesday, and Friday were very difficult days for Jimmy, whereas Tuesday and Thursday were much easier days.

In addition, Jimmy's behavior appears to have worsened by the end of the week, as Friday showed the greatest number of disruptions. What was different on Monday, Wednesday, and Friday (antecedent condition) that set off the disruptive behavior as compared to the other two days of the week? Looking at the data sheet, the teachers could tell

Student: *Jimmy*
Observers: *Mrs. Anderson, Ms. Walker*
Behavior: *disruptive behavior toward others and objects*

	Monday	Tuesday	Wednesday	Thursday	Friday
Arrival to 10:00 A.M.	3	0	3	0	3
Snack to 12:30 P.M.	1	0	3	0	2
12:30 to 3:30 P.M.	1	1	0	1	3
3:30 P.M. to departure	1	1	0	1	2
Total	6	2	6	2	10

FIGURE 2.2   Event Recording Data Sheet

that Tuesday and Thursday morning went well for Jimmy, with only two disruptive events—both after rest period. Afternoon disruptions were steady for Monday, Tuesday, and Thursday, but there were none on Wednesday. Friday afternoon was filled with disruptions. What changed? That is, what antecedent condition was absent on Wednesday afternoon or present on Friday afternoon?

Anecdotal Report

To shed more light on Jimmy's behavior, Mrs. Anderson decides to keep an anecdotal report on Jimmy's behavior. She focuses on arrival, snack time, circle time, nap time, and outdoor play as she generally describes the disruptive events in writing. Since Robert appears consistently to be associated with Jimmy's disruptions, the teacher makes note of Robert's location during Jimmy's misbehavior. She also records her location and that of her aide.

Monday
Arrival: 7:45 A.M.
Mother brings Jimmy to school carrying six-month-old brother. Jimmy has temper tantrum and pouts. Remains passive until 9:30 A.M.

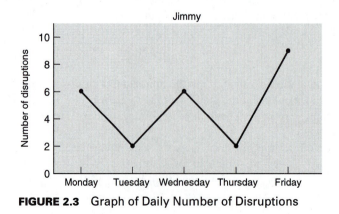

FIGURE 2.3   Graph of Daily Number of Disruptions

Snack: 10:00 A.M.
Knocks over Andy's milk, screams, and throws food at students at his table. Complains that he is not seated by Robert.

Circle time
Kicks Carol, who is seated between him and Robert.

Nap: 12:45 P.M.
Makes noises and disturbs other students. Defiant when told to desist. Ms. Walker supervising.

Playground: 3:30 P.M.
Fights over tricycle with Andy. Wants red tricycle like Robert's.

Playground: 3:50 P.M.
Goes wrong way on path and runs into other cyclists, who scream at him and knock him over.

Playground: 4:00 P.M.
Cries and goes to tire structure. Sits in tire while sucking thumb or biting sleeve for 45 minutes.

Pickup: 5:15 P.M.
Reunites well with father.

Tuesday

Arrival: 7:45 A.M.
Mother brings Jimmy. No infant with her. Jimmy begins playing with Robert immediately after mother departs.

Snack: 10:00 A.M.
Eats well at snack. At his table are Mark, Walter, Carol, Andy, Roosevelt, and Judy.

Circle time
Handles himself well. Robert seated at farthest end of circle from him.

Nap: 12:45 P.M.
Naps well but awakens defiant and moody. Refuses to put on his shoes or put blanket in storage box. Ms. Walker is supervising.

Playground: 3:05 P.M.
Sits passively in sandbox, slowly digging with small shovel in the sand. Throws sand in Mary's face. Runs to opposite side of playground and hides in bushes for 35 minutes.

Snack: 4:00 P.M.
Refuses to eat snack. Sits and pouts.

Pickup: 5:15 P.M.
Reunites poorly with father by kicking at him when he tries to put coat on Jimmy.

Wednesday

Arrival: 7:45 A.M.
Mother brings Jimmy to school carrying baby brother. Jimmy has temper tantrum and pouts passively after mother leaves. Injures his hand while hitting door as mother departs. Does not begin active play until 8:30.

Free play period: 8:45 A.M.
Using paint easel and brushes, repetitively attempts to stab passerby with paint-covered brush. Paints on neighbor's paper to displeasure of classmate.

Snack: 10:00 A.M.
Is first at snack and grabs snack basket. Shoves much of snack into his mouth and refuses to relinquish basket so others may share food. During tussle, knocks milk container from Ms. Walker's hand, spilling milk on floor.

Circle time
Sits in corner by himself. Appears withdrawn and sucks fingers.

Nap: 12:45 P.M.
Falls asleep quickly and is slow to wake up. Mrs. Anderson supervising.

Playground: 3:30 P.M.
Spends most of time on swing by himself.

Pickup: 5:15 P.M.
Reunites well with father without speaking, but appears flat and expressionless as father takes his hand to go.

Thursday

Arrival: 7:45 A.M.
Father brings Jimmy to school with no infant. Jimmy departs well and begins building LEGOs with Robert and three other boys immediately after father departs.

Snack: 10:00 A.M.
Eats well at snack, sitting with Robert at two-person table.

Circle time
Handles himself well at circle time. Robert is seated beside him and they chat in a friendly manner.

Nap: 12:45 p.m.
Naps well but awakens defiant and moody. Refuses to put on shoes or put his blanket in storage box. Begins game of "catch me if you can" by jumping from cot to cot out of Ms. Walker's reach. One cot turns over and strikes him in the face (nosebleed quickly stopped when attended to).

Afternoon
Sits in outdoor tires passively, sucking his thumb with flat expression. Participates in no activities.

Snack: 4:00 p.m.
Refuses to eat snack. Sits and pouts.

Pickup: 5:15 P.M.
Reunites warmly with father, indicating he wishes to be carried to the car "like a baby."

Friday

Arrival: 7:45 A.M.
Father brings Jimmy to school, carrying baby brother. Jimmy has temper tantrum over who will open classroom door. Refuses to hang up coat and lies on floor crying as father departs.

Snack: 10:00 A.M.
Pushes Wayne out of chair next to Robert, which develops into hair-pulling fight with Wayne. Calls other students at snack table "butt-face" and "fart-breath." Takes large bite out of Ellen's fruit, upsetting her.

Circle time
Pinches and pulls others' hair, makes noises with such volume that group activities cannot go on. He is removed from circle and moved to another area of the room by the aide, whom he attempts to bite.

Nap: 12:45 P.M.
Makes noises and disturbs other students. Is defiant when told to desist. After nap time, refuses to put on socks, shoes, and coat. Ms. Walker supervising.

Playground: 3:30 P.M.
Starts "run and chase" game, putting himself into danger positions (attempting to climb over the school fence, running into the path of students on swings, and jabbing pet rabbit with a stick). When Ms. Walker approaches, he runs to the other side of the playground and starts game again.

Playground: 4:00 P.M.
Falls on playground steps, scratches knee, and cuts chin (both bleed slightly).

Pickup: 5:15 P.M.
Cries when father appears. Continues crying as father carries him to car.

The anecdotal data, when added to the accounts of daily disruptions, suggest a number of hypotheses to the teacher:

1. Generally, on arrival, Jimmy had temper tantrums when his baby brother was in a parent's arms. This suggests a series of antecedent events that set a negative tone for the entire day. This possibly calls for a conference with the parents to show them the data and suggest a morning arrangement without the infant in tow.

2. Waking up from rest period was difficult for Jimmy, except on the day when Mrs. Anderson was supervising. More data are needed before any conclusions can be drawn.

3. Jimmy appears to want friendship with Robert. Their relationship is warm and cooperative at some times and hostile at others. More data and observation are needed, but at this early stage we might see the goal of teaching the two boys how to work together.

The teacher now has solid data related to Jimmy's level of functioning and the antecedent conditions leading to his misbehavior. She can now establish goals for dealing with Jimmy, and out of these goals she can set clear behavioral objectives. The objectives, which should be stated positively, might involve helping Jimmy:

- Arrive at school more effectively.
- Play and work with Robert.
- Wake up from rest period in a cooperative manner.
- Acquire social skills as identified by social competency levels.
- Follow group rules in group settings such as circle time and snack.

Understandably, the teacher cannot achieve all of these goals at once. But she can select the more immediate behavior to work on and then, over time, gradually make real and lasting changes with Jimmy by achieving each of the goals.

The teacher should continue collecting and graphing data on Jimmy. Valuable insights may be obtained regarding the frequency of conflicts with Robert; how long Jimmy can play with blocks (duration recording), paint, or engage in sociodramatic play; how long it takes to wake up (latency recording) and become productive; the loudness of his rest-time noises that disturb others (measure of intensity); and whether he has acquired certain defined skills, such as tying his shoes, pouring his juice at snack, and so on (simple yes-no measurement-criterion recording). All these measurements can be graphed to display the data in a manner that enables the teacher to see if the behavioral procedures are effective.

Reinforcement and Other Consequences

The basic view of behavior analysis is that good behavior and misbehavior are learned. In other words, Jimmy's behavior occurs as a result of the consequences of his preceding behavior. Behavior that is followed by a desired consequence, or positive reinforcer, tends to be repeated and thus learned. Behavior that is followed by an unpleasant consequence, or a punisher, tends not to be repeated.

Jimmy's stabbing with the paintbrush and mixing paints together, failing to follow the teacher's commands, and painting on the neighbor's paper were the result of Jimmy's having learned to behave this way. The peers (Robert and the attack squad), the screaming neighbor, and, most important, the teacher have unknowingly reinforced Jimmy's misbehavior by giving him the attention he was seeking.

Reinforcement is a behavioral principle that describes a direct relationship between two real events: a behavior (any observable action: Jimmy stabs at Robert with a paintbrush) and a consequence (a result of the action: Robert screams and runs away). There are two kinds of reinforcement: positive and negative. Care should be given in using these terms, for positive reinforcement is not always good for a student and negative reinforcement is not always bad. The key is what kind of behavior increases when these reinforcers are applied.

Positive Reinforcement

Positive reinforcement is observed when a behavior is followed by a consequence that increases the behavior's likelihood of reoccurring. That is, Jimmy gets a strong response to his actions, and his actions increase.

In our scenario, Jimmy was reinforced at least 10 times in a very short time period. Let's look at just one behavior and a few of the reinforcers (in italics) that follow:

Behavior: Jimmy pumps the paintbrush up and down in each pot, rotating his brush from one pot to the next.

Consequence: The teacher reprimands (*provides attention, a positive reinforcer for Jimmy*), "Jimmy, look what you have done. You have mixed all four paints together. You have made them look like mud, and people can't paint with colors like this!"

Consequence: The teacher takes away the ruined paints and replaces them with fresh pots. (*By replacing the paints, the teacher has unknowingly positively reinforced and concretely rewarded Jimmy for his inappropriate actions.*)

Consequence: The teacher stresses, "Now, Jimmy, do not mix these colors!" (*The teacher rewards Jimmy by talking and interacting with him.*)

A reinforcer can only be judged as positive or negative based on its effect on an individual student in a specific time context and situation. On the surface, all of the teacher's reprimanding statements ("Jimmy, behave yourself!" "Jimmy, look what you've done…") may seem like negative reprimands or punishing statements. For this particular student, however, they are really positive reinforcers. The true test for defining a consequence as a positive reinforcer, then, is if the behavior followed by a consequence increases over time.

Punishment

On the other hand, an event is viewed as punishment only if it is followed by a consequence that decreases the behavior over time. Thus, paddling, for example, may be seen by the general public as punishment, but for some students getting paddled enables them to gain status in the eyes of their peers. So the action may actually be a positive reinforcer resulting in increased misbehavior. Getting paddled for misbehaving might positively reinforce a student whose father rarely pays attention to her, even though she cries during and after the paddling. But if she continues the misbehavior, then punishment is really not taking place—reinforcement is actually occurring.

Note: The general public often confuses negative reinforcement, explained later, and punishment. When reinforcement is used, a behavior will increase. When punishment is used, a behavior will decrease. Behavior analysts use the word *punishment* to describe a specific, observable, and concrete relationship: punishment has occurred only when the behavior followed by punishment decreases.

Much of the so-called punishment delivered in schools today is ineffective because it generally does not decrease target behaviors, and there is little observation to determine the real effects in terms of the student's actions. The common use of time out, for example, can be considered punishment only if a functional relationship can be established between the student's behavior and the application of the consequence, resulting in the decrease in the behavior's rate of occurrence.

Negative Reinforcement

The concept of negative reinforcement is somewhat more difficult to define than punishment. Essentially, it involves steps designed to lead the student to appropriate action (i.e., increase certain kinds of behavior) in order to escape or avoid an unwanted consequence.

For example, Margaret, when awakened from her nap, is generally noncompliant and refuses to leave her cot, put on her shoes and socks, go to the toilet, and move outside for the daily routine of playground period and snack. The teacher says, "Margaret, we are having juice Popsicles (her favorite) at the picnic table on the playground today. If you get up and move soon, you can get to the playground before they melt or have to be put away, and you won't miss out on your treat today."

The use of negative reinforcement enables the teacher to avoid or terminate an unpleasant situation if the behavioral goal is achieved. It is the contingent removal (if you get up and act, this will not occur) of an aversive stimulus (missing out on the treat) that increases the probability of the response (the student gets up, uses the toilet, and quickly moves outside). The student must act to avoid the aversive stimulus. In this way, appropriate behavior will increase. In contrast, punishment is intended so that the consequences will decrease the inappropriate behavior.

Use Negative Reinforcement and Punishment Sparingly

Suppose you ask other teachers for solutions for dealing with a student who is causing considerable difficulty. Many of their solutions are likely to involve punishment. In some cases, these suggestions will involve aversive stimuli following an inappropriate behavior, such as striking the back of the student's hand with a ruler or squeezing the student's shoulder. When such aversive stimuli are overused, the student may begin to flinch when the teacher approaches.

In the short term, negative reinforcement and punishment are the easiest solutions and often get immediate results. However, there are long-term side effects to the use of these two techniques. The negative consequences, especially if strongly aversive, are paired through associative learning with the teacher, the classroom, and the school itself.

Margaret was told she would miss a juice Popsicle as a treat. She now watches to see what the snack is going to be that day. If it is something she likes, she refuses to take a nap and may even refuse to remain in the room where the other students are napping. In the short run, we have won a quick victory by getting the student to get up from the nap promptly. In the long run, we have lost the campaign because the student has learned to avoid a nap altogether.

Negative reinforcement is an effective tool if used correctly with students, but it must be used sparingly and with an awareness of the degrees of intrusiveness associated with different aversive techniques.

Emphasize Positive Reinforcement

Students learn positive behaviors by seeing positive models from teachers or peers. A classroom filled with positive reinforcement creates an environment where there is a strong emotional attachment to the teacher and fellow classmates. The experiences and materials are welcoming and satisfying to the student, and the student loves to come to school to be with teachers and peers. So, on balance, positive reinforcement should dominate classroom behavioral procedures.

For the noncompliant student who refuses to join activities after a nap, one teacher may be freed up to stay with that student after nap time for a few days. During this period, the teacher gives this difficult riser more time to wake up, perhaps reading a favorite story or sitting closely with her on the floor near the student's cot. On subsequent days, the teacher moves to a rocking chair, and the student gets up and goes to the chair to be read to. Next, the teacher takes the student to the toilet and then reads to her. Next, the student uses the toilet and goes outside for the teacher to read the story on the school steps. Eventually the reading is phased out. The student can now follow the normal routine of getting up from a nap.

Negative reinforcement and punishment can inadvertently spread very quickly into classroom procedures. Hence teachers would do well to keep track of all of the punishment and negative reinforcement being used each month in order to design shaping strategies to teach the desired behavior through positive reinforcement.

Types of Reinforcers

Primary Reinforcers The student's natural, unlearned, or unconditioned reinforcers are called primary reinforcers. These are reinforcers that appeal to the five senses (the sight of a favorite character, the sound of music or mother's voice, the taste or smell of food, the feel of the student's favorite blanket, etc.). These reinforcers are central to the student's basic early survival needs and life experiences and provide the student with pleasure, making them very powerful reinforcers for the student (see Figure 2.4).

Secondary Reinforcers Secondary reinforcers include tangible reinforcers, such as stickers and badges; privilege reinforcers, such as the opportunity to be first or to use a one-of-a-kind toy; activity reinforcers, such as the chance to help make cookies; generalized reinforcers, such as tokens, points, or credits; and social reinforcers, in which the teacher gives her attention and reinforces the student through such things as her expressions, proximity to the student, words and phrases, and feedback. Social reinforcers may also come from classmates.

Taste	Smell	Sound	Sight	Touch
fruit juice	garlic clove	party blowers	flashlight	balloons
flavored gelatin	vinegar	push toys	mirror	breeze from
raisins	coffee	whistles	pinwheel	electric fans
cereal	perfume	bells	colored lights	air from hair
honey	cinnamon	wind chimes	bubbles	dryers (on low)
pickle relish	suntan lotion	tambourines	reflector	body lotion
peanut butter	oregano	harmonica	strobe lights	electric massager
toothpaste	after-shave lotion	car keys	Christmas tree	body powder
lemon juice	flowers	kazoo	ornaments	feather duster
bacon bits	vanilla extract	bike horn	wrapping paper	water
apple butter			rubber worms	sand
				burlap
				Silly Putty

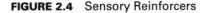

FIGURE 2.4 Sensory Reinforcers

Class	Category	Examples
Primary Reinforcers	1. Edible reinforcers	Foods and liquids (e.g., crackers, juice, pudding, Popsicles)
	2. Sensory reinforcers	Exposure to controlled visual, auditory, tactile, olfactory, or kinesthetic experience (e.g., face stroked with furry puppet, student's security blanket, mixing colors of paint)
Secondary Reinforcers	3. Tangible (material) reinforcers	Certificates, badges, stickers, balloons, status clothing (e.g., a police hat)
	4. Privilege reinforcers	Being first to share at circle time, setting the table for snack, holding the teacher's book while she reads
	5. Activity reinforcers	Play activities, special projects such as making cookies
	6. Generalized reinforcers	Tokens, points, credits, reinforcers that can be traded for other valuables
	7. Social reinforcers	Expressions, proximity, contact, words and phrases, feedback, seating arrangements

FIGURE 2.5 Types of Reinforcers

Secondary reinforcers are not basic to the student's survival and initially may be of little interest. The value that the student places on them is acquired, not inherent. After some previously neutral event or stimulus is learned to have reinforcing value, it is considered a conditioned (learned) reinforcer. For example, in rewarding appropriate behavior, the teacher may state how successful the student has been, may gently pat the student's back, and may place a sticker on the student's hand. Soon the statements, physical contact, and stickers will become powerful secondary reinforcers.

Since primary and secondary reinforcers have been paired in their early and repetitive presentation, the primary reinforcer can be gradually dropped. The secondary reinforcer is now conditioned and is just as powerful as the original primary reinforcers. If the secondary reinforcer begins to lose its effectiveness, it can be paired again with a primary reinforcer now and then. This is sometimes necessary until the secondary reinforcer regains its strength for the student. Figure 2.5 summarizes the types of reinforcers.

Thinning Reinforcement by Using Schedules

Let's now consider a case in which we have established a target behavior and have written behavioral objectives. The student does perform the behavior and we positively reinforce it. As a result of the reinforcement, the student repeats the desired behavior. We now reinforce again and again. Soon, however, the process gets too time consuming and exhausting to keep up. If we abruptly stop the reinforcement, the student's performance of the desired behavior will begin to weaken.

Instead, we begin thinning the reinforcement. We gradually make the reinforcement available less often for a given behavior or else contingent on a greater amount of appropriate behavior, until the need for the reinforcement is eliminated altogether. The reinforcer must be thinned based on a methodical process using intermittent schedules in which reinforcement is given following some, but not all, appropriate responses (see Figure 2.6).

Name	Description/example	Advantage/disadvantage
Fixed-ratio schedule	The number of times the student performs the target behavior will determine when he will receive the reinforcer (e.g., for every four math problems completed, the student is reinforced). Thinning may now occur by increasing the number of times the student must perform (from four math problems to six) in order to receive reinforcement.	Since time is not critical, the student might take far too long between tasks (e.g., complete a puzzle and then pause an hour before starting the next puzzle). If the number of tasks is too large, the student may even stop responding. The key is to seek the right amount of work given the reward schedule. Normally a ratio schedule produces consistent work.
Variable-ratio schedule	The target response is reinforced on the average of a specific number of correct responses, about once every 10 times. This makes it unpredictable for the student.	A student operating under a fixed-ratio schedule may realize that it will be a long time between reinforcers and may therefore work slowly. The variable-ratio schedule is done in such a manner that the reinforcer is not predictable, so the student maintains or increases the pace of his output. Normally under this type of schedule behavior is persistent.
Fixed-interval schedule	The student must perform the behavior at least once, and then a specific amount of time must pass before his behavior can be reinforced again. The student is reinforced the first time (does one puzzle), and then a specific time must pass (four minutes); on the very next puzzle completed after the four-minute wait, the student is again reinforced. This reinforcement arrangement will be thinned by increasing the wait to six minutes, then eight, and so on.	The student can become aware of the time length and, knowing he has to perform just once, will wait for the time schedule to almost run out before beginning his next task. This kind of schedule is easiest for teachers to use, since it is based on the passage of time. A teacher does not have to monitor each piece of work, only the clock and the work performed at the moment.
Variable-interval schedule	The interval between reinforcers will vary and be unpredictable to the student, with the interval differing but maintaining a consistent average length.	The student's behavioral performance is higher and steadier because he cannot determine the next time interval that will be used to make the reinforcement available.

FIGURE 2.6   Types of Schedules

Shaping

Behavior analysis is employed to bring behavior under the control of time, place, and circumstances. Yelling outside on the playground is perfectly acceptable, but loud talking at nap time is unacceptable. Varying types of reinforcers, as previously described, can help bring the student's existing behavioral skills under the control of the teacher and will result in well-disciplined behavior.

Another aspect of behavior analysis is the teaching of behaviors that are not in the student's existing repertoire. New behaviors are often acquired through a process called shaping. Shaping is much like the children's game in which one person is "it" and others hide an object, such as a coin under a chair cushion. "It" wanders around the room and when he moves in the direction of the hidden coin, all the students shout, "You're getting hotter!" (a positive reinforcer). When "it" turns away, the response is, "You're getting colder!" This continues until the student locates the chair and finds the hidden coin. The verbal feedback has now shaped the student to move in the correct direction. The student's reinforcements have shaped a new behavior, leading the subject student to the new positive actions.

Let's take the example of Adrienne. After saying good-bye to her parents in the morning, Adrienne spends an hour doing nothing but sucking her thumb. Her behavior is flat and expressionless. When the teacher attempts to cheer up Adrienne, the child only withdraws further. The teacher's target behavior is to get Adrienne to leave her parents and be active in the classroom. It is very important for the teacher to have chosen a target behavior, in the form of a behavioral objective: "Adrienne (1. identify the learner), when departing from her parents in the morning (2. identify the conditions), will go to materials and objects and begin to use them or will verbally interact with a classmate (3. identify the target behavior) within five minutes (4. identify criteria for acquisition)." With the target behavior stated in the form of a behavioral objective, the teacher is ready to reinforce Adrienne as her behavior gradually changes step by step.

1. Adrienne leaves her parent, but is in tears and sits passively.

2. She stops crying. (The teacher socially reinforces.)

3. Her eyes drop and she turns her face into the wall. (The teacher withdraws her presence and stops reinforcement.)

4. Hearing students laugh, Adrienne turns and looks intently at what is occurring. (The teacher catches her eye and smiles, stating, "Your friends are doing fun things"—social reinforcer.)

5. Adrienne stands to get a better view of her classmates' activities. (The teacher stands by the play activity and holds out her hand—social reinforcer.)

6. Adrienne walks across the room and grasps the teacher's hand with both of hers and buries her face behind the teacher's back, away from the classmates. (The teacher stands still and does not reinforce the "looking away.")

7. Adrienne stands erect, and still holding the teacher's hand, takes a sustained look at the classmates playing. (The teacher states, "Ah, see what they are doing. Carol is a nurse, Jane is the doctor, and Mary is the patient, and they are pretending to wrap Mary's injured arm.") At the same time, the teacher drops Adrienne's hand and affectionately strokes her head; the student moves next to her as the teacher sits herself on a small chair nearby (social reinforcer).

8. Adrienne runs to the play area, picks up the stethoscope, and runs back to the teacher, attempting to crawl onto the teacher's lap. (The teacher subtly closes her lap, denying Adrienne the use of it, and places her hand in her pocket—differentially stopping reinforcement that would continue to permit Adrienne to be dependent.)

9. Finally, Adrienne moves into the play area, picks up a toy doll, pretends to listen to its heartbeat with the stethoscope, and plays parallel with the classmates. (The teacher catches her eye, smiles warmly [social reinforcement], looks on at Adrienne, and then moves to another area of the room to help another student [the natural reinforcement of playing with others takes over—the target behavior has been obtained].)

ce is provided below to help the teacher determine what gradual step-by-step actions a student might take
ard acquiring target behaviors. Go first to Step 7 and write a behavioral objective, then return to Steps 1 to 6
roject shaping steps that the student might take. Also write at the bottom the types of reinforcers you will
As an alternative, it often helps to work backward and think of the behavior that comes just before the last
you want. Continue the process until you are at the student's current behavior.

ping Steps:

1. _____
2. _____
3. _____
4. _____
5. _____
6. _____
7. Behavioral Objective
   a) Identify the learner _____
   b) Identify the conditions _____
   c) Identify the target _____
   d) Identify the criteria for acquisition _____

What reinforcers will be used?

(Check)   (Describe)

1. Edible reinforcers
2. Sensory reinforcers
3. Tangible (material) reinforcers
4. Privilege reinforcers
5. Activity reinforcers
6. Generalized reinforcers
7. Social reinforcers

FIGURE 2.7 Shaping Planning Worksheet

Shaping involves clearly stating a behavioral objective with a target behavior, knowing when to differentially deliver or withhold reinforcement, and being able to shape the student into gradual successive approximations of the target behavior. Figure 2.7 illustrates a shaping worksheet.

DECREASING MISBEHAVIOR: STEPS AND PROCEDURES

When we want to increase a student's behavior, we present a positive reinforcer after the behavior. In contrast, when we want to decrease a student's misbehavior, we present an aversive stimulus after the misbehavior occurs. We have seen that aversion associated as punishment or negative reinforcement can have its fallout effects; thus, we cautiously limit the use of any form of aversion. To give us guidelines, we may establish a continuum consisting of five steps, moving from the use of minimally to maximally intrusive procedures (see Figure 2.8).

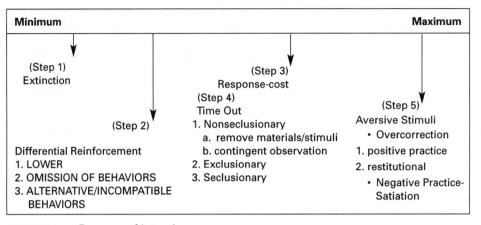

FIGURE 2.8 Degrees of Intrusiveness

Step 1: Extinction

Extinction is simply stopping the positive reinforcers that have been maintaining an inappropriate target behavior.

Peggy does not raise her hand and wait to be called on at circle time. Instead, she shouts out the answer. The teacher tolerates Peg's behavior during the first few days of class, accepting her shouted answers. By the fourth day of school, the teacher decides to use extinction to stop Peg's shouting. The teacher will not respond when Peggy shouts, instead calling on those with their hands in the air and reinforcing those complying. When Peggy shouts, the teacher ignores her. When the teacher's reinforcement stops, Peggy shouts louder and pushes her way to the front of the circle. When the teacher continues to ignore her, Peggy physically moves the teacher's head to look at her. The teacher gently moves Peggy aside and out of her view. Peggy has a full-blown temper tantrum. The teacher ignores Peg's tantrum and moves her own chair to another section of the circle so that all of the students are looking at the teacher with their backs to Peggy. When extinction is used, you may anticipate a number of behaviors:

1. The student's behavior will get worse before it gets better.
2. Extinction can induce aggression in some students.
3. Other students might begin to imitate the misbehavior you are attempting to eliminate. Normally, an assertive command will stop the copied behavior quickly.

One of the criteria for using extinction is whether the increased disruption can be tolerated for a period of time. Extinction will be effective only if the teacher "holds tough" and does not give in.

Step 2: Differential Reinforcement

Differential reinforcement reinforces certain behaviors selectively. This process can utilize three techniques: (1) reinforcing decreased rates of the misbehavior, (2) reinforcing the omission of the misbehavior, and (3) reinforcing incompatible and alternative behaviors.

Lowered Rates of the Misbehavior   The school's student safety rules require that young students remain seated while eating, especially when chewing a mouthful of food. Event recording by the teacher shows that Kevin was out of his seat at snack time 15 times in a 30-minute period, nearly every time with a mouthful of food. The teacher decides to use differential reinforcement to reduce the rate of the misbehavior. The teacher establishes a specific objective: "While at the snack table, Kevin will leave his seat five times or less during a 30-minute period."

The teacher knows that stopping the misbehavior completely is impractical. She begins a system of positive reinforcement—Kevin being able to help the janitor after his snack if he gets out of his seat five times or less. Every time Kevin leaves his seat, the teacher notes it on a card. She also reinforces Kevin every five minutes for being in his seat by commenting on how he is remembering the rule, touching him on the shoulder, and smiling. At the end of snack time, the janitor appears—and so does Kevin. The teacher has Kevin count the marks indicating the number of times he was out of his seat. He is allowed to help the janitor on Monday, Wednesday, and Friday because he has five marks or less on those days. The next week, the teacher drops the number of times Kevin is permitted to be out of his seat to three, and during the third week, to one. By the fourth week, Kevin is now able to follow the rule.

The teacher may not wish to totally eliminate a behavior. Consider Mary, who cannot stop talking to the teacher throughout recess. She assaults the teacher with a verbal barrage and no opportunity for a give-and-take exchange. The teacher does not wish to eliminate Mary's enthusiasm for talking, but wants to bring Mary's behavior to a more reasonable level.

The teacher states, "Mary, you have lots of wonderful things to tell me, but sometimes I get tired and I need to talk to other students. (Teacher holds up five fingers.) You may tell me five things that interest you today, and then I need to be with other students and you need to go off and play." As Mary speaks, the teacher closes one finger at a time, visually counting off the five items Mary tells her. The teacher reduces the number gradually until Mary is limited to two items. The teacher verbally reinforces Mary when the girl stops herself. From then on, when Mary regresses, the teacher simply holds up two fingers and says, "Mary, two!" Finally, the teacher does not need to speak, but gains Mary's compliance simply by holding up two fingers. Finally, Mary is able to speak to the teacher in a normal manner, without any finger prompts from the teacher.

Omission of the Misbehavior   Another method of differential reinforcement is omission of the misbehavior. In the example of Kevin, the teacher could establish six time intervals of five minutes each over the 30-minute snack time. The teacher tapes a 3×5 card in front of Kevin and places a check mark on the card if Kevin has not gotten out of his seat (omission of the misbehavior) for that five-minute interval. Kevin turns in the card at the end of snack time, and if there are two checks on the card during the first week, he earns the activity reinforcer. The next week, there must be three checks, then four, until Kevin finally stays in his seat for the entire 30-minute snack period.

One difficulty in requiring a student to omit a behavior is that the student may not have a repertoire of other behaviors he can perform instead. For instance, Jimmy comes to the edge of the block area and watches for most of the morning as Robert and his friends build a structure with blocks. Finally, without provocation, Jimmy kicks the blocks over.

He then runs off to hide in a corner. Jimmy has just shown a behavior vacuum. Omission of the misbehavior could be applied, but Jimmy still has no understanding of how to behave to join Robert and the other boys in block construction. He needs to learn how to make social overtures to be an associative player.

Both lowering the rate of misbehavior and omitting the misbehavior accept the position that the student cannot abruptly stop the behavior immediately and completely. However, by changing the criteria, the teacher can place more and more demands on the student until the final terminal behavior is reached.

Incompatible Behavior and Alternative Behavior When differentially reinforcing an incompatible behavior, a response is chosen and reinforced to make it physically impossible for the student to engage in the inappropriate behavior. In differential reinforcement of alternative behaviors, an appropriate behavior is reinforced. This behavior is not one that eliminates the physical possibility of exhibiting the target behavior. At times the two techniques can be combined. Remember Peggy, from our earlier example, who shouts her answers at circle time? In response, for a few weeks the teacher gives the students new instructions: When they have the answer and want to speak, they are to cover their mouth with their left hand (incompatible behavior, making it impossible to speak) and raise their right hand (alternative behavior). The teacher ignores anyone who does not have his or her mouth covered and hand raised—including Peggy. In her desire to be heard, Peggy quickly learns the proper procedure. Soon her impulsive responses lessen and finally stop. Before long, the students will no longer be required to place their hands over their mouths, and the class will return to simply raising hands. Often only alternative behaviors can be differentially reinforced since there is not always an incompatible behavior available for every target behavior.

Step 3: Response-Cost Procedure (Removal of Desirable Stimuli)

Paul, a most unruly student, treasures wearing the school's police officer outfit, which consists of a hat, a badge, and a belt with a set of handcuffs snapped on it. The teacher tells Paul that he needs to "police" his own behavior if he wants to continue wearing the outfit—he must not hit or destroy others' things, and he must obey the school rules. By 9:30 A.M., Paul has taken another student's toy. The teacher removes the handcuffs from Paul's belt and states, "If you want to wear these items, you must obey school rules." By 10:00, Paul has kicked a neighbor, and he loses his belt. At snack time, he throws food and loses his badge. At noon, he is found throwing water at his peers, and he loses his hat. This produces a temper tantrum. After nap time, all four items are returned to Paul, but the process can be repeated if necessary. It is important that the teacher also reinforce Paul by "catching him being good" and reminding him to control or "police" his own behavior. During the afternoon, Paul loses no items.

What we see the teacher doing is removing desirable stimuli. This requires that the student have within his possession certain tangible items that he treasures and that serve as reinforcers for him. The dilemma for the student is, how much is he willing to lose in order to continue with his misbehavior? In this response-cost procedure, the teacher has the ability to take away a reinforcer once given.

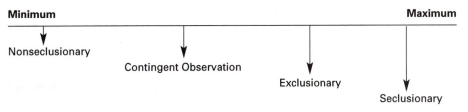

FIGURE 2.9 Time Out and Degrees of Aversion

Step 4: Time Out

Time-out procedures serve as punishment by denying a student a reinforcement for a fixed period of time. This removal of stimuli is actually a time out from positive reinforcement. Time out generally is used when the social context is so reinforcing that the teacher's application of other reinforcers is ineffective. There are four categories of time out (*see* Figure 2.9).

Nonseclusionary Time Out To deal with some minor disturbance, the teacher takes some physical intervention to deny the student reinforcement by removing the materials that are being used inappropriately (eating utensils at snack time, water play toys, or paints and brush) or by having the students put their heads down on their desks and turning off classroom lights. This is called nonseclusionary time out because the misbehaving student is not removed from the classroom or immediate environment.

Consider again Paul and his police outfit. Paul, an aggressive and difficult student, clearly desires to wear the police hat. Paul is given a police hat with his name taped in it, and the teacher tells him, "If you want to wear the police officer's hat, you must police your own behavior. If you hit, destroy, or disrupt the activities of other students, then you will lose your hat." (This is called an if—then statement: "If you do X, then Y consequences will happen.")

In the first few days, when Paul forgets and is disruptive, the teacher takes away his police hat, places it within his view on a hook too high for him to reach, and sets a timer for five minutes. When the bell rings, the hat is returned to him. On the first day, Paul loses the hat six times; on the second day, two; and in the remaining three days of the week, the hat is removed only once.

Contingent Observation Contingent observation is another form of nonseclusionary time out. In contingent observation, the student is removed to the edge of the activity so he can still observe the other students being reinforced. For example, the school has a circular tricycle path with arrows pointing the direction in which the students are to ride (visual prompt). Harold has been taught how to use the track, but he repeatedly seems to enjoy going the wrong way and colliding with playmates. The teacher pulls Harold and his tricycle to the school steps where he can observe the others riding and having fun. The teacher reinforces the other students (models) as they correctly obey the direction rule. After a few minutes, she asks Harold, "Do you see now how our rule works?" If Harold answers yes, he is permitted to return to the activity. If he answers no, he stays on the steps for another two minutes and again is asked if he is ready to comply.

Contingent observation is nonseclusionary because the student is not removed totally from the environment. Instead, he is placed at the edge of the activity so he may observe others being reinforced.

Note: The criterion for being released from contingent observation is the student's maintaining nondisruptive behavior for a specific amount of time. The student is then asked whether he understands the rule and if he will obey it if allowed to return to the activity.

When nonseclusionary time out fails, two other forms of time out are available: exclusionary and seclusionary.

Exclusionary Time Out   This involves removal of the student from an activity as a means of denying access to reinforcement, but it generally does not deny access to the classroom. For example, the student may be placed near a corner facing the wall or in an area of the classroom that is screened off from the room activities so that the student's view is restricted.

Seclusionary Time Out   This is the complete removal of the student from the classroom or environment. This denies the student access to any reinforcement from the classroom, including peers, adults, objects, or activities. When the time-out period is over, the teacher should return the student to the classroom in a calm manner with no extended conversation. Otherwise, the teacher may actually set up a chain of events in which the student learns to misbehave and be placed in time out in order to get into a conversation with the teacher. Some teachers use a bell timer to indicate when time out is over, and the student is informed that she can rejoin the group when the bell sounds. Again, the teacher should interact minimally with the student.

Note: Justification for use of any form of time out is not for retribution based on the idea that the student has failed morally or has not lived up to the adult's values and expectations. From a behavior analysis standpoint, the justification is that the environment and social context are strongly reinforcing the student to continue his or her misbehavior. The objective is to remove that reinforcement. Time out and time-out rooms have historically been misused or mismanaged by teachers, causing great mistrust of the technique by parents and the general public. In no case should students be put in time out for a long period of time. Generally, time out should be limited to one to six minutes; it is doubtful that any period beyond 10 minutes would be effective for the young student. Figure 2.10 presents some guidelines for the time-out room. A time-out record form (see Figure 2.11) should be required for each staff member who uses time out.

A time-out room should meet these minimal requirements:
1. Be at least 6-by-6 feet in size.
2. Be properly lighted.
3. Be properly ventilated.
4. Be free of objects with which students can harm themselves or use for play.
5. Provide the means by which an adult can continuously monitor, both visually and by sound, the student's behavior.
6. *Not* be locked.

FIGURE 2.10   Guidelines for Time-Out Room

Student's Name	Date ___/___/___	Time of Day	Total Time in Time Out _____ Number of Minutes
Teacher's Name			Type of Time Out (check one) _____ Contingent Observation _____ Exclusionary _____ Seclusionary
Other Adult Witness			
Description of the Situation:		State Behavioral Change Wanted:	

FIGURE 2.11 Time-Out Record

Step 5: Aversive Stimuli

Overcorrecting When Johnny arrives at school, he runs down the hall and stairs to the playground. This practice is dangerous and should be stopped. When the teacher has delivered the other students to the playground and another teacher's supervision, she takes Johnny by the hand and walks him to the classroom. The teacher verbally states the school rule to "walk in the hall and on the stairs" and, still holding his hand, walks Johnny out to the playground. She then returns him to the hallway, repeats the rule, and makes Johnny walk down the hall and stairs without holding her hand. He is made to walk the hall and stairs three more times, each time returning to the classroom. This is a behavioral procedure called positive-practice overcorrecting, which teaches the student how to perform correct behavior through an element of aversion.

Mark has just finished eating his Popsicle and discards the stick by simply dropping it on the playground as he always does. The teacher takes him by the hand and states, "When we have trash, we throw it in the waste can." She has him pick up the stick and throw it in the can. She now walks him to a second piece of trash and has him pick it up and throw it in the trash can. The teacher takes him around the playground, requiring him to pick up trash six more times as she states the rule. This procedure is called restitution overcorrecting, which requires the student to make amends by restoring the object, materials, or environment he may have destroyed or disrupted back to its original condition and then going beyond that to do more.

Negative Practice-Stimuli Satiation When Lisa does not get her way with classmates or the teacher, she spits at them. The teacher decides to use negative practice-stimulation satiation to deal with Lisa's spitting. She takes Lisa to the toilet and gives her a large cup filled with water, then asks her to take a large mouthful and spit it into the toilet. The girl complies with a little giggle. She is asked to continue taking water from the cup and spitting it into the toilet until the cup is empty. A second cup is presented to her, and her demeanor changes to reflect a sense of drudgery. At this point, the teacher accompanies each spit by stating, "Spitting is against the rules." With the use of negative practice-stimulation satiation, there is no intent to teach a new behavior. Instead, the idea is to have the student repeat the inappropriate behavior over and over until the act becomes tiresome and punishing and the student becomes satiated.

Sensory Insult In the vast majority of cases, the techniques previously discussed will be sufficient to put an end to most forms of misbehavior. However, there are occasional extreme cases that call for extreme measures. When extreme measures are required, they must be used with the utmost care and with the full participation of the student's parents.

Martha is a new student. During her first two weeks, the teacher discovers that Martha bites and chews her right hand until the flesh is actually torn and bleeding. This occurs repeatedly throughout the day. The teacher determines that this behavior occurs six or seven hours per day over a five-day period, and Martha's biting behavior is increasing.

A meeting is called, bringing together Martha's classroom teachers, a school administrator, the student's parents, a special education teacher (when possible), and a local psychologist (or school counselor). The teacher passes out records on the aversion steps she has attempted and graphs she has made to track Martha's biting. With the parents' permission, a videotape of Martha's behavior is shown to the group. The group recommends approval of the use of sensory insult. The group, including the parents, approves and signs an individualized educational plan (IEP), stating a new goal (e.g., reduction of self-abuse). The members of the group permit the teacher to use such aversion stimuli as putting a lemon into Martha's mouth when biting (aversive taste stimulus); using bright food coloring to paint the area of her hand that Martha tends to bite (possible visual aversion); painting Martha's hand with a quinine liquid (aversive taste stimulus); and/or if necessary, putting the hand into a leather glove Martha could not remove. The IEP indicates that any or all of these aversion techniques may be used for a period of 10 days, with the teacher recording data and graphing the results. A second IEP meeting is set for the end of the 10-day period.

These extreme strategies can leave the teacher open for the risk of being accused of abuse and possible assault charges. When allegations of aversive tactics are brought into court or circulated by the news media, the general public might be shocked and feel that the teacher is being inhuman and using excessive punishment. In reality, however, it would be no less inhuman to permit Martha to suffer potential physical pain and health risks of repeatedly abusing herself by biting her hand and disfiguring her body. It is highly recommended that if a teacher is faced with the need to utilize such aversive techniques, the student should immediately be referred to a psychologist or behavioral specialist, as the student's needs may be beyond the classroom teacher's skills and abilities.

These techniques should be used rarely, and only when adhering to strict guidelines requiring that:

1. The failure of alternative nonaversive procedures is demonstrated and documented.

2. Informed written consent is obtained from the student's parents or legal guardians, through due process procedures and assurance of their right to withdraw such consent at any time.

3. The decision to implement an aversive procedure is made by a designated body of qualified professionals.

4. A timetable for reviewing the effectiveness of the procedure is established.

5. Periodic observation is conducted to ensure staff members' consistent and reliable administration of the procedure.

6. Documentation of the effectiveness of the procedure and evidence of increased accessibility to instruction is maintained.

7. Only designated staff members who are knowledgeable and skilled in behavior analysis perform administration of the procedure.

8. Incompatible behavior is positively reinforced whenever possible as part of any program using aversive stimuli.

Note to the wise teacher: Never use aversive stimuli as punishment techniques without strictly following all of these guidelines as well as any adopted by school administrators.

STRENGTHS AND LIMITATIONS OF THE MODEL

There are many benefits to the behavior analysis model. General behavior is broken down into smaller parts so that students have ensured success. A student can feel successful as he learns appropriate behaviors and receives verbal, social, and material rewards. Standards of behavior are uniform, consistent, and clear to all students. The teacher does not need to spend any time in class discussions about rules or to conduct individual conferences dealing with problem solving, thereby freeing her to spend more time on instructional matters. Behavior analysis can be used with all students, regardless of their age or cognitive and language abilities. A reinforcement schedule can be implemented with a nonverbal, passive student as well as with a highly articulate, aggressive student. The classroom teacher can scientifically test positive use of behavior analysis.

The limitations of the model are both philosophical and practical. Behavior analysis is an approach that attempts to change a student's observable behavior. However, some misbehavior may be the result of "inner" problems. A student who is being physically abused at home may be taking his hostility out on classmates. A reinforcement program that conditions cooperative class behavior and extinguishes physical aggression may be beneficial to the teacher, but it does not help the student (or parents) resolve the underlying home problem. Therefore, in many cases, behavior analysis approaches may change the symptoms, but do little to alleviate the actual problem. There is also the argument that, in a democratic society, it is unethical and unacceptable for schools to control an individual's behavior. Limiting behavior so that destruction or harm can be avoided is necessary in any society, but the notion of conditioning specific behavior would be more applicable to a totalitarian society. Educational concerns with behavior analysis are that learning "to behave" is an important cognitive task, just as important as learning such school subjects as reading and mathematics. Therefore, if a student is not allowed to bring her mental operations into use by learning to clarify emotions, weigh alternatives, and decide on solutions, then a major area of intellectual or rational development would be neglected. Another concern is more immediate to teachers in that such a scientific approach is predicated on precise delineation and measurement of a student's pretreatment behavior. To do this, a teacher needs to write down misbehavior in clear terms and to keep an accurate tabulation of frequency. Some teachers would resist spending the time and effort that this ongoing record keeping involves.

Alfie Kohn's Criticism on Behavior Analysis

On rewards:

...how long rewards last, and to learn that they rarely produce effects that survive the rewards themselves is to invite curiosity about just what it is that rewards are doing. Why don't people keep acting the way they were initially reinforced for acting? The answer is that reinforcements do not generally alter the attitudes and emotional commitments that underlie our behaviors. They do not make deep, lasting changes because they are aimed at affecting only what we do. If, like Skinner, you think there is nothing to human beings other than what we do—that we are only repertoires of behavior—then this criticism will not trouble you; it may even seem meaningless. If, on the other hand, you think that actions reflect and emerge from who a person is (what she thinks and feels, expects and wills), then interventions that just control actions wouldn't be expected to help a child grow into a generous person or even help an adult decide to lose weight. (Kohn, 1993, p.41)

What makes behavioral interventions so terribly appealing is how little they demand of the intervener. They can be applied more or less skillfully, of course, but even the most meticulous behavior modifier gets off pretty easy for one simple reason: rewards do not require any attention to the reasons that the trouble developed in the first place. You don't have to ask why the child is screaming, why the student is ignoring his homework, why the employee is doing an indifferent job. All you have to do is bribe or threaten that person into shaping up. (Kohn, 1993, p. 59)

On time out:

The consensus [among early childhood educators] seemed to be that sending someone away and forcing him to sit by himself does nothing to resolve whatever the problem was. I "cannot give a child new standards of behavior, insight into how one's actions affect others, or strategies for coping with an uncomfortable or painful situation," as Lilian Katz (1985, p. 3) has observed. The adult is not asking, "Why have you...?" or even saying, "Here's why you might..." She is simply telling the child, "Do it my way or leave." Yes, it's true that exiling a disruptive child can make everyone else feel better, at least for a while. But this means that time out acts as "a wedge that pushes persons into opposite directions. Some are feeling relieved at the same time that another person is feeling oppressed." (Lovett, 1985, p. 16)

Problem: Chris and Pat, who are sitting next to each other, are making an unusual amount of noise. Maybe one is annoying the other, or maybe the two are simply talking together, oblivious to everything else going on in the room. Solution: The teacher points to one of the students and then to a distant chair. "Chris, sit over there." ... As educators, our responses to things we find disturbing, our approach to both academic and nonacademic matters, might be described as reflecting a philosophy of either doing things to students or working with them. (Kohn, 1996, p. 23) ... When the teacher separates them, does either student come away with any understanding of, or concern about, how his or her actions may affect other people in the room? Have the two learned how to negotiate a solution, attend to social cues, or make the best of sitting next to someone who is not a friend? Hardly. But they, like the other students watching, have learned one important lesson from this intervention. That lesson is power: when you have it (as the teacher does, at the moment), you can compel others people to do whatever you want. (Kohn, 1996, p. 24)

SUMMARY OF KEY CONCEPTS

anecdotal reports	duration recording	nonseclusionary time out	schedules of reinforcement
antecedent condition	event recording	overcorrecting	seclusionary time out
assertive command	exclusionary time out	pairing	secondary reinforcers
aversive stimulus	extinction	permanent product	shaping
baseline data	fixed-interval schedule	recording	social reinforcers
behavior	fixed-ratio schedule	pinpointing	target behavior
behavioral objective	frequency	positive reinforcement	thinning
broken record	functional relationship	primary reinforcer	time out
conditioned reinforcer	interval recording	prompt	unconditioned aversive
consequence	latency recording	punishment	stimuli
contingency	modeling	reinforcer	variable-interval schedule
deprivation state	negative practice	response-cost	
differential reinforcement	negative reinforcement	satiation	

CASE STUDIES

James, a second grader, as of the fourth month of the school year, has done no homework and is generally failing most school subjects. His mother, who works two jobs, cannot be contacted by telephone or for a school appointment. He has no classroom friends and is routinely excluded from most playground games. While the teacher is teaching a small group, he either appears at the teacher's side to seek answers for questions that the teacher has just given, or, when told to return to his seatwork, he begins disturbing other children seated nearby—taking their pencils, making silly guttural sounds, and creating other noisy disruptions that force the teacher to stop and attend to him.

How would the discipline/management systems be applied to James using behavioral analysis techniques?

Limit-setting System

Drawing from the techniques of behavior analysis for a limit-setting system, defined here as verbal confrontation, would provide little help. Speaking in the form of commanding, questioning, or encouraging the child to name problems, or even looking at him, would reinforce his misbehavior. Therefore, rather than setting limits by attending to the child, the behaviorist would say to ignore his actions after they occur. This is the process of extinction, or simply stopping all reinforcement that has been maintaining this inappropriate target behavior.

Backup System

If James's behavior dramatically escalated, there might be a need for a form of seclusionary time out, such as removal from the classroom or being sent home by the principal.

Incentive System

Applying an incentive system would involve all students in the classroom and would be specifically designed to shape James's and other class members' behavior. The incentive system gives numerous techniques—an interval contingency (an egg timer set for 30 minutes) could be set up to reward the whole class for total class compliance for a period of time, and the teacher could provide a primary or secondary reinforcer (when the timer bell rings, a "poker" chip is added to a seesaw-balance. After many token rewards the balance tips over from the weight, and the students get a reward—sugarless lollipops), or a PAT (preferred activity time) could be scheduled, such as playing a game. Over a period of time these group rewards would be thinned (more weight is added to the scale, requiring more chips and greater times between rewards).

Encouragement System

The teacher would pick one important target behavior to work on with James, at first ignoring other misbehaviors—

this may be staying in his seat for a period of time, desisting in annoying his peers, or completing one or two problems of homework. A behavioral objective would be stated: "James (the learner), during seatwork period (antecedent condition), will remain in his seat (target behavior) for 20 minutes (criteria)." Baseline data would be collected, and interventions would be scheduled with positive reinforcers (teacher paper-punches a hole on James's reward card, which is pinned to his shirt—once he gets 10 hole punches he can turn in the card and "purchase" a toy in the classroom store). New data is counted to see if change is occurring, and with success this reinforcer is faded.

Management System

The teacher has mounted at the edge of the chalkboard a paper "traffic light" with green, yellow, and red lights.

On a poster nearby are children's names with a clothespin clipped before each name. When James disturbs others, the teacher takes the clothespin with his name and clips it to the yellow circle on the "traffic light." This is a visual prompt and a warning to James (behaviorally considered a mild form of punishment). If he disrupts the class again, the teacher moves the clothespin, clipping it to the red light. The "red light" contains three zones—a 5, a 15, and the word "recess." When the pin is placed on the "5," this means that James is to go to the time-out chair at the back of the room, and the teacher sets the egg timer for five minutes. When the small bell rings, he returns to his seat. If this disruption continued for that day, this time out could escalate to 15 minutes, and finally to the loss of recess. This is done without any acknowledgment of James, as the teacher maintains her momentum of teaching.

EXERCISES

What actions would the behaviorist teacher take using the five systems (limit setting, backup, incentive, encouragement, and management system) for each of the following:

1. A sixth-grade special needs student daily chews her hand until, near the end of the day, it is bleeding.
2. The industrial arts teacher, who has a classroom filled with power machines (drill press, table saw, sander, etc.) has one child who refuses to wear protective glasses because it is not "cool" and runs in the classroom with the danger that he will bump a classmate using the power equipment.
3. A kindergarten child, to amuse his peers, pushes an entire peanut butter sandwich into his mouth and is in danger of choking.

4. A high school student, while in the hall unsupervised, but with a hall pass to the restroom, lays a sheet of newspaper flat on the floor before a classroom door, covers it with lighter fluid, lights it, and pushes it under the door through the small space between the floor and the door. This causes four-foot flames to jump up inside the classroom, frightening the students, damaging the door, and causing a fire drill.
5. The teacher requires students to raise their hands to be called on, giving everyone time to think of an answer. A bright middle school student repeatedly breaks this rule and shouts out the answer instantaneously each time any question is asked.

NOTES

1. P. A. Alberto and A. C. Troutman, *Applied Behavior Analysis for Teachers,* 3rd ed. (New York: Merrill-Macmillan, 1990).

REFERENCES

Alberto, P. A., and Troutman, A. C. *Applied Behavior Analysis for Teachers,* 3rd ed. New York: Merrill-Macmillan, 1990.

Engelmann, S., and Carnine, D. *Theory of Instruction: Principles and Application.* New York: Irvington, 1982.

Katz, L. G. "Katz Responds to Daniels." *Young Children* (January 1985): 2–3. Washington, DC: National Association for the Education of Young Children.

Kauffman, J. M., Mostert, M. P., Trent, S. C., and Hallahan, D. P. *Managing Classroom Behavior: A Reflective Case-Based Approach,* 3rd ed. Boston: Allyn and Bacon, 2002.

Kohn, A. *Punished by Rewards: The Trouble with Gold Stars, Incentive Plans, A's, Praise, and Other Bribes.* Boston: Houghton Mifflin, 1993.

Lovett, H. *Cognitive Counseling and Persons with Special Needs.* New York: Praeger, 1985.

Madsen, C. H., and Madsen, C. K. *Teaching/Discipline: A Positive Approach for Educational Development.* Raleigh, NC: Contemporary Publishing, 1981.

CHAPTER 3

TOOLS FOR TEACHING: DISCIPLINE, INSTRUCTION, AND MOTIVATION

Theorist/Writer: Fredric Jones

▦ *Positive Classroom Discipline, Positive Classroom Instruction*

▦ *Tools for Teaching: Discipline, Instruction, and Motivation*

OUTLINE OF THE TOOLS FOR TEACHING MODEL

Basic Assumptions about Motivation

▦ Based on behavior analysis principles and constructs

▦ Attempts to make behavioral principles practical

▦ Eclectically borrowed elements from neurobiology and anthropology to round out and justify his practices

▦ Uses teacher proximity and eye contact as a mild form of punishment to get students back on task

▦ Uses various systems: limit setting, backup, responsibility training, omission training, and classroom structure

Teacher Behaviors
Limit Setting

▦ fight-or-flight response

▦ triune brain theory

▦ pheasant posturing

▦ snap and snarl

▦ silly talk

▦ cardinal error

▦ back talk

▦ Parry reflex

▦ proximity

- camping out
- relaxing breaths
- body movements
- moving in/moving out
- palms
- relaxing breaths
- noncompliance by students
- helpless handraisers
- praise, prompt, and leave
- body language
- working the crowd
- zones: red, yellow, and green
- camouflage
- bop 'til you drop
- proactive vs. reactive
- no means no
- ineffective stages
- Ph.D. in the Teacher Game
- low roller vs. high roller

Guidelines, Planning, or Preparatory Teacher Actions

- Controlling the seating arrangement
- Organizing the space and other classroom actions that can be taken before the students arrive.

Backup Responses (private/semiprivate)
Small Backup Responses

- ear warnings
- private meetings
- think and talk
- warning and delivery

Medium Backup Responses
Large Backup Responses
Responsibility Training (stopwatch)

- incentive system
- bonuses

- give time
- hurry-up bonus
- automatic bonus
- penalties
- PAT or preferred activity time

Omission Training

- private meeting
- class meeting

Structure (management)

- teach rules/structure
- say, show, do
- desk arrangement: forward and packing
- interior loop with ears
- work the crowd
- desk creep
- bell work
- general rules versus specific procedures and routines
- visual instructional plan or VIP

OVERVIEW

The following is a classroom discipline incident involving a teacher using the *Tools for Teaching,*[1] previously known as Positive Discipline, techniques of Fredric Jones. Boldface words highlight the techniques or processes being utilized and will be defined later in this chapter.

> *Ms. Dumas has just finished teaching a new concept to her algebra class and has assigned the class to do seat work to practice applying this concept. She moves around the room,* **working the crowd,** *and checks each student's work. She hears muffled whispers, and the slight movement of a chair coming from the far side of the room. She looks up* **(checks it out)** *to see Nancy's eyes appear above her textbook and then disappear behind it. Again there are whispers, and Ms. Dumas sees Nancy physically turn toward Martha, her neighbor. Nancy is busy giggling and talking to Martha, who appears to be writing. Nancy is clearly off-task, requiring Ms. Dumas to take some action to get her to use the seat-work time constructively.*
>
> *Ms. Dumas (1) slowly stands fully erect, (2) turns her body and feet so that she is* **squared off** *with Nancy, (3) takes two controlled* **relaxing breaths,** *and attempts to (4) make eye contact with Nancy, who is not looking in her direction. Ms. Dumas's voice (5) broadcasts across the classroom, "Nancy," but there is no response from the girl. Again she calls, "Nancy"; the neighbor hears and sees Ms. Dumas's cues and signals Nancy to look in the teacher's direction. Nancy now makes eye contact with*

Part	Definition	Knowledge Base	Example of Techniques
Limit Setting	Actions taken by the teacher to control the student's natural reflexes and prompt students back to work while (1) students are doing seat work or (2) teacher is lecturing	Neurobiology (brain functioning) — fight/flight — modality of functioning Proximity	— relaxing breathing — slack jaw — speed of movement — inhibit talking — body-telegraphing — working the crowd — eye contact — posture — facial expression — closing distance (far, near, and intimate, "in the face")
Classroom Structure	The arrangement of objects and furniture and the teaching of rules and procedures	Behaviorally Discriminate Teaching	Three-step lesson: say, show, do
Responsibility Training	The use of an incentive system for increasing existing or obtaining new behaviors	Behavior Modification	Group incentives Preferred Activity Time Differential Reinforcement
Omission Training	Getting very difficult student to desist	Behavior Modification	Differential Reinforcement, group incentives
Backup System	Three levels of intervention from private to public sanctions	Traditional school practice	Office referral, time out, expulsion, suspension, staffing, parent conferencing

FIGURE 3.1   Positive Discipline. Parts, Definitions, Knowledge Base, and Examples

*Ms. Dumas and sees the teacher looking straight at her; she wiggles in her chair and turns her upper body toward Ms. Dumas, but her lower body (knees and feet) still faces her neighbor. She picks up her pencil and places it on her paper as if to write (**pseudocompliance: pencil posturing**). She looks again to see Ms. Dumas still holding the same unwavering eye contact. Nancy meets Ms. Dumas's eye contact directly and smiles at her with an open-mouth-and-teeth smile, with a slight cock of her head and raised eyebrows (**"smiley face"**). The endearing smile is one that would encourage anyone to automatically or reflexively smile back, but Ms. Dumas holds her same upright posture. She maintains the same visual lock with Nancy, but returns Nancy's smiling overture with a flat facial expression that clearly communicates, "**I am not amused!**" or "**I am bored!**" while taking two more **relaxing breaths**.*

What we see Ms. Dumas doing is applying Fredric Jones's visual *limit-setting* techniques to deal with student misbehavior. The Jones model is premised on the belief that teachers should not get bogged down in the use of language, such as nagging, and negotiations with students, but should use the powers of proximity and vision to assert their will. The Jones model features four legs to his "chair of discipline and management," and each leg must be intact and functioning to make the Tools for Teaching process work: (1) limit setting, (2) responsibility training, (3) omission training, and (4) a backup system (Figure 3.1). In addition, Jones asserts that classroom structure, while not one of these four legs, sets a foundation that allows good discipline to occur. We will first discuss details of limit setting and backup systems, followed by discussion of the remaining two legs.

Jones draws theoretically and conceptually from the knowledge bases of behavioral analysis, proximity research from anthropology as a study of animal behavior, and neurobiology as to how the human brain functions. Each set of techniques and practices is grounded in a justification drawn from these three knowledge sources, as well as from the practical teacher folklore and classroom traditions Jones has gathered from his many years of observation in classrooms at all grade levels. The model is surprisingly void of traditional psychological behavioral terminology, but is chock full of "Fredisms," coined by Fredric Jones to describe techniques, philosophies, or personal wisdom statements drawn from his rural Kansas upbringing and his interest in athletics.

LIMIT SETTING

The objective for all limit setting is to calm the students and get them back on task, as with Nancy earlier. But when we think of discipline problems we usually think of the "big ticket" items of physical aggression, overt defiance, and destruction of property. Jones uses time as a central variable for justifying and thinking out the value of the teacher's action. That is, we may have wonderful discipline procedures, but, if they eat up so much of the teacher's time that none is left for instruction, the techniques are of no value to the Jones model.

To follow Jones's reasoning, these big-ticket discipline actions normally are very rare occurrences. These incidents take five minutes or less, and generally are seen by teachers no more than five times in a school year. If we count up the five incidents multiplied by five minutes, we see that we may spend a great deal of time worrying about the big-ticket discipline incidents that might actually involve 25 minutes or less of our teaching time in an entire school year. What is more important is to watch the "nickel-and-dime" actions of talking and out-of-seat behavior, which combined might eat up one-third or more of our total class time if there is poor discipline. At the same time, it is these nickel-and-dime misbehaviors that consume the teacher's energies and eventually wear the teacher down. Nancy and Martha's talking may be seen as a minor incident, but it caused the teacher to stop her instruction. Multiply that by eight to ten of these incidents in a relatively short span and they will add up, wear the teacher out, and cut deeply into "time on task."

Jones sees the Nancys and Marthas of the classroom as playing a power game and doing penny-ante gambling. When these girls face Ms. Dumas for the first time they ask, "Does she really mean what she says? Do we have to work in this classroom or can we play?" Nancy has a *"Ph.D. in the Teacher Game"* and, as a *low roller* or gambler, will see who will hold the power in this classroom. She has learned a host of pseudocompliance behaviors to sidetrack the teacher during power plays. If she can get the teacher to buy into these behaviors, the teacher will lose the game and control will shift to the student. Although these student behaviors look different and take various forms of being negative or positive, the techniques are all labeled as "back talk." All the students know the power game that is proceeding, with the ultimate prize being to see the teacher "lose her cool" and signal a complete victory for the students and a total lack of control of the classroom. *My life is in the hands of any fool who makes me lose my temper. Calm is strength. Upset is weakness.*[2]

Fight-or-Flight Response

Think back to a time you may have tried hard to forget. You were driving your car and stopped at a red light. The light changed and you slowly pulled into the intersection, but another driver ran the light and barreled through the intersection at excessive speed. If you had not suddenly jammed on your brakes and turned your wheel quickly, you would have had a very serious accident. The adrenaline pumped through your body, your heart was in your throat, your face was warm, and you clenched your teeth. For a moment you weren't sure if you were going to throw up, and 15 minutes later as you got out of your car your legs were still wobbly. You were experiencing the results of a fight-or-flight response.

What your body had experienced is an *adrenaline dump,* causing a reflex body action triggered by an external stimulus. Rational thinking is too slow for sudden emergencies, and your body has a built-in survival process that shuts down higher order thinking so the defensive reflexes can act to save us. When animals are cornered, their lack of language skills and rational thinking leaves them with only two choices—they can fight, or they can flee. Humans experience a similar response when events push them out of rational thinking. This fight-or-flight response exacts a high price in our level of stress and burned-up energy.

Theoreticians suggest that humans have what may be thought of as three brains. This *triune brain* contains (1) a reptilian brain located at the base of our brain stem, (2) a paleo-cortex, an ancient cortex or "doggy-horsey brain," and (3) a neocortex, or new cortex of higher intelligence. The Triune Brain Theory (see Figure 3.2) suggests that each of these three brains has its own functions, but under stress our brain downshifts to lower primal brain centers for purposes of survival. Under moderate arousal the management of behavior shifts from the neocortex to the paleocortex. Under extreme arousal, the management of behavior shifts from paleocortex to the reptilian brain. This means that when we are angry, frightened, and upset we are noncortical, animal-like beings and that higher think-

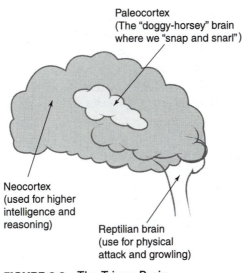

Paleocortex
(The "doggy-horsey" brain
where we "snap and snarl")

Neocortex
(used for higher
intelligence and
reasoning)

Reptilian brain
(use for physical
attack and growling)

FIGURE 3.2 The Triune Brain

ing in our cortex is unavailable to us until we calm down. The downshift occurs in two forms: an *adrenaline dump* or a *slow "bleeding"* of adrenaline into our body system, maintaining us in a constant defensive stressful state.

We have seen, in the automobile near miss, a full regression or downshifting to the reptilian brain is a result of a full adrenaline dump. In classrooms we may have students who are extremely confrontational toward us. More likely for most teachers are the day-in, day-out moderate arousals that cause the *slow bleeding* of adrenaline into our system. This constancy, because of small "nickel-and-dime" discipline incidents such as Nancy's chatting and off-task behavior, causes us to constantly teach and function at a moderate arousal level. For the teacher partially in a fight-flight stance with its accompanying stress, classroom life has been compared with the soldier who begins to suffer battle fatigue—a constant draining of energy.

The central contribution of the Jones Discipline Model is the acknowledgment of this "slow bleed" phenomena and clear practical actions to control this stress and maintain the teacher's classroom power and effectiveness. In the student power game, the ultimate way for students to win control of the classroom is to have the teacher regress to a state where she has "lost her cool." When the teacher has regressed, *going brain stemmed,* it is *"show time"* for the students. The teacher is now out of control and the students are in control, and the teacher's behavior will be quite amusing to the students as she struggles in an attempt to regain classroom control. Remember: *Calm is strength. Upset is weakness.*[3]

Since talking to a neighbor is regarded as the most frequent off-task behavior by students, Jones see ineffective teachers progressing through four ineffective stages as they lose control: as green as grass, do something, sick and tired, and laying down the law.

- *as green as grass*—the new teacher wanting not to nag and to be liked by the student simply ignores off-task talking. The students, seeing her take no action when they or others do talk, now take advantage until the talking is so excessive that teaching cannot happen.

- *do something*—the teacher confronts the talking and off-task students and they respond with a pseudocompliance (smiley face, book posing, pencil posing, and pseudoscholarship) and the teacher believes it by returning to her teaching activities, with the students starting up their talking a few minutes later.

- *sick and tired* and *laying down the law*—the teacher becomes "sick and tired" of this misbehavior and begins brain regression.

Let us see an example of the behavior of a teacher who has *"gone brain stem"* or *"gone chemical"* (meaning physically full of adrenaline and overcome by a fight-flight posture), as Jones would label it.

> *In a harsh voice one step short of actually shouting, Ms. Hopkins says, "If I have told you once, Wanda, I have told you a hundred times. (The teacher stands with left hand on left hip, balancing on one leg and hip and tapping the toe of her right foot, as she points and shakes her index finger across the room at the girls in an action called **pheasant posturing**). This is work time and I don't want to see you two talking, and I don't want to have to come over there! This is valuable class time and you, young ladies, are losing it. I am sick and tired of having to stop my work because of you two girls."*

This teacher who is under stress has regressed to a *fight-flight position,* probably with only her paleocortex, or *doggy-horsey brain,* in gear. The teacher, much like an animal, "snaps and snarls" and does what Jones would label *silly talk,* meaning that the words she says mean nothing, but are even poor examples of threats. The hand pointing and similar physical actions are nonverbal territorial actions, used in the animal kingdom by creatures such as the male pheasant, to intimidate and scare off a rival (thus Jones's term, *pheasant posturing*). Students see these behaviors in teachers and are not fearful, but are entertained by the sight of a teacher who is so weak that the students can "push her button." "It is *show time,* classmates." This is all reactive teacher behavior with little to no proactive actions to really get the students to stop their talking and get back to work.

Eye Contact and Proximity

In animal species and also among humans, contact with another individual is accomplished by reading nonverbal body messages, and the eyes are the most expressive nonverbal communication tool. An unswerving eye lock with an individual is the most powerful confrontational stance. Eye contact with another individual is a direct challenge or exercise of power, and when the other individual breaks the visual lock it is read as capitulation and subservience. ("I don't wish to fight; I yield to your power.") We literally stare them down. The dominant person looks, and the other person smiles back as a signal of capitulation, or "I wish to be your friend." If the dominant person smiles back, the offer of friendship is accepted. If the other person does not smile back or break eye contact, then we have a direct power challenge.

> *Nancy meets Ms. Dumas's eye contact directly and smiles at her ("**smiley face**"). Ms. Dumas holds her same upright posture and maintains the same eye-to-eye visual lock with Nancy. She returns Nancy's smiling overture with a flat facial expression that clearly communicates, "I am not amused" or "I am bored!" At the same time, the teacher takes two more relaxing breaths.*

The "heat" that the other person will feel emotionally from being visually confronted will depend on the spatial distance between the two people or a *concept of proximity*. Across the classroom, the challenge can be very strong, but it can be fended off by many game-playing students. But when the teacher moves to the end of the student's desk and leans over it, the visual heat is turned up dramatically and the student's inner kettle of emotions begins to bubble—fueled by the output of adrenaline and stress within the student. The student is now in a fight-flight confrontation with the teacher.

> *Ms. Dumas now leans or eases over in a slow controlled manner, places the palms (**palms**) of her two hands flat on the far sides of Nancy's desk and paperwork, and takes two relaxing breaths. The teacher remains palms-down on Nancy's desk and watches with unwavering eye contact.*

Most people have around them personal space, much like an invisible three-foot bubble in which they feel safe. When others invade this space, the person becomes emotionally uncomfortable and potentially threatened. When we touch students, place our hands on what they touch, or place our face inches from theirs, we burst their bubble and the protective safety of their personal space. We force them to back down or resist (fight or flight). This will be especially true for adolescents, who are struggling with their own sexual and physical body changes and their new interest in intimacy with members of the opposite sex.

> *Ms. Dumas, in a slow controlled manner, stands erect, takes two relaxing breaths, and then slowly moves behind and between the two girls. Ms. Dumas eases between them, placing her elbow on Nancy's desk; she leans over, meeting Nancy in a face-to-face,*

eyeball-to-eyeball fixed stare, with her back to Martha (camping out from behind). She creates a wall between Nancy and Martha and points to Nancy's paper (prompt).

We may classify space distances when visually confronting a misbehaving student as *proximity-far* for across the room, *proximity-near* when we are within three feet or at the edge of the student's *comfort bubble,* and *proximity-intimate* when we are inches from the student's face. The teacher actually uses these three distances as a technique of signaling students to desist and return to their work and escalates the intrusion by doing a slow *High Noon* walk. The teacher begins a process of *"closing space"* and begins to turn up the heat in the confrontational process. The slow movement of walking and all other easing movements are to permit the student to have time to recognize and understand the challenge and to enable the teacher to maintain and body-telegraph a calm message: "I am in charge, and I mean business."

STEPS IN LIMIT SETTING

Step 1: Eyes in the Back of Your Head

Effective teachers have *"with-it-ness,"* meaning that at all times they are perceptually and cognitively aware as to what is occurring in their classroom. They repeatedly check out what students are doing. To be effective in this technique, the teacher must be careful where she *parks her body.* If Ms. Dumas is helping Mark and is bent over with her head down and her back to 80 percent of the classroom, she will not see Luis tearing out a piece of notebook paper to make spitballs, or Stan creeping among the desks to snatch Harold's ball cap from his back pocket, or Angelica abandoning her math problems to snap open her purse in order to put on more makeup for the thousandth time. The with-it teacher *parks her body* with her back to the closest wall so that with her peripheral vision she can see as much of the classroom as possible. A good classroom arrangement will facilitate the teacher's body positioning. Additionally, the teacher must never get "lost" perceptually in the one student she is helping. If one student is standing before us, we may step back, take him by the shoulder, and turn him around so we are able to look at him and over his shoulder at the class at the same time. If we are bending down looking at a student's papers on his desk, we must heighten our hearing awareness to make up for our loss of vision. We should then periodically bob our head up like radar to make a 270-degree scan of the classroom so we may make quick eye contact with any student who is giving some thought to gambling on a fun off-task behavior. If we have the classroom furniture, especially the desks, arranged properly, and if we park our body with our backs to the wall and face students, we are now in the best position to see what is happening in the classroom.

Jones's use of the term *"check it out"* means simply that we need to keep our broad perceptions running even when we are focused on one student or activity, and we must "surface" regularly to visually scan and check things out. (See Figure 3.3.)

Step 2: Terminate Instruction

With her body still bent over the student's desk, Ms. Dumas takes two more relaxing breaths and stretches her neck up to scan the classroom to discover that Nancy is again off-task. Staying down, she (1) excuses herself from the student she was helping,

Proximity: Far				Proximity: Close		Proximity: Intimate		
Start: "Working the crowd" (eyes, modulation of voice, and moving)	Step 1: Eyes in the back of your head (with-it-ness)	Step 2: Terminate instruction	Step 3: Turn, look, and say name Student Response: smiley face or back talk	Step 4: Walk to the edge of student's desk (closing space)	Step 5: Prompt, break the "comfort bubble" of omnipotence (what they touch)	Step 6: Palms (what they touch)	Step 7: Camping out in front elbow down	Step 8: Camping out from behind (one may also consider "Moving-out" as a Step 9) elbow down, put up wall
Modality (felt by student)	Hearing	Visual	Visual and auditory	Visual	Visual and touch	Visual and touch	Visual, touch, and smell	Visual, touch, smell, and hearing

FIGURE 3.3   High Profile (Visual) Desist

(2) takes two more relaxing breaths, and (3) stands gradually to an upright position where for the second time she takes on the "I am not amused" facial expression. She (4) stares directly at Nancy across the room while (5) placing her hands behind her back (body-telegraphing).

Discipline comes before instruction is the Jones model's cardinal rule. The teacher is instructing Mark at his seat and is just getting to the point of closure on her mini-lesson when the discipline situation surfaces. The teacher may think, "I will just ignore Nancy for another minute until I finish this instruction with Mark, and then I will go and take care of the problem involving Nancy." No, no, and no! The students will then learn that instruction is more important than classroom discipline, and once learned they will take every opportunity to misbehave with nickel-and-dime misbehavior; they will gamble that they can get away with it, and the teacher will get little instruction done in the future. "Pay now with small change, or pay later with big dollars to remediate the problem." Step 2 requires us to apologize to students such as Mark and tell them we are done with them for the moment, and then "announce" that we are about to escalate our power by dealing with the misbehavior.

Step 3: Turn, Look, and Say the Student's Name

Turn and Face
The teacher stands, turns around completely, and faces the student in a square stance (the teacher's feet are parallel and facing the student). If Ms. Dumas has one foot pointed to Nancy and the other foot pointed in a second direction, making an "L" shape, experts in nonverbal behavior would say this body posture is ambivalent and will body-telegraph that the teacher is not committed to the confrontation with Nancy.

Look Them in the Eye   Make unwavering eye contact with the misbehaving student and do not drop the stare. If she is not looking, say her name in a flat nonhostile voice. Again, in contrast, if we drop our eyes, we communicate subservience and fear.

Facial Expression (the Teacher)   Again, in confronting Nancy, Ms. Dumas is struggling to control the fight-flight response, which causes her eyes to widen and her teeth to clench, producing a "fight-flight" face. To stop this from occurring, Jones suggests that the teacher permit her face to relax and unclench the teeth by becoming *"slack jawed."* The teacher is advised, while standing and staring, to take her tongue and curl it back in her mouth until she can touch the beginning of the soft tissue at the back of the mouth. This opens up the jaw and creates the "slack jaw" effect, ensuring that in a confrontation the teacher will not grit her teeth as a result of fight-flight reflex.

Now the student, under the heat of eye contact, will do a *"silly" smile,* which is described as an open-mouth-and-teeth smile with a slight cock of the head and raised eyebrows, much like a young baby might smile at his parents. The *smiley face* communicates to the adult from the child, "Look at me, aren't I cute and adorable and don't you just love me!" The teacher is to return the silly smile with a flat facial expression to send a message, "I am not amused" or "I am bored and will wait right here until you comply." At the same time, the teacher maintains eye contact, providing the visual heat.

Additional Body Cues Every part of the body communicates and telegraphs, and it is difficult to hide internal tension. Jones suggests taking a wide foot stance, placing the hands, which are normally a giveaway for tension, behind the body and clasping them together simply, and standing as relaxed as possible.

Saying the Student's Name If Ms. Dumas cannot get the acknowledgment and attention of the misbehaving student, she broadcasts to the student across the classroom by saying only her first name, using a flat nonhostile manner: "Nancy. Ah, Nancy."

Ms. Dumas stands, turns, squares off, goes slack-jawed, and says the student's first name. What is critical in this is that all of these actions are taken slowly. *Slower is better. Calmness is strength and communicates power.*[4]

Relaxing Breaths Any teaching of how to self-master tension and control emotional and physical action—such as relaxation therapy, stress management, and prepared childbirth training—involves teaching the person to breathe properly during a stressful situation. This is done by taking two controlled slow, shallow breaths, filling about 20 percent of your lung capacity and letting it out slowly, then resting for a few seconds and repeating the sequence. Normally, a breathing coach counts while you inhale and exhale. The exhaling is critical, relaxing the body and mind and slowing down the pace of all actions.

The uninitiated reader may have little appreciation of the value of controlled breathing or even find it humorous: "Wha-at, I need to be taught how to breathe? Ha!" In the Jones model, controlled breathing is the anchor and central technique on which all control is based in a stressful confrontational situation.

In on-site training sessions taught personally by Fredric Jones, all the techniques including relaxed breathing are taught to teachers through a process of *Say* (describes the technique), *Show* (models it), and *Do* (has groups of two teachers enact the techniques). Considerable time is spent on training "how to breathe." The reader who wishes to put the Jones *Tools for Teaching* techniques into practice would be advised to find a person who has had childbirth training and have that person explain, model, and coach you through the process until you feel comfortable and in command of these techniques. The vignette with Ms. Dumas and Nancy shows how the teacher needs to punctuate every new action by first taking two relaxing breaths and then moving slowly in a controlled manner.

To Move In, or Not to Move In

Nancy sees Ms. Dumas and quickly returns to her "pencil posturing." Ms. Dumas takes two more relaxing breaths and waits. Seconds, or more likely minutes, click by with Nancy being aware of the visual heat from Ms. Dumas. She tears out a sheet of paper, takes a second pencil from her purse, folds the paper, and appears to put her pencil to paper (pseudocompliance), all for the purpose of convincing Ms. Dumas that she is now working and that the teacher can turn off the visual heat.

This time Ms. Dumas is not fooled. She takes two more of her controlled breaths and then, still not breaking her visual stare, begins to walk slowly across the room straight toward Nancy. She moves with her High Noon gait. She stops and squares off inches in front of Nancy's desk, again with her hands behind her back and her face flat and expressionless. Finally, her eyes are fixed, looking directly down at Nancy. Ms. Dumas takes her two relaxing breaths and waits. Nancy responds, "Wha-a-t?"

Once you have broadcast the student's name and made eye contact, your next decision is to determine whether the student has "gotten the message" and is complying or whether you need to escalate the confrontation by *"closing space,"* or moving spatially closer to the misbehaving student. The student will perform a host of *pseudocompliance* actions, such as *pencil posturing,* paper shuffling, or pretending to read, in an attempt to convince you that he or she is now working and to get out of your visual fix. One way of determining if the student is complying is to compare the positions of the student's upper and lower body.

Nancy now makes eye contact with Ms. Dumas and sees the teacher looking straight at her; she wiggles in her chair and turns her upper body toward Ms. Dumas, but her lower body (knees and feet) still face her neighbor. She picks up her pencil (pseudocompliance: pencil posturing) and places it on her paper as if to write. She looks again to see Ms. Dumas still maintaining the same unwavering eye contact.

Ms. Dumas notices that under the table Nancy's lower body, especially her knees, is still pointing to the neighbor who was the target of her talking. This position seems to say, "I'll return to my talking once I get you out of my face."

The student's upper body position is for show and attempts to convince the teacher that the student is cooperating, but the position of the lower body nonverbally indicates the student's real intention. It is not until later that the student moves her legs under her desk and begins real work.

Nancy turns her lower body so her legs are now fully under her desk, and does a second, third, and fourth algebra problem while Ms. Dumas is "camped out." When Nancy is halfway through the second line of problems, Ms. Dumas speaks to her for the first time, "Thank you, Nancy." The teacher smiles.

The teacher will need to read the student's posture messages and not be fooled by the pseudocompliance behavior in the discipline poker game. If the student does comply and returns to work, the incident is over and the teacher returns to her previous activity. The basic goal, always, in limit setting is to *calm the students and get them back on task.* We would like to avoid any behaviors that would cause an *adrenaline dump* or *a fight-or-flight response* in the misbehaving student or other class members because, after such negative incidents, it can take 20 to 30 minutes for them to be relaxed enough to do real work. *Do not go any further with the limit-setting sequence than is required to produce the desired result.*[5] But, if the student does not comply and is playing a game of discipline poker with you, you may be forced to escalate your intervention by *closing space—moving in.*

Step 4: Walk to the Edge of the Student's Desk

The teacher walks slowly to the student, never breaking eye contact. She stops when her legs are touching the front of the student's desk and assumes an erect posture and flat facial expression. Repeated relaxing breaths are used, and once in front of the desk, the teacher simply waits and permits the student to sizzle in the teacher's visual heat.

At this point we are most likely to get varying forms of *back talk* (helplessness, denying, blaming, etc.), with the student playing a host of recognizable games to divert us from her real behavior and intent. Do not be taken in by these student maneuvers, especially the helpless statements that suggest the student does not understand the assignment and needs your help—this is a distracting ploy.

One of the most difficult forms of back talk is profanity. Maintain unwavering eye contact, and deal with the profanity later, being certain that the offending student is not allowed to get away with it. When students become verbally abusive to us, we maintain our stance and eye contact. We keep repeating our relaxing breaths, but now we add a *focal point* in order not to hear the harsh words the student is hurling at us. We pick out a small point *(focal point)* on the student's forehead and stare at that point. This permits our mind to bring forth a pleasant scene and mentally leave this confrontational situation—in essence, we allow our mind to take a brief vacation. Do not respond to any form of back talk, no matter how clever or offensive, but stand your ground and be prepared to *"camp out."* [*Note:* If in your judgment there is any chance that closing space is likely to cause the student to assault you, stop and drop the limit-setting approach; you will need to move to a backup system, which will be described later.]

Teachers by their nature are verbal people. We make our living by talking, but Jones would say, "No, not at this time!" Do not speak … say nothing … shut up … keep quiet. There are no words that we can use to be effective in this confrontation. It is the power of the teacher's calmness, eye contact, and use of spatial proximity that will induce the student to capitulate and "get back to work." Jones says, "Any fool may speak, but it takes two people to speak foolishly." If we venture to verbally debate the student's back talk, we will be hooked by the student into playing the game on his or her ground. We would produce "silly" talk and lose the confrontation. Keep quiet—do not speak—shut up!

Step 5: Prompt

Nancy whines, "I wasn't doing anything. What? (back talk: denial) Martha wanted a pencil (back talk: blaming), that's all." Ms. Dumas maintains her posture and stares. Nancy drops her eyes and becomes passive. Ms. Dumas reaches out with her right hand, turns Nancy's textbook to page 45, and points to the first problem (prompt). She then returns to the same upright stance.

Having moved across the room to stand before the student's desk, we are now in new territory *(proximity-near)*. We have broken the student's *comfort bubble* by reaching in with our hands and signaling a prompt to an action that we want. Ms. Dumas reaches out with her right hand, turns Nancy's textbook to page 45, and points to the first problem. If we are successful and the student does begin to work, we can start our steps for *moving out* (described later), but if are not successful we will continue our spatial escalation.

Step 6: Palms

By reaching our hands into the student's comfort bubble to *prompt,* we now get into that bubble with the student. Ms. Dumas now leans or eases over in a slow controlled manner and places the palms *(palms)* of her two hands flat on the far sides of Nancy's desk and paperwork and takes two relaxing breaths. The teacher remains with her palms down on Nancy's desk and watches with unwavering eye contact with Nancy *(camping out in front).* Ms. Dumas is still looking when Nancy whines, "I don't know how to do this " *(back talk: helplessness).* Ms. Dumas waits *(camping out in front).*

The teacher leans over, placing his or her hands palms down on each side of the student's desk with the student's papers and work between these hands. The *palms* on the desk say to the student that you are willing to *camp out in front* as long as it takes. Remember to keep taking your relaxing breaths and maintaining your eye contact, now from a distance of approximately one foot from the student's face (nose to nose). At this point the new modalities of smell and even the sound of your breathing join the modality of looking. This *proximity-intimate* is generally very unnerving for the adolescent student.

Caution: The female teacher must be careful to wear high-buttoned blouses so that when she leans over she does not reveal herself. The male teacher dealing with a female student wearing an open-top blouse should stop at the previous step and not use palms down or get closer, in order to avoid the improper appearance that he is looking down the student's blouse. The adolescent will find this close spatial proximity unnerving and will blame your actions on voyeurism. We don't want to give the student this type of excuse. The teacher who cannot advance further on the steps will be forced to go to the Backup System.

Step 7: Camping Out in Front

We are now at *palms* and the student is "mouthing off" with a barrage of *back talk.* After a period of time, the teacher now eases in by lifting one hand, bending an elbow, and placing her weight on that elbow, which is now on one edge of the desk top *(camp out in front).* While maintaining relaxed breathing and unwavering eye contact, she remains quiet and waits.

Step 8: Camping Out from Behind

If there is a neighboring student such as Martha involved, most likely the second student will join the first student's *back talk* to gang up on you.

> *"Martha asked me for a pencil, I was only giving Martha a pencil." (**Back talking: blaming.**) Martha now joins Nancy and attempts to gang up on Ms. Dumas, stating, "Yeah, get out of her face." (**Back talk.**)*
>
> *Ms. Dumas, in a slow controlled manner, stands erect and takes two relaxing breaths. She then slowly moves behind and between the girls. Ms. Dumas eases between the girls, placing her elbow on Nancy's desk; she leans over, meeting Nancy*

in a face-to-face, eyeball-to-eyeball fixed stare, with her back to Martha (camping out from behind). She creates a wall between Nancy and Martha, thus splitting up the gang of two.

When two students gang up on us, we will not win if we deal with both of them at the same time. We divide and conquer by putting up a wall between them and dealing with one student at a time.

Step 9: Moving Out

By this point, the student has capitulated and begins to work. We then need to begin *moving out,* which is also a controlled process of steps. Before we move out, however, let's deal with the second student.

> *Nancy turns her lower body so her legs are now fully under her desk, and does a second, third, and fourth algebra problem while Ms. Dumas is camped out. When Nancy is halfway through the second line of problems, Ms. Dumas speaks to her for the first time, "Thank you, Nancy." The teacher smiles, then picks up her elbow and turns around to face Martha. She places her elbow on Martha's desk. Martha does not look up and is obviously working like an eager beaver on her algebra problems. Ms. Dumas smiles and says, "Thank you, Martha."*
>
> *Ms. Dumas slowly stands (moving out), breathes, turns, and walks to the front of Martha's desk. She takes two relaxing breaths, assumes her stance, and looks directly at Martha. Ms. Dumas slowly walks away from the girls (moving out), but first she takes five or six steps, stops, turns, takes two relaxing breaths, and looks at Nancy and then Martha. Both students are now too busy to look up.*

We must use the moving-out process step by step in a slow, skilled manner or we will lose everything we have established to this point. Slowly, we stand and begin to move back to our original position, where we were working with a student across the room. But we will stop, posture, breathe, make eye contact at each of the proximity points of *close* or *intimate* (at the edge of the students's desk, or approximately eight feet in front of the teacher is also called the red zone, meaning the student will not chance being off-tasked), *near* (approximately 15 feet from the teacher is the yellow zone where the students will chance off-task behavior when the teacher is not looking), and *far* or the green zone where the student feels free to be off-task without being caught. Much like a stoplight's red, yellow, and green, the teacher's movement while walking about the room, *working the crowd,* uses proxemics by keeping all or most all of the class in the red or yellow zone.

> *Ms. Dumas walks back to the student she was helping, but before bending over to help, she again assumes her erect posture, looking at Nancy and Martha. After finally being reassured, she takes two more relaxing breaths and bends over to help the nearby student, placing herself beside the new student but again in direct view of Nancy and Martha, as well as the remainder of the class (tailhook).*

The visual proximity confrontation process is now completed but will continue to be maintained through the teacher's walking about the classroom looking and checking the students' work *(working the crowd).* When confronted for compliance in our example, Nancy and Martha began a conscious and unconscious series of back-talk maneuvers to take Ms. Dumas down a blind alley toward powerlessness and defeat. This *back talk* took the following forms:

• Helplessness	"I don't know how to do this."
• Denial	"I wasn't doing anything."
	"Wha-at?"
• Blaming	"Martha wanted a pencil—that's all!"
• Accusing the teacher of professional incompetence	"You went over this so quickly I didn't understand it."
• Excusing the teacher to leave	"Yeah, get out of her face."

Back talk may even escalate into insults or profanity. Other forms of *back talk* that do not appear as such to most teachers include:

• Crying	Attempt to get our sympathy
• Compliments	Making flattering statements to the teacher
• Tangential statements	Asking a question about a topic not under discussion
• Pushing you aside	When the teacher puts her hands on the desk *palms down,* the student pushes them aside and off the desk
• Romance	Student actually kisses the teacher or makes a sexual overture

Weaning the Helpless Handraisers

Every teacher has had the experience of explaining an activity to a class and then assigning them to carry out the practice of this concept at their desks, and having one student raise a hand to ask, "How do I do this?" Jones calls these students helpless handraisers who have learned to be helpess, and that if we individually go to them to teach the same concept or direction again we are falling into a trap of reinforcing these students for their learned helplessness. He humorously describes the handraising behavior as having four positions as the student physically tires from having his hand in the air: beginning position (arm straight up), half-mast (lowering the arm and providing some support), broken wing (rotating the arm a quarter turn and relaxing, laying their head on their desk), and finally the out-cold (maintaining the broken wing that they "lose their train of thought" and are "out-cold" when you get to them).

Limit Setting on the Wing

Proximity is accountability. Distance is safety.[6] The teacher who has been trained in *Tools for Teaching* will not be found lecturing from in front of her desk, seated on top of her desk, or seated in a chair. This style of teaching requires the teacher to be on her feet slowly walking and *working the crowd,* moving among the students who are seated at desks or tables. When walking, or *on the wing,* the teacher is aware of and uses eye contact and proximity to maintain the attentiveness or work activity of each and every student. The walking and looking combination creates a conscious ballet of movement that will bring the teacher in *proximity-far* (as far as 10 feet) and *proximity-near* (at the edge of the three-foot *comfort bubble* of each student). Periodically when the teacher bends over to help one student for a few moments, the teacher is in *proximity-intimate*. Throughout the entire class period, students will always feel the presence of the teacher, while the teacher is instructing or even while the student is doing independent seat work.

> *Once she has helped this student, Ms. Dumas slowly walks through the students' pre-arranged desks, traversing an interior circle around the classroom as she passes among the working students. She checks on students' work, and passes again before Nancy and Martha. She stops, looks, checks, and in a voice soft enough that a neighbor cannot hear makes comments about a particular student's work, before moving on* (**working the crowd**). *In all, she speaks to five to seven students. When she comes to Martha, three minutes before the bell is to ring, she appears to stop, look, check, and comment in a similar fashion, but this time she whispers a different nonacademic statement: "Martha, after the bell rings I would like you to stay behind. We need to talk."* (**Camouflage.**)

In order for the teacher to perform this walking ballet, it is critical to have a well-designed staging of the students' desks, chairs, or tables. Traditionally we think of all classrooms as six rows of five or more chairs with the teacher's desk before a chalkboard in the front of the classroom. Such a room arrangement, however, puts walls between the teacher and the students and always maintains the teacher at the *far proximity*. Jones arranges the students' desks with an interior loop as a pathway for the teacher to walk through. (See his double-E classroom in Figure 3.4.)

The use of an interior loop of free floor space where the teacher can walk without obstruction permits easy teacher movement and excellent supervision through the use of proximity and eye contact.

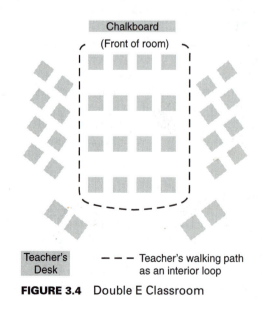

FIGURE 3.4 Double E Classroom

Guidelines for Room Arrangement/Space Use

- Don't let the janitor dictate the desk arrangement.
- Furniture arrangement is best when it puts the least distance and fewest barriers between teacher and students.
- Place the teacher's desk on the side or in the rear and get the entire class as close as possible to the chalkboard.
- Compact the students' desks together as much as possible.
- The teacher goes to the students; students do not come and wait for the teacher.
- Place well-behaved, cooperative students in the most distant seats from the teacher.
- Place misbehaving students in the middle of the interior loop and as close to the teacher as possible.[7]

THE BACKUP SYSTEM

When one student is a chronic discipline problem and our limit-setting techniques fail despite being correctly applied, we are now required to drop limit setting and move to something else. That something else is the use of either a backup system or omission training (OT). We will describe the back up system here and later will fully explain omission training, as well as the incentive program and responsibility training—the final legs of the discipline stool necessary for the total Jones discipline program to work.

Typically, most schools by default have a backup system that is neither systematic nor well thought out, but apply certain traditional sanctions to students, generally arranged in increasing severity. They typically are, in sequence:

- Warning
- Conference with student
- Time out, being sent to the office, detention
- Conference with parent
- Conference with teacher, parent, and principal or vice principal
- In-school suspension
- Out-of-school suspension (one day)
- Out-of-school suspension (three days)
- Expulsion and/or a special program such as "continuation school"

Most of these progressively more punitive sanctions are overused by the majority of schools and simply do not work. They are self-perpetuating, and do not "self-eliminate." On pages 260–265 of his book, Jones gives a solid description of why these sanctions fail, based on behavioral theory, reinforcement scheduling, and reinforcement error. His explanation is a "must read" for any teacher and school continuing to use such useless traditional practices. Jones simply and concisely summarizes what these practices are really saying to a chronically misbehaving student. Jones's message can be paraphrased as, "You know what we're going to do to you? We're going to send you to the office, where you'll have nothing to do but watch all the activity that goes on there. And then we may have to suspend you—to deprive you of the opportunity to sit in your math class, your English class, your social studies class, and your science class. In other words, we're going to punish you by making you go out and have a good time."

Essentially, this says to the misbehaving child that if he escalates the level of his obnoxious behavior, authorities will have no choice but to grant him freedom. The sanctions basically fail because the teacher and school have little or no system or technology and are blundering through the application of these sanctions. Jones proposes a methodology by defining three levels of the backup system as Level 1: Small Backup Responses, which take place in the classroom and are private between the teacher and student; Level 2: Medium Backup Responses, which are mostly carried out by the teacher, but are now more public; and Level 3: Large Backup Responses, a time-costly process that will involve high public visibility and the participation of others such as a counselor, the principal, or even the judicial system.

Backup Responses in the Classroom

*Once she has helped this student, Ms. Dumas slowly walks through the students' pre-arranged desks, traversing an interior circle around the classroom as she passes among the working students. She checks on students' work, and passes again before Nancy and Martha. She stops, looks, checks, and in a voice soft enough that a neighbor cannot hear she makes comments about a particular student's work before moving on (**working the crowd**). In all, she speaks to five to seven students. When she comes to Martha three minutes before the bell is to ring, she appears to stop, look, check, and comment in a similar fashion (**camouflage**), but this time she whispers a different nonacademic statement: "Martha, after the bell rings I would like you to stay behind. We need to talk." (moved to **Backup System: Level 1, Small Response—"Ear Warning"**).*

The bell rings and the students depart, passing Ms. Dumas as she stands at the door. When Martha arrives, the teacher signals her to move to a nearby desk, then closes the door to the now empty classroom (private meeting). It is time for Ms. Dumas to deal with Martha regarding her confrontational behavior. (Don't go public!) Ms. Dumas has not forgotten Martha's words, "Yeah, get out of her face!"

After-Class Meeting: Example 1

Ms. DUMAS: "Martha, the use of such harsh language toward me today suggests to me that you may be angry, or there is some problem occurring with you. Can I help?"

MARTHA: "Well, things are not good at home these days. My father was arrested last night. We were at the jail all night, and I'm really exhausted. I don't know what got into me today."

Ms. DUMAS: "Well, sometimes no sleep and such problems do rattle our nerves and make us edgy. An apology would be welcomed by me!"

MARTHA: "Well, I am REALLY sorry. I don't know why I acted so rude to you."

Ms. DUMAS: "Your apology is accepted, and if things really continue to be rough for you I can extend your deadline for the class project. You also may wish to stop by and talk with the school counselor, Mr. Evans. I'll write you a pass to get out of study hall so you can talk to him."

After-Class Meeting: Example 2

Ms. DUMAS: "Martha, the use of such harsh language toward me today suggests to me that you may be angry or there is some problem occurring with you. Can I help?"

MARTHA: "Dumas, get out of my face!"

Ms. DUMAS: "Martha, I will not accept such rudeness from you. This is your warning. If you speak to me like that again, I will need to take actions that you will not like, and which I would prefer not to take. It is now your choice. I would prefer to settle this calmly between the two of us. But it is your choice. Do you wish to talk to me about anything that can be causing you to be so angry?"

MARTHA: "NO!"

Ms. DUMAS: "Okay, you have had your warning. You may now go to class. I will be watching your behavior in the future, and I hope that we have settled this matter with this warning."

(Martha departs)

Small Backup Responses   The Level 1: Small Backup Response is a quiet and private confrontation between the teacher and the misbehaving student. The teacher continues to *work the crowd,* walking around the classroom to supervise, using eye contact and proximity to keep the student working. The teacher periodically speaks softly to the various students about their work, which is her standard routine. When the teacher wants to use a backup response by warning the student about the misbehavior, she first camouflages her intent by stopping at three or four students' desks to talk about academic matters. But when she comes to the misbehaving student, she issues a nonpublic warning: "Nancy, this is the second time class has been disrupted by your talking. If this occurs again, I will need to think about taking some actions to get you to stop this." *(Ear warning.)* The teacher stands, makes eye contact, assumes an erect posture, and then moves on to another student. The *ear warning* is not heard by any neighbors, thus is done in such a *nonpublic manner* that the student does not need to act back in order to save face.

The idea of the ear warning is to get the student to stop while still saving face. If necessary, a *private meeting* would be held between the student and the teacher out of the view and hearing of peers, as Ms. Dumas did with Martha regarding her swearing. In these conferences we teachers have two choices: either *"think and talk"* or *"warn and deliver."* In the after-class meeting with Martha in example 1, we see the teacher talking to Martha supportively, and listening and thinking about what she is hearing from the girl. In example 2 we see the "warn and deliver" actions by Ms. Dumas; she warns Martha about the swearing and is prepared to "deliver" if it occurs again.

Quiet Time   As part of her working-the-crowd supervision techniques, the teacher whispers in Nancy's ear, "Nancy, you are having a hard time staying at your work and you're about to get in deep trouble with me. I would like you to have some quiet time to think this over and decide to change your behavior. Go to that chair at the back of the room, and I will signal you in five minutes. Then I want you to return to your seat ready to work."

Quiet time is a technique that requests that the student go to an out-of-the-way area and become quiet and reflect on his or her actions and decide to change. The time should not exceed five to 10 minutes.

Medium Backup Responses

Ms. Dumas has arranged to have a professor of ornithology from a local university give a guest lecture in her biology class this morning. Bird study is Ms. Dumas's passion, and she is both excited and a little nervous about having such a renowned national expert in her classroom. During the lecture the guest demonstrates a number of bird calls to the class, to the amusement of Nancy. In the middle of each call, Nancy erupts into a large belly laugh that stops the demonstration. She then leans over to her neighbors and makes odd whistling and mouthing sounds, causing everyone on that side of the room to "crack up." Ms. Dumas walks to the classroom door and signals with one finger for Nancy to follow her. Nancy is quickly escorted to the end of the hall and placed on a lone chair at the back of Mr. Fox's class. She is now in time out.

Medium backup responses are those sanctions that have traditionally been used in schools. These include time out, loss of privileges, parent conferences, and detention. Classroom teachers, without the aid of school administrators, still primarily carry out the *medium backup responses.* These methods are considered risky because they may produce feelings of hostility and nonacceptance in students, they are time consuming, they have a high probability of failing, and they are much more public. Before the teacher moves to a medium backup response, it is best to revisit the practices of limit setting, omission training, and the incentive program to see if those processes are working. *Medium backup responses* are not ray guns that we quickly pull out when the occasion arises and use to zap the misbehaving student. They must be well thought out, used systematically, and done in as *private or semiprivate* a manner as possible.

The rule of thumb is to deliver a nonpublic warning to students in preparation for a medium backup response, as far as it can be done. Don't go public; stay private. Putting the student's name on the board as a warning, for example, would be public and destructive to the student–teacher relationship and eventually will cost the student. Use private talks out of the view and hearing of peers. Before using medium backup responses, always reevaluate to see if your entire management system is working: perhaps you are moving too fast and short-cutting your other systems.

The following are some medium-level sanction listed by Jones:[8]

1. Time out in the classroom
2. Time out in a colleague's classroom
3. Public warning
4. Threat
5. Being sent to the hall
6. Detention after school
7. Loss of privilege
8. Parent conference

Items considered to be very poor practice:

9. Lowering the student's grade
10. Extra homework

Time Out   Time out is the temporary removal of a student from an activity as a consequence of his inappropriate behavior, usually not to exceed five minutes. Normally the place of time out is a neutral isolated chair. But Jones feels this is an overused and mis-used process, with many teachers unaware of the requirement for time out to be truly effective. The following is an overview of guidelines for the use of time out:

- Rules and expectations must be spelled out clearly in advance.
- Consequences for unacceptable behavior must be described and demonstrated in advance.
- An appropriate time-out place that denies the student substitute means of reward must be selected.
- The problem behavior must be responded to early with limit setting followed by warning.
- There must be consistency.
- The student must be effectively delivered to time out if she resists. If the student refuses, we are into a time-costly and emotionally charged confrontation that will cause much damage to the teacher–student relationship. Don't take middle backup responses lightly.
- Effectively respond to problems that the student might cause while in time out (our response must be clearly thought out beforehand).

Public Warning and Threats   Public warnings and threats in which the teacher uses pheasant posturing, nagging, and silly talk are costly to the teacher, ineffective, and destructive, and they will eventually require an escalation to a large backup response. Don't use them.

Being Sent to the Hall   This is a time-honored practice that takes a dangerous gamble. The student is humiliated by being seated in the hall, is reinforced by activity going on in the hall, is unsupervised and can wander about causing real mischief, or will be a "runner." Don't use it!

Detention after School   Jones questions the real value of after-school detention. Only the students who don't really need it show up for detention, and it teaches them that being in a classroom and in a school setting is punishment. As a result, through associative learning all school attendance becomes a punishment. In addition, many teachers overuse detention. Rarely use it. Jones says that, if it is necessary, it should be employed in a well thought-out, systematic manner.

Loss of Privilege   On the surface this looks like a good sanction, but it will cause resentment from the student, and eventually the student will seek to make the teacher pay. An escalating battle will develop and eventually lead to a large backup response.

Parent Conference   Many of today's teachers feel they get very little support from parents. A parent conference used by the teacher costs much time and hardly ever produces meaningful results. Jones feels that the misbehaving student is one who has learned to mis-behave at home under the ineffective discipline techniques of his parents. What makes a teacher think that if he or she cannot control the student at school, the parents have the par-enting skills to effectively get the child's behavior to change? To help parents remediate the negative behaviors of their child requires professional counseling or therapy, and the teacher does not have the necessary skills or time to be effective with parents. You may try parent conferences, but don't expect much help from this approach. Jones, who is a family psychologist and therapist, says, "Get what you can out of a parent conference and keep your hopes modest. In most cases it's cheaper to fix it yourself."[9]

Lowering Student's Grade/Assigning Extra Work   Lowering a grade and giving extra work as a discipline sanction are widely used but highly destructive practices that condition students to hate schoolwork and resent the teacher.[10] Don't do either.

Large Backup Responses   The large backup response to discipline situations is the very public action of sending the student to the office, which has a high probability of escalating to more extreme sanctions including suspension or expulsion.

Sending Students to the Office   Jones says, "Indeed sending a student to the office may have the dubious distinction of being the most overused and overrated discipline technique in education."[11] Let us give up the myth that the vice principal or the school counselor has a magic ritual that will change the misbehaving student into an angel. Let us also give up the idea that being sent to the office is or can be a punishment. It is not and cannot be. In the student's mind, the message is, "If I get sent to the office, I escape for an entire period of American History, and I am entertained by the office's social happenings. I get rewarded by being able to talk to my friends who are also sitting on the bench waiting to talk to the administrator."

So what can the professionals in the office do to help the teacher? The answer is that they usually do have behavioral and counseling skills that can be useful to the teacher, but they rarely get a chance to use these skills. Jones reports that in a typical large high school the office referrals, counting tardies, run between 2,500 and 5,000 per school year. The vice principal is running a revolving-door referral service with no time to really counsel the students, who receive a bunch of "silly" talk and are sent back to their classrooms.

Why are so many students referred to the office, creating this gridlock? Jones says it is because of the "bouncers." Excluding tardies, 90 percent of all office referrals are sent to the office by the same five percent of teachers, and the effective teachers who rarely use the office don't know the facts regarding this overuse by the "bouncers." The teachers who are not willing to take the time to use limit setting, omission training, an incentive program, and teacher responsibility are the very ones who, in the face of some minor misbehavior, "bounce" the students down to the office. The bouncer is rewarded by being rid of the difficult student for the remainder of the period. It is easy for the bouncer-teacher: Just zap them with a pink slip, send them to the office, and you are done with it.

Sometimes the committed teacher with a genuine discipline system in place does rightfully need the office's help. Larry in Mr. O'Donald's class has been back talking and appears irritable. Mr. O'Donald is aware that Larry's father is an alcoholic and is violent with Larry. Last night his father fought with Larry and literally kicked him out of the house. As a result, Larry slept in the bus station. Today, as he arrived for second-period English class, someone had taken his normal seat. When the classmate refused to move, Larry slugged him. Mr. O'Donald sent Larry to the office, and now needs help from the office staff regarding what to do about Larry. This is a legitimate problem, and the school structure must serve Mr. O'Donald's need. So for office referrals, we have two objectives: (1) set up an omission training program that makes it costly for the "bouncers" to cause gridlock by sending students with minor misbehaviors to the office; and (2) create a system whereby the office staff can help teachers such as Mr. O'Donald who really are conscientious and have legitimate needs.

Office Referral System   The administration, typically the vice principal, establishes the guidelines for referring students to the office. This system, with its paperwork and meetings, will be viewed by the bouncer as a punishing and costly disincentive, but will be seen as a real way of getting office help for the committed teacher (such as Mr. O'Donald, who really wants to get help for Larry). After the second office referral and during the after-school meeting with the bouncer, the principal insists, "Tell me about the limit-setting actions you have taken with the student you referred. Tell me about your omission training and your responsibility training. Oh, you don't have any and haven't done this! Well, here is Jones's book called *Tools for Teaching;* take it, read it, and use it in your classroom, and I will be by to see if you still need my help in implementing such a discipline program. By the way, until we have all four legs of this discipline system working well, please do not refer any students to the office. Thank you very much."

In contrast, the committed teacher now has a structure for getting real help. The disincentive system has stopped the bouncer's trivial referrals, the office gridlock has been broken, and the principal and counselors can now do the job they were really trained to do. Other large backup responses may also be addressed as a part of the staffing process, including notifying parents, in-school suspension, expulsion, or involving the police or juvenile authorities, all of which Jones feels are highly destructive and ineffective. "Are we going to pull out all the stops to keep this student in public education, or are we going to call it off?"[12] The staffing process is a system for working as a group to "pull out all the stops."

Corporal Punishment   Jones does not mince words when discussing the use of corporal punishment: "If the technology of discipline management could be likened to an animal, then corporal punishment would surely be its ass end. Of all the discipline techniques in existence, corporal punishment distinguishes itself as having the fewest assets and the greatest number of liabilities. In terms of locking adult and child into a series of coercive cycles, it is the all-time champion. Those who rely on it swear by it—testimonial to the addictive properties of quick short-term cures."[13]

Many teachers and administrators question, "Where do you stand on corporal punishment?" as a litmus test for whether the discipline system being suggested is a "soft" model or whether it really "means business." Jones uses his behavior analysis construction regarding reinforcement and demonstrates that the whole process of sending a student to the office for corporal punishment is full of reinforcement errors. Unknowingly, those who use corporal punishment fail to see that the student receives constant and positive reinforcement as the process unfolds. The "bad" student gets the entire class to stop and focus on him; he passes classmates in the hall and they give him acknowledgment by their smiles of recognition and comments; the office atmosphere changes when he arrives; he gets to interact with the principal; and he returns to the classroom as a "hero," one who has been through it and lived. One school so clearly failed to see how the student was really being positively and socially reinforced that it actually permitted the student to sign the paddle.

Corporal punishment is the granddaddy of large sanctions. As a part of the backup system, these sanctions will likely (1) be destructive to the school–student relationship, (2) cause the student to feel resentment and withhold all future cooperation, (3) make the student irresponsible, (4) make the student dependent on an external authority, and (5) cause the student to become countercoercive to "get even" with the school or teacher.[14]

RESPONSIBILITY TRAINING

The purpose of limit setting is to stop behavior—to calm the students and get them back on task—but it has its limitations. In order to run a productive classroom, the teacher needs cooperation from students, such as showing up on time, walking in an orderly fashion as they enter the classroom, bringing books and pencils, taking their seats right away, and being at work when the bell rings. The teacher cannot force students to cooperate. Cooperation is always voluntary and under the control of the student. Students choose to cooperate or not cooperate, and responsibility training is *Tools for Teaching's* system for helping the teacher obtain such positive cooperation.

When we seek cooperation from students, they naturally ask, "Why should I?" or "What's in it for me?" Let's look at two toddlers, one lucky to have warm, effective parents, the other an unlucky child who has been neglected and not nurtured. The parents of Lucky see her holding a valuable, breakable knick-knack, and mother asks, "Careful dear, give that to Mommy, please. That is not a toy." Lucky, who has learned to trust and depend on adults, complies and is kissed and hugged by her parent. Unlucky is asked to "give it to Mommy," but there is no trust. He does not trust that he will receive hugs, kisses, and warmth, so he thinks, "I will keep what I have and get as much pleasure as I can from this." He refuses to give it up, throws a temper tantrum, and breaks the item. Unlucky has no trust in the future, and so we see no cooperation.

Many students coming to our schools today are like Unlucky, and they can't have sufficient trust in adults and teachers to accept the demands made of them for school and classroom cooperation. "I will goof off and take as much pleasure with my friends now because I am sure that it will not come to me in the future." These students need to be given to, at the human relationship level, before they can give back with cooperation. Traditionally schools and teachers nag, punish, and coerce these children at a great price, but with no results. Jones says that every classroom needs an incentive system to teach cooperation. Limit setting can be very helpful for stopping misbehavior, but responsibility training is needed to develop cooperative behavior in students.

To put it simply, students have to be given something that they value, something they will strive to conserve once it is in their possession. Jones uses the analogy of teaching a teenager to be responsible with money. The teenager is given a sum of money to spend and take care of necessities, including his school lunch money. He has not earned it, but his parents have given it to him. He is (1) responsible for this finite amount of money, (2) responsible for the control of how the money is spent, and (3) made responsible for living with the consequences if he overconsumes and runs out of the resource. By Wednesday, the teenager has used up all of his monetary resources and asks his dad, "Could you spare some change for my lunch money for the remainder of the week?" Good old Dad says, "No!" He is teaching his child to be responsible, and there is real-life stress in the situation. (It is important to note, however, that the teenager would not starve if he misses lunch; he can take some fruit or other items from home to eat at lunchtime.) This is the basis for Jones's responsibility training. Let us see this in action:

> *"Good morning, eighth graders, and welcome to second-period English class. I am your teacher, Mr. Hansen. I have a surprise gift for all of you. Is there anyone here who does not enjoy watching videos? (No hands go up, but a few giggles are heard.) I am going to start this class off with a video gift to you. (The teacher shows 25 minutes*

of the motion picture To Kill a Mockingbird, which is the first book the class will read.) I can see by your faces that you enjoyed that and are curious to see the rest. Well, you will see it this Friday. In the future, you and I will negotiate on future videos that you might like to see, or other enjoyable activities. Every Friday I will give you a PAT. (Laughter.) No, not that kind of pat, my PAT means Preferred Activity Time. I have chosen the preferred activity this week as a video, but in the future you will help me decide what PATs you like and how you want to use your time. I am awarding you a gift of 15 minutes of class time (writes 15 on the corner of the chalkboard) on Friday this week for you to see more of this video. In the future, you can earn even more time to be added to this 15 minutes by your cooperation in here.

"Now, you may add more 'free' time to this 15 minute PAT in a number of ways, including hurry-up bonuses, automatic bonuses, bonus contests, and individual bonuses. Hurry-up bonuses are given when you hustle. Okay, let's try to see if you can win some hurry-up bonuses right now. On the board I have written jobs that we need to accomplish quickly this morning. They are:

1. Last person in the row get a textbook for each person in that row.
2. Write your name in the book, at the proper location on the front cover.
3. Place your book ID number on the master list that is being passed around.
4. Read the three-paragraph introduction to To Kill a Mockingbird on page 7.
5. No talking or goofing off.

"Now, you can see that in my hand I'm holding a stopwatch. My calculation is that the jobs on the board can be accomplished in five minutes. I will click the stopwatch, and you will begin. When all these jobs are accomplished, you will signal by turning over your textbook. When I see that everyone is done, I will stop the watch. Whatever amount of time is left on the watch will be added to your PAT gift of 15 minutes. During the week you may continue to add more free time for your Friday PAT. Begin now!"

The teacher clicks the stopwatch. During the activities, Jim, who sits in the front row and was one of the last students to get a book, begins to mentally drift off. His book is now in front of him and so is the master list, but he is "spaced out." Quickly, those students around him see that the master list is stalled on his desk and he is not working. The neighbors gently poke him, frown, and point to the list. Startled, Jim quickly "gets with the program."

This example uses peer pressure rather than teacher nagging, threats, or coercion. Several minutes later, Mr. Hansen says:

"Oh, I see you are all done, let me check my watch. Ha! One minute and twenty seconds remaining! You have earned this time and I will write it here on the board under the 15 so we will remember, and on Friday we will add up the minutes. By the way, no cheating. I keep a record of this in my grade book, so I don't want anyone changing times up here. (Laughter.) Now, you will also earn time through Automatic Bonuses. For example, if each of you is in your seat and working when the bell rings, this will be an automatic two minutes added to your PAT. You will see that cooperation will result in other ways to earn automatic bonuses. I am also going to keep the time awards up here for all three of my English classes, so you can see how your competitors are doing. Whichever of the three classes has scored the highest points will receive a bonus of five minutes, and second place will get three extra minutes."

What we have just seen is Jones's responsibility training, and the use of incentives (the PAT, or Preferred Activity Time). Time is the currency that students will earn. Just like the teenager learning to be responsible with money, the students are given 15 minutes of time-currency as a gift from the teacher. They are (1) responsible for this time-currency and there is a finite amount, (2) responsible for controlling how the time-currency is spent (consumption), and (3) made responsible for living with the consequences if they overconsume and run out of the resource (time).[15] This spending of the time-currency may occur in two ways, through penalties or use on the PAT.

Penalty

"Students, you now have your time, and all the other time during our class period is mine for instruction. Your job is to work hard during my time. Sometimes, some students like to play games and use up their time before the end of the week, which is when most PATs are done. When they poach on my time like this, they are penalized by losing some of their time."

Let's look at an example of the awarding of penalties by the teacher. It is the second day of English class, and the students are busy working when Laverne decides to get a dictionary. She stands, but instead of walking straight to the shelf holding the dictionary, she takes the "scenic" route past a friend and drops off a note on the friend's desk. She then flips through the dictionary for a number of minutes. Mr. Hansen stands, takes two relaxing breaths, assumes his best posture, and calls across the classroom, "Laverne." The girl looks up at him. He holds up the stopwatch and states, "Laverne, you are on your own time," and clicks the watch. Laverne freezes like a deer caught in headlights, but the students nearby whisper, "Sit down, Laverne, you're wasting our time. Sit down, now!" Laverne scurries to her seat, opens her book, and begins the work. Mr. Hansen clicks the timer off, goes to the chalkboard, and writes −45 seconds.

Through her behavior, Laverne began to play a game of noncooperation by killing time and not working. Rather than nag her, Mr. Hansen simply starts the stopwatch, which makes a small beeping sound all can hear, and begins counting the off-task student's penalty time. This is then displayed on the board and subtracted from the total time accumulated to that point. Since the "free" time or PAT belongs to all class members, Laverne is selfishly using up everyone's time. This creates social pressure, but not from the teacher as an authority figure toward whom Laverne could target her anger. Instead, it comes from her peers. Thus the class, rather than enjoying one student's challenge to the teacher's authority *(show time),* now becomes a part of the socialization process; misbehavior is just too expensive for the individual student to engage in because she is just hurting herself and must endure the wrath of her peers. Jones would say that social pressure is very strong among peers, but through this incentive system, the pressure is rendered benign and harnessed to support productive cooperative behavior. Penalties are used in conjunction with bonuses to give the teacher considerable control in obtaining cooperation from the students. Jones says, "It allows the teacher to combat the countless scams and flimflams which students devise with a calm that can only come from having discovered the perfect antidote."[16]

The "Rule of Penalties"

Let us see an example where penalties are abused by a negative, personal teacher. "Class, I am counting to 10. I want everyone in their seats, all paper off the floor, and the desks in neat, orderly rows. For each number I count before this is accomplished, you will lose that much time from this afternoon's pep rally. One … two…" This is not what Jones is proposing in his incentive system. Therefore he has created a rule to eliminate teacher abuse of this system by teachers who repeatedly zap students with more and more penalties, until the students know they will not win a PAT. This rule is simple: *Every penalty implies a corresponding bonus.* This is done to prevent the system from degenerating into negativism whereby the students begin to feel resentment, undermining their relationship with the teacher and causing rebellion and very negative peer pressure. The idea is that students should and must accumulate PAT time for the fun of it, in order to serve as an effective incentive.

Preferred Activity Time (PAT)

Preferred activity time is not "kicking back" time permitting students to "rap" with each other and do nothing. If adolescent students are given the freedom to do nothing, that is exactly what they will do. Jones would clearly admit that the use of PAT with students is really a "shell game." Such activities as a "popcorn" party would be permitted as PAT, but would be considered a poor or weak use of PAT. Under Jones's definition, PATs are fun activities that hold high interest for students but have embedded in them a routine of drill and practice, or even content review of the subject matter. In short, they are thus process activities involving elements of learning. The PAT of watching the video of *To Kill A Mockingbird* involved a book the students will read this semester; seeing the video is a motivating, high-interest activity that the teacher simply turned into a PAT.

Jones permits much feedback from students in choosing and modifying the activities for their own interest. Historically, games with rules are passed down from one generation of children, beginning in the upper elementary grades, to the next generation of children. They normally are not taught by adults, but are strictly dependent on the child culture (remember Red Light–Green Light or Red Rover). Because of television, mall arcades, and the general marketing of childhood leisure activities, these traditional games are being lost and not passed down by many children today. The commercial games, such as Nintendo or its sibling Game Boy, are isolated activities, and therefore children are losing out on the very valuable social interaction that traditional games have long taught them. According to Jones, children, especially adolescents, simply do not know how to have fun in the sense that fun for hundreds of years has been centered around group games. Jones's PAT approach is literally attempting to save children's cultural heritage and get teachers and students to socially enjoy themselves, while at the same time slipping in some academic training and review.

Finally, this incentive system of awarding time-currency and using a stopwatch to give bonuses and penalties will gradually fade. Once the students have developed normal classroom habits that will begin on the first day of school, the stopwatch can be put away—but not the PAT. The PAT should continue throughout the year with normal classroom teaching and learning becoming more fun and game-like until Jones's wish is met: teaching and having fun begin to blend into one activity.

OMISSION TRAINING

As noted earlier, the *Tools for Teaching* system is a four-legged chair, and we have reviewed three of those legs: limit setting, backup systems, and the incentive system as a part of responsibility training. The fourth and final leg is omission training, but it is important to remember that all four systems are interrelated and all must be functioning in order for the system to work.

Omission training (OT) is used with the one or two students who are chronically provocative toward the teacher or toward peers, who take the attitude, "I don't care about PAT, and you can't make me!" By his (or her) behavior, this difficult student is causing penalties for his classmates; he is alienated and typically has few or no social skills or friends. He is bitter and revengeful, and he wishes to get even with others for the social isolation he feels. His behavior clearly provokes rejection. This student is taken to a private conference and permitted to move out of the responsibility training process. Then if he misbehaves, his actions will not penalize classmates and destroy the incentive system set up by the teacher. The teacher continues to calmly use limit setting for minor off-task behaviors with this student. By taking this student out of the PAT system, the teacher removes a control lever the student has been using to get even with peers. By creating an alternative omission training system for this student, the teacher has a face-saving course of action that simultaneously deprives the student of the class as an audience.

Omission training is an individualized program of incentives for the very defiant student, encouraging him to earn rewards through the omission of unwanted behavior. We arrange this reward to provide bonuses in time added to the class PAT, thus making the student a hero within the classroom if he is able to control himself. The student may not be interested in adding to the PAT itself, but the "hero" status it will give him among his peers is a strong incentive. This process is established in three ways:

1. **Private Meeting.** The student is told that he may drop out of the normal responsibility training and he may choose to skip the PAT, or he may individualize his PAT to his liking. Either way, a special rewards program is set up for him. A kitchen timer will be set for a period of time, and if he can control himself for this time by not performing certain general categories of behaviors (hitting others, swearing, putting others down, or a host of other unwanted behaviors), he will earn one minute of extra time for everyone. *Note:* He does not earn it individually, but by his actions is able to give bonus gifts to the entire class and is rewarded with feelings of being a hero.

2. **Class Meeting.** A class meeting is held, with the teacher pointing out that Larry has been causing the entire class to lose time because he has had trouble controlling his behavior. From this point on, Larry cannot hurt the class as a whole, but can only help it. When the kitchen timer goes off, a bonus of one minute will be added to the class PAT. So it now becomes the class's responsibility to help Larry. Classmates should not provoke him, but should help and invite him into their activities because they help themselves by helping Larry control himself. This control will bring bonus points to the entire group. Through the OT program, the revengeful student who lacks social skills and acceptance is now placed in the best position for social pressure to help him find this acceptance. Many of these problem students have learned to be the best bad kid and have a sense of status by being the class outcast. They cannot improve their behavior or get better until the class changes its actions toward them, and the OT system places the incentives in front of the group to help change its actions.

3. **Process.** Once the kitchen timer rings, the teacher announces that Larry has given the class bonus time. The teacher writes it on the board and encourages the

class to applaud Larry. With Larry able to maintain good behavior for 30 minutes (as an example), the timer is now set—unknown to Larry—to 35 minutes; it is gradually increased to require longer and longer intervals of good behavior from Larry.

Finally, Larry's behavior has changed so dramatically that the teacher needs to phase out the OT process. First the timer is eliminated, and the teacher begins class by announcing, "Class, Larry has been doing so well that I will give you Larry's gift of seven minutes right now because I am confident he will be able to control his behavior today." Finally, after a private meeting with Larry, he is brought back into the regular responsibility training process.

The central concept of omission training for the very difficult student is: (1) remove him from the responsibility training program so that he cannot use his misbehavior as a power lever to hurt peers; (2) permit him to earn bonus points for the entire class, which includes him; (3) challenge the class to help the difficult student succeed and in turn help themselves; and finally (4) gradually phase out the OT process.

CLASSROOM STRUCTURE

Mr. Fox's Latin class has been in session for 15 minutes when Carol's pencil breaks, leaving her unable to do the written assignment. She thinks, "Can I just get up and go over there and sharpen my pencil? In the past some teachers have permitted me to do this and some have not." Carol stands, makes eye contact with Mr. Fox, points to the pencil sharpener, and takes five steps toward it. Mr. Fox demands, "Young lady, where do you think you are going? I did not give you permission to get out of your seat! Sit down immediately!"

All the students tense up and think, "Ah, Mr. Fox is going to play the game of 'minefield' with us." The students realize that Mr. Fox is going to keep his class rules a secret at the beginning of the semester, and they will have to break a rule ("step on a mine"), causing Mr. Fox to explode and "slam dunk" that person in order for them to learn the particular rule and how to avoid breaking it.

The game of "minefield" will create battle fatigue among the students in this class, and war will be declared between teacher and student because they will never be able to feel comfortable or relax within a predictable structure. The students realize that it may take all semester to learn all of Mr. Fox's rules, and the moment they think they know them all, a new one will pop up from nowhere. If Mr. Fox is erratic and inconsistent based on his mood, the students will have a tremendously difficult time dealing with him. If one day a student breaks a rule, but Mr. Fox does not explode, yet a similar violation by another student the next day makes him erupt and threaten 10 years of detention, the students quickly recognize that this will be a tense, hateful school term. They could easily assume the position that if Mr. Fox is going to play such punitive games with them, they will also play their own, escalating their use of power in order to get even with the teacher. After all, they know he is only one individual and there are 25 to 35 of them; Mr. Fox is outnumbered, and reinforcement troops will be sent in every semester or year. The students figure it won't be long before administrators will be giving Mr. Fox a "Section 8" discharge as emotionally unfit—the students will drive him crazy.

Structure—class routines, the organization of desks and furniture, and general rules—give students a sense of predictability. Once they learn this structure, they are free to act within defined boundaries and have the sense of security that they will be safe and can relax. Many teachers, especially upper level high school teachers, adhere to a number of myths about structure and rules:

1. Students, especially in middle or high school, should already know how to behave. Wrong! Each class is different and every student wants to know where this teacher's "mines" are located.

2. It takes too much time to teach rules and structure. Wrong! The teacher will pay a higher price in time later in remediation—and perhaps with a stomach ulcer—if he does not take the time up front.

3. Rules are general guidelines and need only to be announced. Wrong! Rules must be taught like any other concept in a lesson; they cannot be just verbally announced, but must be specifically taught in the form of what motor actions are needed to comply with this rule.

4. Teach rules well at the beginning and then you can forget about them. Wrong! Rules need to be monitored and retaught after long holidays, when spring weather breaks out, when new students are enrolled, and periodically throughout the year. Rules need maintenance!

5. Teaching rules equates to undue strictness. Wrong! Rules are like the guardrail on a high bridge: They show us where to stop, indicate where we may safely maneuver, and keep us on the proper path.

6. Students hate rules. Wrong! Mr. Fox's students would love to know what the rules are. Students appreciate a certain amount of rules, so they may know how to avoid out-of-bounds behavior.

From the moment the students enter the classroom managed by Jones's *Tools for Teaching* techniques, the teacher shows that he or she means business and teaches through structure. Here are Jones's recommendations for the first day of class:

1. The teacher greets each student by shaking the student's hand, saying the teacher's own name, and asking the student's name. The teacher then gives the student a card with a number corresponding to the seat he or she will take, and asks the student to begin working, following the directions on the board.

2. The board directions will ask the students to fill out a 3×5 card with their name, address, and phone number and their parents' or guardians' names, place of work, and work phone number. These cards will be used as a part of the backup system if and when the student needs to be warned.

In this way, the student has learned that rules begin the moment he or she walks into the classroom. The message delivered by the teacher is, "I care who you are and I want you to care for me, to walk into my class, take your seat, and begin working." The teacher now plays a game (a variety of choices is included in Jones's book) so that everyone in the classroom gets to know everyone else's first and last name. Later the teacher will pass out a seating chart to test whether each student knows everyone else's name. Once everyone passes the name test, bonus points are added to the PAT. Anonymity creates within the student a distance toward the teacher and classmates. "If he doesn't even know my name, he doesn't care about me, and I don't care about him!" This personalizing of each student is critical for establishing a relationship between the teacher and class members and must be accomplished immediately.

Teaching Rules and Structure

The teacher actually teaches all rules and the structure of the classroom—the use of furniture and equipment—just as any other lesson is taught through a Say, Show, and Do process. "Students, in this chemistry class it is critical that all test tubes are absolutely clean or contaminants will destroy new experiments. Let me show you how they are to be washed out each and every time we are done using them. First we get the water hot, then … (Say). Now watch me do it, as I repeat the directions (Show). Now pair up in groups of two, and one of you will become Professor Einstein and the other will be Dr. Schweitzer. Dr. Schweitzer, cross your arms across your chest, and Professor Einstein will show you how to do this. Professor Einstein will teach you the lesson of 'cleaning test tubes' and bring the cleaned-out tube to you. Now, Dr. Schweitzer, you teach this same lesson with a new test tube to Professor Einstein." (Do.). What we see is the teacher not just announcing rules, but actually teaching all rules and procedures needed in this classroom before any instruction can begin.

SCHOOLWIDE DISCIPLINE MANAGEMENT

Most schools do very little planning on how out-of-classroom management will be done. Therefore, when misbehavior does occur, the tendency is for the school to jump right to medium or large backup system sanctions, which are destructive to the school environment. *Tools for Teaching* presents very valuable procedures for dealing with supervision in theses areas (although in very abbreviated form). Primarily, Jones is suggesting the use of limit setting (with eye contact and proximity) and responsibility training for these areas.

JONES AND THE TEACHER BEHAVIOR CONTINUUM

In the early 1990s, an automobile manufacturer made the claim that "Quality is Job 1." For quality classroom teaching, the motto for the Jones model of *Tools for Teaching* could be that Discipline is Job 1. For most middle or high school teachers, their passion is their subject area, be it history, physics, music, or the array of other subjects. They would love to step into their classroom each day and just deal with content. But because of a host of home, community, and societal pressures, fewer and fewer of today's students come with the attitude of really wanting to learn what teachers would like to teach them. When teachers butt their heads again a wall of resentful students, most teachers will take one of two routes: either they lower their standards and make do, or they leave the teaching profession. But the Jones model presents a discipline designed to help teachers reclaim their students' interest and enthusiasm.

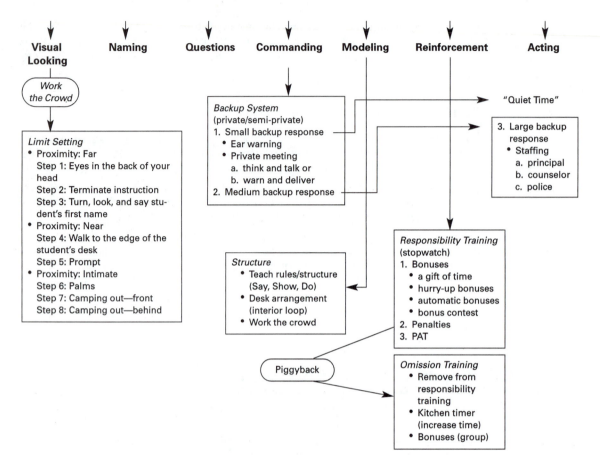

FIGURE 3.5   Teacher Behavior Continuum: Jones's Positive Discipline Model

In many ways, parts of the Jones model parallel elements of the Teacher Behavior Continuum. From the beginning, the teacher informs the students about the structure and rules he or she wants in the classroom, following the pattern of the TBC's *modeling*. This sets the stage for the future classroom drama of limit setting (TBC's *directive statements*) for the high-rolling misbehaviors, and then responsibility training (TBC's *reinforcement*) for all students with an incentive program that creates new cooperative behavior. Finally, for those one or two students with major emotional and social adjustment problems, the teacher piggybacks an incentive system for the purpose of omission training (again, TBC's *reinforcement*). (See Figure 3.5.)

SUMMARY

Good classroom discipline and management start the minute the first student walks through the classroom door at the beginning of the semester. Either the teacher sets the agenda, or the students will set it. From the first day, the teacher must be clearly in charge and mean business by "owning the classroom and furniture." The teacher immediately teaches the classroom structure she will use, and is prepared to use the Jones techniques of limit setting, backup system, and responsibility training to deal with most behavior problems. For the more serious, less frequent problems, the teacher uses a process of omission training. In these limited cases, the teacher wishes to stop the unwanted behavior and get peers to help the misbehaving student find social acceptance.

Strengths and Limitations of the Model

By far the greatest strength of the Jones model is that all of its component parts combine to form a holistic view of how to achieve good classroom discipline and management. While most discipline models focus on limit setting and confronting to deal with a misbehaving student, the Jones model goes far beyond this to include other dimensions—backup, management, incentive, responsibility, and so on. Jones found that after doing "discipline" training with schools, he could go no further unless he also dealt with the aspect of classroom instruction (as he did in his second book, *Positive Classroom Instruction*). In the most recent book *Tools for Teaching* he merges discipline and instruction seamlessly into one process. Another contribution of the Jones model is the concept of the two dimensions of proximity and helping the teacher maintain self-control (to avoid "going brain stemmed"). At a very practical and specific level, Jones demonstrates how the teacher can gain self-control through relaxing breaths, posture, and movement. Confrontation is the most stressful situation for the classroom teacher, and these relaxing behaviors can be central for a teacher to gain control and remain empowered. The use of proximity, or closing space between the teacher and the off-task student, is new and a significant contribution to the classroom teacher's skills. Our tendency as teachers, when challenged by a student, is to react with "flight or fight." Understanding this and having specific techniques to control this "reflexive" reaction can help many teachers with potentially explosive tempers. Again, the suggestions for classroom furniture arrangement and the process of "working the crowd" give meaning to concepts that many teachers have known and used in limited ways.

True to most behaviorists, Jones did not include in his first book any training teacher actions, especially in limit setting, and during backup, that involve the use of language between teacher and student and tapping the rational capacities of the student. The Jones view suggests that if the teacher responds to a student's back talk, he or she is falling into the student's trap and is unknowingly reinforcing the misbehaving student. The new Jones model *Tools for Teaching* provides examples and guidelines for private "heart-to-heart" talks with students as a part of the omission process.

Some have faulted the past Jones model *(Positive Discipline)* for failing to deal with the role of parents as a part of the discipline process. Although he clearly attributes parent "weenie" childrearing practices, especially parents' lack of consistenency (no means no) for the "brat" behavior of their children now our students, he provides solid proactive techniques for gaining parent trust—communicating standards to parents, parent nights, and ongoing communication with parents as a major additive to the new *Tools for Teaching*.

Alfie Kohn's Criticism of Jones' Model On "How-to" Guides:

> *"When a student does such and such, tell me where to stand and how to look and what to say." This is the sort of demand that keeps classroom management consultants in business. But these easy-to-follow recipes are fundamentally insulting to teachers, not unlike attempts to design a "teacher-proof" curriculum. They are short-term fixes, instruments of control intended, at best, to stop bad behavior rather than affirmatively help children to become good people. (Kohn, 1996, pp. xiv–xv)*

Jones clearly insists that the teacher grab control of the classroom the first day and first minutes of the school year; here are more observations and criticisms by Alfie Kohn on these suggestions:

> *Even older children may act in troubling ways because they are wanting for the sort of warm, caring relationships that enable and incline people to act more compassionately. They may have learned to rely on power rather than reason, to exhibit aggression rather than compassion, because this is what they have seen adults do—and perhaps what has been done to them. "Give 'em an inch and they'll take a mile" mostly describes the behavior of people who have hitherto been given only inches. (Kohn, 1996, p. 9)*

SUMMARY OF KEY CONCEPTS

adrenaline dump	closing space	paleocortex	responsibility training
back talk	comfort bubble	palms	say, show, do
back talk: accusing the	eye contact	park the body	"show time"
teacher of professional	fight or flight	"part of a loaf"	silly talk
incompetence	focal point	pencil posturing	slack jaw
back talk: blaming	Fredisms	Ph.D. in teacher game	"smiley face"
back talk: denial	"going brain stemmed"	pheasant posturing	square-off
back talk: helplessness	going public	private meeting	structure
back talk: profanity	"gone chemical"	prompt	tailhook
backup system	high roller	proximity	three-step lesson
body-telegraphing	incentive program	adrenaline "bleed"	triune brain
camouflage	limit setting	proximity-intimate	with-it-ness
camping out from behind	low roller	pseudocompliance	working the crowd
camping out in front	moving in/moving out	relaxing breaths	
check-it-out	neocortex	reptilian brain	

CASE STUDIES

What actions would the *Tools for Teaching* teacher take using the five systems (limit setting, backup, incentive, encouragement, and management systems) for the following discipline incident?

1. **Andrew "Takes Over":** The students return to your classroom after being in the library-media center. The director of the center complains strongly about the poor behavior by your students, but gives you little details. Once the students are settled in their seats, you open a discussion with, "I want to talk to you about your behavior in the media center. (All heads drop.) Does anyone have anything to say?" Andrew is seated in the back of the room, slouched in his chair with his feet in the air propped over the top of the desk next to him. "Yea, I have something to say. Shut up! I hate that ugly bitch, and we aren't going back to the media center again." Most of the other class members respond, with "Yea! We're not going back there again!" Andrew seems to be respected and somewhat feared by the other students, and they often look to him for a signal as to whether they should comply with you as the teacher, and you often have the feeling that he can "take over" your class.

The following are possible actions that could be taken with Andrew using the five systems (limit setting, etc.).

You will notice that the systems parallel nearly exactly the systems suggested in the Jones model.

Limit-setting System

One of the cardinal rules of *Tools for Teaching* is "keep it private or don't go public." Andrew would like to have the teacher lose his composure or "go chemical," meaning the adrenaline floods the teacher's thinking. The teacher begins to use his "horsy-doggie" brain and reprimands the student with "silly talk" or engages him in a power struggle. This leads to "show time" for the class. The teacher would take three relaxing breaths, square off with the class, and give an assignment to get all the students working. Then once everyone is engaged in their seat activity, the teacher watches to see if Andrew "gets to work." If not, the teacher would use the limit-setting techniques in Figure 3.3—relaxing breaths, squaring off, closing space, and proximity, and so on.

Backup System

If the limit setting fails to work, Jones would drop it and move to the backup system. He would move about the classroom, stopping and privately discussing some item with two or three students. When he comes to Andrew he delivers an "ear warning," then uses a private after-class meeting. He then progresses to a small backup response and possibly escalates to medium and large backup responses if things continue to escalate, but the object is to "get the student back to work."

Incentive System

The incentive system is defined differently in Jones's behavioral terms as responsibility training. He feels that Andrew has to be given something that he values and will attempt to conserve once it is in his possession— preferred activity time. Students in Jones's thinking ask, "Why should I work?" The answer is to give them an incentive. The *Tools for Teaching* teacher might place 15 minutes on the board as time given to students, including Andrew, for free use, but when one student is not working, seconds or minutes are gradually taken away. This causes a collective dynamic of students socializing themselves, including Andrew, not to lose this free time. Jones would tell the teacher to use a stopwatch and teach the concept of penalties, much centered around enabling Andrew and other students to "get back to work."

Encouragement System

The encouragement system in Jones's definition is called omission training. When limit setting, backup, and an incentive system do not work with those one or two very difficult students, the teacher is required to use an omission system. Andrew says, "I don't care about PATs" (preferred activity time). Jones takes Andrew into a private conference and out of responsibility training. The teacher creates an alternative individualized system especially for Andrew. Special rewards are set up for him, possibly using a kitchen timer to mark off sections of time that Andrew is requested to work and not disrupt. If he can meet the times (short amounts of time at first, then getting longer), he can earn extra time, not only for himself but for the entire class. This is explained in an open class meeting. The class celebrates with Andrew when he is able to win the reward for the class.

Management System

The classroom structure in the form of furniture is critical to Jones's success with such students as Andrew. We must notice in the example described that Andrew was seated in the back the of the room as far from the teacher as possible. The teacher would change Andrew's seating and place Andrew in close proximity to him near the front of the room. The furniture would be organized with interior circles of open space, permitting the teacher to be in front of any student in one or two steps. Of course Jones would say that all students must be taught the basic rituals and rules of running the classroom on the first day of class as a good management technique.

For Further Discussion

How would the *Tools for Teaching* teacher apply the same systems in the following incidents?

2. **Mike's Clowning:** Mike could be labeled as the class clown. He has been seen blowing chocolate milk bubbles through his nose in the cafeteria; placing his backside on the edge of the stool in chemistry class, using a movable Bunsen burner to lights his "farts" to produce a flame; and often dressing in a T-shirt with the words "suck city" on the front. When asked to stop these behaviors, he gives the teacher the "deer in the headlights look" with a slight smile. He does stop, but within an hour or two he has a new action to "gross out" the class members and disrupt the teacher's teaching. Today, with his hand underneath his armpit, he produces a flagrant sound by pumping his elbow up and down. Using these sounds, he attempts to "play" *Jingle Bells,* "cracks up" the class, and, of course, disrupts your teaching.

3. **Jake the Grenade:** Jake is like a walking grenade. One can never tell when he will explode. He passively seems to withdraw within himself, carrying a large "chip on his shoulder." If he is bumped or jostled accidentally by a fellow student, he will strike out. He has deliberately pulled a chair away from a fellow student just as she was seating herself and caused this student to fall to the floor, striking her head on the way down. He attempts to throw wet paper wads down the open blouse of one of the girls. He likes to draw monster-like cartoon characters on any surface that he can find, including the top of his desk. Today in chemistry class he got up and wandered about the room while the teacher was lecturing, and he opened all the gas jets at the chemistry tables at the back of the room—the smell of gas quickly filled the room.

4. **Linda the Passive:** Linda is a tall thin girl who is nearly always seen with her head down on her desk and her gangly long legs wrapped around the

legs of her chair. She constantly has her first three fingers in her mouth, sucking them to the point that she has sucked off one fingernail. She has a body odor that is noticeable to everyone and often looks as if she has not bathed for many days. It is November, and she has done no homework, answers no questions when called on, and when questioned by the teacher in one-to-one situations, grunts yes or no to all questions. Other children laugh at her, calling her a host of derogatory names. The parents do not have a phone number, and you have not been able to contact them for a conference. Other teachers have never seen the parents, but her address is near the railroad track where there are many trailers.

Jones's *Tools for Teaching* is uniquely designed for example 2, Mike's clowning. He would clearly use limit setting with the "visual burn," proximity as described in the TBC in Figure 3.5, and responsibility training with incentives to deal with Mike's need for attention. The fellow students would not laugh and provide reinforcement for his antics but "punishment" for having lost very valuable PAT times. A backup or omission system would rarely be needed with such students as Mike, but the classroom management structures must be in place.

There is a real possibility that a backup system would be needed for example 3, Jake the Grenade. What system or systems do you believe would be helpful with Linda the Passive?

NOTES

1. F. H. Jones, P. Jones, and J. Jones, *Tools for Teaching: Discipline, Instruction, and Motivation* (Santa Cruz, CA: Fred H. Jones & Associates, Inc., 2000).
2. Frederic Jones, *Positive Classroom Discipline* (New York: McGraw-Hill, 1987).
3. Frederic Jones, *Positive Classroom Discipline: Trainee Manual* (Santa Cruz, CA: Fred Jones and Associates, Inc., 1993), p. 32.
4. Jones, *Positive Classroom Discipline*.
5. Jones, *Positive Classroom Discipline*, p. 93.
6. Jones, *Positive Classroom Discipline*, p. 57.
7. Jones, *Positive Classroom Discipline*, pp. 56–65.
8. Jones, *Positive Classroom Discipline*, p. 281.
9. Jones, *Positive Classroom Discipline*, p. 285.
10. Jones, *Positive Classroom Discipline*, p. 281.
11. Jones, *Positive Classroom Discipline*, p. 289.
12. Jones, *Positive Classroom Discipline*, p. 301.
13. Jones, *Positive Classroom Discipline*, p. 344.
14. Jones, *Positive Classroom Discipline*, p. 342.
15. Jones, *Positive Classroom Discipline*.
16. Jones, *Positive Classroom Discipline*, p. 170.

REFERENCES

Jones, F. *Positive Classroom Discipline.* New York: McGraw-Hill, 1987.

Jones, F. *Positive Classroom Instruction.* New York: McGraw-Hill, 1987.

Jones, F. H., P. Jones, and J. Jones. *Tools for Teaching: Discipline, Instruction, and Motivation.* Santa Cruz, CA: Fred Jones and Associates, Inc., 2000.

CHAPTER 4

ASSERTIVE DISCIPLINE

Writers/Theorists: Lee and Marlene Canter
- *Assertive Discipline: A Take-Charge Approach for Today's Educator*
- *Assertive Discipline: Positive Behavior Management for Today's Classroom*
- *Responsible Behavior Curriculum Guide: An Instructional Approach to Successful Classroom Management*

OUTLINE OF ASSERTIVE DISCIPLINE

Basic Assumptions about Motivation/Philosophy

- Teacher's attention is one of the most powerful forms of reinforcement and can be used by the teacher to gain a positive motivation and productive behavior from most children.

- Once students understand that if they choose to break rules, a corrective action will follow; then their behavior will change and become more positive. Students need limits.

- Students must know and be taught responsible behavior.

- Student misbehavior continues when teachers do not enforce the same standards for all students.

- Teachers have the right to request behavior from students that meets the needs of the teacher and ensures an optimal learning environment.

- Teachers have the right to ask assistance from parents, principals, and other school personnel.

Teacher Behaviors

- Using a warning to alert students that there is a problem with their behavior: "Class, we should be doing…"

- Giving "I"-message ("If you don't stop, then you have chosen…") and "broken record" demands to avoid being sidetracked.

- Using a steady gaze and low voice when talking to students.

- Giving rewards, or positive recognition, for appropriate behavior (positive notes home, calling on a student, token coupons, marble system to reward whole class) and corrective action for inappropriate behavior (loss of privilege, detention, note home).

▨ Using systematic exclusion (to another classroom, principal's office, home, etc.).

Guidelines, Planning, or Preparatory Teacher Actions

▨ Determining differences among assertive, nonassertive, and hostile teachers.

▨ Establishing a uniform classroom discipline plan of relatively few but specific rules and consistent actions for enforcing them.

▨ Writing down the plan and sharing it with the principal and parents.

▨ Using mental rehearsal (mentally thinking it out ahead of time) to explain the classroom plan and enforcement procedures and to prepare for handling student violations.

OVERVIEW

The following scene takes place in an eighth-grade classroom with a teacher who uses the new and improved assertive discipline approach.

Discipline Hierarchy (Student Breaks a Rule)	Assertive Discipline Technique	Teacher or Student's Action	Scattered around the classroom are five students who are off-task. They are talking and generally failing to do the seat work they were assigned.
First Time	Warning or reminder	TEACHER:	*"Students, you should be working on the six problems on page 32—this is your reminder!"*
			(Three of the five off-task students return to their work, while the other two, Janice and Mike, continue to talk.)
	Supportive Feedback	TEACHER:	*"Thanks, guys!"* (to those students that have returned to their work)
Second Time	Minimum corrective action	TEACHER:	*"Janice and Mike, I can see that you have chosen to break the rule, 'no talking during seat work.' You will need to stay in your seats and not depart when the change bell rings until one minute has passed."*
			(The two students become quiet for a few minutes, but when the teacher moves on, the students return to their off-task behavior.)
Third Time	Escalate corrective action	TEACHER:	*"Janice and Mike, you have chosen to break the rule; stay in your seat for two minutes whenever the change bell rings."*
			(Mike complies and begins his seat work. Janice turns around and again tries to chat with the student behind her who is working intently. She is disrupting the student's work.)
Fourth Time	Escalate corrective action	TEACHER:	*"Janice, take your books and move to that chair in the back of the room where no one else is seated."*
			(At the same time Mike is working productively on his seat work.)

Discipline Hierarchy (Student Breaks a Rule)	Assertive Discipline Technique	Teacher or Student's Action	Scattered around the classroom are five students who are off-task. They are talking and generally failing to do the seat work they were assigned.
	Supportive Feedback	TEACHER:	*"Thanks, Mike—working quietly helps all of us here!"*
			(Janice does move to the isolated seat, but does not begin to work and, in fact, deliberately puts out her foot to trip a student who is passing by to sharpen his pencil. The passing student nearly falls on his face.)
Fifth Time	Escalate corrective action	TEACHER:	*"Janice you know my discipline plan! That was your fifth rule broken this morning. After third period and just before lunch, we will meet in my office and we will call your parents."*
		JANICE:	"Aw, she-ee…"! I didn't do anything."
			(She throws her textbook at the nearby wall, producing a loud crashing sound that startles everyone in the classroom.)
	Escalate corrective action	TEACHER:	*"Janice you have chosen by your actions to go to Mr. Walker's (assistant principal) office. Go now!"*
	(Limit Setting: Assertive Command.)	TEACHER:	*"Janice, you knew the rules and you have chosen to break them. Now you must experience the conse-quences.* (Moves to a position in front of the student.) *Janice* (states the student's name, points a finger at her, and then gestures toward the door and makes eye contact), *I want you to stand, go out the door, and go straight to Mr. Walker's office."*
	"Fogging"	JANICE:	*"I wasn't doing anything!"*
	"Broken Record"	TEACHER:	*"Janice* (points a finger at her and then toward the door and makes eye contact), *I want you to go to Mr. Walker's office."*
	"Fogging"	JANICE:	*"Noreen was talkin, and you didn't say anything to her!"*
	"Broken Record"	TEACHER:	*"Janice* (points a finger at her and then toward the door and makes eye contact), *I want you to go to the office."*
	"Fogging"	JANICE:	*"I don't know how to do this work."*
	"Broken Record"	TEACHER:	*"Janice, to the office."*
		JANICE:	(Drops her eyes, but doesn't move.)
	Warning	TEACHER:	*"Janice, this is your last warning. Move now, or I will need to get Mr. Walker and Mr. Coats to come here and we will escort you to the office. This is a promise—you choose!"*
		JANICE:	(Makes quick eye contact, drops her head, and begins to grind her teeth.)
		TEACHER:	(Takes two envelopes from his grade book and addresses himself to a well-behaved student seated near the door) *"Gwen, please take this letter to Mr. Coats across the hall, and then this second letter to Mr. Walker in the office."* (If a classroom telephone was available, he would have used it instead of the letters.)

Discipline Hierarchy (Student Breaks a Rule)	Assertive Discipline Technique	Teacher or Student's Action	Scattered around the classroom are five students who are off-task. They are talking and generally failing to do the seat work they were assigned.
	"Who-squad"	STAFF:	Mr. Coats and Mr. Walker soon appear in the classroom door and ask, *"Who?"*
		TEACHER:	*"Janice, seated there"* (points to Janice).
	"Who-squad"	STAFF:	(The assistant principal approaches Janice, takes her by the elbow, and escorts the student to his office. Mr. Coats stands nearby ready to help if needed. They escort Janice to the office.)

This teacher–student interaction is an example of the teacher practicing assertive discipline techniques. The teacher has determined that he or she has the right to teach, has developed a clear plan for giving supportive feedback (*"Thanks, Mike—working quietly helps all of us here!"*) and a hierarchical discipline plan, and will follow through with corrective actions with a student who violates a rule.

Assertive discipline suggests that most teachers work hard and do much thinking as to their lesson plan design and the carrying out of teaching strategies as they teach their content. But, often these same teachers may not preplan for what they may do in a discipline situation; therefore, they are left with responding in an unplanned and counterproductive *reactive approach* or manner that may be seen as nonassertive (*"Janice, could you please be more quiet and try to get back to your work?"*), or hostile (*"Janice, shut your mouth! I have had enough of you already. I am sick and tired of you and your actions"*).

Assertive discipline wants the teacher to anticipate that students will break rules; this is part of the job of teaching—it *will* occur—so plan ahead. Planning permits the teacher to be *proactive* with concrete actions they might take to be positively supportive (again, *"Thanks, Mike…"*) when students behave appropriately. Planning teaches the students what behavior is expected and that corrective action will be taken when a rule is broken. Proactive teacher responses aim at stopping the disruption and getting students back to work without getting emotionally involved or upset.

An *assertive response* would involve many of the actions we saw in the opening vignette, including statements such as, "Janice, I want you to be quiet. I will not tolerate disruption in my classroom. You know the rules and if you talk again, then you have chosen to go to the principal's office."

The Canters and their associates have applied these assertiveness training concepts[1] to create their Assertive Discipline Model. They base their philosophy on the following value statements as they relate to the classroom teacher:

- You have the right and the responsibility to establish rules and directions that clearly define the limits of acceptable and unacceptable student behavior.

- You have the right and responsibility to be supportive of those students who are not disruptive.

- You have the right and responsibility to teach students to consistently follow these rules and directions throughout the school day and school year.

- You have the right and the responsibility to ask for assistance from parents and administrators.

Establishing a Classroom Discipline Plan

In making a classroom discipline plan, the assertive teacher must (1) *establish rules* that students must follow *at all times,* (2) develop *supportive feedback* that students will consistently receive for following the rules, and define (3) *corrective actions* that the teacher will consistently use when a student chooses not to follow a rule. For those who have read and been trained in early editions of *Assertive Discipline* they will find that the 3rd edition has made dramatic changes to overcome some of the misinterpretations and/or criticisms of the earliest model. The major criticism was that the model often "decayed" into a negative mode, with the teacher forgetting to use the positive reinforcement dimensions of the early model. So, the new edition has placed positive teacher's action "up front" with a less abbreviated and arbitrary explanation of techniques and often cautions the teacher not to get lost in a system of negativity; one chapter is headed "A Balance Between Structure and Caring." This move to a more caring philosophy required a number of vocabulary or word changes—*praise* now becomes *supportive feedback* and *verbal recognition,* and *punishment/consequences* have been changed to *corrective actions.*

Rules

Canter sets out a number of principles to follow in creating rules. First, the rules must be observable. Vague rules such as "Show respect" or "No fooling around" are poor examples because they do not spell out clearly the behavior that the teacher wants. An observable rule such as "Keep your hands to yourself" would replace such vague rules as "Show respect at all times," while "Be in your seats" would be better than "No fooling around." Also, rules created and published by the teacher for the classroom should not involve academic or homework issues because they are not related to observable classroom behavior.

Second, each rule that is posted—ideally no more than four, and never more than six—must be enforceable all day long. Canter would not like a rule that might state, "Raise your hand and wait to be called on before you speak" because he would suggest that many times throughout the day the students cannot fully comply with this rule and we would not really expect them to do so. Therefore, the teacher's rules must be those that can be in effect all day long and in any school location. "No swearing" is a good rule because this rule would be observable and relevant all day long. Finally, Canter would suggest that, when possible, students should be involved in the establishment of rules, although the final say must belong to the teacher.

PREPLANNING

The teacher writes out a discipline plan, gives a copy to the principal for approval, and sends it home to the parents asking for feedback and suggestions. The teacher also teaches the plan, with its accompanying rules, to the students.

The plan must contain a clear statement of classroom rules, which are also posted on the chalkboard; positive recognition actions that the teacher will take to positively reinforce those students who follow the rules; a statement of corrective actions if the rules are broken; and a severity clause allowing the teacher to jump past other steps if the misbehaving student is endangering himself, fellow students, or property. An example of such a plan for a middle school or high school teacher might be as follows:

1. **Classroom Rules**

   Follow directions

   Be in the classroom and seated when the bell rings

   Do not swear or use put-downs

2. **Positive Recognition**

   Supportive feedback

   Positive notes sent home to parents

   Privilege pass

3. **Corrective Actions**

First time a student breaks a rule:	Warning
Second time:	Stay in class one minute after the bell
Third time:	Stay in class two minutes after the bell
Fourth time:	Call parents
Fifth time:	Classroom isolation (could be isolation in a classroom across the hall)
Sixth time:	Send to principal

4. **Severity Clause:** Send to principal[2]

Supportive Feedback

The supportive feedback is defined as "sincere and meaningful attention you give a student for behaving according to your expectations" (Canter, 2001, p. 41) and the examples in the opening vignette (*"Thanks, guys!"* or *"Thanks, Mike—working quietly helps all of us here!"*) are clear ones. This supportive feedback, previously called praise, is seen as feedback that: encourages the student to continue appropriate behavior, helps increase a student's self-esteem, creates a positive classroom climate, and, finally, teaches and establishes positive relationships with the students. The supportive feedback may be done by:

- **Giving verbal recognition**

  The words the teacher uses should communicate the feeling that *"I care about you. I notice the good work you are doing. I'm proud of you, and you need to be proud of yourself, too."* (Canter, 2001, p. 47)

- **Positive notes and phone calls home**

  Often parents only hear from the classroom teacher when their child has done something wrong. Assertive discipline believes that we must quickly (at the beginning of the school year or semester) begin to acquire good relationships with the parents of our students so that we might get their full support for our teaching and discipline efforts. Assertive discipline requires that, as a part of the discipline plan, the teacher send positive notes home and make phone calls to parents telling about authentic behaviors that the child performed in the classroom. Assertive discipline workbooks contain scripts for the phone calls and notes, as well as forms to practice when making original feedback statements to parents.

The following is an example of a note to be sent home.

October 14

Dear Mr. and Mrs. Wilson:

This is a quick note to tell you how I enjoy having Andrew in my Language Arts class. He is always prepared, his homework is complete, and asks many insightful questions. I believe he will have a good school year and you should be very proud of him.

Sincerely

Ms. Jensen

This sounds very time consuming for the middle school and high school teacher who instructs a large number of students each semester, but, again, a structure must be committed to by the teacher to make a specific number of calls or send a certain number of notes home per week.

- **Behavioral awards**

  These are printed forms. Many contain cartoons and lively drawings, which may be found and copied out of the teacher workbooks published by AD, that compliment the students on "lining up correctly, bring materials to class," and a host of other teacher-desired behaviors. The child's name is typed in the appropriate space and the child takes these awards home to be placed on the kitchen refrigerator door or on their bedroom wall.

- **Special privileges**

  Notes of a personal nature to students, about a job well done or how their appropriate behavior is valued by the teacher, are recommended. Also suggested are awards such as a Clock Buster, a ticket that the student may earn and later use to turn in a later paper or to take a test at a later day (or even be excused completely from taking a test). A raffle-ticket combination is suggested whereby the teacher gives a marker or ticket as a recognition award; the student saves this and then, periodically, a raffle is held with one or two markers drawn and the winners receiving a Clock Buster credit. Finally, assertive discipline suggests getting the community involved by contributing free passes (a coupon for free popcorn at a movie theater, free skates at a rink, free shoes at a bowling alley, etc.) to use as recognition for properly behaving students. Again, the assertive discipline workbooks provide examples of awards and coupons that may be copied.

  Finally, a number of in-school special privileges are suggested. This list includes, but is not limited to: be the first one excused from class, choose any seat for a day or week, listen to a cassette with a headset, get 10 minutes free time, and so on.[3]

Here are more examples.

Elementary	**Secondary**
Sit at the teacher's desk for a morning	Be first out of class after the change bell
Be first to use the computer (or any preferred item treasured by peers)	Excused from one quiz (or assignment)
	Choose any seating with a friend
Care for classroom livestock or plants	Have more time on the computer (or any preferred classroom item or activity treasured by peers)
Distribute playground balls and equipment	
Be a helper (or tutor) in the kindergarten	

- **Tangible rewards**

  For some difficult children, these items might not be powerful enough and may require the teacher to use tangible rewards such as giving the students stickers or small trinkets of little value, but highly prized by the students. These rewards must be given right after the observable behavior desired, accompanied by verbal recognition, but given sparingly.

These tangible rewards and positive recognitions have been criticized as "bribes." Assertive discipline provides a good defense and a clear response to this criticism of rewards. It states that a bribe is given in anticipation of a behavior, to entice a person to do something that is not in his best interests, while a reward is given as a result of behavior. A reward is given in recognition for a behavior that *is* in the best interest of the student.

The nonassertive teacher fails to see and give recognition to appropriate behavior. Some teachers believe appropriate behavior is simply to be expected from students, and so it goes unreinforced. But an assertive discipline system requires repetitive and large amounts of *supportive feedback* and *verbal recognition* for appropriate behavior. The *supportive feedback* must be personal and genuine and, for middle and high school students, it must be given quietly out of the hearing of peers or in such a manner that it will not make the older student look as if he or she is "sucking up" to the teacher. Most important, *verbal recognition* must be descriptive and specific. Comments such as "Good work, Carol" are too vague and do not point out what behavioral actions the teacher is recognizing. "Carol, I have noticed that for the last two weeks you have been doing all your seat work and your grades have jumped one grade level. Keep it up!" is a specific *verbal recognition* statement.

Since teachers are busy and can get distracted and forget to give positive recognition, assertive discipline would recommend positive reminders (prompts) on the classroom clock or the teacher's lesson plan or grade book. In essence, the teacher makes a specific agreement with himself to make a specific number of *verbal recognition* statements within a classroom period. Such structure begins to help the teacher shift into a habit of being positive. In the *Assertive Discipline: Secondary Workbook,* a positive parent communication log is provided that allows the teacher to record and keep track of supportive feedback, positive notes, phone calls, or other parent communication. (see Figure 4.1.)

Corrective Actions

Assertive discipline views corrective actions for breaking a rule as a student's choice. For example, when the teacher says, *"Harry, the rule is no profanity, and you have chosen to*

The Assertive Discipline Workbook, in an edition specifically for the secondary teacher, provides examples and "fill-in-the-blank" helpers that give a practical structure to the assertive discipline guidelines. Most of these can be copied by the teacher. This workbook contains:

• Classroom Rules Worksheet
• Posters
• 50 Opportunities to Say "You're Terrific"
• Example of positive notes to parents
• Positive Parent Communication Log
• Positive Memo
• Form for "A Note from the Teacher"
• A postcard from the teacher
• Quick Notes to Parents
• Clock Buster (coupons give special privileges)
• Privilege Pass
• Raffle Ticket (book markers)
• Message from the Teacher (forms)
• School–Community Positive Recognition (forms)
• Wish List of Special Privileges
• You Earned it! (forms)
• Positive Recognition (forms)
• Forms for playing a touchdown classroom game

FIGURE 4.1 Workbook Helpers

break the rule. Therefore you have chosen the consequence of staying one minute after class." In the discipline plan, the corrective actions must be made clear to students so they will know the choice they are making through their behavior. These corrective actions do not have to be severe. Canter points out that one of the most effective corrective actions for middle and high school students is simply requiring the student to remain in the classroom for a few minutes after all other students are dismissed. A child this age seems very much to dislike this rather simple corrective action, and it is used extensively with these older students.

The corrective action should be listed in a discipline hierarchy, moving from a warning, which includes writing the student's name in a grade book or a discipline folder carried by the teacher, to a second violation, which entails a minor corrective action with another check mark beside the student's name. (All future infractions for that day, along with the teacher's subsequent actions, are recorded in the grade book or discipline folder.) The student starts anew each day, getting a "clean sheet" with no infractions or penalties carried over. The third violation generally increases the corrective actions (wait two minutes after class), while the fourth violation requires the student to call his or her parents at home or at work and tell them about the inappropriate behavior. Finally, with the fifth violation, the student is sent to the classroom across the hall or the principal's office and, typically, is awarded some corrective action by the principal. Canter's book provides this particular plan, but suggests that each teacher is free to design his or her own plan using a discipline hierarchy whereby the corrective actions become increasingly severe or place greater demands on the student.

It is important to note that Canter urges a teacher, when carrying out this discipline plan hierarchy, to treat students alike and not be confused by what he refers to as roadblocks. Roadblocks are thoughts by the teacher that individual students cannot behave properly because of factors beyond the teacher's control, ranging from emotional illness or hyperactivity to family conditions and socioeconomic background. Such a defeatist attitude becomes a self-fulfilling prophecy. If the teacher excuses the student from following the rules, then he or she is accepting a discipline problem that will probably affect the entire class for the entire year. Instead, a teacher should expect the same standards from all students, and the teacher should expect to succeed. He or she may have to call in the help of such other resources as parents, counselors, juvenile authorities, and administrators, but this is the teacher's right. The teacher has the right to teach and to have students behave.

Putting Names on the Chalkboard   In the first assertive discipline book and training, it was recommend that the teacher not stop teaching when a student was misbehaving, but simply place the student's name on the board as a visual warning and record check marks beside the student's name in a similar manner. This has been widely criticized as humiliating to the student,[4] and as a backup position Canter now recommends writing the name in a discipline folder or the grade book with an accompanying verbal warning. (The workbook provides a well-developed Behavior Tracking Sheet, which may be copied.) *Note:* Canter does suggest that names be put on the chalkboard by the teacher for good behavior and positive recognition, even recommending that a game be played to see how many names in one day or period can get on the board for appropriate behavior, perhaps earning some sort of reward.

Corporal Punishment/Isolation   During the final step on the discipline hierarchy, the student is sent to the principal's office. Large numbers of schools have interpreted this step as indicating corporal punishment by the principal or in-and-out-of-school suspension/isolation for days at a time. This has resulted in a number of high-profile court cases in which principals have used corporal punishment or long periods of isolation, claiming they were only carrying out a nationally known and respected assertive discipline plan. Canter clearly states that this was a total misinterpretation of the assertive discipline philosophy and has issued a clear disclaimer that corporal punishment is not a part of the assertive discipline techniques. Canter also recommends that time out or isolation be used in a very cautious manner; and, if it is used, the student should be in isolation (a classroom across the hall or the principal's office) for no more than a few minutes, not exceeding an hour at the middle school or high school level. (Criteria for a room or location for isolation is given, and is nearly identical to that previously presented in the Behavior Analysis chapter.)

TEACHER BEHAVIOR CONTINUUM

Applying the Teacher Behavior Continuum as a way of viewing the power techniques inherent in the assertive discipline process includes the following actions.

Looking

Before using the classroom actions and techniques, through preplanning, the teacher covertly (a) establishes a discipline plan that is published to students, the principal, and parents. The teacher also (b) posts the rules on the chalkboard and (c) teaches the discipline plan to the students through a say, show, and check process using the TBC's directive statements or directive teaching. (*Note:* Refer to the techniques displayed on Teacher Behavior Continuum—Figure 4.2.)

Naming/Questioning

The first step in an assertive discipline plan is to give the off-task student a warning. This will range in power as a minimal warning such as, "Class, we should all be doing…!" (Naming)[5] or a similar warning in the form of a question, "What should you be doing now?" (Questioning).

Commanding

Next, the warning becomes quite directive as an *"I"* statement, such as, *"I want you to stop talking now!"* Finally, this warning is labeled as the student's last signal or warning to change the off-task behavior, *"This is your last warning,"* before a corrective action will occur.

Modeling/Reinforcing

In the discipline plan hierarchy, the teacher must follow up a warning with a corrective action. This is generally a negative minor corrective action (i.e., stay after class one minute). After a third violation, the hierarchy moves to an increased negative corrective action (stay after class two minutes), and finally with the fourth infraction the parents are called by the student. The student is taken to the office, the teacher dials the phone to get the parent at work, and the teacher states, "Hello, Mr. (or Mrs.) Parent, this is Mr. (or Ms., Mrs.) Jamerson, your child's teacher, and we are having some difficulty with his behavior in class today. I now will put him (or her) on the phone so he (or she) can tell you about it." The telephone is then turned over to the student to tell the parent what has occurred.

ASSERTIVE COMMAND

At times a desist process between teacher and student becomes confrontational, which undoubtedly will challenge the teacher. Assertive discipline would not want the teacher to retreat to a nonassertive passive stance and behavior or to a hostile response in these taxing interactions. Canter provides clear guidelines for how to give an assertive command—say the student's name, gesture, touch (not for secondary teachers), establish eye contact, and tell the student exactly what to do.

TEACHER: "Janice, you knew the rules and you have chosen to break them, now you must experience the corrective actions. (Moves to a position in front of the student.) Janice (states the student's name, points a finger at her, and then gestures toward the door and makes eye contact), I want you to stand, go out the door and go straight to Mr. Walker's office." (Limit setting: assertive command)

Looking	Naming	Questioning	Commanding	Modeling/ Reinforcement	Acting
a. Establish/ publish discipline plan to: students principal parents b. Post rules Must: • be observable • apply all day • relate to teaching style • involve students • be age appropriate Redirection 1: The "Look" 2: Physical proximity	The Assertive Process After first misbehavior (give warning): (1.1) Warning: Hints) "Class, we should be..." 3: Mention off-task student's name 4: Proximity Praise (praise the appropriate behavior of students on each side of off-task student) 5: Praise the student later (when he or she is on-task)	(1.2) Warning: As a question "What should you be doing now?"	(c) Teach the discipline plan Step 1: Say (1.3) Warning: "I" statement "I want you to stop talking now and...!" 4(1.4) Warning: "This is your warning." (write name in tracking book) 6. Assertive Command — say student's name — gesture — touch (not for secondary grades) — eye contact 7. Broken Record (repeat Assertive Command three times, then follow through with consequence) 8. Promise, "Be quiet now or you'll have chosen to (experience a negative consequence)!"	Step 2: Show (model) Step 3: Check (have student model or demonstrate) — Use positive repetition (teach this four times the first month) 4(2) After second misbehavior: Consequence (2.1) Stay after class one minute (write a check in tracking book) 4(3) After third misbehavior: Consequence (3.1) Stay after class two minutes (write another check in tracking book) 4(4) After fourth misbehavior: Consequence (4.1) Call parents (write another check in tracking book) The Recognition Process a.) Positive Recognition — praise — notes/calls home — certificates/ awards — tangible awards b.) reminder for teacher — Classwide Recognition — use + behavior chart	4(5) After fifth misbehavior: consequence (5.1) Go to office ("Who-Squad" if needed) 6. Severity clause (send to the principal) Go to office (for recognition/praise)
(numbers) = Concrete behaviors, (letters) = Preplanning behaviors 4 = five steps on the discipline plan					

FIGURE 4.2   Assertive Discipline Teacher Behavior Continuum

At times the student will not comply, instead giving the teacher back talk, fogging (attempting to distract the teacher from the main issue), or playing games to divert the teacher from this assertive position. When this occurs, the teacher does not fall into the student's trap by arguing or trying to reason with the student but moves to a "Broken Record" response by saying the assertive command over and over, like a broken record, at least three times before following through with a corrective action.

JANICE: "I wasn't doing anything!"

TEACHER (moves to a position in front of the student): "Janice (points a finger at her and then toward the door and makes eye contact), I want you to go to Mr. Walker's office." (Limit setting: first initiation of a "Broken Record")

JANICE: "Noreen was talking and you didn't say anything to her!"

TEACHER (moves to a position in front of the student): "Janice (points a finger at her and then toward the door and makes eye contact), I want you to go to the office." (Limit setting: second example of a "Broken Record" by repeating the assertive command.)

JANICE: "I don't know how to do this work."

TEACHER (moves to a position in front of the student): "Janice, to the office." (Limit setting: third example of a "Broken Record")

JANICE (drops her eyes, but doesn't move)

Enough is enough. There comes a point when the teacher has escalated to the top of his or her discipline hierarchy and now must follow thorough with physical intervention by removing the student to the principal's office. Before this occurs, the student is given a clear choice through the use of a promise of corrective action that permits the student a final option.

TEACHER: "Janice, this is your last chance. Move now or I will need to get Mr. Walker to come here and we will escort you to the office. This is a promise—you choose!" (promise of a corrective action)

JANICE (makes quick eye contact, drops her head, and begins to grind her teeth)

The Who-Squad

After the fifth infraction or breaking of the rule, the student is sent to the principal's office. If the student refuses to go and directly challenges the teacher's authority, the teacher makes use of three previously prepared letters: one addressed to the principal in charge of discipline and the other two for the fellow teachers across the hall. These have been stored in the teacher's lesson plan book or grade book. A well-behaved student seated near the door is asked to take these envelopes containing letters that state, " need your help to escort a defiant student out of my room." The fellow teachers and principal appear at the classroom door and say, "Who?" and the teacher points and says the student's name—hence the title, The Who-Squad. The squad then escorts the student to the office, where the principal will counsel the student and possibly award some negative corrective action.

TEACHER: "Janice, this is your last chance. Move now, or I will need to get Mr. Walker to come here and we will escort you to the office. This is a promise—you choose!" (promise of a corrective action)

JANICE (makes quick eye contact, drops her head, and begins to grind her teeth)

TEACHER (takes out two envelopes from his grade book and addresses himself to a well-behaved student seated near the door): "Gwen, please take this letter to Mr. Coats across the hall, and then this second letter to Mr. Walker in the office." Mr. Coats and Mr. Walker soon appear in the classroom and ask, "Who?" (the Who-Squad)

TEACHER: "Janice, seated here" (points to Janice). (The assistant principal approaches Janice, takes her by the elbow, and escorts the student to his office. Mr. Coats stands nearby ready to help if needed.) (send to principal)

Severity Clause

If the student were endangering property, himself, or others, the teacher obviously would not take the time to slowly progress up this hierarchy. Instead, the teacher would invoke the severity clause and send the student directly to the principal.

Modeling/Reinforcement

Also, under the reinforcement column of the TBC, we would place the positive feedback or verbal recognition of our assertive discipline plan. This would involve a teacher relating to one student through recognition actions of supportive feedback, positive notes/calls home, certificates/awards, and tangible awards. Again, the teacher would place reminders to himself or herself to give recognition daily, and these teacher actions would be tracked.

The teacher would also use an all-students (entire class) recognition system. This might involve a game of "classroom football" in which the entire class would gain points through the appropriate behavior of all students or by just one student; when the game was won, the whole class would win by having a special privilege (i.e., no homework for one evening or getting free time to do whatever they wanted).

Canter recommends a series of other techniques to create an accepting climate and positive relationship with students, all designed to be reinforcing:

- Take an inventory of student interest and attempt to bring this interest into the classroom activities. (A form for a Student Interest Inventory is included in the text and workbook.)
- Greet students at the door.
- Spend a few special minutes with students in small talk.
- Make home visits.
- Make a phone call to a student who had a difficult day in your classroom to let him or her know that you care.
- Make a phone call to a student when he or she has had a good day.
- Send a get-well card.

Teach the Discipline Plan and Rules

Assertive discipline maintains that a discipline plan, especially the rules, needs to be directly taught to the class just as the teacher would instruct any new knowledge in the subject area. Even in middle school and high school, we cannot assume that just because the students have been in school for many years and are older, they will automatically understand and follow the rules after we have explained them once. Canter provides a teacher lesson plan for teaching discipline to the total class with the lessons covering such points as: (1) explain why you need the rules, (2) teach the rules, (3) check for understanding, (4) explain why you have corrective actions, (5) explain how you will reinforce students who follow the rules, and (6) check for understanding.[6] These direct instructional strategies generally follow the Madeline Hunter[7] approach or instructional procedures as seen in Jones's positive discipline model following the basic three-step lesson of say (verbally explain), show (physically model and demonstrate), and check (test for comprehension). Canter also points out that the teaching of rules, even when following these direct lesson procedures, cannot be done on a one-shot basis, but instead needs positive repetition. At the middle/high school level, this means that once a new rule has been taught, it must be retaught, through positive repetition, at least four times during the month in order to truly reinforce the learning.

Other Suggested Classroom Procedures

In his newest book, Canter has added a number of general classroom practices that look quite similar to those first described in Jones's positive discipline model.

Scanning   This technique is used to get students to maintain a working behavior at their desks or while working in groups. While working with a group of students, the teacher periodically looks up and over the remaining students in the classroom and gives supportive feedback statements to those who are actively working. This alerts the students to the fact that the teacher is still observant.

Circulating the Classroom   "Don't stay seated behind your desk!" directs assertive discipline. Get on your feet and move around the room—in other words, circulate.

Redirection   When a student is off-task, Canter suggests a series of low-profile correction techniques, again similar to those used in the Jones model. In visually looking, the teacher gives the off-task student a "look" to signal them that the teacher is aware of the off-task behavior. Next, the teacher may mention the off-task student's name during the discussion or lecture, again signaling the student. Also, the teacher would use proximity supportive feedback by praising the students on each side of the off-task student for their appropriate behavior, thus attempting in a subtle manner to cue the off-task student. Finally, whenever the student does comply and gets back to work, the teacher finds the earliest opportunity to offer supportive feedback for the cooperative behavior.

SUMMARY

The underlying premise of the assertiveness model is the right of the teacher to teach and the right of the teacher to expect students to obey, with the full support of parents and administrators if needed. An assertive teacher clearly conveys his or her rules for compliance and actions that will greet noncompliance. The assertive discipline teacher does not back down. He or she covertly makes a discipline plan for all students and teaches this plan directly to the class through an instructional process. The teacher gives warnings, and then, if necessary, follows up with preestablished corrective actions, making it clear that the misbehaving student has chosen this negative corrective action by his or her own behavior.

Although the plan clearly delineates negative corrective actions, Canter has outlined a positive recognition system whereby supportive feedback is used and documented by the teacher. The system attempts to train the teacher to repeatedly give reinforcing positive actions toward the class and individual students.

Strengths and Limitations of the Model

Some of the same strengths and limitations of the behavioral analysis model apply to the assertive model. Canter believes in the use of positive rewards, and positive recognition as incentives to comply with the teacher-established rules, but also emphasizes punishment (loss of privileges, detention, notes home). The assertive discipline model is concerned with a teacher asserting his or her rights and putting together a plan of rewards and corrective actions that will enforce the teacher's authority—this is based on the assertiveness training concepts[8] and not on behavior theory. In fact many of the behavior analysis advocates take issue with the use of punishment on the basis of research showing that positive and negative reinforcement (systemic avoidance of an undesirable event) works, but that corrective action does not. Since punishment is commonly used in schools, most teachers would probably side with the assertive discipline position that even though punishment may not have long-term benefits, it does at least give temporary aid to a teacher to be able to use the threat of corrective action with a student.

The model's emphasis on a teacher's assertiveness and clearness in her direction and expectations appears to be a major strength. The use of a uniform plan for all students appears to be the model's greatest liability. Those who believe that a classroom should be a model of democracy, that students should take responsibility for their own behavior, and that misbehavior is often symptomatic of underlying problems will find little comfort with the assertiveness model. Total teacher control, uniform disciplinary actions without regard to individual differences, and a low priority for communicating and understanding a student's behavior are all limitations to those who believe that discipline should include learning about oneself and one's relationship with others and the attempt to behave according to one's own standards.

Alfie Kohn's Criticism of Canter's Assertive Discipline

On teacher-imposed rules:

If, however, the goal is to help students grow into compassionate, principled people, then having students "define the real meaning" of rules is the best way—perhaps the only way—that a list of rules prepared by the teacher can help students become thoughtful decision makers. But such an arrangement can only do so much; it is far better to ask children to create rules. (Kohn, 1996, p. 71)

On Canter's use of "you have *chosen* to break a rule," thus this consequence is occurring:

Adults who blithely insist that children choose to misbehave are rather like politicians who declare that people have only themselves to blame for being poor. In both cases, potentially relevant factors other than personal responsibility are ignored. A young child in particular may not have a fully developed capacity for rational decision-making or impulse control that is implicit in suggesting he made a choice. Teachers who think in terms of a lack of skills would be inclined to respond by trying to help the child develop these facilities, rather than by punishing and blaming. Indeed, two researchers recently discovered that the more teachers resorted to saying that a child simply 'chose' to act inappropriately, the more likely they were to use punishment and other power-based interventions. (Scott-Little and Holloway, 1992; Kohn, 1996, p. 17)

On Kohn's total rejection of Canter's use of punishment (or assertive discipline's corrective actions):

punishment: it must be deliberately chosen to be unpleasant, such as by forcing the student to do something he would rather not do or preventing him from doing something he would rather do or preventing him from doing something he wants to do; and it must be intended to change the student's future behavior. A punishment makes somebody suffer in order to teach a lesson. (Kohn, 1996, p. 24)

On rewards:

Rewards, like punishment, can only manipulate someone's actions. They do nothing to help a child become a kind or caring person. (Kohn, 1996, p. 34)

On supportive feedback:

The message of supportive feedback is: I approve of what you did, so you should do it again. It is a way of reinforcing the act. "Look at Jaime's face!" on the other hand, is concerned with helping the sharer to experience the effects of sharing and to come to see himself as the kind of person who wants to make other people feel good—irrespective of verbal rewards. Even when this particular response isn't used, the goal remains much deeper than buying a behavior; it is nothing less than assisting children in constructing an image of themselves as decent people. (Kohn, 1996, p. 70)

Things [verbal recognition] get even worse when such comments are offered in front of others (e.g., Canter and Canter 1992, pp. 143–145): "I like the way Alisa has found her seat so quickly…" Here the teacher has taken rewards, which are bad enough, and added to them the poison of competition. Children are set against one another in a race to be the first one to receive supportive feedback.. This sort of practice does Alisa no favors; one can imagine how the other kids will treat her later; "Look, it's Miss Found-Her-Seat Dork!" Over time, singling children out like this works against any sense of community in the classroom. What's more, public praise is a fundamentally fraudulent interaction in its own right. The teacher is pretending to speak to Alisa, but is actually using her, holding her up as an example in an attempt to manipulate everyone else in the room. (Kohn, 1996, p. 25)

Finally, Kohn rejects the assertive discipline model with "full force":

Even when judged by the narrow criterion of getting children to conform, the evidence suggests

that Assertive Discipline is not terribly effective. When various approaches to classroom management are examined empirically, some studies typically show "positive" effects while other show no effects. It is rare to discover that a program has negative effects, but they have turned up in some students of Assertive Discipline. Overall, most of the published research shows that technique to be detrimental or, at best, to have no meaningful effect at all (Emmer and Aussiker 1990; Render, Padilla, and Frank 1989). Still, one of the chief selling points of a program like Assertive Discipline is, in the words of one teacher, that "it's easy to use. It's all spelled out for you" (Hill 1990, p. 75). Without a packaged system Canter warns, the teacher would be "forced to constantly make choices about how to react to student behavior" (Canter and Canter 1992, p. 46). In other words, the teacher might have to think about herself or bring students into the process of solving problems. John Nichols spent a year watching a 2nd grade teacher struggle to implement Assertive Discipline and observed that it "stifled her wit and cut her off from the children she communicates with so well" (Nichols and Hazzard 1993, p. 187). Indeed, teachers who have abandoned the program in favor of noncoercive models of teaching sometimes say they would quit the profession before using Assertive Discipline again. (Kohn, 1996, pp. 57–58)

But now we are ready to move beyond a critique of punishment and rewards. The next step is to recognize that trying to keep control of the classroom and get compliance, as virtually every discipline program assures us we must, is inimical to our ultimate objectives. What we have to face is that the more we "manage" students' behavior and try to make them do what we say, the more difficult it is for them to become morally sophisticated people who think for themselves and care about others. (Kohn, 1996, p. 62)

SUMMARY OF KEY CONCEPTS

assertive command	broken record	corrective actions	students privileges
assertiveness	classroom plan	mental rehearsal	
behavior awards	classroom rules	punishment/isolation	

positive notes home and/or phone call to parents	preplanning	rewards	the Who-Squad
	punishment	severity clause	uniform standards
	putting names on the chalkboard	systematic exclusion	verbal recognition
positive recognition		teacher rights	warnings

CASE STUDIES

What actions would the assertive discipline teacher take using the five systems (limit setting, backup, incentive, encouragement, and management system) for the following?

1. **Mike's Clowning:** Mike could be labeled as the class clown. He has been seen blowing chocolate milk bubbles through his nose in the cafeteria; placing his backside on the edge of the stool in chemistry class, using a movable Bunsen burner to lights his "farts" to produce a flame; and often dressing in a T-shirt with the words "suck city" on the front. When asked to stop these behaviors, he gives the teacher the "deer in the headlights look" with a slight smile. He does stop, but within an hour or two he has a new action to "gross out" the class members and disrupt the teacher's teaching. Today, with his hand underneath his armpit he produces a flagrant sound by pumping his elbow up and down. Using these sounds, he attempts to "play" *Jingle Bells,* "cracks up" the class, and, of course, disrupts your teaching.

How would the five discipline/management systems be applied to Mike using assertive discipline techniques?

Limit-setting System

The one clear behavior involving limit setting suggested by *Assertive Discipline* for the teacher is the assertive command—say Mike's name, gesture, touch, make eye contact, and state clearly what actions you wish Mike to do. "Mike, return to your seat open, your workbook, and begin now!" The teacher may repeat this as a broken record, but the basic process that will be used to change Mike's behavior is the incentive system to follow.

Backup System

The concept of backup systems when working with a student such as Mike involves the use of isolation and

removal to the principal's office (the "who-squad"—a team of teachers and/or administrators coming into the room and escorting Mike out if he become defiant or assaultive). Discipline actions and the possibility of sending Mike home to his parents are actions central to this model. Both the principal and Mike's parents got copies and were required to sign the discipline plan that states the steps and procedures for involving the principal and parents. The dealings with the parents follow the same assertive procedures and attitude; that is, the teacher has the perfect right to get assistance from both the principal and parents, and the teacher asserts her- or himself to demand this support. Since we hear that communication with Mike's parents was not accomplished, the strongest backup action would be to take Mike to his parent's place of work during the school day and turn him over to the parents. This is a very strong suggestion, and we would wonder at the practical level how many schools would be willing to take such actions, and, if done, what ramifications would occur.

Incentive System

Most of the techniques and methods presented by *Assertive Discipline* can be placed under the heading of an incentive system—rewards for good behavior and corrective actions for unacceptable behavior. These incentives can be uniformly done with the entire classroom. The TBC in Figure 4.2 provides clear actions with inherent degrees of power available to the teacher when administering such an incentive system involving Mike. When Mike is at the teacher's side disrupting her while she is working with a small group, or when he is disturbing a fellow classmate, the teacher would put his name on the board as a warning and at the same time say nothing. If he disrupted again, a check would be put beside his name, now requiring him to stay after school for 15 minutes (or some similar consequence). If the disruption occurred again, a second check would cost Mike 30 minutes after school. With this second check Mike would be taken by the teacher to the phone and required to call his parents and tell them what he did. The third check would result in the child being sent to the principal's office.

To balance these negative actions, the teacher would be carrying out a group reward system, with *Assertive Discipline* being "famous" for the "dropping the marble" scheme. While the teacher is teaching and no one is disrupting, the teacher periodically verbally recognizes everyone ("Good, I see that everyone is working hard") and drops a marble in an empty fish bowl. Once the bowl is full, the class stops and has a party (i.e., popcorn party) or some other special treat. So the class socializes each other to behave so that the entire class can get this group reward.

Encouragement System

Assertive discipline takes the position that "I will not tolerate anyone stopping me from teaching. I don't care if you are deprived, depraved, or whatever. No one will stop me from teaching." This position does not allow any room for an encouragement system to focus on one student such as Mike, but *Assertive Discipline* would begin a campaign of "catching Mike being good" with the use of verbal recognition. This constant verbal recognition being dispersed minute by minute and hour by hour has caused some critics to label assertive teachers as "praise junkies." "Good work, Mike!" Also, if the incentive system did begin to help Mike comply, the teacher would send positive notes or make calls home, give certificates/awards, and allow other tangible awards (see Figure 4.1) such as applause from his peers.

Management System

Assertive discipline does not give us help for managing objects, materials, time, or students in our classroom. The one minor suggestion that seems widely used by teachers is that no more than five classroom rules should be posted on the wall or chalkboard at the front of the classroom. Mike would have been clearly taught the rules that the teacher wanted him to obey.

What actions would assertive discipline take for dealing with the next three students?

2. **Andrew "Takes Over":** The students return to your classroom after being in the library-media center. The director of the center complains strongly about the poor behavior by your students, but gives you little details. Once the students are

settled in their seats, you open a discussion with, "I want to talk to you about your behavior in the media center. (All heads drop.) Does anyone have anything to say?" Andrew is seated in the back of the room, slouched in his chair with his feet in the air propped over the top of the desk next to him. "Yea, I have something to say. Shut up! I hate that ugly bitch, and we aren't going back to the media center again." Most of the other class members respond, with "Yea! We're not going back there again!" Andrew seems to be respected and somewhat feared by the other students, and they often look to him for a signal as to whether they should comply with you as the teacher, and you often have the feeling that he can "take over" your class.

3. **Jake the Grenade:** Jake is like a walking grenade. One can never tell when he will explode. He passively seems to withdraw within himself, carrying a large "chip on his shoulder." If he is bumped or jostled accidentally by a fellow student, he will strike out. He has deliberately pulled a chair away from a fellow student just as she was seating herself and caused this student to fall to the floor, striking her head on the way down. He attempts to throw wet paper wads down the open blouse of one of the girls. He likes to draw monster-like cartoon characters on any surface that he can find, including the top of his desk. Today in chemistry class he got up and wandered about the room while the teacher was lecturing, and he opened all the gas jets at the chemistry tables at the back of the room—the smell of gas quickly filled the room.

4. **Linda the Passive:** Linda is a tall thin girl who is nearly always seen with her head down on her desk and her gangly long legs wrapped around the legs of her chair. She constantly has her first three fingers in her mouth, sucking them to the point that she has sucked off one fingernail. She has a body odor that is noticeable to everyone and often looks as if she has not bathed for many days. It is November, and she has done no homework, answers no questions when called on, and when questioned by the teacher in one-to-one situations, grunts yes or no to all questions. Other children laugh at her, calling her a host of derogatory names. The parents do not have a phone number, and you have not been able to contact them for a conference. Other teachers have never seen the parents, but her address is near the railroad track where there are many trailers.

Further Discussion

For example 2, Andrew "Takes Over," the assertive teacher would follow the identical procedures as in example 1, Mike's Clowning—assertive command, name on the board, and so on. But, with 3, Jake the Grenade, we would see the assertive discipline teacher apply the severity clause and remove the student from the classroom because of the dangerous aspect of his actions. If Jake were defiant, the "who-squad" or a response team of the principal and possibly the school's officer would be called to escort Jake from the classroom. In example 4, Linda the Passive, assertive discipline gives minimal help because she is not disrupting the classroom. However, assertive discipline would be highly encouraging through "bathing" her in verbal recognition and having her be a part of any rewards. A question that we may ask is: Does assertive discipline teach a new repertoire of behaviors for any of these four students?

NOTES

1. L. Canter and M. Canter, *Assertive Discipline: Positive Behavior Management for Today's Classroom* (Santa Monica, CA: Lee Canter & Associates, 1992), p. 5.
2. L. Canter and M. Canter, *Assertive Discipline: Positive Behavior Management for Today's Classroom,* p. 45.
3. L. Canter, *Assertive Discipline: Secondary Workbook* (Santa Monica, CA: Lee Canter & Associates, 1992), p. 37.
4. D. Hill, "Order in the Classroom," *Teacher Magazine* (April 1990): 70–77.
5. L. Canter, "Be An Assertive Teacher," *Instructor* (November 1978).
6. L. Canter, *Assertive Discipline: Secondary Workbook,* p. 60.
7. M. Hunter, *Teach for Transfer* (El Segundo, CA: TIP Publications, 1971).
8. R. E. Alberti and M. L. Emmons, *Stand Up, Speak Out, Talk Back* (New York: Pocket Books, 1975).

Related Readings

Canter, L., and Canter, M. *Assertive Discipline: A Take-Charge Approach for Today's Educator.* Los Angeles, CA: Canter and Associates, Inc., 1982 (the original text).

Canter, L., and Canter, M. *Assertive Discipline: Positive Behavior Management for Today's Classroom.* Santa Monica, CA: Lee Canter & Associates, 1992.

Canter, L., and Canter, M. *Succeeding with Difficult Students: New Strategies for Reaching Your Most Challenging Students.* Santa Monica, CA: Lee Canter & Associates, 1993.

Canter, L. *Back to School with Assertive Discipline: Grades 1–6.* Santa Monica, CA: Lee Canter & Associates, 1990.

Canter, L. *Homework without Tears for Teachers—Grades 1–12.* Santa Monica, CA: Lee Canter & Associates, 1989.

Parents

Canter, L., and Canter, M. *Assertive Discipline for Parents.* New York: Harper & Row, Publishers, 1982.

Canter, L., and Canter, M. *Parents on Your Side: A Comprehensive Parent Involvement Program for Teachers.* Santa Monica, CA: Lee Canter & Associates, 1991.

Canter, L., and Hausner, L. *Homework without Tears: A Parent's Guide for Motivating Children to Do Homework and to Succeed in School.* New York: Harper & Row, 1987.

Difficult Student(s)

Canter, L. *Succeeding with Difficult Students: Workbook—Grades K–12.* Santa Monica, CA: Lee Canter & Associates, 1993.

Workbooks

Canter, L. *Assertive Discipline: Elementary Workbook—Grades K–5.* Santa Monica, CA: Lee Canter & Associates, 1992.

Canter, L. *Assertive Discipline: Middle School Workbook—Grades 6–8.* Santa Monica, CA: Lee Canter & Associates, 1992.

Canter, L. *Assertive Discipline: Secondary Workbook—Grades 9–12.* Santa Monica, CA: Lee Canter & Associates, 1992.

Canter, L. *Teacher's Mailbox: A Collection of Reproducibles to Facilitate Communication between Teachers, Students, and Parents—K–6.* Santa Monica, CA: Lee Canter & Associates, 1988.

Auxiliary Staff

Canter, L. *Assertive Discipline for the Bus Driver: A Step-by-Step Approach for Managing Student Behavior on the School Bus.* Santa Monica, CA: Lee Canter & Associates, 1987.

Canter, L. *Assertive Discipline for Paraprofessionals.* Santa Monica, CA: Lee Canter & Associates, 1987.

Because of the controversial nature of the assertive discipline model, research and discussion literature regarding this model is provided here as a resource to the reader:

Research and Discussion Papers Related to Assertive Discipline

Allen, R. D. "The Effect of Assertive Discipline on the Number of Junior High School Discipline Referrals." *Dissertation Abstracts International, 44* (1984): 2299A–2300A.

Barrett, E. R. "Assertive Discipline and Research," 1987. Unpublished manuscript available from Canter & Associates, P.O. Box 2113, Santa Monica, CA 90406.

Barrett, E. R., and Curtis, K. F. "The Effect of Assertive Discipline Training on Student Teachers." *Teacher Education and Practice* (Spring/Summer 1986): 53–56.

Bauer, R. L. "A Quasi-Experimental Study of the Effects of Assertive Discipline." *Dissertation Abstracts International, 43* (1982): 25A.

Canter & Associates. "Abstracts of Research and Validating Effectiveness of Assertive Discipline," 1987. Unpublished manuscript available from Lee Canter & Associates, P.O. Box 2113, Santa Monica, CA 90406.

Canter, L. "Competency-Based Approach to Discipline—It's Assertive." *Educational Leadership, 8* (1979a): 11–13.

Canter, L. "Taking Charge of Student Behavior." *National Elementary Principal, (58),* 4 (1979b): 33–36, 41.

Canter, L. "Assertive Discipline: A Proven Approach." *Today's Catholic Teacher* (October 1983): 36–37.

Crawley, K. E. (1983). "Teacher and Student Perceptions with Regard to Classroom Behavior Conditions, Procedures, and Student Behavior in Classes of Teachers Trained in Assertive Discipline Methods." *Dissertation Abstracts International, 43* (1983): 2840D.

Emmer, E. T., and Aussiker, A. "School and Classroom Discipline Programs: How Well Do They Work?" In *Student Discipline Strategies: Research and Practices,* ed. by O. C. Moles. Albany: State University of New York Press, 1990.

Ersavas, C. M. "A Study of the Effect of Assertive Discipline at Four Elementary Schools." *Dissertation Abstracts International, 42* (1981): 473A.

Fereira, C. L. "A Positive Approach to Assertive Discipline." Martinez, CA: Martinez Unified School District, 1983. (ERIC Document Reproduction Service No. ED 240058).

Henderson, C. B. "An Analysis of Assertive Discipline Training and Implementation on Inservice Elementary Teachers' Self-Concept; Locus of Control. Pupil Control Ideology; and Assertive Personality Characteristics." *Dissertation Abstracts International, 42* (1982): 4797A.

Hill, D. "Order in the Classroom." *Teacher Magazine* (April 1990): 7–77.

Mandelbaum, L. H., Russell, S. C., Krouse, J., and Gonter, M. "Assertive Discipline: An Effective Classwide Behavior Management Program." *Behavior Disorders, 8,* 4 (1983): 258–264.

McCormack, S. L. (1985). "Students' Off-Task Behavior and Assertive Discipline." *Dissertation Abstracts International, 46* (1985): 1880A.

Moffett, K. L., Jurenka, D. J., and Kovan, J. "Assertive Discipline." *California School Boards* (June/July/August 1982): 24–27.

Nichols J. G., and Hazzard, S. P. *Education as Adventure: Lessons form the Second Grade.* New York: Teachers College Press, 1993.

Parker, P. R. "Effects of Secondary Level Assertive Discipline in a Central Texas School District and Guidelines to Successful Assertion and Reward Strategies." *Dissertation Abstracts International, 45* (1985): 3504A.

Render, J.G.F., Padilla, J. M., and Krank, H. M. "Assertive Discipline: A Critical Review and Analysis." Paper presented at the annual meeting of the Northern Rocky Mountain Educational Research Association. Park City, UT, October 1987.

Render, G. F., Padilla, J. M., and Krank, H. M. "Assertive Discipline: A Critical Review and Analysis." *Teachers College Record, 90* (1989): 607–630.

Smith, S. J. "The Effects of Assertive Discipline Training on Student Teachers' Self-Perceptions and Classroom Management Skills." *Dissertation Abstracts International, 44* (1984): 2690A.

Ward, L. R. "The Effectiveness of Assertive Discipline as a Means to Reduce Classroom Disruptions." *Dissertation Abstracts International, 44* (1984): 2324A–2325A.

CONFRONTING-CONTRACTING

WE NOW PRESENT the chapters on confronting-contracting. The philosophies of the confronting/contracting models suggest shared power with the student for behavioral change. These discipline models attempt to maintain an adult accepting relationship with a misbehaving student by requesting the student to stop and change. The solution for how the student will change remains in the student's hands or control.

CHAPTER 5. The Adlerian models, which include those by Dreikurs, Nelson, and Albert *(Cooperative Discipline),* are based on the idea that misbehaving students are those who cannot find social acceptance. The model provides practical techniques to confront these students and encourage them to change.

CHAPTER 6. The Curwin and Mendler *Discipline with Dignity* model first published by the Association for Supervision and Curriculum Development (ASCD) appears to be widely known, and presents three systems: prevention dimension (what can be done to prevent a discipline incident), action dimension (what to do when an incident is occurring.), and resolution dimension (establish contracts with the very difficult student).

CHAPTER 7. *Love and Logic: Taking Control of the Classroom* by Fay and Funk places a high priority on establishing a positive relationship with a misbehaving student, seen as hurt and discouraged, and guides the teacher away from power conflicts. Since the philosophy and methods parallel those of Glasser's reality therapy, we have embedded Glasser's ideas within the Love and Logic model.

Mr. Garcia ignores Ronald's lack of a solid response, finishes calling the roll, and finally introduces himself and the content of the course. He turns his back to the class and begins to write the name of the textbook across the chalkboard. Before he can finish, the same girlish scream is heard, but this time with such intensity that it signals something more serious. The girl seated in front of Ronald jumps to her feet, crosses her arms across her chest, and runs frantically to the classroom door. As she passes before Mr. Garcia and the front of the class, everyone can see that her bra is open in the back. A few nervous giggles come from the class, and now all eyes focus on Ronald and then, unfortunately, back to Mr. Garcia.

Mr. Garcia is quite obviously "on the spot." It is the beginning of the semester, and he faces a troublesome male student, a distraught female student, and a class of 31 teenagers waiting to see what will transpire. What specific steps should he take to defuse this situation, get the class back on track, help the girl, and eventually aid Ronald in improving his behavior? This chapter will explain Rudolf Dreikurs's techniques as we apply them to Mr. Garcia's treatment of Ronald. As the techniques are explained, you will see a particular application of the teacher's behavior as it relates to Ronald's misbehavior and motivation.

ALBERT/DREIKURS'S AND ADLER'S SOCIAL THEORY

The writings of Rudolf Dreikurs and Linda Albert, author of *Cooperative Discipline,* flow out of the work of the noted social psychologist Alfred Adler. Adler believed that the central motivation of all humans is to belong and be accepted by others. Humans are, foremost, social animals. Books written by Dreikurs and his various associates *(Children: The Challenge; Logical Consequences; Encouraging Children to Learn; Psychology in the Classroom; and Discipline without Tears)* all have a common bond with Adler. This bond is that all behavior, including misbehavior, is orderly, purposeful, and directed toward achieving social recognition.[1] Each action taken by such students as Ronald Foster is goal directed. The "inner" goal results in the "outward" behavior. The teacher must have a student like Ronald recognize his inner goal and then help the student change to the more appropriate goal of learning how to belong with others. This is the rationale for placing Albert/Dreikurs under the Confronting-Contracting orientation. They believe in an underlying cause for misbehavior (similar to Relationship-Listening), yet they believe that its correction is the result of a teacher actively showing a student how to belong.

Since Dreikurs's death in 1972, two writers have built on his work and expanded on it. They are Linda Albert, whose *A Teacher's Guide to Cooperative Discipline: How to Manage Your Classroom and Promote Self-Esteem* presents readable and practical suggestions for classroom teachers, and Donald Dinkmeyer, author of *Systematic Training for Effective Parenting (STEP),* who has written a host of books for parents dealing with differing ages of children and has conducted many valuable workshops for parents. Both writers build their suggestions, techniques, and practices solidly on the Adlerian-Dreikurs theoretical constructs, with Albert's work speaking clearly to the classroom teacher. The following is a presentation of Dreikurs's methodology as it relates to discipline; where

Albert has expanded the practical methods, I have added her suggestions in an outline-block format throughout this chapter.

METHODS AND PHILOSOPHY

When a student is unsuccessful in obtaining social acceptance (sometimes as early as her infant or toddler years at home), a pattern of misbehavior begins. One way of analyzing this is through a sociogram (see Figure 5.1). The student is left with the recourse of trying to fulfill inner needs by annoying, destructive, hostile, or helpless behavior. If we, as teachers, can help misbehaving students understand their mistaken faulty goals and provide them with avenues for group acceptance, then such students will rationally change their own behaviors. These subconscious goals that motivate misbehavior are (1) attention getting, (2) power and control, (3) revenge, and (4) helplessness and inadequacy.[2]

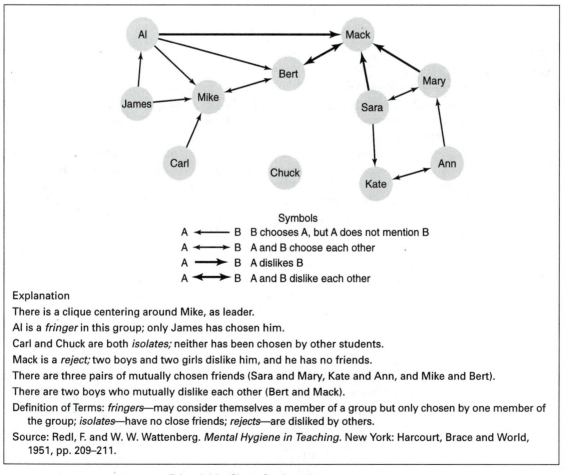

Symbols

A ◄——— B   B chooses A, but A does not mention B
A ◄——► B   A and B choose each other
A ——► B   A dislikes B
A ◄——► B   A and B dislike each other

Explanation

There is a clique centering around Mike, as leader.

Al is a *fringer* in this group; only James has chosen him.

Carl and Chuck are both *isolates;* neither has been chosen by other students.

Mack is a *reject;* two boys and two girls dislike him, and he has no friends.

There are three pairs of mutually chosen friends (Sara and Mary, Kate and Ann, and Mike and Bert).

There are two boys who mutually dislike each other (Bert and Mack).

Definition of Terms: *fringers*—may consider themselves a member of a group but only chosen by one member of the group; *isolates*—have no close friends; *rejects*—are disliked by others.

Source: Redl, F. and W. W. Wattenberg. *Mental Hygiene in Teaching.* New York: Harcourt, Brace and World, 1951, pp. 209–211.

FIGURE 5.1 Friendship Chart Sociogram

1. **Attention Getting:** This is evident when a student is constantly looking to belong and be recognized in the class. Instead of receiving such recognition through productive work, often a student will resort to acting in ways that demand incessant praise or criticism. Both praise and criticism of an incessant nature are equally undesirable.

2. **Power and Control:** This is a goal for a student who feels inferior, who feels unable to measure up to the expectations of others or of self. It makes no difference whether the student is actually handicapped in some way or has only a false perception of being inferior. In either case, the youngster will try to remedy this perception of inferiority by trying to get his own way, being the boss, forcing himself on others, or by bragging and clowning.

3. **Revenge:** This is a goal for the student who feels unable to gain attention or power. This student sees herself as having unequal status because of what others have done to her. This student places the blame for her plight on those outside. She feels hurt by others and compensates by following the philosophy "an eye for an eye." In other words, "If I'm hurting, then I have the right to make others hurt." The student goes beyond the desire for attention and power, beyond the desire to win. She resorts to achieving status not by merely winning over others, but by beating others with maliciousness and humiliation.

4. **Helplessness and Inadequacy:** The student operating with this goal is the most pathetic. He has given up on the possibility of being a member of or of gaining any status in the group. This student not only feels incapable of doing anything (either constructively or destructively) about it, but has accepted the feeling of being a nobody and no longer cares what happens.

Since Adlerian-Dreikurs-Albert theory places membership and belonging as the primary motivator, teachers may wish to study the social makeup of the class with the use of a Friendship Chart (sociogram). This may be done by asking the students to state preferences for other members of the class in response to such questions as: whom would you like to sit beside? Who would you like to work with in a study group or laboratory? Which student would you most like to visit at home? Which boys or girls do you like least? Based on the results, the teacher constructs a diagram similar to the one shown in Figure 5.1.

With this beginning understanding of Albert/Dreikurs, let us move to the Teacher Behavior Continuum with Mr. Garcia and Ronald Foster.

THE TEACHER BEHAVIOR CONTINUUM

To begin, the teacher must determine which of the four faulty goals is motivating the student. This determination is basically a four-step process, as follows:

1. The teacher observes and collects information about the student in situations involving peers and family.

2. After gathering information about the student, the teacher can then hypothesize or guess which of the underlying goals is held by the student.

3. This goal can be verified by the teacher by reflecting on what feelings arise within the teacher as a result of the student's behavior.

4. Final verification is achieved by confronting the student with a series of four questions and looking for the student's recognition reflex.

In carrying out this procedure, the teacher moves through silent looking, questioning, commanding, and back to questioning.

Looking

Mr. Garcia, in the immediate situation with 31 pairs of eyes peering at him, disinvolves himself emotionally from Ronald's behavior. He has noted the first impression of rudeness, braggadocio, and flashiness that Ronald has created. Mr. Garcia makes a mental note to himself to search for more information by looking at school records, talking to former teachers, and possibly making a home visit. For now, though, with limited information, he suspects that Ronald's goal may be attention getting, power, or revenge. It certainly is not helplessness!

It is important to remain calm during the beginning encounter with a student operating under any of the faulty goals, and not to give the student what he seeks. For example, the worst thing Mr. Garcia could do is call out loudly and angrily to Ronald. To do so would give Ronald the attention he seeks (attention getting), or it would accelerate the battle of who will win out (power), or it would drive Ronald into physically lashing out (revenge).

Mr. Garcia can remain calm because he knows rationally that Ronald's behavior is not directed at him personally but is simply the student's previously learned mode of responding in groups. Of course, a quite human reaction from a teacher would be to explode, but this urge must be held in check. Examining this emotional urge or feeling toward the student will be most helpful in narrowing down and identifying the student's goal.

Questions (Covert)

Now Mr. Garcia can assess the inner emotions that Ronald's behavior has evoked. Albert/Dreikurs suggested that teachers covertly ask themselves four questions related to the goals.[3]

Introduction: Teacher Beliefs on Discipline

1. Do I feel annoyed? If so, you may have reason to suspect attention getting as a goal.

2. Do I feel beaten or intimidated? If so, you may have reason to suspect power as a goal.

3. Do I feel wronged or hurt? If so, you may have reason to suspect revenge as a goal.

4. Do I feel incapable of reaching the child in any way? If so, you may have reason to suspect helplessness as the goal.

Mr. Garcia analyzes his feelings as "annoyed," to say the least, and even slightly intimidated, which suggests that Ronald's goal was attention getting or power.

Let's see what Ronald's probable responses would have been if the teacher had given free rein to his first impulses. If Mr. Garcia had yelled at him, Ronald might have responded with, "Chill out, chill, man, no need to lose it, just chill!" In other words, if Ronald's goal were power, he would have won at that point. He would have "shown up" Mr. Garcia in front of the class as a teacher who becomes easily flustered while he, a 17-year-old student, was more of a man, with calm and collected reactions. If Ronald's goal was to get attention, he would have responded in a different way. Mr. Garcia's yells might have caused Ronald to put his head down sheepishly and grin to himself. The rest of the class would be observing Ronald, and as soon as Mr. Garcia turned away, Ronald's head would be back up, face smiling and looking around to make sure that everyone had seen him. In both cases, Mr. Garcia's primary reaction would have done little to prevent numerous future occurrences. Mr. Garcia knows he can't play into the student's scheme and is ready now to take specific action. He makes a guess that Ronald's primary goal is to seek attention.

Command

The previous reflective and covert behaviors of silent looking and questioning were primarily enacted to gather information, to narrow down and identify the student's possible goal, and to make a tentative plan for action. A teacher trained in Albert/Dreikurs's approach would take only a split second from first witnessing the girl running out of the classroom to begin action with Ronald.

Having identified attention getting as Ronald's underlying goal, Mr. Garcia acts in a way that deprives Ronald of the attention related to his misbehavior. Mr. Garcia turns to the girl and quietly tells her to come back in the classroom when she is ready and to take another seat away from Ronald. He then turns to the class and states, "Class, I would like to introduce you to some of the laboratory equipment you will be using this year. In a few minutes I would like you to break up into groups of four people and gather around the lab tables at the back of the room. When you get settled, open to the first page of your lab manual, where you will find pictures of the various kinds of equipment. As a group, see if you can first learn the equipment names, then I will join each group briefly to demonstrate how to use some of the more dangerous equipment, such as the Bunsen burner. OK, class, find your groups of four and move to your tables." Turning to Ronald, he adds, "Oh, Ronald Foster, your behavior has told me that you are not ready to work with others. I want you to remain in your seat. When you think you can join a group without being disruptive, you may do so."

Having attended to the class, Mr. Garcia gives Ronald a directive statement. He has told Ronald that he can join the group if and when he is ready to contribute in an appropriate way. This is an example of a teacher applying logical consequences rather than punishment. (I will explain this difference more fully later. For now, let us say that Mr. Garcia has employed as a logical consequence the loss of the student's right to engage in an activity as a result of a behavior that would be counterproductive to performing that activity.) Before Mr. Garcia can conclude definitely that attention getting is Ronald's goal and continues with a long-range plan based on that goal identification, he needs further verification. He can achieve this by turning to overt questioning with Ronald.

Questions (Overt)

Ronald has stayed by himself, slouched down with his hat over his face for nearly half the period. This is a further sign that Mr. Garcia has correctly identified Ronald's goal. If Ronald had wanted power, he would have continued to defy the teacher's rules. If Ronald had wanted revenge, he would have physically retaliated against the girl or teacher. Mr. Garcia eyes Ronald slowly getting out of his seat and moving toward the lab table. There is only one spot open in the groups of four, and he heads toward that spot. When this group of three notices that he is ready to join them, one of the girls at the table (the very one that Ronald bothered) begins to complain and shout, "No, no, you don't! You're not joining our table." Ronald then turns to another nearby group and is greeted with, "You're not coming into our group. There is dangerous stuff here—you'll get us killed!" With a parting shot, "You're a bunch of jerks," Ronald returns to his desk. Mr. Garcia moves toward him, takes a seat nearby, and in a voice that cannot be heard by anyone else begins to question Ronald:

TEACHER: "Do you know why you acted like you did this morning?" (Confronting)

RONALD (simply shrugs his shoulders)

TEACHER: "I have some ideas. Would you like to know?"

RONALD (nods yes)

TEACHER: "Could you want special attention?" (Verifying)

RONALD (For the first time, his eyes look directly at Mr. Garcia, and he gives a slight smile.) (Recognition reflex)

During a discussion in a calm setting, Albert/Dreikurs proposed that the teacher does as Mr. Garcia has done.[4] The teacher should ask the student if she is interested in knowing why she behaves as she does. If the student does not resist, the teacher asks one of four questions. Albert/Dreikurs listed them as:

(Attention)	**1.**	Could it be that you want special attention?
(Power)	**2.**	Could it be that you want your own way and hope to be boss?
(Revenge)	**3.**	Could it be that you want to hurt others as much as you feel hurt by them?
(Helplessness)	**4.**	Could it be that you want to be left alone?[5]

After the teacher asks each of these questions, he looks (silent looking) for behavior verification. If the student smiles, laughs, looks up suddenly, moves her shoulders, or shows other signs of response to the implied goal, then the teacher has conclusive evidence that his hypothesis is correct and treatment can proceed. The teacher formulates a plan and returns to appropriate command.

Command

Now that Ronald has given the "recognition reflex" to question 1, Mr. Garcia can be confident that attention is Ronald's goal. Mr. Garcia's task now becomes one of finding ways for Ronald to receive attention through constructive social behavior. In other words, he needs to give Ronald the attention that he craves. Following are descriptions of treatment for each of the four goals that correspond with Albert/Dreikurs's prescriptive chart for teachers.[6]

Attention   A student who seeks attention should not receive it when he acts out. To give attention to the student for inappropriate behavior would be playing into the student's plan and would not help the student learn how to behave productively in the group. Instead, the teacher might use some of the techniques shown in Figure 5.2.

Power   A student who wishes to possess power should not be able to engage the teacher in a struggle. The teacher who falls for this "bait" and gets pulled into the battle is merely continuing the excitement and challenge for the student. The student becomes increasingly bolder and pleased with trying to test the teacher. The teacher should attempt to remove the issue of power altogether and force the student to look for some other goal for behaving.

Student's Motivation	Behavior Characteristics	Teacher's Feelings
Attention-getting	Repetitively does an action to make himself the center of attention. When asked to stop, will comply but will start again later.	Annoyed

Techniques with the Attention-getting Student
Minimize the Attention
  Ignore the behavior
  Give the "The Eye"
  Stand close by
  Mention the student's name while teaching
  Send a secret signal
  Give written notice
  Give an "I-"message
Legitimize the Behavior
  Make a lesson out of the behavior
  Extend the behavior to its most extreme form
  Have the whole class join in the behavior
  Use a diminishing quota
Do the Unexpected
  Turn out the lights
  Play a musical sound
  Lower your voice
  Change your voice
  Talk to the wall
  Use one-liners
  Cease teaching temporarily
Distract the Student
  Ask a direct question
  Ask a favor
  Change the activity
Notice Appropriate Behavior
  Thank students
  Write well-behaved students' name on the chalkboard
Move the Student
  Change the student's seat
  Send the student to the thinking chair

Source: Albert, L. *A Teacher's Guide to Cooperative Discipline: How to Manage Your Classroom and Promote Self-Esteem.* Circle Pines, MN: American Guidance Services, 1989, pp. 31–41. Reprinted with permission.

FIGURE 5.2 Techniques for Dealing with Nonsocially Adaptive Students' Attention-Getting

Revenge   In this case, the teacher is dealing with a more difficult task. A student who feels hurt and wishes to retaliate must be handled in a caring, affectionate manner. It is probable that this student appears unloving and uncaring, and is very hard to "warm up to." But this is exactly what the student needs—to feel cared for. Figure 5.3 discusses some techniques that are helpful with students who are seeking power and/or revenge.

Student's Motivation	Behavior Characteristics	Teacher's Feelings
Power	Repetitively does behavior to make him the center of attention. When asked to stop, he becomes defiant and escalates his negative behavior and challenges the adult.	Annoyed
Revenge	Hurts others physically or psychologically.	Hurt

Techniques with the Power and Revengeful Student
Make a Graceful Exit
  Acknowledge students' power
  Remove the audience
  Table the matter
  Make a date
  Use a fogging technique
    Agree with the student
    Change the subject
Use Time-Out
  Time out in the classroom
  Time out in another classroom
  Time out in a special room
  Time out in the office
  Time out in the home
  Enforcing time-out
    The language of choice
    The Who Squad
  Setting the duration for the time out
Set the Consequence
  Establishing consequences
  Presenting consequences
  Guidelines for effective consequences
    Related consequences
    Reasonable consequence
    Respectful consequences
  Consequences versus punishments
  Choosing the consequence
    Loss or delay of activity
    Loss or delay of using objects or equipment
    Loss or delay of access to school areas
    Denied interactions with other students
    Required interactions with school personnel
    Required interactions with parents
    Required interactions with police
  Restitution
    Repair objects
    Replacement of objects
  Student response to consequences

Source: Albert, L. *A Teacher's Guide to Cooperative Discipline: How to Manage Your Classroom and Promote Self-Esteem.* Circle Pines, MN: American Guidance Services, 1989, pp. 72–83. Reprinted with permission.

FIGURE 5.3   Technique for Dealing with Nonsocially Adaptive Students' Power and Revenge

Helplessness The student who shows inadequacy or helplessness is the most discouraged. She has lost all initiative of ever trying to belong to the group. The teacher must exercise great patience and attempt to show the child that she is capable. Some practices that might assist a helpless student are discussed in Figure 5.4.

Student's Motivation	Behavior Characteristics	Teacher's Feelings
Helplessness	Wishes not to be seen, passive and lethargic, rejects social contact, refuses to comply or try most educational demands.	Inadequate-incapable

Techniques for the Helpless (avoidance-of-failure) Student
  Modify Instructional Methods
  Use Concrete Learning Materials and Computer-Assisted Instruction
    Attractive
    Self-explanatory
    Self-correcting
    Reusable
  Teach One Step at a Time
  Provide Tutoring
    Extra help from teachers
    Remediation programs
    Adult volunteers
    Peer tutoring
    Learning centers
  Teach Positive Self-Talk
    Post positive Self-Talk
    Require two "put-ups" for every put-down
    Encourage positive self-talk before beginning task
  Make Mistakes Okay
    Talk about mistakes
    Equate mistakes with effort
    Minimize the effect of making mistakes
  Build Confidence
    Focus on improvement
    Notice contributions
    Build on strengths
    Show faith in students
    Acknowledge the difficulty of a task
    Set time limits on tasks
  Focus on Past Success
    Analyze past success
    Repeat past success
  Make Learning Tangible
    "I-Can"
    Accomplishments albums
    Checklist of skills
    Flowchart of concepts
    Talks about yesterday, today, and tomorrow
  Recognize Achievement
    Applause
    Clapping and standing ovations
    Stars and stickers
    Awards and assemblies
    Exhibits
    Positive time out
    Self-approval

Taken with permission from: Albert, L. *A Teacher's Guide to Cooperative Discipline: How to Manage Your Classroom and Promote Self-Esteem,* Circle Pines, MN: AGS: American Guidance Service, Inc., 1989, pp. 98–104.

FIGURE 5.4 Technique for Dealing with Nonsocially Adaptive Students' Helplessness

Ronald is obviously interested in Mr. Garcia's idea that Ronald is seeking attention, but he jars Mr. Garcia back to the immediate situation with a sarcastic, "Well, that sounds cool, but there's one big problem. I can't do all these things without equipment, and no one wants me in their group. What do you suggest? Maybe you'll buy me my own laboratory?"

Mr. Garcia, as a Albert/Dreikurs teacher, knows that he must capitalize on using the group as a model to help Ronald adjust.

Modeling

Mr. Garcia informs Ronald that at the end of class today, and on every Friday, there will be a short class council meeting to discuss problems that are of concern to the members of the class. He adds that Ronald could bring up his problem at that time and see what he and the class might work out.

Albert/Dreikurs believe that Western schools and classrooms, as part of a democratic society, need to be models or laboratories of that society.[7] In other words, students need to practice democratic principles in school in order to learn how to contribute later to society as a whole. The central process for carrying out this modeling of democracy is the use of the class meeting, which Mr. Garcia refers to as the class council. Regular meetings should be held to discuss everyday occurrences as well as long-range policies. We will see in the next chapter how William Glasser has further refined and elaborated on this concept of classroom meetings.

Meetings can be conducted informally without a designated leader, or formally with a rotating president, recorder, and treasurer. Voting should be avoided, as it has a tendency to alienate the minority. Instead, decisions should be made through arriving at a consensus of all members. When many people agree with a decision, peer pressure tends to influence the one or two "holdouts" and thus makes the decision unanimous. (We see this at political party conventions. After a hard battle among several candidates, one individual finally emerges a winner and all opposition evaporates. A united party once again emerges.) Let's see how Mr. Garcia capitalizes on the group process.

Mr. Garcia calls the class back to their seats and tells them that, in his classes, he always has a class council meeting on Fridays for the last 20 minutes of the period. However, since this is the first week of a new semester and they have a lot of problems to work out, they will have a meeting every day of this week, beginning today. The class is then encouraged to begin an open general discussion. One or two students bring up different problems pertaining to missing lab equipment, how they are going to be graded, and whether the lab could be open during their free period after lunch. Finally, Ronald raises his hand, and everyone turns to look at him. "I have no equipment and I'm in no group." The girl he previously embarrassed shouts, "Serves you right." Mr. Garcia interjects, "What Ronald has done is in the past. What can we do about his not having a group to join?" The class begins in earnest to discuss the issue. Most students express the feeling that if Ronald has no equipment, then he cannot pass the course and that would be unfair. Some members ask the three-member group if they would let Ronald into their group. Again, the girl who had been embarrassed states, "No way! He will bug us and keep us from our work. Those chemicals are dangerous!" However, the other two members of the group say that they would be willing to work with him on a trial basis. Finally, after much discussion, it is decided that the girl will change places with a student in another group and

Ronald would now have three people with whom he could work at the laboratory table. Ronald appears greatly relieved to hear this decision.

Up to this point, everything seems to have been resolved. But what happens if Ronald continues to misbehave? What recourse does the teacher or class have? We need to look at Albert/Dreikurs's interpretation of logical consequences to answer these questions.

Reinforcement

Albert/Dreikurs did not believe in the use of punishment, negative reinforcement, praise, or positive reinforcement. Instead, they substituted natural/logical consequences and the process of encouragement. Each of these will be explained as it applies to Ronald.

Natural/Logical Consequences

If Ronald should create a commotion after becoming accepted in the group, he could be disciplined as a result of some of the following logical consequences:

- Have the group of three decide what should be done with Ronald.
- Have Ronald work alone and have him use the laboratory equipment on his own time (at lunch, study hall, after school).
- Bring Ronald's misbehavior back to the entire class in a classroom meeting to decide on future consequences.

Specifically, for Ronald, this means:

- If Ronald has been causing a disturbance by poking students with a pencil, take away all his pencils and tell Ronald that whenever he needs to write, he'll have to come to the teacher's desk to ask for a pencil.
- If Ronald has been constantly moving out of his chair and distracting others, tell Ronald that he does not seem to need a chair and take it away from him. Let him stand until he requests to have it back and stay in it.

A natural consequence is defined as that which happens as a result of one's behavior. If a student is rushing to get into line and trips and falls, we call this a natural consequence. On the other hand, if a student is rushing and pushing others in order to be first in line and is removed by the teacher to a place at the end of the line, then this would be identified as a logical consequence. In other words, a natural consequence is an inevitable occurrence that happens by itself, whereas a logical consequence is arranged but directly related to the preceding behavior. Albert/Dreikurs believes that, in a democratic society and in a democratic classroom, students must be responsible for how they behave. There is no room for autocratic punishment, as such punishment further alienates and discourages the child. Extensive punishment serves as a force to drive a student toward a goal of revenge. Punishment is not seen as being logically related to a student's behavior. It is inflicted as a reaction to personal dissatisfaction felt by the teacher. Punishment says to the student, "You had better behave or I (the teacher) will make life miserable for you." If the student does "knuckle under," it is because of the power of the teacher and not because the student has learned how to be a productive member of the group. If one accepts Albert/Dreikurs's definition of human behavior as a purposeful attempt to belong, then a teacher who uses punishment blocks a student's purpose. Punishment "plays back" into the student's misdirected goals. It gives attention, enhances the power struggle, stimulates further revenge, and keeps the helpless child in his or her place.

In addition, Albert/Dreikurs rather pragmatically pointed out that, in today's age of equal rights and militancy, students are not easily coerced by the use of authoritarian power. Not only does punishment thwart a student's ambition but it simply does not work.[8] Let us further explore the operational distinction between punishment and natural/logical consequences. Sending a student home with a note, keeping her after school, paddling, scolding, ridiculing, or standing the student in a corner are all forms of physical or psychological punishment. The teacher's actions are aimed at hurting the child or making her feel bad. Punishment is the teacher's vengeance for a committed crime. On the other hand, students who clean up the mess they created, who are put at the end of the line for shoving, who miss a pep rally because of tardiness with their assigned work, or who are barred from using certain materials until they chose to use them properly are all actually involved in the effects of logical consequences. Logical consequences are not always easy to tailor to every disruptive action. However, it is the teacher's task to arrange the situation that follows the disruption in a way that the student can see a relationship between the consequences and her behavior. (This is a further break from the Relationship-Listening position, particularly Gordon's, which would criticize logical consequences as being false, contrived, and manipulative.)

Finally, it is important to note the differences in a teacher's attitude and manner in the application of logical consequences as opposed to the act of punishment. Two teachers might arrive at the same solution for a problem caused by a child's behavior, but one will be an example of logical consequences and the other will be an example of punishment. Sounds confusing, but it really isn't. For example, during quiet work time, Sue Ann continually pokes Ernie with a pencil. One teacher, "Mr. Matter-of-Fact," tells the girl, "Sue Ann, if you do that again, you are showing that you cannot control your pencil, and I will need to take it from you. You will be able to finish the pencil and paper task here in this classroom while the others are at the pep rally." The other teacher, "Mr. How-Dare-You," says, "Sue Ann, I have told you a thousand times not to do that. Can't you understand anything? If I catch you once more, I'll take all your pencils away and you'll stay in at recess. Maybe being alone is the only way that you can work!" Mr. Matter-of-Fact has calmly told the student to use the pencil correctly or give it up. Mr. How-Dare-You acts as though he has been personally affronted and that Sue Ann's misbehavior is a direct challenge to his authority. He tries to hammer her down by scolding, questioning her competence, and challenging her. The same outcome has occurred, the student has had the pencil confiscated, but Mr. Matter-of-Fact has used logical consequences and Mr. How-Dare-You has applied punishment.

Encouragement

At the same time that the class and Mr. Garcia are applying logical consequences to Ronald's behavior, Mr. Garcia is also using the encouragement process. Mr. Garcia asks Ronald to keep an inventory of all laboratory equipment and to prepare an order of new supplies for the class. Mr. Garcia also makes a mental note to greet Ronald warmly each day.

The encouragement process is an attitude taken with a misbehaving student that results in a climate of respect and optimism.[9] One must remember that a student whose goal is attention feels stifled by authority, and may retreat to the even more destructive goal of power. When that goal is "beaten down" by an overbearing, punitive teacher, the student may then resort to the goal of revenge to retaliate. When revenge is crushed by even more coercive means, we may finally have the most pathetic result, a student who has simply given up and has internalized the goal of helplessness. This lowering of goals is the result of a student becoming further discouraged. Not only does the student retreat further back into gloom and despair but so does the teacher. The vicious cycle compounds the problem.

The role of the teacher is to stop this dissipation of hope by using encouragement. This is accomplished by such teacher action as:

- Emphasize improvement rather than expect a perfect product.
- Criticize the student's actions, but not the student (i.e., "I like you, but I don't like to hear you shouting").
- Keep the student in a group with other students who are willing to help. Determine those peers who are most accepting and tolerant of the student in question. Seat the student with them and arrange for him to work with them in groups. Find a companion or friend for the student.
- Refrain from having the student compete against others. Do not compare the student to others ("Why can't you behave like Rufus?") or constantly single out for praise others who outperform the youngster. Deemphasize grades; try to grade the student on effort, not her rank in relation to others. Avoid contests for the best-behaved student or citizen of the week, when the student has little chance of winning.

Albert/Dreikurs believed that the provision of positive reinforcement is generally a desirable method. Encouragement is much broader than in the Rules and Consequences use of verbal praise, materials, or situational rewards as conditioning to achieve appropriate behavior. In 1963, Dinkmeyer and Albert/Dreikurs wrote:

Unfortunately, even the well meaning and sincere educator may often fail to convey much needed encouragement if he tries to express his approval through praise. ... Praise may have a discouraging effect in the long run, since the child may depend on it constantly and never be quite sure whether he will merit another expression of special approval and get it.[10]

Dinkmeyer and Albert/Dreikurs were not saying that praise should be totally avoided, but what they were suggesting is that too much praise makes a child dependent on the teacher. The student who is "won over" by the teacher to work quietly due to the teacher's praise ("Oh, look at Hillary! What a fine student to be working so quietly! I am so proud that you're being so quiet!") has not learned social behavior. Instead of learning how to act out of consideration for others, the child is learning how to act for purposes of receiving the teacher's special compliments and dispensations. In other words, the child behaves well, but for all the wrong reasons. If the teacher is removed from the scene, the child's behavior will deteriorate. The child needs to internalize the correct motivation for being well behaved (acting as a productive member of the group) in order for it to be lasting.

In addition, the child who sees himself as a failure and is motivated by revenge or helplessness will tend to disbelieve the authenticity of the teacher's words. A child who refuses to work and "gives up" on carrying out any order may have reason to speculate on why the teacher makes such an effort to praise her ("Oh, Sam, look what a good job you did! You make me so pleased when you hang your coat up!" Or, "Margie, it's great the way that you answered that question!") The student will, in effect, believe that the teacher is overcompensating and that she is being singled out because she is indeed inferior. The child may think, "Why make such a big deal about hanging my coat up or answering a simple question? The teacher must think I'm a real nincompoop (idiot, jerk, bozo, etc.)." Thus, the opposite effect of what the teacher intended will result—a further sign that reaffirms the child's inferiority. In this vein of thought, Dreikurs and Grey wrote that there is a fundamental difference between the act of reward and the act of encouragement. Few realize that, at times, success can be very discouraging. The child may conclude that, although success was achieved once, it could not happen again. The student's recent "success" may become a threat to her future ability to succeed. But what is worse, such an event often conveys to the child the assumption, which actually is shared by most of her teachers and fellow students, that she is worthwhile only when she is successful.[11]

What we have, then, is the premise that praise or other forms of reward seem to heighten a child's anxiety about always having to "measure up." It puts constraints on a child who feels such pressure. He feels comfortable only when being successful. The discomfort with being unsuccessful further discourages a child from feelings of being accepted and of being an acceptable person. He feels accepted only when successful, but not when something less than success occurs as a result of efforts expended. The child who needs to learn to be a member must learn to accept his individual self as being a person capable of both success and failure but who, despite outcomes, is still worthy of being loved and accepted by others.

A child who is always dependent on being rewarded for what he does is in a bind when it comes to taking a risk. The child who is learning how to belong must be encouraged to try new ways of behaving. The student who learns that it is safe and rewarding to be meek and passive will not easily venture into the unknown by being assertive and active. He won't venture into untried areas. This is the danger of having "failure-proof" programs or "praise-laden" teachers.

The teacher must not stress the concept of success but instead promote a climate of always accepting the student as worthwhile. This happens when a teacher uses encouragement rather than such reinforcement as praise.

Following are two contrasting lists that give examples of praise versus encouragement. Praise focuses on the teacher being pleased by the child and on the child achieving a completed product. Conversely, encouragement focuses on the student and on the process of the student trying.

Praise	*Encouragement*
1. "I (teacher) like what you have done."	1. "You're trying harder."
2. "Great job! What a smart person."	2. "You must be happy with (playing that game, being with others, etc.)."
3. "You get a star (token, free time) for doing that."	3. "It must be a good feeling to know you're doing well."
4. "I'm going to tell everyone how proud I am of you."	4. "You have every reason to be proud."

Acting (Physical Intervention) and Isolation

Forms of teacher intervention such as paddling or shaking a student would be rejected by Albert/Dreikurs. Such treatment would be seen as a form of punishment that would drive a student further away from social cooperation. Pain experienced as a natural consequence (without the possibility of serious harm) could be allowed. Some examples of this might be a student who recklessly rushes to be first in line and falls and is bruised, or the student who repeatedly provokes the science class gerbil and is bitten. On the other hand, there are some natural consequences that can occur when a student precariously tilts back in her chair, or when a "90-pound weakling" begins to taunt and enrage a 250-pound high school football tackle. There could be dangerous consequences, and the teacher would be wise to prevent them from occurring. It is also important to note that a teacher should carefully judge the natural consequences before deciding to act or not act in a given situation.

Isolation must also be used judiciously by the teacher. Albert/Dreikurs advocated the use of isolation only as a logical consequence. We saw that Ronald was isolated temporarily by Mr. Garcia when his behavior was immediately disruptive of others. However, Ronald was given the opportunity to join the group once he decided that he wished to belong.

It is obvious that if being part of a group is the ultimate goal for all individuals, then each person needs to learn to relate successfully to others. One only learns such relationships by practicing appropriate behaviors with others. One does not learn cooperation by being lectured to or having to sit by oneself. For these reasons, instead of relying on isolation, the teacher is required to look constantly for ways to encourage attachments between the offending child and other members of the class.

Classroom Meetings

Jane Nelson et al.[12] a Dreikurs-Adlerian writer, adds a much needed practical process to the model—classroom meetings. Young people have major influences in their lives: home, school, peer group, and (sometimes) religion. As teachers, we cannot do much about the home or religion, but we are in the position to have a positive effect on the school and peer-group experiences that constitute a large portion of the student's day. Nelson believes in using much classroom time to hold daily and weekly classroom meetings with students, which she views as teaching children life skills that are in many ways more important than reading, writing, arithmetic, or academic subjects. Rather than lecturing students on respect and empathy for others, classroom meetings with open uninhibited discussion, including discussions about the behavior and misbehavior of class members, will enable the teacher and the students to make choices as well as:

- Understand themselves, others, and situations through their own experiences
- Explore what happened, what caused it to happen, how behavior affected others, and how we feel about it
- Determine what students can do to solve their problems[13]

Nelson defines eight building blocks for carrying out effective class meetings:

1. **Form a circle:** Students are brought together in a tight circle so that everyone sees everyone else's face with the arrangement suggesting that everyone's ideas

and expressions are equal and valued. In elementary school it is suggested that meetings be done daily. In middle or secondary school, 45 to 50 minutes of class time would be used at the beginning of the semester and then possibly moved to 10 minutes at the end of the period.

2. **Practice compliments and appreciation:** Through the activities suggested in the class meetings, children are encouraged to be supportive of others through the practice of compliments and appreciation. Out of these meetings there should come three empowering perceptions for each student:

   • Perceptions of personal capabilities: "I am capable."
   • Perception of significance in primary relationships: "I contribute in meaningful ways, and I am genuinely needed."
   • Perceptions of personal power and influence in life: "I use my personal power to make choices that influence what happens to me and my community."[14]

3. **Create an agenda:** Students are encouraged to bring conflicts and problems to the class meeting and these items are placed on the agenda to be solved. For example, a fifth-grade class had only one kickball on the playground so groups of friends are fighting over who gets it first; or middle school girls dislike the whistling and sexually suggestive comments made by boys as they walk down the hall. These problems and concerns were put on the agenda by dropping a card into the "agenda box," sometimes anonymously. Also, out of these agenda ideas come classroom rules for behavior jointly developed by all parties, including the teacher.

4. **Develop communication skills:** Much emphasis is put on learning to speak about problems and feelings and the ability to truly listen to what others are saying, especially to you.

5. **Learn about separate realities:** Nelson presents a series of activities to be done in class meetings to demonstrate how each individual might see situations or realities differently. These insights are then used to have members develop empathy for others and to see that others might view happenings very differently than they do.

6. **Recognize the four purposes of behavior (attention getting, power, revenge, and helplessness):** Students learn and become able to spot the four inappropriate motivations in themselves and others. One class had small flags with symbols to represent these four motivations, and when someone appeared to be motivated by one of these purposes, they would "flag" that behavior to give insight to the individual and for discussion. This would not be a form of "put-down," but would lead to real problem solving as to how the student must gain attention, power, and acceptance in a positive manner.

7. **Practice role-playing and brainstorming:** Nelson has students in class meetings role-play problems and interactions between individuals that could occur in the classroom or in the outside world. Often, after these role-playing sessions, students would brainstorm to consider how these incidents could be handled in a different or creative manner. The middle school girl who receives unwanted sexual advances role-plays this and the class helps her consider how she may respond rather than simply getting angry or embarrassed.

8. **Focus on nonpunitive solutions:** Although logical consequences are a sanctioning technique in Dreikurs-Adlerian theory, Nelson tends to deemphasize logical consequence because it becomes a hidden form of punishment. She has created a "wheel of choice" from which students may consider several actions before they seek adult help: apologize, walk away, put on the agenda for the class meeting, use an "I"-message, tell the person to stop, count to ten and cool off, go to another activity, or shake hands and take turns. Nelson presents the "four Rs of solutions" as guidelines for actions or consequences: related (directly connected to the misbehavior), respectful (with manner and tone that the student involved feels respected), reasonable (no punishment dimension), and revealed (students should know in advance that if they fail to do something or misbehave, a consequence will follow).

These open class meetings create a context for developing empathy and group membership so that some of the following dynamics, such as the "outside aggressor" phenomenon, do not occur.

THE "OUTSIDE AGGRESSOR" PHENOMENON

In the eleventh-grade art class the students are allowed to select their own seats among the many tables in the room. Five girls have sat together at a round table for four weeks so far. Amy, an attractive new student at the school, has been sitting by herself but has started to become friendly with some of the girls at the "in" table. After class, Marcia, one of the girls at the table, tells Amy to make sure to get to class early tomorrow and to grab a seat at the round table. She confides that she and three others will also be early so they can all sit together. The next day Amy and the four girls are already seated by the time Julie, a past member, walks in. She seems startled and walks up to Amy and says, "Pardon me, but you're in my seat!" Amy isn't too sure what to say and looks around at the other girls who are smiling at her. Marcia looks up at Julie and says, "We've invited Amy to join us. I'm sure you can find somewhere else to sit where you'll fit in." Stunned, Julie walks away.

During the class that same day, Julie's teacher is placing paints before her on her table when one pot accidentally tips and spills, making a small yellow paint mark on Julie's blouse. Julie shouts at her teacher, "Look what did, you damn stupid old cow!" The entire class quiets while "the gang" giggles and laughs at Julie.

The incident with Julie and "the gang" shows clearly that Julie has lost her past friends and companions and is now being socially isolated. The Confronting-Contracting position would be that Julie's "acting out" (the verbal aggression, "you old cow") was a result of built-up "revengeful" feelings being directed at an innocent party, the teacher. All misbehavior by children in our classroom—whether attention-getting power acts, revengeful acts, or passive behavior—is seen by Confronting-Contracting as a failure to find social acceptance. However, we rarely get such a clear observation as in the Julie incident to actually verify this position. Instead, we typically see a repetitive host of misbehaviors and aggressive actions that, on the surface, do not appear to be related to immediate behavior by other children. "He hits other students without any provocation." Students' first feelings of acceptance come out of the home setting with parents and siblings. If they felt they were rejected in early family interaction, they will assume that they will be rejected in a class-room situation and will set out with negative actions to prove that others do not like them.

The less skilled teacher might bring "the gang" aside and verbally reprimand and lecture them for their actions, applying large doses of guilt for their behavior. Such actions might unknowingly make members of "the gang" even more hostile to Julie, and now they will be revengeful toward her in more subtle ways that we will not see or detect. Julie needs to acquire social skills that will enable her to find acceptance.

There are a number of techniques that enable the teacher to be proactive in helping children to acquire social skills. Before they are presented, however, it may be helpful to first explain the "outside aggressor" phenomenon.

> *A visitor to an early childhood center is asked on the playground by a three-year-old, "What's your name, Mister?" The man responds, "Mr. Wolfe." The child, hearing woof, jumps up and runs screaming to the opposite end of the playground, shouting, "Woof, Woof!" Then each member of his group picks up a light twig that had fallen during a storm the night before. They "stalk" the visitor, walking up behind him on tiptoe, and then each child forcefully strikes the man in the back with the sticks. They run off, again screaming, "Woof!"*

We have just witnessed the phenomenon of the "outside aggressor."

Since young children still have two large islands of emotional extremes—when they love, they love totally and when the hate, they hate totally—and their feelings of rivalry are still very strong, they have a difficult time coming together in groups. One of the more primitive and base levels of social interaction, which first begins during the early years, is coming together in a group and finding an outside person, object, or fantasy object against which to project their strong competitive feelings and aggression. This creates an implicit agreement not to aggress against each other and establishes a temporary feeling of belonging. Julie became the common outside aggressor object to "the gang," just as Mr. Wolfe did to the three year olds.

Although the "outside aggressor" phenomenon begins in early childhood,[15] examples can still be seen among adolescents and adults. One can recall the interaction at a dinner party when one person must depart early, leaving behind everyone else to talk about him in the most negative manner. The "leaver" becomes the dinner group's outside aggressor. Members of the group, by default, have informally agreed to project their aggressive criticism at the departed person and not to speak ill of each other. The game works if nearly everyone says something derogatory. Thus, for a short period of time, the members of the "dinner gang" have a superior feeling of being above someone else—a feeling of primitive belonging to this "in" group. Politicians throughout history have used this outside aggressor phenomena to gain control of groups; perhaps the most glaring and frightening example was the way in which Hitler controlled an entire nation by casting one ethnic group as the outside aggressor.

Banding together against an "outside aggressor" is normal for many adolescents. Our role, of course, is to engineer ways through which students can learn to be social in a healthier manner and to help children like Julie find belonging and acquire social skills.

Social Engineering

After the "we don't want you in our group" incident, but before any actions like the "you old cow" verbal aggression could occur, Mrs. Anderson calls Julie to the art table. She has seen Julie being made the outside aggressor and she summons her in a voice loud enough for "the gang" to hear. She states, "Julie, we are going to make the centerpiece for the Christmas dance, and I am going to let you be the chairperson of this project. I will arrange with the principal and your study hall supervisors to have this committee released from study hall for the next three weeks. You may choose helpers to work with you!" Every member of the class is eager to be on this committee, and everyone begins waving their hands to be chosen. Julie selects six nearby students. "The gang" sees what is happening. Their facial expressions show that their excitement has been deflated; they begin to wander over to the art table and look on as this new project is being organized. They loiter about, and then gradually plead in a whining voice, "Mrs. Anderson, can we be on the committee, too?" The teacher responds, "I don't know, I am not the chairperson of this project—Julie is! You will have to ask her." The gang approaches Julie and asks, "Can we join your committee?" Julie hesitates for a few seconds, then smiles and says, "Yes." The teacher hovers nearby watching all the committee members working on the art arrangement, her presence helping Julie to maintain her power. Later, when the dance programs are made, Julie's name will be listed as the chair of this committee, and she has her photograph taken while working on the project for the local newspaper and for the class yearbook. Later, during the class discussion, Mrs. Anderson will encourage other students to express their joy at being a part of the project and working under Julie's leadership (encouragement).

In the use of social engineering, we consider that a misbehaving child is powerless, lacking the skill to find social belonging. We deliberately "engineer" or set up activities whereby we empower children such as Julie and help them enjoy the experience of successfully working within a group. We deliberately point out to classmates how she has contributed to making the classroom a happy and accepting place. Thus, we deliberately engineer positive experiences for misbehaving children. After the centerpiece experience, we may question Julie with Confronting-Contracting "What" questions, such as "Julie, what did you do as committee chair? What worked for you as you worked with friends? What did not? What will you do next time when you want friends?" Notice that we did not tell Julie how well she did, or make any value judgments, or offer a prescription for her in further interactions. Through our questions and counseling of children who are having social difficulty, we want them to become reflective after social experiences, to become consciously aware of their own behavior, to evaluate their success, and to come up with ideas of how they may be even more effective the next time.

Disengaging

Teachers are not robots who are emotionless, never get angry, and always have good feelings toward all children. Some children are appealing and some are very unappealing; the unappealing children generally are the ones who cannot find acceptance in their homes and from fellow classmates. We have stated that the nonsocially adjusted misbehaving child in our classroom, because of feelings of rejection, begins to seek excessive attention and power, becomes revengeful, and, finally, retreats into a passive state of helplessness. If we as teachers acknowledge that we are human beings with a range of feelings, we will allow that the excessive attention-getting child produces feelings of annoyance in us, that we feel at times beaten by the power-needy child, that we feel hurt by the revengeful child, and that we feel inadequate in working with the helpless child.

We must acknowledge to ourselves that we have these feelings toward these children. Our feelings only become a problem when we ourselves begin to regress into becoming revengeful and feeling helpless toward these children. Therefore, we now have a good reason to use isolation techniques—that is, in order to get ourselves disengaged. If we are angry and overcome by our own feelings because of the repetitive demands that the problem child is presenting to us (being called an "old cow"), we may become emotionally flooded in the middle of a teachable moment. We need to do skilled confronting, yet we are not able to handle this successfully and professionally because our clear thinking has been flooded by emotions. We then may consider placing the misbehaving child in isolation for a period of time, or moving the child temporarily to another room or building area under the supervision of another teacher or school authority. As emotionally flooded individuals, we must spatially move away from this student for a period of time until we have disengaged from these strong emotions. Once we are calm and relaxed, we will have energies to reapproach the difficult child to begin our steps of confronting. We cannot do Confronting-Contracting when angered.

Unknowingly, the entire school staff can collectively begin to have these same angry, revengeful, and helpless feelings toward this one student. The child with an attitude of, "If I can't be the best good student, I will be the best bad student" is known in schools by the bus driver, guidance counselor, and cafeteria worker, and even the parents of other students. The student has a reputation that precedes him or her. If we analyze the staff and the reaction of the problem child's classmates, we begin to see that after a period of time we have made the "Ronalds" of this world the outside aggressor in our classroom. He gets blamed by all students and staff for all accidents and negative occurrences. Others, including teachers, do not want him at their table or sitting near them at social events. Most everyone, including adults, has unknowingly begun a process of "shunning" the problem student. This "shunning" and being the object of the "outside aggressor" phenomenon now severely complicates the intervention and dynamics of ever helping this child to change. The difficult child has dug a deep social hole that he will never be able to climb out of by himself.

Besides disengaging if necessary before confronting such a child, how then do we handle this collective anger and shunning toward the child?

The Most Wanted

A staff meeting must be called involving all adults who come into daily contact with the difficult student (if you are one teacher by yourself, you may need to sit down during a quiet period and in essence have this meeting with yourself). At the start of this meeting it might be helpful if members of the group of adults are permitted some time to express their honest feelings toward the student. Staff members who are frightened by their own negative feelings toward the difficult child might receive some reassurance if they hear a skilled and respected teacher state, "I am wondering how you are feeling about Ronald Foster these days. I must confess that at times I find myself getting angry and even frightened by him. At times I don't want him in my class, and at times I am having a hard time liking him." The first step in changing staff's negative behavior toward a difficult student is to get honest feelings "out on the table."

As we noted, the problem student has dug a deep social hole that he cannot climb out of by himself. Because he feels rejected, he sits about day in and day out, his negative actions evoking further rejection from classmates and adults. After all, adolescents are still children. Our problem student is still in the formative years of development, and these stormy adolescent years are the most robust years for making a positive impact on the child's development that will serve—or misserve—him for the remainder of his life. As the expression goes, "Love begins with love!" The very nature of our jobs, and the central role as teacher, is to make a lasting contribution to these difficult children. Almost all adults can recall one significant experience where a teacher has befriended and helped them at a difficult point in their life. We must understand what a lasting impression this can have and how it can make long-term positive results for the child's well-being.

That is the challenge—and the opportunity—before us as we deal with this one particular difficult problem child. If we do not do it, who will? Literally, anyone can teach the child who has been well mothered and fathered, but it is the difficult child who enables us to "earn our stripes" as teachers. This is a big responsibility, but we may be their only and last hope, because once they get into the real adult world, rarely will they find another person willing to take the time to help them.

Now, exactly how do we do this? We do it in a staff meeting by using the Confronting-Contracting procedures on ourselves, much as Glasser reality therapy questions. We ask, "What are we and his classmates really doing to Ronald Foster?" The answer is that we are, unknowingly, shunning him and making him the "outside aggressor." We want most staff members to verbally express past incidents in which they have moved away from this problem child. Mrs. Anderson confesses, "I am embarrassed to admit it, but one time when I was seated at the table with a group of students, we had one chair remaining at our table. I saw Ronald approaching, and—again, I'm embarrassed to admit it—but I grabbed another student and had him take this free seat so that Ronald would not be at my table." This outward admission is most important! (The teacher working alone might want to write this out.) Mrs. Anderson's candor may then encourage other staff members to share similar experiences or feelings.

We then move to, "What will we do to change?" The answer is that for the next two weeks we will put Ronald, as our difficult problem child, on the Most Wanted list. Unlike a police Most Wanted list, however, this list will single Ronald out for special positive behavior. We may have witnessed the behavior of staff and students when we have had a visiting student, perhaps visiting from another country. Visitors enjoy special status while spending the day in our classroom. We roll out the "red carpet" for them: They are greeted warmly at the door, shown where to be seated, and told how and where things work. Placing our difficult student on our Most Wanted list means treating him as an honored guest throughout the two-week period. When every staff member—even those who do not have him in their group or classes—sees the difficult child passing by, they are to give him or her the "time of day." The teacher says hello, makes eye contact, says the child's name, and makes some pleasant verbal overture. The teacher helps him and invites him to be a part of any group activities. During every time period throughout the day for the two weeks, some adult should be helping him as if he were new to school procedures and practices, a stranger visiting without friends. At any discussion groups involving the entire class, the teacher will provide statements of encouragement by pointing out to classmates any and all positive behaviors by the difficult child.

Almost as if a whistle has been blown, we all as adults deliberately change our behavior toward the difficult student. If we, as teachers, don't change, then classmates and the student himself cannot change. We help the problem student "climb out" of the deep social hole in which he was imprisoned by changing the entire social environment in the school. At first we will feel phony acting in such a manner, but we must push and commit ourselves to perform such "motor actions." A campaign of welcoming the child day in and day out can have a real impact on changing a problem student's behavior and helping him gain a feeling of acceptance. In contrast, if we use the social engineering techniques described previously, but the school climate—the actions of adults and classmates—still shuns the difficult student as an object of "outside aggression," it will be unlikely that progress can be made. At the end of the two-week period of the Most Wanted program, another staff meeting must be held. This will be a follow-up meeting to evaluate the success or lack of success of our welcoming process. The remainder of the staff meeting should follow the Six Steps to Staffing described in later chapters, through which we focus

Silently Looking	Naming	Questions	Commands	Modeling	Reinforcement	Acting (physical intervention and Isolation
(a) Observe and collect information about the student — with peers — with family — with other teachers		(b) Ask yourself "Do I feel…" 1) "annoyed?"—attention getting 2) "beaten?"—power 3) "hurt?"—revenge 4) "incapable?"—helplessness	(1) According to the hypothesized goal, give logical consequence. ("Class continue. Ronald, you have shown by your behavior that you are not ready to join the group.")	(5) Use the classroom as an example of democratic living. — allow class to discuss and propose ways to help the student.	(6) Natural/logical consequences — do not punish arrange outcome as immediately related to student misbehavior (7) Encouragement — recognize student's attempts to improve, not the end product. "You are trying…" — Avoid teacher praise. "I like what you have done…"	— as a natural/logical consequence — in times danger
(c) Recognition reflect after verifying questions (smiles, laughs, looks up, shrugs shoulders, etc.)		(2) Confronting "Do you want to know why you are behaving like this?" (3) Verifying "Could it be that you want — special attention"—Attention — to be the boss"—Power —to hurt others."—Revenge — to be left alone"—Helplessness	(4) Make a plan according to verified goal. Attention—Give at appropriate times. Power—Let student have power, do not fight. Revenge—Do not show hurt; give affection. Helplessness—Show the student he/she is capable; do not do for him/her		(8) — Social Engineering — Most Wanted	
The Social Discipline Model Author: Rudolf Dreikurs number = overt behaviors letter = covert behaviors						

FIGURE 5.5 Teacher Behavior Continuum (TBC): Social Discipline

on the child's problem behaviors and address what actions can be taken individually by the teacher or staff in dealing with misbehavior. Also, it is a given that the welcoming and accepting attitude toward the difficult child should and must continue.

SUMMARY

We have positioned Albert/Dreikurs as the initial example of Confronting-Contracting for three reasons. First, closely aligned with the Relationship-Listening orientation, they had an optimistic belief in the child's rational capacities. Second, unlike those models under Relationship-Listening, they believed that such a development must occur in a social milieu where adults or peers need to intervene and redirect the child's misplaced goals. Third, Albert/Dreikurs instructed the teacher to use specific actions to redirect the child's misdirected goal. The use of such actions is much more assertive than the Relationship-Listening orientation's nonjudgmental approaches. Albert/Dreikurs has directed the teacher to use strategies that personally combat the child's game and aim consciously to pull the group to her side. The teacher then arranges logical consequences for the offending student to experience. Albert/Dreikurs believed that every student can attain her place in life but needs the active help of the adult. These approaches therefore are more intrusive than Relationship-Listening, but could hardly be described as the shaping mechanisms of Rules and Consequences.

Looking at Figure 5.5, we can now identify the teacher behaviors and guidelines of a teacher using this model. The teacher begins by covertly observing and collecting information about the student by (a) silently looking. This is followed by the teacher's analysis of his or her own feelings toward the student's behavior by (b) asking himself or herself such questions as "Do you feel … annoyed (reflecting the student's goal of attention getting); beaten (the goal of power); hurt (the goal of revenge); or incapable (the goal of helplessness)?" The teacher can then make an immediate guess at the student's goal and respond with (1) an appropriate directive statement that includes a logical consequence. In order to determine the student's goal and to plan accordingly, the teacher will choose a calmer moment and use questions that (2) confront the student as to whether the student wishes to know why she behaves as she does, and then (3) verify the suspected goal by asking one of four questions that correspond to the elements of attention, power, revenge, or helplessness. Immediately after each question, the teacher will be silently looking for the student to

exhibit a "recognition reflex" identifying her goal. With the goal verified, the teacher can (4) initiate a long-range plan by conferring with the student and describing, through the use of command, how the student can successfully have her needs met through socially appropriate ways. The classroom group can serve as a model of democratic living by (5) proposing ways to help the student. Finally, the teacher builds the use of (6) natural/logical consequences for those misbehaviors that may continue into the plan, while simultaneously using the process of encouragement. This combined approach prevents the student from becoming discouraged, even though there may be future instances when natural/logical consequences occur as a result of socially inappropriate behavior.

Strengths and Limitations of the Model

The strength of the Albert/Dreikurs/Adlerian model is in the concreteness of its application. It tells the teacher how to uncover the student's mistaken goal and how to plan according to that goal. Among the techniques a teacher can employ are confronting, class meetings, role-playing, and sociometric testing. It advocates a system of mutual respect in which natural or logical consequences replace punishment. The model is predicated on an optimistic outlook by the teacher who does not "give up" on a student. The teacher becomes sensitive and appreciative of a student's struggle and attempts to improve rather than concentrating on the improvement itself. The limitation of this model is that it may be difficult to determine the student's mistaken goal. Albert/Dreikurs makes limited demands on the student to achieve. Finally, the use of logical consequences is difficult for the teacher to determine.

Alfie Kohn's Criticism on Albert/Dreikurs

On logical consequences:

The … most widely cited distinction between punishments and logical consequences is that the latter are related to what the child did wrong; there must be some connection between the child's action and the adult's reaction. By definition, a "consequence" fits the crime (Dreikurs and Grey 1968, pp. 73–74; Nelson 1987, p. 73). This is really the linchpin of Dreikurs's system because of his core belief that "children retaliate [when they are punished] because they see no relationship between the punishment and the crime" (Dreikurs et al. 1982, p. 117). If this premise is wrong, then the whole house of cards—the distinction between consequences and punishment, and the rationale for the former—comes crashing down. I believe it is wrong. To contrive some sort of conceptual link between the punishment and the crime may be satisfying to the adult, but in most cases it probably makes very little difference to the child. The child's (understanding) anger and desire to retaliate come from the fact that someone is deliberately making her suffer. That person is relying on power, forcing her to do something she doesn't want to do or preventing her from doing something she likes. The issue here is not the specific feature of the coercive action so much as the coercion itself; "You didn't do what I wanted, so now I'm going to make something unpleasant happen to you." This power play invariably enrages the person who is being discomfited, in part because she is forced to confront her helplessness to do anything about it. We would not expect her anger

to vanish just because of modest modifications in the implementation. (Kohn, 1996, p. 43)

What Dreikurs and his followers are selling is Punishment Lite. (Kohn, 1996, p. 42)

On Dreikurs's form of class meeting, democracy, and compliance:

"Democratic Practices" could contain such suggestions as using a class meeting to drive "a wedge between the participants, splitting them [so as] to weaken their power. The moment the teacher wins one or more of the students, it fortifies her position" (Dreikurs et al. 1982, p. 237). But the apparent contradiction dissolves once we recognize the very specific, and rather peculiar, meaning Dreikurs gives to democracy. In a pivotal sentence, he declares: "It is autocratic to force, but democratic to induce compliance" (Dreikurs et al. 1982, p. 67). And later: "Children should be stimulated to want to conform" (pp. 85–86). Given this perspective, it makes sense that discussion sessions would be used strategically by teachers to "induce compliance." Dreikurs is decidedly not talking about offering students a genuine opportunity to participate in decision making. … What counts is that the teacher has never given up any real control. What matters is that the goal is not learning: it is obedience. (Kohn, 1996, p. 60)

SUMMARY OF KEY CONCEPTS

attention getting	hidden motivation	respectful	recognition reflex
classroom meetings	logical consequences	reasonable	revenge
encouragement	natural consequences	revealed	role-playing
helplessness	related	power and control	sociometric test

CASE STUDIES

What actions would the Dreikurs-Adlerian teacher take using the five systems (limit setting, backup, incentive, encouragement, and management) for the following discipline incidents?

1. **Mike's Clowning:** Mike could be labeled as the class clown. He has been seen blowing chocolate

milk bubbles through his nose in the cafeteria; placing his backside on the edge of the stool in chemistry class, using a movable Bunsen burner to lights his "farts" to produce a flame; and often dressing in a T-shirt with the words "suck city" on the front. When asked to stop these behaviors, he gives the teacher the "deer in the headlights look" with a slight smile. He does stop, but within an hour or two he has a new action to "gross out" the class members and disrupt the teacher's teaching. Today, with his hand underneath his armpit he produces a flagrant sound by pumping his elbow up and down. Using these sounds, he attempts to "play" *Jingle Bells,* "cracks up" the class, and, of course, disrupts your teaching.

2. **Andrew "Takes Over":** The students return to your classroom after being in the library-media center. The director of the center complains strongly about the poor behavior by your students, but gives you little details. Once the students are settled in their seats, you open a discussion with, "I want to talk to you about your behavior in the media center. (All heads drop.) Does anyone have anything to say?" Andrew is seated in the back of the room, slouched in his chair with his feet in the air propped over the top of the desk next to him. "Yea, I have something to say. Shut up! I hate that ugly bitch, and we aren't going back to the media center again." Most of the other class members respond, with "Yea! We're not going back there again!" Andrew seems to be respected and somewhat feared by the other students, and they often look to him for a signal as to whether they should comply with you as the teacher, and you often have the feeling that he can "take over" your class.

3. **Jake the Grenade:** Jake is like a walking grenade. One can never tell when he will explode. He passively seems to withdraw within himself, carrying a large "chip on his shoulder." If he is bumped or jostled accidentally by a fellow student, he will strike out. He has deliberately pulled a chair away from a fellow student just as she was seating herself and caused this student to fall to the floor, striking her head on the way down. He attempts to throw wet paper wads down the open blouse of one of the girls. He likes to draw monster-like cartoon characters on any surface that he can find, including the top of his desk. Today in chemistry class he got up and wandered about the room while the teacher was lecturing, and he opened all the gas jets at the chemistry tables at the back of the room—the smell of gas quickly filled the room.

4. **Linda the Passive:** Linda is a tall thin girl who is nearly always seen with her head down on her desk and her gangly long legs wrapped around the legs of her chair. She constantly has her first three fingers in her mouth, sucking them to the point that she has sucked off one fingernail. She has a body odor that is noticeable to everyone and often looks as if she has not bathed for many days. It is November, and she has done no homework, answers no questions when called on, and when questioned by the teacher in one-to-one situations, grunts yes or no to all questions. Other children laugh at her, calling her a host of derogatory names. The parents do not have a phone number, and you have not been able to contact them for a conference. Other teachers have never seen the parents, but her address is near the railroad track where there are many trailers.

Discussion

The four examples fit clearly into the Albert/Dreikurs/ Adlerian model with its four mistaken goals—Mike's clowning (need for excessive attention getting); Andrew's taking over (power), Jake the grenade (revenge), and Linda the passive (helpless).

Limit-setting System

For Mike, Andrew, and Jake, the teacher using this model would employ the limit-setting techniques of confronting as outlined in Figure 5.5.

Backup System

This model would use isolation, not as punishment, but to permit the teacher to continue teaching and getting the student to relax and discuss his actions and goals. With such students as Mike (attention getting), isolation would rarely be needed. Isolation would be used with Andrew (power) and Jake (revengeful) with great care because both students would likely become very defiant or assaultive. When possible, if we cannot go on with our teaching, it might be wise to have the other students move away from them (moving to their lab tables or the playground) and not "take on" these two with an audience. The major backup process is to bring Andrew, Jake, and Mike and their behaviors to a classroom meeting. Other students will be fearful of such students, but with a classroom of students previously taught the four mistaken goals, solutions can be sought. For example, if the library-media specialist's behavior were demeaning to

Andrew and fellow classmates, an open discussion with role-playing and brainstorming would help the students learn how to deal with a difficult person in the future. After brainstorming, one class member, such as Andrew, made the suggestion that they were not going to the center again. Others pointed out that they had reports to do and they needed to go. Andrew said he would do his report by going to the public library. The teacher indicated that the students' library time was her teacher-planning period and that there would be no one to supervise Andrew in the homeroom. He suggested that he could sit quietly in the back of Mr. Anderson's classroom across the hall and work independently. The classroom discussion also revealed that the students were aware that Ms. Miller, the media specialist, had been arrested for driving under the influence, and they speculated that she was an alcoholic and often hungover, thus the reason for her irritability. The students developed empathy for Ms. Miller and said that they enjoyed it when she read to them. They asked if they could invite her to come to their room and read rather that going to the center. A delegate of students did ask her, and she did come to the classroom with great success. Out of this discussion, the students, on their own, began to bring flowers to Ms. Miller from home; eventually this class became her favorite, and her behavior improved. What started as a discipline problem involving Andrew's swearing and defiance turned around to be a real bonding for the class and Ms. Miller, but Andrew never did return to the center and was responsible while being unsupervised.

Encouragement System

Encouragement as defined by this model is needed for all four students but especially Linda (helplessness). Near the Christmas holiday, the class was making a mural and they needed someone who was a good artist to draw the outline on a wall-sized sheet of hanging paper. When the teacher brought that to the class for a solution, they chose Linda. It surprised the teacher that she had not seen this strength in Linda, but the class had. Linda was the class's best artist, and now the teacher knew how she could be encouraging to Linda—by having her develop this talent as a positive form of identity.

Incentive System

The Dreikurs-Adlerian model is clearly against rewards and incentives.

Management System

Figures 5.2 for Mike, 5.3 for Andrew and Jake, and especially 5.4 for Linda make concrete suggestions for changes in academics and management.

Techniques for the Attention-getting Student

Minimize the Attention
>Ignore the behavior.
>Give "the eye." (Look straight at the child till he stops.)
>Stand and move physically close by. (Move into the personal space.)
>Mention the student's name. (Called "low profile desist." Makes the student aware of his behavior, but does not disrupt the thought process of the other class members.)
>Send a secret signal. (Wink or make a similar humorous nonverbal signal that says, "I see you and I recognize you," but continue your teaching.)
>Give written notice. (Have previously made and stored in your lesson plan book a small Post-it note with a desist message, humorous if possible, and simply slip it to the child with no break in the continuity of your teaching.)
>Give an "I"-message. (A statement containing the teacher's reference to him- or herself, the child's behavior, its effect on the teacher, his/her feelings, and a request for the child to desist.)

Legitimize the Behavior
>Make a lesson out of the behavior. (The math teacher makes spitball throwing permissible by making it a part of the math lesson with the children counting distances, graphing each person's throw, and teaching probability concepts related to hitting a target with the spitballs.)
>Extend the behavior to its most extreme form. (A child making spitballs now must make 500. A child who is constantly out of his seat must stand for the period.)
>Have the whole class join in the behavior. (When a student does some annoying behavior, tapping pencils, burping, the entire class is ask to do it so that it steals the attention from the misbehaving child.)
>Use a diminishing quota. (Make a contract that the child can do the attention-getting behavior, but

25 percent less times in the class period. Put a check on the board for each time he may do it and continue to teach, erasing the checks until he runs out of his allotted quota. Continue every day from this point on, dropping the permitted number of times until the behavior becomes zero.)

Do the Unexpected. (Steal the attention from the student.)

Turn out the lights.

Play a musical sound.

Lower your voice to a whisper.

Change your voice. (Pretend a silly accent.)

Talk to the wall. (Tell the wall that so-and-so is doing specific things to get attention and you wish he/she would stop. This steals the attention from the student.)

Use one-liners. (These are jokes, maybe about the teacher himself, that do not ridicule or make fun of the student.)

Cease teaching temporarily. (Simply stop and say nothing until the attention-getting child stops. Students will stop and look at him, but not in a supportive way.)

Distract the Student

Ask a direct question.

Ask a favor.

Change the activity.

Notice Appropriate Behavior

Thank the students.

Write well-behaved students' names on the chalkboard. (May or may not be a good idea for middle and high school students.)

Move the Student

Change the student's seat.

Send the student to the thinking chair. (This chair is located at the back of the room out of the view of other students.)[16]

Techniques for the Power-seeking and Revengeful Student

Make a Graceful Exit

Acknowledge the student's power. (You may actually say, "You can beat me on this—I have no wish to take you on!")

Remove the audience.

Table the matter. (State that you will not deal with this now, but at a later date decided by you.

You can calm down and assert you power in a different context on your ground.)

Make a date. (Tell the child when you wish to deal with him—time and place.)

Use a fogging[17] technique:

Agree with the student. (Revengeful student: "You're an ugly bitch!")

TEACHER: "Well, I probably wouldn't win a beauty contest."

Change the subject.

Use Time Out

Time out in the classroom.

Time out in another classroom.

Time out in the office.

Time out in the home.

Set the Consequence

Loss or delay of activity.

Loss or delay of using objects or equipment.

Loss or delay of access to school areas.

Denied interactions with other students.

Required interactions with school personnel.

Required interaction with parents.

Required interaction with police.

Determine Restitution

Repair of objects.

Replacement of objects.[18]

Techniques for the Helpless (Avoidance-of-Failure) Student

Modify Instructional Methods

Use concrete learning materials and computer-assisted instruction.

Teach one step at a time.

Provide Tutoring

Extra help from teachers.

Remediation programs.

Adult volunteers.

Peer tutoring.

Learning centers.

Teach Positive Self-talk

Post positive classroom signs. (Posted in the classroom are signs such as "I can do it!" "With a little effort, I'll succeed," etc.)

Require two "put-ups" for every put-down. (Make a rule that every negative statement that the child says out loud, he/she may say two positive statements.)

Encourage positive self-talk before beginning tasks. (When a task is given, require the discouraged child to make two positive "I can" statements into a tape recorder.

Make Mistakes Okay
    Talk about mistakes.
    Equate mistakes with effort.
    Minimize the effect of making mistakes.

Build Confidence
    Focus on improvement.
    Notice contributions.
    Build on strengths.
    Show faith in students.
    Acknowledge the difficulty of a task.
    Set time limits on tasks.

Focus on Past Success (remind student of past successes)
    Analyze past success.
    Repeat past success.

Make Learning Tangible
    "I-Can"
    Accomplishment albums.
    Checklists of skills.
    Flowchart of concepts.
    Talk about yesterday, today, and tomorrow.

Recognize achievement
    Applause.
    Clapping and standing ovations.
    Star and stickers.
    Awards and assemblies.
    Exhibits.
    Positive time out.
    Self-approval.[19]

NOTES

1. R. Dreikurs, *Children: The Challenge* (New York: E. P. Dutton, 1964).
2. R. Dreikurs, *Psychology in the Classroom: A Manual for Teachers,* 2nd ed. (New York: Harper & Row, 1968), pp. 16–17.
3. R. Dreikurs and P. Cassel, *Discipline without Tears: What to Do with Children Who Misbehave,* rev. ed. (New York: Hawthorn Books, 1972), pp. 34–41.
4. Dreikurs and Cassel, *Discipline without Tears,* p. 41.
5. Dreikurs, *Psychology in the Classroom,* p. 55.
6. Dreikurs and Cassel, *Discipline without Tears,* p. 42.
7. Dreikurs and Cassel, *Discipline without Tears,* p. 44.
8. Dreikurs, *Psychology in the Classroom,* pp. 71–73.
9. Dreikurs, *Children: The Challenge,* p. 76.
10. D. Dinkmeyer and R. Dreikurs, *Encouraging Children to Learn: The Encouragement Process* (Englewood Cliffs, NJ: Prentice-Hall, 1963), pp. 45–56.
11. Dinkmeyer and Dreikurs, *Encouraging Children to Learn,* p. 121.
12. J. Nelson, L. Lott, and H. S. Glenn, *Positive Discipline in the Classroom: Developing Mutual Respect, Cooperation, and Responsibility in Your Classroom,* rev. 3rd ed. (Roseville: CA: Prima Publishing, 2000).
13. Nelson et al. (see above)
14. Nelson et al. (see above)
15. R. Dreikurs and G. Loren, *Logical Consequences* (New York: Meredith Press, 1968), p. 157.
16. S. Isaacs, *Social Development in Young Children* (New York: Schocken Books, 1972).
17. L. Albert, *A Teacher's Guide to Cooperative Discipline: How to Manage Your Classroom and Promote Self-Esteem* (Circle Pines, MN: AGS: American Guidance Service, 1989), pp. 32–41.
18. R. Alberti, and M. L. Emmons, *Your Perfect Right: A Guide to Assertive Behavior* (San Luis Obispo, CA: Impact Publishers, 1978).
19. Albert, *Teacher's Guide*, pp. 72–83.

REFERENCES

Albert, L. *A Teacher's Guide to Cooperative Discipline: How to Manage Your Classroom and Promote Self-Esteem.* Circle Pines, MN: American Guidance Service, 1989.

Dinkmeyer, D., and Dreikurs, R. *Encouraging Children to Learn: The Encouragement Process.* Englewood Cliffs: Prentice-Hall, 1963.

Dreikurs, R. *Children: The Challenge.* New York: Hawthorn Books, 1964.

Dreikurs, R. *Psychology in the Classroom: A Manual for Teachers,* 2nd. ed. New York: Harper & Row, 1968.

Dreikurs, R. *Discipline without Tears: What to Do with Children Who Misbehave.* New York: Hawthorn Books, 1972.

Dreikurs, R., and Loren, G. *Logical Consequences.* New York: Meredith Press, 1968.

Books written for parents on the STEP Program (Adlerian–Dreikurs-based theory):

Dinkmeyer, D., and McKay, G. D. *Systematic Training for Effective Parenting (STEP).* Circle Pines, MN: American Guidance Service, 1976.

Dinkmeyer, D., and McKay, G. D. *Padres Efficacies Con Entrenamiento Sistematico (PECES).* Circle Pines, MN: American Guidance Service, 1981.

Dinkmeyer, D., and McKay, G. D. *Systematic Training for Effective Parenting of Teens (STEP/Teen).* Circle Pines, MN: American Guidance Service, 1983.

Dinkmeyer, D., and McKay, G. D. *Systematic Training for Effective Parenting (STEP) of Children under Six.* Circle Pines, MN: American Guidance Service, 1989.

Dinkmeyer, D., Sr., McKay, G. D., Dinkmeyer, D., Jr., Dinkmeyer, J. S., and McKay, J. L. *The Next STEP.* Circle Pines, MN: American Guidance Service, 1983.

CHAPTER 6

DISCIPLINE WITH DIGNITY

Theorist/Writers: Richard L. Curwin and Allen N. Mendler,
Discipline with Dignity

THE CURWIN/MENDLER MODEL

The following is a classroom that is using the Curwin/Mendler techniques suggested in their book *Discipline with Dignity* (1999).

> *Good morning, students! Welcome to my class! We will be working together this year (this semester for the secondary teacher), and we will need some rules so that this year will go smoothly and productively. Let us have a class meeting now and discuss what rules we will need both for you and me. I will place two columns on the board and I will head them with "Rules for students" and "Rules for the Teacher." The students look surprised, but one student smiles broadly and ventures to speak. "I don't like it when teachers give homework; we should have a rule against homework." The teacher responds, "Ah, we need a rule that governs how I, the teacher, will give homework. Let me put that on the board." The teacher writes under the rules for the teacher, "Homework rules." "What other rules can we suggest, which will make us able to live together this year (semester)?" Another child speaks up, "I don't like to be hit, put down, or called names!" The teacher places under "Rules for Students" hitting, put-downs, and name calling. Another student speaks, "I don't like it when the teacher punishes me for something that another student does!" This is added to the list. A group of students speak up. "I don't like it when my homework is not returned by the teacher. I don't like it when the teacher calls my parents." This continues with the teacher adding items to both the teacher's and students' list. Finally, the teacher joins in with her needs: "I need students to come to class on time" and "I need students to come with paper and pencil." After the discussion and the list of items seem to stop, the teacher returns to each item to discuss it in more detail, again encouraging the students to speak and discuss until there appears to be an agreement upon a list of rules for both students and the teacher.*
>
> *The teacher states, "OK, let us return to 'rules needed for homework.' Homework for me permits the student to practice the new concepts that I have taught, and is needed." The students carry on a discussion about "it ain't fair" criticism of how past teachers have used homework. "They give us homework over the weekend. They give us too many problems to do. They do not return the homework checked in a timely manner. The grade on homework counts too much for the final grade. At times I have sports practice (or any other extracurricular activity) and do not have time to do homework." Out of this discussion comes an agreement that homework will count for*

20 percent of the final grade and it will be checked by the teacher and returned within three days. A student will have two extra days to do homework when faced with a major school event, etc. In contrast, the student rules become, "Be in your seat when the second bell rings, have pencils sharpened before class starts, have pencil and paper available for each class, treat others with respect, when two students have a conflict that might lead to a fight they ask for mediation with a teacher, etc." Each of these rules was voted on, with the teacher accepting a 70 percent agreement to keep it as a rule.

During the next class periods (or days) the students are given a test on these rules and the teacher requires 100 percent correct for passing. The student may take this classroom rule test over and over until he or she obtains the 100 percent and, once passed, they have earned the privilege of going to recess (or a pep rally). Periodically, throughout the year (or semester), the rules are revisited with some dropped, others added or modified, based on the evolving needs of the teacher and students.

What we see here is the classroom teacher establishing a *social contract* with his or her class following the discipline practices of Curwin and Mendler, based on their discipline model named *Discipline with Dignity*. Although it not clear as to the theoretical or psychological principles (Rogerian, Adlerian, behavioral, etc.) on which they base their practices, their value statements and suggested practices clearly place them in the Confronting-Contracting school of thought. Central to their discipline practices is the idea of *three-dimensional discipline:* (1) the prevention dimension, (2) the action dimension, and (3) the resolution dimension.

- The prevention dimension is all the activities that the teacher may take beforehand to prevent misunderstanding and discipline problems. This prevention, when well planned, informs students that they will be dealt with in a reasonable and orderly manner and has the added benefit for the teacher that such preplanning can eliminate much teacher stress when discipline actions do occur.

- The action dimension is the action the teacher will take when faced with a discipline situation, including keeping records and preventing minor problems from becoming major discipline situations.

- The resolution dimension is the action that the teacher can take with or toward an "out-of-control" or chronic rule-breaking student.

The writers of *Discipline with Dignity* are concerned about not destroying the motivation of a student through discipline actions. There are some sanctions that are effective in stopping the negative behaviors in classrooms, but they destroy the dignity of the student. Therefore, after the sanction or consequence is administered, the student loses all interest in school and learning. The central goal of all the discipline actions must be to preserve the student's interest in learning and life in school—thus their dignity. The dignity writers believe in a 80–15–5 principle reflective of three groups of students in our classrooms. They see 80 percent of the students rarely breaking a rule or being a discipline problem, while 15 percent break rules on a regular basis and fight restrictions. Finally, only 5 percent are seen as chronic rule breakers who get out of control. The goal is to deal with the 15 percent without alienating or overcontrolling the 80 percent, while being careful not to get cornered by the 5 percent of uncontrolled students. The three dimensions—prevention, action, and resolution—are designed to do this.

Curwin and Mendler do not like "systems" of discipline, which they view as arbitrary formulas for teacher's actions because they depersonalize the actions of teachers and make them unthinking and uncreative about considering the students' needs. Organizations establish systems to help their employees carry out the institution's policies. Every reader has had a negative experience dealing with a "system" in attempting to get a new drivers license after his/hers was lost, returning a purchase to a store, attempting to get a loan, rectifying a mischarge on a credit card, and similar actions. So "dignity" is *more concerned* about the process, such as the opening school meeting depicted earlier, than the rules that are established.

The Prevention Dimension

The prevention dimension attempts to answer the question, "What can be done to prevent discipline problems?" The following suggestions and techniques are used in *Dignity*'s prevention dimension.

1. **Be aware of self (the teacher's self).** It is suggested that teachers need to become aware of the degree of value they hold related to democratic ideas, authoritarian practices, or moderate views. The model provides a survey instrument to increase one's self-awareness related to these issues (see Figure 6.1).

2. **Be aware of the students.** It is highly advised that teachers familiarize themselves with student records, discover any unhappy or unsuccessful prior school experience, and find out about the students' interests or hobbies, so that when teachers come in contact with students (especially the 15 and 5 percent misbehaving ones), they can personalize themselves to those students. The model provides a Student Awareness Inventory for guidance in carrying out this action.

3. **Express genuine feelings.** This model shows us that many teachers have difficulty expressing genuine feelings; Curwin and Mendler see a direct connection between expressing feelings and successful classroom teaching. The model provides a structured activity to help teachers gain a conscious awareness of their feelings.

4. **Become knowledgeable about alternative theories.** The dignity model suggests that teachers become knowledgeable in many alternative discipline models and theories such as those found in this book. With the widest understanding of the many alternatives, teachers can find techniques that are congruent with their values.

---

1. Be aware of self (the teacher's self).
2. Be aware of the students.
3. Express genuine feelings.
4. Become knowledgeable about alternative theories.
5. Establish social contracts.
6. Implement social contracts.
7. Reduce stress.

FIGURE 6.1   Prevention Dimension

5. **Establish social contracts.** Central to this model is the establishment of a social contract with the students in the teacher's class. The opening example provides a fairly clear outline as to how to accomplish this contract.

6. **Reduce stress.** It is suggested that a host of stress reduction techniques be researched and used by the teacher to deal with daily stressful activities.

7. **Implement social contracts.** While implementing the social contract, rule breaking will occur and it is the use of this foundation of agreement through the contract that enables the teacher to move to the action dimension when dealing with a misbehaving student.

The meeting with the class of students to establish rules for the students and the teacher is basic to a prevention dimension. This process of working together to come to an agreement on guidelines for living together in the classroom is central to effective classroom discipline. Consequences are also established for these rules with the help of these same students, including consequences for teachers if they break rules (more will be said about that later). Once the social contract has been created, the teacher would take these actions:

- The students are tested on the rules with 100 percent correct answers required. If the child fails, the teacher may reteach these rules to the student, possibly through role-play, then the test is taken over and over until passed.

- The rules and consequences social contract is shared with (1) principal, (2) parents, (3) substitute teachers, (4) other teachers, and (5) school counselor.

- If the rules and consequences are not working, have another meeting to modify them—rules may be added or deleted.

Consequences

The "dignity" definition of consequence is similar to those defined by Dreikurs's punishment versus logical consequences. They describe how punishment destroys the student's dignity and motivation and is destructive in the classroom. They give these guidelines for consequences.

- They are clear and specific.
- They have a range of alternatives.
- They are not punishment.
- They are related to the rule.

Consequences must also:

- Preserve the student's dignity.
- Increase internal locus of control when appropriate.
- Increase student motivation.

An important contribution by Curwin and Mendler is the concept of "fair and not equal." Many classrooms and a large number of schools attempt to set up a "system" with a rule and a parallel sanction. "Fighting will mean a three-day suspension. If homework is not in on time, student must stay after school to finish it (or miss the pep rally)." Such systems govern people, and "individual needs are sacrificed for impartiality and efficiency replaces common sense" (Curwin and Mendler, 1999, p. 48). This arbitrary one (rule) to one (punishment) is set up so that the teacher and school cannot be criticized for showing favoritism. But now a straight A student, Sally, who has always had her homework completed, appears before you and indicates that her father was taken to the hospital the night before and the student and mother slept in the hospital waiting room all night. Thus, in the confusion of the emergency, she did not have her textbooks and was not able to do her homework. Do we make her stay after school (or miss the rally) to complete the homework? If we do not apply the rule and consequence to her, the next child, Jane, who does not have her homework done seven out of ten times, now charges you with being unfair. After all, you did not keep Sally after school. In order to deal with this dilemma, "dignity" sets up a range of consequences and permits the teacher flexibility to choose. The consequences for failing to have homework in on time are as follows:

- Reminder
- Warning
- Student must hand homework in before close of school that day
- Stay after school to finish work
- A conference between teacher, student, and parent to develop an action plan for completing homework on time

For Sally, because of the circumstances, the teacher chooses to simply remind her or asks her to get it done by the end of day. But Jane, often late with homework, is required to say after school. When Jane complains about fairness, the teacher states that, "I am fair, but not always equal." This concept is taught early to the class during the first class meeting when establishing the social contract. The students are told this story:

> I am a medical doctor and I have four patients in my office with the following ailments: poison ivy, a broken arm, a severe cut that is bleeding, and someone with the flu. Would it be fair to put a tourniquet on all four patients? Of course, the answer is no. The doctor is the professional; he or she is fair by giving the patient the medical action needed for each individual case. The teacher is a professional as well. She applies the sanction, drawing from a range of them to be fair, and the students know the consequences ahead of time. The teacher meets the needs of the particular student with whom he or she is dealing: Sally gets a warning, and Jane stays after school. This is "fair, but not equal."

Praise

Similar to the Dreikurs's concept of praise versus encouragement, Curwin and Mendler strongly criticize the use of praise as an adult-imposed value judgment, with the exception that they do approve of it for students with special needs or major self-concept problems. Instead they suggest using a form of praise called "I-statements" (not to be confused with the "I"-message as defined by Gordon in *T.E.T.* in Chapter 8). The I-statement has three components: the *behavior* (what the student did), *feeling* (how the teacher felt about the behavior), and the *reason* (why you felt this way). While praise is judgmental and nonspecific, an I-statement specifically says what can be appreciated about another's behavior. Praise would be, "James you behaved very well today," while an I-statement might be, "James, I am pleased that you were able to complete all your worksheets this morning because now I can see that you understand that math concept." The praise I-statement should include:

1. (Student's name) _____, when you did _____,

2. it made me feel _____

3. because _____.

The Action Dimension

Once the teacher has established the social contract through a class meeting, which contains rules and range of consequences, the teacher's behavior to the student becomes orderly and predictable with the understanding that the classroom will not be a place to be feared. But when rules are broken and the teacher must take action, there is a possibility that this can be done in such a hostile or nonassertive manner that poor discipline will occur. "Dignity" establishes nine principles of consequence implementation:

1. Be consistent by always implementing a consequence.
2. Simply state the rule and consequence (when rule is broken).
3. Use the power of proximity by being physically close to the student when implementing a consequence.
4. Make direct eye contact when delivering a consequence.
5. Use a soft voice.
6. Catch a student being good.
7. Don't embarrass the student in front of his or her peers.
8. Be firm and anger-free while giving the consequence.
9. Do not accept excuses, bargaining, or whining.

And finally, Curwin and Mendler describe how, unknowingly, we may get into a power struggle while implementing consequences. When a student breaks a rule, which she clearly knows because she has passed the social contract test, she may then refuse to take the consequence. The student may then challenge the teacher with the statement, "You can't make me." It is suggested that the scene may progress in this manner: student has refused to take the consequence, insults teacher, makes a scene in class, or tries to hook the teacher into a power struggle. The teacher may then use a deescalation strategy, such as:

- Active listening (label or verbally encode the student's feeling)
- Ignoring attempt by student to fight
- Speak with the student later
- Give student time out (to cool down)

The teacher gives the student time to think about whether or not to accept the consequence, and, if the student fails to comply, the administration intervenes with the *insubordination rule*. The insubordination rule is the principal's manner of supporting the teacher with a defiant student. The student may not return to class until willing to accept the consequence.

Traditional behavior modification methods also are suggested, along with a host of other actions such as videotaping the child, the teacher performing an "old-fashioned" tantrum, role reversal (having the misbehaving student "teach" the class) with the use of humor and nonsense statements. For example, when a student is late, rather than stating that to him, respond with a nonsense statement such as, "Peter piper picked a peck of pickled peppers".

The Resolution Dimension

The resolution dimension is the action that the teacher can take with (or toward) an "out-of-control" or chronic rule-breaking student. The Curwin-Mendler resolution presents a laundry list of activities:

1. **Positive student confrontation strategies** (a meeting to attempt to work out a compromise between teacher and student needs). The teacher and the "out-of-control" student are brought to a conference with a third person (an administrator, another teacher, guidance counselor, or any other neutral adult), and taken through a prescriptive series of steps for mediating an agreement. (*Note:* this process appears almost identical to peer mediation [chapter 10], with the exception that an adult is the outside mediator or coach.)

   a. The mediator or coach describes the problem, process, and his or her role.

   b. The teacher and student take turns sharing feelings of dislike, resentment, anger, and frustration. The coach acts as the counterpart to repeat or paraphrase what the other has said so it is assured that he or she is listening.

   c. The teacher and student are now required to state what they like about the other person.

   d. Teacher and student state their demands. ("Tell what you want!")

   e. Teacher and student negotiate a solution.

   f. An agreement is put into writing and signed.

   g. A meeting for follow-up is scheduled. (Curwin and Mendler, 1999, p.140)

2. **Family intervention process** (a behavioral incentive system with rewards and consequences monitored by a daily student rating system). At times, especially with the very difficult student, the family intervention process is required. Both parents, the student, and the teacher come together and follow a step-by-step procedure similar to the previous mediation. Added to this parent–student–teacher plan resulting from the meeting is a Daily Student Rating Card to be completed by the teacher for the parents so that progress can be monitored. Privileges and consequences for the student may be attached to the success or lack of success in carrying out this plan.

3. **Comprehensive social contract** (involves student, attendance coordinator, administrators, and parents) to monitor school attendance. Finally, a comprehensive social contract that will involve the student, attendance coordinator, administrators, and parents is established through a major conference. The goal of this contract is to have everyone claim ownership for helping to solve the student's behavioral problem and keep him in school.

	Looking	Naming	Questioning	Commanding	Acting/Reinforcement
Prevention Dimension	4. Learn alternative discipline theories	3. Teacher expressing feelings	question 1. Self-values (democratic ideals) 2. Background of students 5B. Test on social contract	5A. Establish social contract Rules • for students • for teacher	5C. Share social contract • principal • parents • substitute teacher • other teachers • school counselor
Action Dimension	Out-of-control child • active listening • ignore attempts to fight • speak later • give time out			Apply consequences (example: failing to do homework) • remind • warning • require by end of day • stay after school • conference with parents	Praise I-statement • Behavior • Feeling • Reason Use insubordination rule • videotape student • teacher does "temper tantrum" • role reversal • use humor • use nonsense statements
Resolution Dimension				Mediation • State feelings and dislikes • State what is liked about the other • Both state demands or wants • Negotiate a solution • Write/sign agreement • Meet later as follow-up	Family Intervention Daily Student Rating Card Comprehensive Social Contract • Student • Attendance coordinator • Administrators • Parents

FIGURE 6.2 Teacher Behavior Continuum—*Dignity*

STRENGTHS AND LIMITATIONS

Discipline with Dignity, in its attempt of "not wanting to be a systems model of discipline" is laudable, but because of its lack of a clear theoretical or conceptual framework on which to base its actions and suggestions, is at times difficult to follow as well as contradictory. For example, much is made of helping students develop an internal locus of control. Curwin/Mendler are critical of the "systems" model with its external locus of control models such as behavior modification suggesting that the teacher may get an immediate desist in the student's misbehavior but will not have long-term effects. When talking later about the "out-of-control" 5 percent student, a systems model of behavior analysis is suggested.

The book is a collection of personal wisdom, suggestions, and a host of techniques such as "active listening" from *T.E.T.,* logical consequences from Dreikurs, proxemics from Jones, behavior analysis techniques, and many others. It is as if an attempt were made to create an eclectic discipline model by selecting methods and techniques from various other models or traditional practices used in schools. The Teacher Behavior Continuum, Figure 6.2, provides a visual display of these methods.

Curwin and Mendler would probably defend themselves by saying that many actions and techniques may be used to deal with limit setting with a difficult student, but they must be carried out in such a nonpunitive manner so that the student's dignity is not destroyed. The use of advance organizers—(1) prevention dimension, (2) the action dimension, and (3) the resolution dimension—are the major contributions of this model, but these three constructs get smothered and lost in the writing style.

If the teacher were to read the book for guidance in being more successful with a difficult student, he or she would find some help with the activity of the "social contract" and a process for finding logical consequences by enlisting assistance from a host of others, including fellow teachers, parents—even students. But the bulk of the concrete suggestions on what to do with a misbehaving student gets lost in the guidelines of "don't do this, do this." In fact, 80 percent of the writing is one personal wisdom idea after another without any coherent organizer to give meaning and relationship to the suggested actions. The videos are helpful in gaining respect for Curwin and Mendler's real positive regard for students and defending student's dignity, but offer the teacher minimal aid in implementation.[1] Often, techniques are presented with inadequate definition, such as the *insubordination rule* (Curwin and Mendler, 1999, pp. 111–112) or active listening. Many of the other more developed models might be more helpful, especially for the beginning teacher. The personal experiences of Curwin and Mendler provide some insightful ideas to ponder.

SUMMARY OF KEY CONCEPTS

action dimension	daily student rating card	mediation	social contract
comprehensive social contract	insubordination rule	prevention dimension	
	I-statements	resolutions dimension	

NOTE

1. R. L. Curwin and A. N. Mendler, *Curwin and Mendler's Discipline with Dignity* (Bloomington, IN: National Educational Service, 1991), Part I: Overview, Part 2: Prevention, Part 3: Action & Resolution.

REFERENCE

Curwin, R. L., and Mendler, A. N. *Discipline with Dignity.* Alexandria, VA: Association for Supervision and Curriculum Development, 1999.

CHAPTER 7

LOVE AND LOGIC DISCIPLINE (INCLUDING GLASSER'S REALITY THERAPY STEPS)

Theorist/Writer: Jim Fay, Charles Fay, and David Funk

- Fay, J. and D. Funk, *Teaching with Love & Logic: Taking Control of the Classroom.*
- Fay, J. and C. Fay, *Love and Logic Magic When Kids Leave You Speechless.*

Other titles from Love and Logic

- *Meeting the Challenge*
- *Hope for Underachieving Kids: Opening the Door to Success with Love and Logic*
- *Pearls of Love and Logic for Parents and Teachers*
- *Quick and Easy Classroom Interventions: 23 Proven Tools for Increasing Student Cooperation*
- *9 Essential Skills for the Love and Logic Classroom: Low Stress Strategies for Highly Successful Educators*

Theorist/Writer: William Glasser[1]

- *Reality Therapy: A New Approach to Psychiatry*
- *Schools without Failure*
- *Control Theory in the Classroom*
- *The Quality School: Managing Students without Coercion*

OUTLINE OF LOVE AND LOGIC

Basic Assumptions about Motivation

Love and Logic

Students who disrupt or misbehave are viewed as covering up their fear of being seen as incompetent and are feeling hurt by their lack of success; thus they have a poor self-concept. Although there may be several [reasons for the child's misbehavior], two that significantly impact classroom

Glasser

- The student is a rational person who deserves to be appealed to in such a manner.
- The student has the capabilities to be responsible, but needs to learn moral or acceptable boundaries of living.
- The student must live in a society with others and satisfy his own needs in

performance are the issues of autonomy and self-concept. We all want to have some control over our lives and when we feel we are losing that control, we will fight to the end to get it back. Likewise, if our sense of self-worth is being attacked, we will rise at all cost to defend it (Fay and Funk, 1996, pp. 68–69).

such a manner that this does not infringe on others.

■ Each person has basic needs of belonging, freedom, power, and fun.

■ The student needs to acknowledge his own behavior, then commit himself to more logical and productive forms of behavior.

Teacher Behaviors (Love and Logic)

■ The "evil" eye

■ Moving in

■ Proximity

■ Eye contact/ "no" headshake

■ "Let's talk about this later."

■ "I" message

■ "Can you save that for later? Thanks!"

■ Change location

■ "Is this the right place for that?"

■ Enforceable statement

■ Provide choices

■ Make an appointment

■ Applying consequences

■ Remove to time out

■ Creating a new plan

■ Evaluating time out

■ What happened?

How did you feel?

What did you do?

How did it work out?

What are you going to do next time?"

"Will you try that just for me!"

Write a plan for change

■ Give permission to student to solve the problem "Good luck, I hope it works."

■ Information letters/telephone call

■ Use administrator

■ Systematic suspension

Guidelines, Planning, and Preparatory Teacher Actions

■ Learn to make your decisions and act on a "principled approach"

■ Be prepared to give power and decisions away by giving students choices

OVERVIEW

What we see in the following classroom actions is a teacher using the model called *Love and Logic* and its suggestions and practices.

> *This is a ninth-grade English classroom. The teacher has slightly dimmed the classroom lights in order to use an overhead projector. As she lectures, she turns her back to make reference to the information on the screen. She is unaware that James, who has a small pen-size laser light, proceeds to shine a spot on her back to the amusement of his peers. The laughter of the class brings the teacher's attention back to the students to attempt to discover the object of their amusement, but James quickly turns off the light. The teacher is baffled by the class's actions. The class sits silently with broad knowing smiles on their faces. The teacher continues. Ten minutes later she turns to the screen again and the laser light on her "back side" brings more laughs. The teacher stops to ask the class what is happening and what is causing them to laugh. No one speaks, but their eyes flash in James's direction, and then most of students drop their eyes. It becomes apparent to the teacher that James is doing something behind her back. She returns to her lecture and when needing to turn her back again to the screen, she turns in such a manner that she can see the student's reflection in the wall of glass windows to her left. She could see James again turning on the laser light and pointing it at her back.*

TEACHER (The teacher turns, continues to lecture, and walks slowly down the aisle, passing James; she then moves beside his desk. She bends down and whispers in his ear.)

TEACHER: *"James—that behavior is not acceptable in this classroom. I'm going to have to do something about it. I don't know what it will be because I am teaching right now. I will let you know when I decide tomorrow. Don't worry about it tonight."*

Fay and Funk's model of *Love and Logic* is placed within the Confronting-Contracting school of discipline and human relationship models because the role of the teacher is to help the student attempt to find solutions to life's problems. The teacher's primary action is one of *confronting through questioning* while attempting to lead the student to logical and more productive social actions. Misbehavior is seen as a result of the student's poor sense of self-worth and the desire to avoid pain. The misbehavior is viewed as enabling the difficult student to avoid or mask a sense of failure.

> *Although there may be several [reasons for the child's misbehavior], two that significantly impact classroom performance are the issues of autonomy and self-concept. We all want to have some control over our lives and when we feel we are losing that control, we will fight to the end to get it back. Likewise, if our sense of self-worth is being attacked, we will rise at all cost to defend it. Our needs for autonomy and self-concept are so powerful that we will sometimes engage in conduct that is detrimental to ourselves in order to hang onto them. Consider the teenager who drives recklessly to show how tough he is or the student who fails a class to prove the teacher can't make her do anything she doesn't want to do. (Fay and Funk, 1996, pp. 68–69)*

The misbehaving student comes to feel that, after a number of years in a school (if it is one of high competition with norm-based evaluation), his or her personal worth or value depends on accomplishments (e.g., grades, athletic achievement, etc.), and that ability is

The Glasser philosophy, seen in *Reality Therapy,* is regarded as being complementary to a Love and Logic orientation. The student is rational, must be confronted for misbehavior in a supportive, nonjudgmental manner, and given "the time of day"—a teacher–student relationship must be established. Glasser emphasizes changing school structures to build on the students' interest and strengths rather than creating a competitive school environment in which students get a feeling of failure—thus the title of his earlier book, *Schools without Failure.*

critical in attaining these accomplishments. If the student fails in academic success, he assumes that he does not have that ability that is perceived as an inherited, inborn given, and may choose to minimize these feelings of lack of ability by appearing apathetic, aggressive, or passive-resistant to protect his self-worth. The difficult student does not connect the choices he makes or the effort that he gives as central in their accomplishment, but simply blames a given lack of ability. "I'm not good at that—I can't do that!"

Love and Logic says that discipline involves building students up so that they feel more capable—and even better about themselves—even after a discipline situation (Fay and Funk, 1995, p. 64). The "building up" must consider internalized control versus external enforcement. When punishment or positive and negative reinforcements such as those used in behavior analysis or the assertive discipline model are tried, this would be viewed as dealing only with the symptoms of behavior problems rather than the source of these problems, and they will likely have no long-term effect. What is needed is a long-term process to change misbehaving students' perceptions that drive their behavior. This is done by:

- Building positive relationships with the students (rebonding with the student).
- Setting enforceable limits through enforceable statements (the ability to make wise and effective limits and to use language in a skilled and creative manner).
- Sharing control (especially for establishing classroom rules, and making decisions on changing their behavior in a conflict situation).
- Implementing discipline interventions that stop undesirable behaviors in their infancy, avoiding the need for consequences.
- Delaying consequences (as seen in our opening vignette—*"I don't know what it will be because I am teaching right now. I will let you know when I decide tomorrow. Don't worry about it tonight"*). (Fay and Funk, 1995, p. 44)

Control and Rules

A major exclamation used by students or parents to unnerve a teacher is, "It ain't fair!" This statement weighs heavily on teachers' shoulders, with most teachers and school officials making great attempts to "be fair." We often hear teachers and school officials state, "We cannot let you do that (or get away with that) or everyone will want to do that (or attempt to get away with that). We have a rule (policy) against that." Love and Logic states, *"'Fair' is often not identical treatment, but is, rather, giving what is needed"* (Fay and Funk, 1995, p. 100). In a day care/preschool classroom, parents of the children are often expected to send lunches from home. One father, having just become a single parent, began forgetting his child's lunch because he was still adjusting to this new demand. The head teacher brought up this problem in a staff meeting. The director stated, "I will purchase some frozen healthy lunches, so just 'nuke' one and give it to the child with a glass of milk or juice that we have for snacks." The teacher responded, "If you do that for him, all the other parents will hear about it and they will want you to do it for them!" The tyranny of fairness takes the position that we must deny everyone equally and enslaves the teacher to treating everyone the same. Similarly, a teacher might discipline one student for "breaking a rule" differently than another student who breaks the same rule—this might occur in the Love and Logic process and be seen as quite fair. Love and Logic would hold class meetings at the beginning of the year and encourage students to come up with the rules or evaluate the teachers' rules that will govern them, but the teacher will not be forced to publish an arbitrary punishment for a specific misbehavior (i.e., talking in class equals one-hour detention, talking in class a second time three hours of detention, etc.). This action of misbehavior with specific punishment would be labeled a *systems approach* to school management and discipline. In the Love and Logic model we see the teacher saying:

TEACHER: Here are the rules that I think are most important as we work together this semester. What do you think about them?

STUDENTS: What if you break one of these rules, what will happen?

TEACHER: I expect that no one will break a rule and, if someone does, I will do something.

STUDENT: What will this something be?

TEACHER: I don't know. It will depend on how this rule is broken. I treat everyone in this room as a unique individual and each misbehavior as a unique incident. I will try to treat everyone fairly, and if you ever feel that I am unfair, I want you to tell me. (Fay and Funk, 1995, p. 13)

Love and Logic sees schools as either warm and friendly or cold and uncomfortable. The uncomfortable ones are run by a "systems approach" in which rules are established by the staff and the staff and teachers are required to take action when there is a violation. Discipline actions are based on a specific punishment for a given infraction. Staff, either from the administration or the collective pressures from fellow teachers, are encouraged to impose uniform punishment regardless of their comfort level with predetermined rules and punishment administered to every student with no individual consideration for differences.

The warm and friendly schools, in Love and Logic's definition, are seen as following a "principled approach" whereby rules are established and teachers are expected to take action when violations occur, but consequences are based on an accepted set of principles. Teachers vary their discipline actions based on the student's individual situation and adherence to a set of values. These principles are:

1. **A student's self-concept needs to be either maintained or enhanced.** (This is especially true when dealing with a student concerning a discipline incident.) Love and Logic would describe the students' view of themselves as, "What I think about myself is highly determined by what I think other people think about

me" (Fay and Funk, 1995, p. 120). The view of oneself as an effective, competent person cannot be accomplished through being told that one is good or through some packaged self-concept program, but must be learned from experience. The basic and central experience is through school achievement. Most schools are focused on helping students overcome "deficits," and this can be overdone to the extent that a student feels inadequate. If students are to be successful, they must reach that success through their strengths. The role of a supportive teacher is to help students with a poor self-concept come to a perception of knowing their own strengths and how to use them. A fourth-grade score on the state standardized test produces a score of second-grade reading, but the same student scores an eleventh grade level in math. Love and Logic would say that the child needs help in reading, but he or she will probably always be a slow and tedious reader. The student will need more time in reading in the subject areas, but the student's real strength is math. Educators will need to help the child celebrate this math strength, and, most likely, future success will come by developing, elaborating, and finding outlets for this math ability.

If we accept that self-concepts are our view of how we think others view us, then the teacher becomes a mediator for these perceptions. The positive and outward actions by the teacher, especially those involving discipline, must help the student know that the teacher "unconditionally accepts [him or her] as a worthy person, even while rejecting the [their] questionable behavior" (Fay and Funk, 1995, p. 129). "I like you and value you too much to let you get away with that behavior." The teacher's objective should be to have the child come to the positive self-concept view that (1) "I'm loved by the 'magic' people (the teacher being one of them) in my life," (2) "I know more about my strengths than my weaknesses," and (3) "I can handle the consequences of my own behavior" (Fay and Funk, 1995, p. 128).

2. **Control is a shared commodity.** (The teacher uses only the amount of control absolutely needed, permitting students much control over their decisions and actions.)

- "Class, here are 40 math problems to do for homework tonight (moans from the class). You may choose to do the odd or even ones!"
- "Class, we have 10 minutes before the bell rings for you to do some of your assignment; would you rather do reading or social studies first?"
- "Would you speak quietly so others are not disturbed or sit here by yourself where you can work quietly?'

All these teacher statements give the student a choice, thus granting autonomy. The motto is "Teachers gain control by giving some of it away." The Love and Logic major technique, as a form of setting limits, in both giving directive or command statements on a day-in and day-out basis related to teaching math, reading, or social studies or when they see misbehavior (speaking so others are not disturbed) is to change the command mode to a questioning mode, granting the student choices within limits. The command is seen as "fighting" words whereby the teacher will tell students what the adult is going to *make them do*. "Thinking" words tell the student *what the adult will do*.

Fighting Words	**Thinking Words**
You are going to (clean your desk, do your work, get quiet, etc.) or I'm not letting you go to recess.	I'll be happy to send you to recess just as soon as (the desk is cleaned, your work is done, you get quiet, etc.).

When fighting words are used, we are sending threats. Although most students will obey them, many challenging students will not, and they, in their own minds, say, "She can't make me do that!" The defiant child who is passive-aggressive will use such behaviors as getting even or asserting passive power by "accidentally" breaking school equipment, refusing to participate or answer questions, and engaging in a host of other difficult-to-detect that actions, you might not recognize as occurring. A second group of defiant students takes teachers on aggressively.

Rules for Giving Choices

1. *Always be sure to select choices that you, the teacher, like, because if you give one that you do not like, the student will inevitably choose that one.*

2. *Don't give a choice that you are not prepared to follow through with by permitting the student to experience the consequence of that choice.*

3. *Never give a choice while the student is angry; delay until they have calmed down.*

4. *Never give a choice unless you are prepared to choose for them if they do not make a choice in a reasonable period of time.*

5. *Try to start your verbal statement with:*
   - *You're welcome to_____or_____.*
   - *Feel free to_____or_____.*
   - *Would you rather_____or_____?*
   - *What would be best for you_____or_____?* (Fay and Funk, 1995, p. 31)

3. **Consequences must be served up with compassion, empathy, or understanding, rather than anger.** (Children need to learn from the consequences of life. You touch a hot stove, you get burned. You disrupt the classroom activity, you are removed or some similar action occurs, but the adult does this without anger.)

Love and Logic basically takes a position that all change in student behavior must involve some feeling of hurt. That hurt can be viewed from two locations—inside or outside the self. When students are punished for misbehavior, they hurt; they look about for someone to blame for that hurting. This is directed at the teacher, who is especially blamed if the punishment has been delivered with anger. This situation will cause no behavior change on the child's part because he or she accepts no responsibility; he or she will blame the teacher or principal who has shown the student no compassion, empathy, or understanding. If the teacher, with a student, labels an action a "consequence," not "punishment," this will permit the student to reason, "I am hurting, and what is the cause of my hurting? I have two choices: I can wait till the hurting stops or I can see that my actions are causing this hurt and, if I change, the hurting will stop." The sanction or action is in the "eye of the beholder"—that is, the student—and, depending on how the teacher *deals with the student doing the critical limit setting,* this becomes a teachable moment if it is done with empathy or compassion, rather than anger.

Here are the guidelines for the teacher:

1. Give the child the opportunity to be involved in the solution/decision making.

2. Administer consequences with calm interest.

3. Give students the opportunity to develop a new plan of behavior.

4. Let students make their own value judgments.

5. Demonstrate problem-solving techniques.

6. Allow students to feel empowered. (Fay and Funk 1995, pp. 168–169)

4. **Thinking needs to be shared.** (Especially in rule-making or discipline situations, students must be asked to think about their actions, decisions, and their effects on their life.) (Fay and Funk, 1995, pp. 109–110)

When there has been a "breaking of a rule" or some classroom disruption, the natural tendency is for the teacher to "go to work," thinking about how to deal with this incident and get a change in the students' behavior. This means that the teacher is doing all the work. Love and Logic wishes to turn this around and share the thinking, or even induce thinking in the student and encourage the student do the work. A schoolwide rule is "No wearing of baseball caps in the classroom." A student is wearing a hat today.

TEACHER: "What is that?"

STUDENT: "Hat."

TEACHER: "Why?"

STUDENT: "'Cause I like wearing it and it doesn't hurt nothin'."

TEACHER (Smiling): "On a scale of 1 to 10, how good a decision do you think it would be to keep it on your head? Thanks for giving it some thought." (Fay and Funk, 1995, p. 180)

(*Note:* Ten minutes later the student takes the hat from his head and sticks it into his pocket.)

The cold and uncomfortable classroom teacher would have approached the student with a command, possibly threatening punishment. That teacher would be teaching in a straight-jacket of school rules and enforcement. In Love and Logic, commands are used in a very limited manner and replaced with questions. Questions induce student thinking. Here are some "magic" words and phrases for beginning these questioning techniques:

Love and Logic's Magic Words and Phrases

- *What would you like to happen?*
- *Would you like my thinking on that?*
- *Is it possible that...?*
- *How do you feel about...?*
- *Is there any chance that...?*
- *How do you suppose that might work out?*
- *What do you think I think?*
- *On a scale of 1 to 10, how good a decision do you think that is?*
- *Would you like to hear what others have tried?* (Fay and Funk, 1995, p. 179)

Questions verses commands require the teacher to understand the theories and concepts about the nature and form of questions developed for teachers by Bloom (1956) in his taxonomy (see Figure 7.1). As we move up the pyramid in Figure 7.1, we see the type of questions that would require the student to think in higher and higher level of abstractness or "higher order thinking." The lowest level 1—Fact questions—simply asks the student to name and label.

TEACHER: "What's that?" (level 1—Fact question)

STUDENT: "Hat."

This requires little real thinking and is mostly a reflex response. Moving up to the higher thinking level 2—Convergent question—requires that students put facts together and communicate a possible reason in the form of cause and effect.

TEACHER: "Why?" (level 2—Convergent question)

STUDENT: "'Cause I like wearing it and it doesn't hurt nothin'."

The level 3—Divergent question—asks the student to creatively go beyond fact and make something new from ideas previously unrelated. And, finally, the highest form of question, level 4—Evaluative—asks the student to make judgments, put opinions in order, and apply standards.

TEACHER (Smiling): "On a scale of 1 to 10, how good a decision do you think it would be to keep it on your head? (level 4—Evaluative question) Thanks for giving it some thought." (Fay and Funk, 1995, p. 180)

The goal of Love and Logic is, of course, to share power, induce thinking, and model for the student how to solve problems through rational reasoning, thus helping them to develop a more positive self-concept. This will take some time, and limit-setting incidents are not rushed to an immediate conclusion. In the previous example, after the teacher says, "Thanks for giving it some thought" and the student has had some time to think, he does remove his hat and puts it in his pocket. Again, in our opening example, with the student using a laser light on the teacher's back, we hear the teacher saying: *"James—that behavior is not acceptable in this classroom. I'm going to have to do something about it. I don't know what it will be because I am teaching right now. I will let you know when I decide*

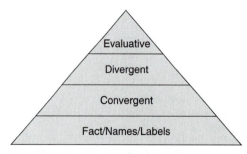

FIGURE 7.1   Bloom's Taxonomy

tomorrow. Don't worry about it tonight." The laser-light student now has much time to reflect on his behavior.

The title of this model uses the word *love.* So if we were to ask just what is the most important concept, technique, or value in the Love and Logic model, the answer would be "Make them, the students, fall in love with you, the teacher." Everyone has felt the distance of institutional behavior when dealing with waitresses, check-out persons at a grocery store, workers at an airline counter, or auto-repair mechanics, plus a host of other service people who help us as quickly as possible to get a specific need met. Then we move on, never to see them again. The teacher cannot deal with misbehaving students in such an institutional manner. The majority of students, who have had excellent parenting with much love and affection, can accept this institutional "standoffish" relationship from a teacher and be comfortable with it. But the students who are disruptive and causing most of the discipline problems lack this secure self-concept, and they will put up barriers of rude behavior to increase this distance. The student with a poor self-concept thinks, "I feel no warmth or acceptance from your businesslike manner and thus I feel rejected, so I will show you how I can reject you with my negative behavior." But the opposite, worth and acceptance, is what they really want and need. They need an adult who cares about them and will take the time to personalize that relationship—a difficult task for a teacher who sees many students in one day.

Here are a few relationship actions, but teachers must be creative in developing their own approaches.

- First day of school, stand at the door and shake their hands.
- Look in their eyes, smile, and say, "I'm glad you're going to be in my room."
- Say, "Give me five!" and clap hands with them.
- Learn their names.
- Notice things about them and ask questions about their personal life.
- Approach student deliberately to personalize yourself to them.
- Take all necessary personal actions to cut through the shell of their rudeness or outward coldness that they hide behind.

These statements are labeled "one-sentence intervention(s)" (Fay and Funk, 1995, p. 21) for dealing with the difficult student. They help to build up a positive relationship with the student that Love and Logic calls the "savings account." When we want a change in an off-task student, we then draw on this savings account or the positive personal relationship and may request, "Would you do this just for me?"

If there is an incident when the student is off-task, being disruptive, or you sense a potential conflict is about to begin, it is important in Love and Logic to head this off before it becomes a major disruption. The teacher may use some of their interventions under the Teacher Behavior Continuum (TBC) heading of "looking" shown in Figure 7.2.

SPECIFIC LOVE AND LOGIC INTERVENTIONS

The fairly nonintrusive interventions are (1) the "evil" eye, (2) moving in on the student, (3) proximity, (4) eye contact and "no" headshake. The following labels of looking, naming, and so on permit the reader to view these actions on Figure 7.2, and thus get a feel for the amount of power the teacher is using.

Looking	Naming	Questioning	Commanding	Reinforcement or Modeling	Acting
1. The "evil" eye 2. Moving in 3. Proximity 4. Eye contact/"no" headshake (Have class make or evaluate rules based on principles) Take care of yourself in front of students (don't get pulled into a power struggle with students) **Step 1. Reflect: "What am I doing?" (Glasser)** **Step 2. "Is it working?"**	5. "Let's talk about this later." 6. "I"-message (Behavior/effect/feeling) (Savings account: "One-sentence" intervention) **Step 3. Recognition (Glasser)**	7.1. "Can you save that for later? Thanks!" (Whispered in ear) 8. "Is this the right place for that?" (Whispered in ear) 12.3 Evaluating time out a. "What happened?" b. "How did you feel?" c. "What did you do?" d. "How did it work out?" use high-level Bloom's questioning) e. "What are you going to do next time?" f. "Will you try that just for me?" g. Write a plan for change h. Give permission to student to solve the problem, "Good luck, I hope it works." 12.4. Creating a new plan **Step 4 + 5: "What are you doing? Is it against the rules?" (Glasser)** **Step 6. Work it out—make a plan**	9. Enforceable statement (Delay the consequence: "Don't worry about it.") 10. Provide choices 11. Give an appointment	12.1. Applying consequences 13. Information letters/telephone call	7.2. Change location 12.2. Remove to time out 14. Use administrator 15. Systematic suspension (Apply consequences with empathy—"We will miss you—come and see us when you get back!") **Step 7. Classroom isolation** **Step 8. In-school isolation** **Step 9. Sent home** **Step 10. Get professional help**

FIGURE 7.2 Love and Logic (with Glasser)

Looking 1—"Evil" eye

Fred, our student, is inattentive and beginning to "horse around." We move so that Fred can see our face and we make eye contact while at the same time we do not stop the flow of our teaching. We maintain an unbroken eye-to-eye contact with him, signaling him that he is off-task. This *evil eye* continues until he returns to on-task behavior. A more positive or sophisticated form of this is to give Fred a smile and a wink or, as Love and Logic would say, send "a hug from across the room."

Looking 2—Moving in on the student

While I am continuing to teach, I move about the room and when coming to off-task Fred, I lightly place my hand, almost in an absentminded manner, on his shoulder.

When he looks up at me I smile at him authentically. This is most effective when we previously have established a relationship with this student. For other students, this may be a very dangerous action because many students have been physically punished in their life. The only touching they ever get is a hurting touch. They may become verbally or physically aggressive as a result of this minor and gentle touch, so professional judgment is needed related to touching. Another point to consider that may be dangerous is when a male teacher touches a female student.

Looking 3—Proximity

Another nonintrusive action to get students to stop and get back on-task is to move physically close in *proximity to* them. Standing near and teaching over them may settle them down, but also may require an eye-to-eye contact with an accompanying smile.

Looking 4—"Eye contact and "no" headshake"

If evil eye, moving in, and proxemics have not worked, the teacher might move away from Fred, make eye contact, and in a very minimal way use a clear back-and-forth head movement, making a *"no" headshake.* It is best to do this as privately as possible, attempting not to embarrass the student, but meaning, "I have had enough of this—now, get back to work."

Naming 5—"Let's talk about this later"

If by chance the teacher misjudges Fred and the touch, eye contact, or proxemics produce defensive statements from him—"don't touch me, what did I do?" or similar refrains—we slowly move out of the student's private space, but just before we do we whisper to him as we move up the TBC to naming: *"Let's talk about this later."* We want no power struggle with a student with the classroom as an audience. If Fred escalates his verbal response, wishing for a power struggle, Love and Logic would simply state, as part of TBC naming, "This sounds like an argument. If it is, I schedule arguments at 12:15 and 3:15 daily. Which time is best for you? Let me know later." The teacher returns to teaching.

Naming 6—"I"-message

Love and Logic suggest the use of Thomas Gordon's "I-messages" taught to us in the *Teacher Effectiveness Training* model. The purpose of an "I"-message is not to tell the student how to change, but to give them information. It generally follows the three parts of (1) describe what is happening *(when pencil tapping occurs),* (2) describe how that makes you feel *(I feel distracted),* and (3) identify the tangible effect of the other person's behavior *(and seem to lose track and focus as I am lecturing).* This model cautions against wanting immediate change and compliance after the teacher delivers an "I"-message. It may take some students some time to contemplate the information in the "I"-message that we are giving them and they may want to maintain their power. They may wish to stop their behavior or change in their "own good time." Often Love and Logic might respond to the power student who is not complying immediately with "I just wanted you to know how I felt, and I hope you will give it some thought. Thank you" and then the teacher moves on.

Questioning 7.1—"Can you save that for later? Thanks."

Although intervention techniques one to five involving looking and naming are rather private, if the student escalates and appears to want a conflict, we may move to the TBC's questioning while maintaining a natural smile yet using the following language:

- "Fred is this really necessary? Thank you."
- "Fred could you *save this for later. Thanks.*"

Acting[2] 7.2—Change location

Finally, we may add to the questioning intervention the idea of acting by *changing the location* of the student's space. "Would you mind, Fred, sitting over there? Thank you." A minor technique that has a limited "shelf life" is to have the confrontational student physically move. If he complies, that somehow breaks the tension and may calm him down. If this confrontational behavior begins to be a repetitive action by Fred we might, at the next class meeting, reseat everyone with a new seating chart that moves him across the room but is done in such a whole-group manner that this will not embarrass him.

Questioning 8—"Is this the right place for that?"

There are a host of small student behaviors that disrupt teaching, but if they were done anywhere else no one would label them as "bad." This could be chewing gum, talking to a friend, passing a note, and similar minor actions that are not wanted while the teacher is teaching, and most students know that these are not wanted. If the teacher needs to stop the flow of her lecturing in order to move to this "misbehaving" student, we try to get the entire class occupied in a worthwhile task to free up the teacher to reach the target student. The teacher may state, "Class read page 52 and when you can find three actions in this story that cause the main character to be fearful, raise your hand with three fingers up." The teacher moves to off-task Fred and states, "Hey, could you save that for the playground, or *is this the right place for that?*"

Naming 9—Enforceable statements

The next and much more powerful teacher action is the teacher setting limits by stating or describing what she or he will allow or provide, and is labeled *enforceable statements.*

- I give full credit for assignments that are turned in on time.
- I dismiss my class when I see all lab equipment cleaned up and back on the storage shelves.
- I listen to those students who raise their hands.

These enforceable statements must only be given for those behaviors over which the teacher has total control.

Questioning 10—Provide choices

When Love and Logic moves to powerful steps in limit setting that may be viewed as questioning but are very close to a covert command, this is nearly always done with choices.

- Would you rather study with a friend or by yourself? (Wanting the student to get to work.)
- Should we do math first or social studies?
- Do as many of the homework problems as you need to be sure that you know the concept.
- Would you like to choose your partners or would you like me to choose?

We attempt to break the cycle of defiance with a student or with the whole class by giving away some of our teacher power by offering students choices, thus sharing power. By *"providing choices"* we move the student away from an emotional response, which we would most likely receive if we had given a direct command—"Get to work now." To this command the student's emotional thinking is, "You can't make me!" These choices, known as thinking words, encourage students to move beyond defiance to really thinking about the real decision they have been given to make.

Acting   11—Give an appointment

The previous techniques of changing location and giving time to think are seen in the process called *"Give an appointment."* We have a "hit-and-run" student who causes small disruptions and then quiets. These "nickel-and-dime" actions are too small to stop our teaching, but at the same time they are repetitive and disruptive. The teacher, while keeping her teaching momentum, moves through the classroom and when she comes to the Sonny or Sally "hit-and-run" simply whispers, *"We'll have an appointment to discuss that. Would you like to meet at the end of lunch period at 12:25 or at the end of the day at 3:15?"* Note that the teacher again shares the power by giving the student a choice. At that meeting, the teacher simply keeps it short and to the point: *"Sonny (or Sally), thanks for coming in. I wanted to let you know that when you did (so-and-so), it disrupted my teaching. I lost my continuity and did a poor job of teaching after that. I just want to give you that information. Thanks for coming in. Have a nice afternoon."* The student is then dismissed and that is that! The objective is to get the student thinking, not create a power struggle or conflict.

Acting   12.1—Applying consequences

When there is an established school rule, such as fighting will get a student three-days' suspension, the manner in which this is delivered to the student is critical and the teacher or administrator is encouraged to use maximum empathy.

TEACHER: Ah, you were fighting at the water fountain. You must have been really angry. What a shame. Fighting means how many days' suspension?

STUDENT: Three.

TEACHER: Yes, we will miss you. We will see you back on what day?

STUDENT: Thursday.

TEACHER: Yes, I will see you when you get back. Stop in before the bell rings on Thursday morning and let's talk.

The student might be angry for having the consequence applied, but the goal for the teacher is not to show anger for the past misdeed, but to maintain an empathic relationship.

Acting   12.2—Remove student to time out

Time out, in Love and Logic's opinion, has been misused. Rather than a place you go to be punished, they wish to characterize this "away space" as a place to "think-it-over" or as an "office of productive thinking." It is suggested that this space could be humorously named by the students. One class called it "hit the beach" and a canvas beach chair was placed in the corner with a large beach umbrella over it. The duration in time out should be very limited and the student should have the right to decide when to return to class. Doing schoolwork in the time-out space is not recommended because students are meant to be thinking about their actions. If a student returns and disrupts again, and is put repetitively and daily in the time-out place, the teacher using Love and Logic would now involve the parents.

In a meeting with the student, parent, and teacher, the parent is asked to listen and help if possible. The teacher goes through a series of questions about what is a reasonable number of times the student would think that they would go to time out before it was too often—two or three times. The discussion then goes to how the parent and teacher can work together and send the student home under certain conditions, or, with the parent signature, have the student be isolated in an unused room in the school. Sending a student to another teacher's room, with that teacher's cooperation, as a form of escalated time out is also suggested.

Questioning   12.3—Evaluating time out

To help get the student thinking while in time out, Love and Logic suggests the following five questions:

1. What happened?
2. How did you feel?
3. What did you do?
4. How did it work out?
5. What are you going to do next time?

The student is permitted time to think about answers to these questions or even write them out.

Acting   12.4—Creating a new plan

When the student shows some dramatic misbehavior, such as fighting, outside of the classroom such as on the playground, in the hallway, in the cafeteria, or any other place, Love and Logic calls in that student for a conference at the beginning of this activity. *"You are welcome to go out to the playground and play whenever we have <u>created a new plan</u> for your actions here. Fighting on the playground needs to change to some new behaviors for you to settle conflicts. What are your ideas? Take your time. No hurry here."* The goal is to have the child think through new actions to settle his needs, and his plan should be written down either by the teacher or the student. Through questioning, the student is asked to think through what positive things will happen (getting to play on the playground) if the plan is lived up to, or what happens if the plan is broken (is not able to play).

Acting 13—Informational letters

An interesting technique not suggested in other models is to have the student send an information letter or call home. The student may be doing Step 12.4, Creating a new plan, by writing a letter home to their parents explaining the situation and giving examples of past behavior and how they will change. If this is done by phone, the teacher calls the parents first to explain the situation and alerts them that the child will call. We ask the parents not to accept any responsibility for the child's problem, but allow it to stay in their own hands or those of the student for solving it. Ask the parents to show the child empathy and offer to talk it out with them if they need help.

Acting 14—Use of the building administrator

There are times when, in this model, students are sent to the building administrator for a "cooling down" period. The role of the administrator is not to counsel or talk to the student at this time, and simply says, "Oh, I see you (the student) have a problem—good luck in solving it." When students are sent to the office, the teacher may appear to be saying to the student and the administrator, "Student, I can't handle you, pal!" Thus, the teacher may be giving away his or her authority. If support from the administrator is needed by the teacher, the teacher meets with the administrator beforehand to talk things out and then brings in the student for a meeting, by appointment, in which the teacher is in charge and does the questioning. The teacher may ask the administrator in front of the student, "Do you have any ideas regarding the issues that we are trying to solve here?" Teacher and administrator are thus united.

Acting 15—Systematic suspension

The final action defined by Love and Logic is the very powerful systematic suspension. The position is that school is not therapy, and some students, because of past life experience, need specific and long-term therapeutic intervention. The school's responsibility to these children is to allow them to stay in the school setting as long as their behavior does not take away the learning rights of other students as well as the teacher's right to teach. A meeting between the teacher, the administrator, the parent, and the student must occur to help make a plan (putting it in writing) as to under what conditions the child is permitted to stay in school for the day, and at what point he or she is sent home. It is highly likely that the parents will voice a strong negative response, often making school officials frightened. Fay and Funk state, "The interventions (listed above) we have covered are not therapy. We need to always be aware that some kids may still need intensive and specialized professional help. These interventions will, however, help maintain the classroom. And they will build better relationships" (Fay and Funk, 1995, p. 364).

Step 1: What am I doing? (The teacher asks this question of himself to gain an intellectual awareness of himself, rather than a stereotypical reflex response involving a narrow set of predictable teacher behaviors that are not working and may be making things worse.)

Step 2: Is it working? If not, stop doing it. (A directive by the teacher to himself, based on Step 1.)

Step 3: Recognition (The teacher should give the student "the time of day" and establish an informal relationship with the misbehaving student during the times that child is not misbehaving, in order to personalize himself to the child.)

Step 4: What are you doing? (This question is directed to the child, delivered without guilt as a genuine request for the child to reflect cognitively on his or her own behavior. If the student cannot remember, remind what he or she did.)

Step 5: Is it against the rules? (The teacher asks the student this question, again for cognitive reflection.)

Step 6: Work it out and make a plan. (The student is counseled on how he or she may act whenever this incident occurs again. The teacher and student now have an agreement on what the student's behavior will be in the future. The plan may be solemnized with a handshake or written out and signed by both parties.)

Step 7: Isolate from the class: Within the classroom (elementary school only—what Glasser calls "off to the castle" or to a chair at the back of the classroom)

Step 8: Isolate from the class: Out of the classroom (in-school suspension or a time-out room in the building)

Step 9: Send the student home.

Step 10: Get professional help. (Ask parents to get psychological help for the child, and possibly improve parenting skills through counseling for themselves.)

FIGURE 7.3   Glasser's 10 Steps to Discipline

SUMMARY

The Teacher Behavior Continuum shown in Figure 7.2 provides a visual summary of the teacher techniques or interventions as they are labeled by Love and Logic. For display purposes, the interventions are numbered, and generally we view them on the TBC as a gradual move from minimum power to stronger techniques of systemic suspension. Love and Logic rejects a systems approach, and therefore would not suggest that a teacher slavishly move across this intervention in a lockstep manner. The display shows teachers the amount of power they are using in their actions. Added to the Love and Logic Teacher Behavior Continuum are Glasser's 10 steps to discipline shown in Figure 7.3. One can see the direct and complementary parallels between Glasser and Love and Logic.

Strengths and Limitations of the Model

Many of the looking, eye contact, proxemics, and "I"-messages are better described and applied in other models, and the text *Teaching with Love & Logic: Taking Control of the Classroom* is interesting to read with its vignettes and boxed-off suggestions, but various authors have apparently written different chapters, and as a result it is very difficult to follow when asking the question, "What do I, as a teacher, do on Monday morning?" The text needs much editing for it to be practical. Although heuristic values are stated as a philosophy for this model, it is not made clear which psychological theory is influencing its concepts and practices. One can only speculate that Fay and Funk have been trained in attachment theory with a psychoanalytical background.

The choice of the words *love* and *logic* is reflected in the model orientation. Many suggestions are given to the teacher for develop logic in students, but outside of the "one-sentence" intervention and the idea of a "savings account," which are meaningful and not found in other models, the model shortchanges the love dimension and how to fully accomplish it. More processes for establishing teacher and student relationships would be helpful.

The strength of this model is the use of questioning, and the delay of sanctions or consequences. Most teachers, and most models, wish to solve a conflict or discipline situation at the very moment it is happening. The giving of power to the student to logically think about his or her behavior through teacher questioning, and a delay in time—"See you at the end of day, or see you tomorrow"—can be very powerful. It gives both teacher and student time to cool down, and to be ready to deal effectively with conflict and behavior.

SUMMARY OF KEY CONCEPTS

"Can you save that? Thanks."	Bloom's Questioning Taxonomy	Use enforceable statements	magic words and phrases
"Fair is not often identical treatment."	Facts questions	"evil" eye	moving in on the student
"Is this the right place for that?"	Convergent questions	eye contact with "no" headshake	one-sentence intervention
"Let's talk later."	Divergent questions	fighting versus thinking words	Provide choices
"Magic" people	Evaluative questions	Give an appointment	proximity
Applying consequences	building administrator, use of	"I"-message	systematic suspension
	Change locations	information letters	systems versus principled approach
	Create a new plan	love	Thinking needs to be shared
	Delay consequences		time out

CASE STUDIES

1. Mike's clowning (see previous chapters describing Mike's blowing bubbles of chocolate milk through his nose, making "fart" sounds, etc.).

Encouragement System

For the Love and Logic model, the encouragement system is placed first in our discussion because this model would see Mike as a student with a poor self-concept, who is covering that up by his attention-getting behavior. For the following limit-setting actions to be effective, the teacher would have to personalize him or herself to Mike through "one-sentence intervention," labeling and acknowledging his interests, and our interest in him. The teacher would attempt to build up a "savings account" of goodwill with Mike from which to draw later by such requests as, "Mike, could you do this for me?" This also would involve helping Mike to find his strengths and obtain attention and acknowledgment for these abilities and talents. Even when rebonding is established, most likely Mike will need "consequences to be served up with compassion, empathy, or understanding, rather than anger."

Limit-setting System

Love and Logic would see itself as offering very meaty intervention, under limit setting, when dealing with Mike's clowning. One would begin with (1) "evil" eye, (2) moving in, (3) proximity, and (4) headshaking "no." If this low-profile correction didn't work, Love and Logic would move to (5) "Let talk about this later," (6) "I"-message, (7) "Can you save that for later?" (8) "Is this the right place for that?" (9) enforceable statements, (10) providing choices, and finally (11) give an appointment. If all these failed to work, one would move to the backup system.

Backup System

Mike may need to be sent to time out, giving him time to think about his behavior with the help of evaluating time-out questions (What did you do? How can we work this out? etc.) If the behavior dramatically escalates or continues in such a manner that the teacher cannot teach, the teacher may move to contacting parents, information letters/telephone call, using the building administrator, or systematic suspension.

Incentive System

No incentive techniques are suggested by the Love and Logic model, and a clear statement is given in opposition to their use.

Management System

Love and Logic presents limited to no management techniques with the exception of changing locations. That is, in order to break the tension inherent in a conflict, Mike is requested to physically move to a new desk, or the entire seating arrangement of the class is changed to see if this might positively impact Mike.

Multimedia Training Packages

Address: Love and Logic Press, Inc.
            2207 Jackson Street
            Golden, CO 80401
Phone: 1-800-338-4065
Email: www.loveandlogic.com

- *Parenting with Love and Logic: Teaching Children Responsibility*
- *Parenting Teens with Love and Logic: Preparing Adolescents for Responsible Adulthood*
- *Grandparenting with Love and Logic: Practical Solutions to Today's Grandparenting Challenges*
- *Love and Logic Solutions for Kids with Special Needs*

NOTES

1. In past editions of this book a full chapter on Glasser's writings was included, but his recent books have focused less on school discipline while new models such as *Love and Logic* have subsumed most of the Glasser school ideas and follow nearly the same orientation. So Glasser's 10 steps, which are his best contribution, have been included here because they still represent an insightful series of concrete actions that give practical guidance to teachers.

2. Notice that as we escalate up the TBC with Love and Logic techniques we skipped the Commanding category. Directive commands are rarely if ever recommended with questioning.

REFERENCES

Bloom, B. *Taxonomy of Educational Objectives.* New York: Longman, 1956.

Fay, J., and C. Fay. *Love and Logic Magic When Kids Leave You Speechless.* Golden, CO: Love and Logic Press, 2000.

Fay, J., and D. Funk. *Teaching with Love & Logic: Taking Control of the Classroom.* Golden, CO: Love and Logic Press, 1995.

Glasser, W. *Reality Therapy: A New Approach to Psychiatry.* New York: Harper & Row, 1975.

Glasser, W. *Control Theory in the Classroom.* New York: Harper & Row, 1986.

Glasser, W. *The Quality School: Managing Students without Coercion,* 2nd ed. New York: HarperCollins, 1992.

Related Readings (Glasser)

Glasser, W. *Schools without Failure.* New York: Harper & Row, 1969.

RELATIONSHIP-LISTENING

THE LEAST intrusive of the three discipline orientations or faces is that of Relationship-Listening (RL), which views students as inherently good. If students are misbehaving, it is because they are suffering from the blockage of some inner need. The teacher's role is to establish a nonjudgmental relationship and encourage the student to "talk out" the problem while the teacher listens; this talking out helps empower the student to solve his own problems. The RL model is:

CHAPTER 8. Thomas Gordon's *Teacher Effectiveness Training (T.E.T.)*. Gordon's model can be characterized as a humanistic model that has operationalized for the teacher the nondirective therapy practices of Rogerian theory.

TEACHER EFFECTIVENESS TRAINING MODEL (OR ROGERIAN MODEL)

Writer/Theorist: Thomas Gordon

▓ *Teaching Children Self-Discipline: At Home and at School*
▓ *T.E.T.: Teacher Effectiveness Training*

OUTLINE OF TEACHER EFFECTIVENESS TRAINING

Basic Assumptions about Motivation

▓ The student is seen as motivated by the internal desire to be good.

▓ He or she is helped by a warm accepting nonjudgmental relationship with another.

▓ The student is rational—capable of solving his or own problems.

Teacher Behaviors

▓ Critical listening

▓ Acknowledgements

▓ Door openers

▓ Active listening

▓ "I"-messages

▓ Influencing

Guidelines, Planning, or Preparatory Teacher Actions

▓ Method III (no-lose) problem solving

▓ Reorganize space

▓ Reorganize time: diffused, individual, and optimal

▓ Six Steps to Problem Solving

▓ "Areas of freedom"

The scene is a high school classroom where a student and teacher are involved in a discipline situation. As we watch the situation unfold, we will see the teacher use Rogerian

Emotionally Supportive techniques (**boldface** words are names for techniques used by the teacher, which will be defined and explained in more detail later).

> *The students are talking and laughing as they enter Ms. Walker's chemistry lab. As they move to their assigned seats, Ms. Walker is already checking the roll; at the bell she double-checks and marks two students as absent, sets the roll book down, and brings the class to order.*
>
> *Two minutes after the bell, while Ms. Walker is still giving the class instructions, one of her absentees walks in. His clothes are baggy and unkempt as usual, and he is playing "air drums" with two pencils. He heads to his assigned place without looking at the teacher. Ms. Walker states, "Darrin, you're late and I do believe that this is your third tardiness. You know the rule!" Darrin stops and listens to her, with his head dropped and eyes looking at the floor. He turns and yells, "Lay off, bitch, I ain't going to no detention or the office. You think I give a shit about any of y'all?" He takes his seat and slouches deep into it.*
>
> *Ms. Walker says, "Class, yesterday, I introduced you to all of the concepts you need to know for experiment number 34 B on page 120 of the Chemistry Lab Workbook. I want you to now move to your lab tables and your work groups and do this experiment as we have done in the past with other similar activities. Darrin, I need you to stay where you are, at your seat, so that we may talk." The students move to their lab tables and begin to work while Ms. Walker approaches Darrin and seats herself "knee-to-knee," facing him. She speaks in such a manner that other student cannot hear her words.*

Ms. WALKER: "When I am called such a name, it shows me much disrespect and causes me to lose respect from other students, and it angers me."(**"I"-message**)

Darrin slouches deeper into the chair and under his desk.

Ms. WALKER: "Darrin, we need to talk. Apparently you are quite upset. Would you like to talk about it?" (**Door Opener**)

Darrin shifts his weight from hip to hip, makes eye contact with Ms. Walker, and then drops his eyes, saying nothing.

Ms. WALKER: "You are obviously having a very bad morning, and are having some difficulty. (**Active Listening**) I am here to listen to you!" (**Door Opener**)

DARRIN: "Get the f——k out of my face!"

Ms. WALKER: "You're angry and upset and are having a very difficult time talking. (**Active Listening**) There are a number of ways we can handle this. One, I can call the assistant principal, Mr. Mack, and he will remove you from my classroom, which will only result in even more problems for you. (**Method #1: Teacher Wins**) Or, two, I can just ignore this name-calling and behavior (**Method #2: Student Wins**), but that is unacceptable to me as a teacher. There is a third way that we can handle this difficulty. If we can talk this out, we might be able to find a 'no-lose' solution where you don't get into more trouble, and I can get the respect that I need as a teacher." (**Method #3: No-Lose Problem Solving**)

DARRIN: "I don't want to see 'Mack the Knife' again."

Ms. WALKER: "OK, can we talk about this now?"

Darrin shakes his head no.

Ms. Walker: "When do you think you will be ready to talk about this—just before you go to lunch this morning, or after school?"

Darrin: "Before lunch."

Ms. Walker: "OK, I now want you to go quickly to the office and get a late pass and come right back and join your lab table. I will see you here in my classroom at 11:45, just before lunch period."

Darrin nods his head in agreement and departs the classroom; he soon returns from the office with a late pass and joins the other students.

The techniques used here by the teacher come from Rogerian theory and writers such as Thomas Gordon in his book *T.E.T.: Teacher Effectiveness Training* and Clark Moustakas in *The Authentic Teacher: Sensitivity and Awareness in the Classroom*. To set the tone for understanding Rogerian Theory, let's listen to the words of Moustakas:

> *When the adult [the teacher] loses sight of the child [the student] as a human being, when the adult fails to gather in the child's presence as a person, there is no reality between them, there is no relationship. There is no mutuality.*
>
> *And this is what happens in many situations [such as the Darrin incident] where potential growth and love exist between persons. The persons are lost. The discrepancy or issue [disrespect] becomes all that matters. And the loudest voice, the strongest figure, the person in authority carries out his office of command. Gradually the child [student] is forced into a process of desensitization where feelings and senses are muffled and subdued until eventually he is no longer aware that he is not experiencing from within. When people [teachers] reject, humiliate, hurt, belittle, control, dominate, and brutalize others [students], without any awareness of what they are doing, when there is no concern on the part of others [students] for what is being done to them, there is extreme danger that man will cease to be man, that whatever is distinctly human will be impaired or so significantly reduced that the life of man [teacher] will be as automatic as a self-moving machine and as mechanical as counting beads on an abacus.[1]*

ROGERIAN THEORY

Such popular and practical discipline books as Gordon's *T.E.T.* and Moustakas's *Authentic Teacher* are based on a school of thought first conceptualized and popularized by Carl R. Rogers in his books *Client-Centered Therapy, On Becoming a Person,* and *Freedom to Learn*. Rogers's therapeutic concepts, focused on self-concept and emotional development, marked a departure from the highly deterministic Freudian therapy based on innate inner aggressive drives.

Although the belief in the inner person remained, Rogers did not accept the position that the child is inherently ruled by destructive forces. Instead, he aligned with A. H. Maslow's belief that the child is born "prior to good and evil."[2] The child does have an inherent capacity, but it is a capacity for being rational and capable. Rogers believes that given empathetic understanding, warmth, and openness, one will choose what is best for oneself and will become a fully functioning person, constructive and trustworthy. The child is seen as "exquisitely rational," and it is believed that problems arise from the conflict that occurs when the inherent rationality is stifled. It is felt that this "stifling" happens in the classroom when teachers set about to order, direct, or force a student to behave according to the teacher's will.

The underlying assumption of Rogerian theory is that each person is unique and thus it is impossible for one person to make appropriate decisions for another. Any two people in a given situation will experience that situation in different ways. This is because people experience and interpret stimuli based on prior encounters, goals, expectations, and attitudes. Each person will "screen" the event according to who he or she is as a person, and this screening, to a great extent, occurs at the unconscious level. Life, then, according to Rogerian theory, is a process of continually changing situations and continually changing problems in which one must make a multitude of decisions based on individual experiences and perceptions. Many of these factors about making personal decisions are hidden from one's consciousness. Therefore, within the Rogerian theoretical framework, the process or goal for the individual experiencing problems is consciously to process his or her difficulties through the vehicle of language. By expressing feelings and concerns, an individual can make decisions that will result in the most appropriate rational solution.

Let's return to our earlier example of Ms. Walker and Darrin's statement, "Lay off, bitch. I ain't going to no detention or the office. You think I give a shit about any of y'all?" This statement and Darrin's repeated lateness are seen by Rogerians as just the tip of the iceberg. Underneath these aggressive words and behavior is a collection of fears, disappointments, and deeply angry feelings of not belonging or being rejected. "You think I give a shit about any of y'all?" might be more appropriately interpreted as a message to the teacher and anyone willing to listen that "I am deeply unhappy, isolated, and cut off from others, and I don't expect anyone to concern themselves with me!"

A teacher such as Ms. Walker, if she is using this Rogerian Model, would hear a wider message and would not fall into the trap of denying the child's underlying message by lecturing or responding with similar hostility. This model requires a very secure teacher who isn't frightened by such hostility, especially if it is expressed in front of an entire class of onlooking students.

The teacher, as we saw, took an empathic, nonjudgmental position. She simply mirrored the student's statement, behavior, and feelings ("You are obviously having a very bad morning and are having some difficulty"), attempted to encourage the child to "talk out" his concerns, offered to share her power (Method #3: No-Lose Problem Solving), and offered her listening and empathetic help. Rogerian teachers like Ms. Walker believe that, given a supportive nonjudgmental climate, the student will be able to express his problem(s) and feeling(s) and then suggest his own solutions. Whether the solutions are successful is not as important as the student being able to trust his own capacities to eventually master his problems.

This theory holds that faith in the student's own problem-solving capacity relates directly to the idea of "self-concept." Self-concept can be defined as a set of ideas and feelings that one holds about oneself as a person. You may see yourself as basically competent or incompetent in meeting life's continual challenges. It is only through the opportunity to wrestle with your own daily problems that you become master of your own destiny. In the Darrin example, the student can only enhance his self-concept by realizing that he can define his own problems and make attempts to solve them. If the teacher had lectured or advised him, the opposite effect might have occurred, and the student's self-concept would have been weakened in the process.

Based on this theoretical position, the teacher's role is primarily one of being a supportive, noncritical facilitator with a total commitment to the rational ability of a child to identify and solve his or her own unique problems. With this understanding, we may now turn to the techniques of Gordon and observe how he has operationalized Rogerian theory into specific teacher practices, as described in *T.E.T.: Teacher Effectiveness Training.* We will follow Gordon's procedures, using the Teacher Behavior Continuum (TBC) as our organizer in comparing the central elements or behaviors. Keep in mind that these behaviors are (1) silently looking, (2) naming statements, (3) questions, (4) directive statements, (5) reinforcement, (6) modeling, and (7) physical intervention and isolation. The ranked order of these behaviors suggests an increasing use of power by the teacher and a decrease on the part of the student. It should be obvious that, given Gordon's theoretical framework, he will stress those behaviors (1, 2, and 3) that give the most control to the child. With this in mind, let us begin.

T.E.T. AND THE TEACHER BEHAVIOR CONTINUUM

Looking

Central to the T.E.T. model is the expression of open and authentic communication between teacher and student. By definition, the word *communication* suggests an exchange of ideas between people. Obviously, there is a difference between talking and hearing versus communicating. Communicating is a process whereby each party understands what the other has to say and formulates responsive messages in a way to create further understanding. Of course, all teachers will "hear" what a child says. The child who screams an obscenity is clearly heard, but, according to Gordon, the child is often not understood in terms of the meaning of the "real" message and the impact of strong feelings being expressed. Stress is placed on the teacher to use the least control possible in the process of understanding a student. That minimal control is described as *silently looking* as the teacher *critically listens* to what a student is trying to say.

The first step on the Teacher Behavior Continuum is for the teacher simply to look at a misbehaving child. The look should be one that says, "I see what you are doing. I have trust in your ability to correct yourself. If you need my help, I am here." The student who cannot achieve his or her own immediate solution to the problem should then be encouraged to verbalize the issue. The teacher gives the student much time and encouragement to express what is troubling him or her, with the teacher nodding or using various gestures to encourage the child to continue.

STUDENT: "Janie is a stuck-up snob. She wouldn't go to the game with us!"

TEACHER: "Uh-huh." (Teacher nods while looking at the child.)

Gordon, in *T.E.T.: Teacher Effectiveness Training,* stated, "Saying nothing actually communicates acceptance. Silence—critical listening—is a powerful nonverbal message that can make a student feel genuinely accepted and encourages him to share more and more with you. A student cannot talk to you about what is bothering him if you are doing the talking."[3]

Questioning (Skipping Naming Statements Temporarily)

At times, when students are talking to teachers they seem to have trouble beginning, or, once started, they pause in the middle of what they are saying and cannot appear to get started again. In these instances, it may be necessary to use what Gordon call "door openers or reopeners." Examples would be such questions as "I'm interested, would you like to talk more about that?" or "Would you like to go on?" Such door openers (questions) are of a nonevaluative nature. They encourage the student to explore his or her feelings more fully.

TEACHER: "Hello, Tommy. I think I see a worried look on your face. Would you like to talk about it?" (This is the use of *questioning* as a door opener.)

STUDENT: "Someone stole my pencil. This has happened three times this week!"

TEACHER: "Uh-huh." (Nods while silently looking: *critical listening.*)

Using these supportive questions as door openers is quite different from using those kinds of questions that Gordon calls "roadblocks to communication." The latter are questions that probe, cross-examine, or accuse and are of little help to a student trying to find his or her own solutions. For example, "How much time did you spend on this project?" or "Did you ask permission before you did that?" are questions that impose the teacher's will and dominance. These are really camouflaged directive statements that say, "You are wrong. You need me to tell you what to do." Gordon is adamantly opposed to the use of questions or directive commands that diminish the student's capacity to rationally alter his or her own behavior. On the other hand, making naming statements is seen as a more active way of helping the student.

Naming Statements

The question now arises as to exactly how to use language to communicate with students most effectively. The most important use of language by the teacher within the T.E.T. model is called *active listening.* To employ silence, to acknowledge responses by silently looking, or to use door openers as questions have a positive but limited use and, in general, reflect passive behavior on the teacher's part. Effective communication between the teacher and student involves a much more active response by the teacher through active listening and the use of *naming statements* or nondirective statements. The teacher can actively communicate to the student that he or she is being understood by summarizing or mirroring the student's feelings or problems, as the teacher comprehends them.

It may be helpful to look more closely to see how true communication really works, or, in short, "why people talk." Gordon says that people talk when they have an internal need, either physical or emotional, and that people encode need in the form of spoken language so that others can understand them. Unfortunately, many needs, especially those related to feelings, are difficult to express in language.

The philosophical orientation of these Rogerian techniques views the child as an inherently good and rational being. If his behavior is destructive, the Rogerian explanation would be that the child is having some form of inner turmoil, which we call flooding, and this inner tension comes out as "acting out" behavior. Thus the student, under the Rogerian position, should never be viewed simply as being naughty. The teacher's helping role is to establish a nonjudgmental supportive relationship with the child and encourage the child to communicate these feelings in words, by using the teacher as a sounding board.

Communication is a very difficult process among adults, but it can be even more difficult for students, with their limited intellectual knowledge and verbal ability. Gordon suggests that we constantly maintain one of two internal states: we are at either equilibrium or disequilibrium. A child who is full and not hungry, and who is playing happily, is at equilibrium. An hour or two later the child begins to tire and gets inner messages that he is beginning to get hungry, indicating a growing disequilibrium. When this hunger is very strong, the child attempts to communicate this inner need to his mother. As seen below, the first and surface communication, when heard by the mother, is not always what the child really means.

CHILD (in a whining, demanding voice): "Mom, when is Dad going to get home from work?"

MOTHER: "Ann, you know that Dad always gets home at six o'clock."

The child has failed to communicate her real need, and the mother has failed to hear what was _really_ being said—thus poor communication. What the child really meant to say was, "Mom, I am very hungry, and I don't think I can wait until Dad gets home to eat." When the child has an inner need she must express it externally, and so she tries _verbally encoding_ that need to express her wants.

Now, let's replay the discussion, this time with the mother using _Active Listening:_

CHILD (in a whining, demanding voice): "Mom, when is Dad going to get home from work?"

MOTHER: "At six o'clock, but you would like Dad to get home sooner?" _(Active Listening)_

CHILD: "Ah, he'll be late again!"

MOTHER: "You are worried that he might not be on time today." _(Active Listening)_

CHILD: "I don't think I can wait for Dad if he's going to be late."

MOTHER: (Looks at child, nods, and smiles—_Acknowledgments._)

CHILD: "I'm starving!"

MOTHER: "You are very hungry, and you'd like to eat now and not wait for Dad because he might be late?" _(Active Listening)_

CHILD: "Yeah. A-a-ah…"

MOTHER: "Would you like to tell me more?" _(Door Openers)_

CHILD: "Yeah, while I was waiting for the bus it rained and I forgot to bring my lunch into the shelter. It got wet and was ruined, and all I had to eat for lunch was a banana."

MOTHER: "Oh, that *does* make a difference. The rule is that we wait for Dad so we can all eat dinner together, but because you missed out on lunch today why don't you have a glass of milk and two oatmeal cookies to tide you over."

Active Listening is a technique for improving communication between child and teacher whereby the child is encouraged to repeatedly "talk out" a problem, and the adult's role is to attempt to mirror back to the child the feelings we think we are hearing from the child. (See Figure 8.1.) If we take first or surface communication statements from the child as fact, especially when the child is flooded, we may not hear what the child is really attempting to communicate. The adult's nonverbal behavior of nodding the head is called *acknowledgment*, and questions like, "Would you like to tell me more?" are called *door openers* and simply serve to encourage the child to continue to talk and attempt to communicate.

Let us return to our opening vignette, where Darrin asked his teacher, "You think I give a shit about any of y'all?" We must realize that it will only be after much active listening that we may discover Darrin's real feelings and the problems he is facing. The student's first attempt to **encode** his feelings by using this hostile verbal aggression is considered a **unique coding** and reveals only the surface of the deeper problems he is facing. We must not take such "uniquely coded" statements at face value, but permit the student to continue expressing through language while we mirror with **active listening** (naming) our understanding of what the child is attempting to really say. Figure 8.2 provides examples of feeling words that the teacher may use when doing **active listening** and mirroring the student's feelings.

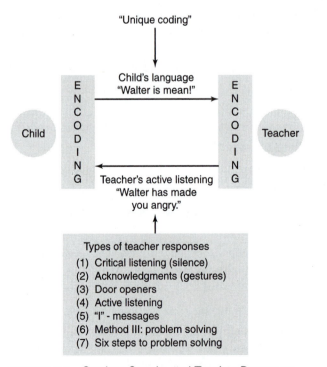

FIGURE 8.1 Student Speaks and Teacher Response

Negative Feelings		Positive Feelings	
angry	sad	appreciate	happy
confused	scared	better	joyful
disappointed	sorry	cheerful	like
frightened	unfair	enjoy	love
hate	unhappy	excited	pleased
hurt	want to get even	glad	proud
left out	want to give up	good	successful
mad	worried	great	wonderful

FIGURE 8.2   Examples of Feeling Words

Ms. Walker enters her empty classroom at 11:45 and finds Darrin, as they had agreed, seated at his desk, with his lunch and soda unopened before him.

MS. WALKER: "Oh, Darrin, I see that you have brought your lunch—well, I have mine too." She seats herself knee-to-knee (**knee-to-knee conferencing**) before the boy. "Feel free to eat your lunch. I'm going to eat mine as we talk. I'm stuck with a peanut butter and jelly sandwich today. What do you have?"

DARRIN: "Meat, I guess … baloney."

MS. WALKER: "Well, I think that's better than mine. Gee, were you angry this morning. We need to talk about what is going on!"

DARRIN: (Drops eyes.)

MS. WALKER: (Three very long minutes pass with total silence—**critical listening.**) "Would you like to tell me what is happening with you these days?" (**Door opener**)

DARRIN: "I hate this f——n' school."

MS. WALKER: (Silence as she munches on her sandwich—**critical listening**)

DARRIN: "Everybody's on my case!"

MS. WALKER: "You feel that everyone is telling you what to do." (**Active listening**)

DARRIN: "Yeah, I get crap from my mom and crap at school!"

TEACHER: (Silence—**critical listening;** makes eye contact with Darrin and nods her head—**acknowledgment.**)

DARRIN: "Christ, the crap my mother makes me do!"

TEACHER: "Your mother is requiring you to do things that you dislike." (**Active listening**)

DARRIN: "Shit, Jimmy isn't my kid, why do I have to watch him?"

TEACHER: "You are responsible for Jimmy and must take care of him." (**Active listening**)

DARRIN: "The guys are always bustin' my chops about that. Yeah, I never get to hang out."

TEACHER: "You are required to watch Jimmy, and your friends tease you about it."

DARRIN: "Yeah, and that goddamn bus."

TEACHER: (Silence—**critical listening**)

DARRIN: "This is the fourth freakin' time it's been late!" (Three minutes of silence) "Goddamn bus!"

TEACHER: "Would you like to tell me about that?" (**Door opener**)

DARRIN: "Well, I'm stuck with watching my little brother when my mother leaves. That damn day-care bus was late picking him up. Now I'm late and get detention after class. I ain't going to no detention, my mother will whip my ass."

TEACHER: (Nods—**acknowledgment**)

DARRIN: "My mother will whip my ass if I don't watch Josh."

TEACHER: "Let me see if I understand what you are telling me. You must watch Jimmy, and the day-care bus is late, which makes you late for school, and you also have to watch Josh or you will be in big trouble with your mother." (**Critical listening**)

DARRIN: "I can't stay in no detention. I have to get Josh, or the big kids will pick on him."

TEACHER: "Oh, I see. Staying after school for detention keeps you from picking up and watching Josh, and that will get you in trouble with your mother." (**Critical listening**)

In the preceding dialogue, we see the teacher helping the student express feelings that were "uniquely encoded" and unclear at first ("Damn bus!"), and through "critical and active listening" the teacher finally hears the student's central problem and the feelings that were deeply troublesome.

Now that the teacher has some understanding as to the problems of this student, what should the teacher do? Should the teacher call Darrin's mother, tell a school counselor or administrator, or tell Darrin to find a solution for his difficulties? Gordon would say "no." He would describe such a response as a "roadblock," called "advising, offering solutions, or suggestions." *T.E.T.* provides a helpful construct for the teacher to use in answering these questions and for defining what the teacher's response should be.

Who Owns the Problem?

The key to these issues in T.E.T. is: Who owns the problem—the teacher or the child? As shown in Figure 8.3, all behaviors of the student can be placed on a "window" and divided into three areas: (1) those behaviors that indicate the student is having a problem (i.e., other students will not pick him as a team member), (2) a no-problem behavior (i.e., a child works quietly at his desk), and (3) those behaviors by the student that have a direct and concrete effect on the teacher, causing the teacher to "own" the problem (i.e., student interrupts while another child is being helped).

When the problem belongs to the student (I can't find my pencil" or "Mrs. Jones won't let me do so-and-so"), the role of the teacher is to use critical listening (silently looking) and door openers (questions), and to periodically mirror the child's concerns or messages with active listening (naming statements). If the problem is owned by the teacher, in that it has a concrete effect on the teacher, then she may introduce an "I"-message. This is a matter-of-fact naming statement containing the word *I* that expresses to the student the description of the student's behavior and how the teacher feels about these actions; for

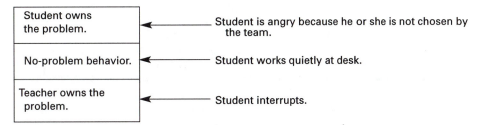

FIGURE 8.3 Problem Ownership

example, "When gym equipment is left in the aisle, I might trip, and I'm afraid I might fall and be hurt." The "I"-message must contain the sequence of *behavior, effect, feeling*. Once an "I"-message is expressed and the student has heard how her behavior is interfering with the teacher's needs, the teacher returns to critical listening (silently looking), active listening (naming statements), and, if need be, door openers (questions). The following dialogue provides examples of each of these behaviors.

TEACHER: "Carol, when lunch trash is left on the table instead of being thrown away, I must pick it up before the next lunch group can be seated. I find this frustrating!" *("I"-message)*

STUDENT: "I'm always getting picked on! Everyone *always* picks on me!"

TEACHER: "You feel that everyone is making unfair demands on you." *(active listening, naming statement)*

STUDENT: "Well, everyone picks on me."

TEACHER: "Uh-huh." *(critical listening, naming listening)*

STUDENT: (Silence)

TEACHER: "Would you like to tell me more?" *(door opener, question)*

STUDENT: "Well, Mrs. Jones makes me pass out the papers and lots of other donkey jobs for her, and Mrs. Anderson made me clean out the animal cages in the biology lab for the last two weeks."

TEACHER: "You feel that it is unfair for you to be given extra jobs by teachers, and therefore you do not need to clean up after yourself at lunchtime." *(active listening, naming statement)*

STUDENT: "Well, it is unfair, but I guess I could throw my lunch trash away. Gee, I didn't know it was such a problem for you. But I'm going to tell Mrs. Anderson, 'No more hamster cages for me!'"

The preceding dialogue reveals a problem clearly owned by the teacher. The student's *behavior* (leaving behind lunch trash) had a concrete effect on the teacher (the teacher had to pick it up and it interfered with her ability to seat other children), and in turn the teacher described her feelings (frustrated). We can also see that the teacher did not use any forms of power-related behavior to manipulate the outcome. After delivering an "I"-message, the teacher returned the problem to the student, and the teacher maintained a nonjudgmental stance (see Figures 8.4 and 8.5).

Poor Example: *"I want you to get your feet off that table now!"*

This is a "you" message implying guilt. It contains a poor definition of the improper behavior, no example of the effect, and a lack of expression of the teacher's feelings.

Good Example: *"When feet are put on the table* (behavior), *they scratch and destroy the table surface, and I am responsible for protecting school property. I get in trouble with my administrators* (effect), *and I therefore am fearful and annoyed* (feeling)."

Poor Example: *"When students run in the hall* (behavior), *I don't like it!"*

The message starts effectively with a good statement of behavior, but no effect is given, and "I don't like it" is a value judgment rather than an expression of the teacher's feelings.

Good Example: *"When students run in the hall* (behavior), *they may fall and get injured or injure others, and I am responsible for keeping students safe* (effect), *and that makes me frightened* (feeling)."

Good Examples of "I"-Messages

"When trash paper is left on the floor (behavior), *I am responsible for cleaning up my class-room for the next teacher before I leave. It causes me lots of extra work and makes me late for my next class* (effect), *and I get annoyed and exhausted* (feeling)."

More Examples of Good "I"-Messages

"When tables are not cleaned after lunch (behavior), *it will make these tables unusable for the next group of students* (effect). *I am afraid* (feelings) *that the extra cleaning will slow down the cafeteria schedule and everyone will not have time to eat."*

"When I am told to 'shut up' when I am carrying on a discussion with the class (behavior), *I am not able to explain the lab rules to everyone* (effect), *and I am fearful* (feelings) *that someone will get hurt using the acids and chemistry equipment."*

"When students lean out the classroom windows (behavior), *I am afraid* (feeling) *that they will fall out and get seriously injured* (effect)."

"When people scream indoors (behavior), *it hurts my ears* (effect) *and I get angry* (feelings)."

"When people write or scribble in our good school books (behavior) *it destroys them* (effect). *I am responsible for their care, and I am afraid* (feeling) *we soon will have no books to share or read."*

"When objects are thrown (behavior), *they may hit people's eyes and hurt them* (effect), *and I am the teacher who must keep people safe, and that scares* (feeling) *me."*

"When students are late to class (behavior), *I need to repeat my first instructions, which wastes of lot of classroom time* (effect), *and that exhausts and frustrates* (feeling) *me."*

FIGURE 8.4   Examples of Poor and Good "I"-Messages

There are other behaviors engaged in by students about which a teacher might hold very strong feelings. However, when these are investigated closely, it may be found that they do not have a concrete effect on the teacher, in which case an "I"-message would have little impact. Students' hairstyles, weird clothing, hand-holding in the halls, poor posture, and the choosing of friends all may evoke strong feelings in a teacher, but are simply matters of personal taste. Gordon has warned against trying to change students to conform to a teacher's values by "I"-messages or "roadblocks."

Notice that in our vignette Darrin had two problems—he wanted to "hang out" with his friends, and he was late for school—but the teacher did not solve the problems for him. Darrin owned these problems, and the teacher facilitated his process of thinking through and then acting on the problems. We as teachers are solidly motivated to

Student's ACTION	Teacher's "I"-MESSAGE
Joe starts to talk to Ryan while the teacher is lecturing. He talks loud enough that he starts to disturb everyone listening to the story.	"When students talk while I am lecturing (behavior), I have a hard time speaking so everyone can hear (effect), and that makes me frustrated (feeling)."
Katy, after getting up from her lab table, leaves her equipment scattered across the table while she returns to her seat and readies herself to depart.	"When students leave equipment out on the lab tables (behavior), I am fearful (feeling) that others will knock them over them and get hurt and I am responsible for keeping equipment and students safe (effect)."
When the school bell rings, Caroline runs at full speed through the door and down the stairs.	"When students run down the stairs (behavior), I am fearful (feeling) that people will fall and get injured (effect), and my job is to keep people safe."
Mary appears in front of the teacher and begins speaking so hysterically that the teacher cannot understand her.	"When students shout (behavior), I can't understand what is being said (effect), and I am disappointed (feeling) that I can't help."
Teacher is talking to a parent when a student interrupts her and starts talking.	"It makes it hard for me (feeling) to understand two people who are talking to me at the same time (behavior), and I become confused (effect)."
A child deliberately pushes a second student while lining up at the water fountain.	"When students are pushed (behavior), it is dangerous (effect), and that frightens me (feeling) because I need to keep people safe."
Two children fight over a book, pulling it back and forth.	"When books are pulled (behavior), I am fearful (feeling) that they will get damaged and destroyed and we will not have them anymore (effect)."

FIGURE 8.5 "I"-Messages

nurture and help children. We may wish to be a Super-teacher and see our role as the person who solves all problems in the classroom. But if we do that, we rob the children of the real experience of clashing and interacting with others—an essential process that enables them to acquire the skills necessary to solve their own problems and become autonomous. In dealing with problems that involve students, it is important to determine whether it is the student or the teacher who owns the problem. These questions will help:

1. Does the student's action or problem take away the teacher's or classmates' rights? (The student takes three handouts while others have had only one or did not get one, and by his actions he is moving to take a fourth. This requires teacher intervention.)

2. Is the safety of materials, classmates, the teacher, or the student himself involved? (In industrial arts class the student uses the band saw without wearing a face mask. This requires teacher intervention.)

3. Is the student too young and thus incapable of "owning" or solving this problem? (The student wishes to move a friend's car on the school parking lot, but does not have a driver's license. This requires teacher intervention.)

If the answer to any of these questions is yes, then the teacher owns the problem and must respond. Response techniques will be "I"-messages, active listening, door openers, acknowledgments, and possibly the Six Steps to Problem Solving (discussed later).

The concept of problem ownership clearly tells teachers to inhibit their "rescuer" tendencies.

STUDENT: "Mr. Johnson, my pencil is missing!"

TEACHER: "What are you going to do to get another?" **(Door opener)**

In reality, 80 to 90 percent of all problems faced by students in the classroom belong to them. Our guidelines for problem ownership suggest that we must not allow our need to help or our fear of chaos to prompt us to move too quickly and without thinking, thus robbing children of the experience of solving their own problems.

Emotions, Anger, and Feelings

Everyone who has driven a car has experienced another driver cutting in front of them too quickly or having a similar near-accident because of another driver's poor driving actions. We quickly respond by swerving out of the way, and then perhaps sounding our car horn, visually glaring, shouting, or even swearing at the other driver. For the next 10 minutes we remain very angry before gradually calming down. Our actions—sounding the horn, glaring, shouting, even swearing at the other driver—were for the purposes of making the other person feel guilty for the careless behavior and clearly sending a message of anger—"you dummy."

In sending an "I"-message to students that expresses anger, we will produce guilt in students and they will hear this message as a "You"-message. Anger is almost always expressed and directed at another person and involves guilt.

But there are two forms of feelings: *primary feelings* and *secondary feelings*. Looking at the dangerous driver example: We may really see that our first or primary feeling was fear, arising from the genuine risk of an accident. Then once the incident has passed and we are relieved to see that we have avoided the accident, we now become angry. We want to show our secondary feeling of anger to the "dummy" as a way of punishing that driver. In dealing with students, then, Gordon[4] requires us to first determine our primary feelings and express the "I"-message with the use of a primary feeling, rather than expressing it with anger—a secondary feeling—in order to minimize the guilt that the student will feel.

Recall our opening vignette: "Darrin stops and listens to her, with his head dropped and eyes looking at the floor. He turns and yells, 'Lay off, bitch. I ain't going to no detention or the office. You think I give a shit about any of y'all?' He takes his seat and slouches deep into it."

Much like the close call while driving, we may feel—and rather quickly—the secondary feelings of anger at Darrin, but there was a primary feeling of embarrassment or fear that preceded the feelings of anger. It is this primary feeling that needs to be delivered in an "I"-message, rather than anger. "When I hear such harsh fighting names directed at me (behavior), I am embarrassed and fearful (feelings) that this will hurt my relationship with the person and hurt my authority and respect with the students in my class (effect)." (See Figure 8.2 for examples of feeling words that may indicate primary feelings.)

Commands as Directive Statements

I can imagine some readers shaking their heads in amazement and asking, "You mean to say that this fellow Gordon says for me never to tell students what to do?" Actually, Gordon does believe that there are times when teachers must use very strong commands. When commands are used correctly, they are described by Gordon as strong "influencing attempts" by the teacher. If a student is in some immediate danger, naturally it is appropriate for the teacher to give a command: "Turn down the flame quickly. It is in danger of exploding!" or "Don't jump now—someone is climbing underneath!" or "Watch your head!" Such "influencing attempts" are generally acceptable to students as a result. The difficulty occurs when teachers overuse commands. Then, in reaction, students begin to resist, and the teacher and students find themselves in conflict. When this occurs, such commands again become roadblocks, and the teacher will need to return to active listening to reestablish the relationship. Gordon cited the following examples of commands that should be avoided by teachers:

1. Ordering, commanding, directing. *Example:* "You, stop playing with your pencil and finish that test right now."

2. Warning, threatening. *Example:* "You had better straighten up, young man, if you want to pass this course."

3. Moralizing, preaching, giving "shoulds" and "oughts." *Example:* "You know what happens when you hang around with 'that gang'—you get into trouble. You ought to choose your friends more wisely."

4. Advising, offering solutions or suggestions. *Example:* "What you need to do is to make a list and then put yourself on a time schedule to get these things done on time."

5. Teaching, lecturing, giving logical arguments. *Example:* "Let's look at what is going to happen. If you do not bring your gym clothing, you will not be able to take PE and you will fail that class."

Each of the preceding roadblocks presents a teacher's solution to a student's problem. The next five communicate judgments, evaluations, and, at times, put-downs.

6. Judging, criticizing, disagreeing, blaming. *Example:* "You're just not the student that your sister was."

7. Name-calling, stereotyping, labeling. *Example:* "You're always acting like the class clown. When are you going to grow up?"

8. Interpreting, analyzing, diagnosing, *Example:* "You're always trying to find the easiest way to get around your homework."

9. Praising, agreeing, giving positive evaluation. *Example:* "You are the best student I have in this class. I'm sure you will want to be the chairperson of this committee."

10. Reassuring, sympathizing, consoling, supporting. *Example:* "I also found that course difficult when I first tried it, but once you get into it you'll find it easier."[5]

Reinforcement

The resolution of conflict within *T.E.T.* models relates to Gordon's definition of two types of authority and how the teacher uses his or her power with students. Type I authority is desirable and is based on a person's expertise, knowledge, and experience. An individual obtains the power inherent in Type I authority by being judged as one who is wise and expert enough to be listened to by others and is an individual sought after for advice. Type II authority is undesirable. It is aligned with a power-based position that enables a teacher to (1) dispense certain benefits that students need or want (rewards or positive reinforcement) or (2) inflict discomfort or painless punishment on students (negative reinforcement). In previous chapters that have endorsed the Rules-Consequences techniques, reinforcement and rewards have been used as central tools in getting students to change. The Relationship-Listening writers such as Gordon and Bailey (2000) dramatically disagree with such an approach. Gordon sees the use of both positive and negative reinforcements as a manipulation and misuse of power by a teacher, which will eventually produce defensive reaction mechanisms in students to deal with such authoritarian power. Gordon would suggest that if we see the following behavior in our students, we may need to investigate our use of power. These following behaviors may provoke the use of Type II authority:

- Rebelling, resisting, defying
- Retaliating
- Lying, sneaking, hiding feelings
- Blaming others, tattling
- Cheating, copying, plagiarizing
- Bossing, bullying, pushing others around
- Needing to win, hating to lose
- Organizing, forming alliances
- Submitting, complying, buckling under
- Apple polishing
- Conforming, taking no risks, trying nothing new
- Withdrawing, dropping out, fantasizing, regressing[6]

Finally, even the teacher who has Type I authority and uses looking, naming, door openers, and "I"-messages will still run into conflict with an individual student. The occasions will be less frequent but still inevitable. The T.E.T. model provides a resolution for such conflict. Gordon has defined *conflict* as a collision occurring between teacher and student where their *behaviors* interfere with each other's attainment of their own needs, and thus *both parties own the problem.* For example:

TEACHER (returns to the classroom to discover a student taking a pencil from the teacher's desk): "When pencils are taken from my desk, I cannot find one to do my work, and I must pay to purchase new ones. This has happened a number of times, and I find it annoying." (**"I"-message**)

STUDENT: "Well, each time I return from music class, I find someone has taken my pencil. This has happened three weeks in a row."

In this example, both teacher and student own the problem, and they find themselves in conflict. Gordon suggests that such problems are usually resolved by using two methods that result in either the teacher or the student winning. In Method I, the teacher wins by using authority and power, and the student loses.

TEACHER: "Well, you're just going to have to learn that you cannot be permitted to steal from the teacher's desk. For the remainder of this week, you will not be permitted to go to recess (or the pep rally)." (Judging, criticizing, blaming, and punishing are creating an obstacle to the student's rational capacity to solve his or her problems.)

We can restate the dialogue to show Method II, where the student wins and the teacher loses.

TEACHER: "Someone has taken your pencil on a number of occasions" **(active listening).**

STUDENT: "Yes, and if you had not left class to go to the teacher's lounge, you would have been here to prevent someone from taking my pencil. My father is really angry, and he said if I have one more thing stolen from my desk he is going to come to see the principal."

TEACHER: "Well, uh, I don't ever want you to take things from my desk again."

Here the student wins when the teacher gives up or ignores the student's actions. These win–lose methods both centered on a "power struggle" between teacher and student, and in each case the loser goes away feeling angry and resentful. Many teachers unknowingly use one of these methods. Some teachers use both, which is even more destructive, as the teacher swings from an authoritarian position to one of being permissive. Gordon proposes an alternative solution called Method III, where the conflict is resolved without the teacher or student using or losing power.

TEACHER: "Someone has taken your pencil." **(Naming: active listening)**

STUDENT: "Well, I probably shouldn't have taken yours, but I really need a pencil for the test next period—and someone keeps stealing mine."

TEACHER: "Can you think of how we may solve this problem for now so we will both have our pencils and both feel OK about it?"

STUDENT: "Well, it only happens on Tuesday when I go to music class. I could take my pencil with me, but I don't use pencils in music class, and I really don't want to carry it around."

TEACHER: "Taking your pencil to music class does not seem to be the solution." **(Naming: active listening)**

STUDENT: "Yeah, I was wondering if I could put my pencil somewhere else in the classroom on Tuesdays when I go to music—somewhere where it will be safe. And I'm going to bring this problem to our class meeting to see if we can get people to stop taking my pencil, or see if others are having this problem."

TEACHER: "It sounds like you have begun to solve your problem." **(Naming: active listening)**

STUDENT: "Could I put it in your desk?"

We can see that Method III—"no lose"—is a conflict-solving process in which the teacher actively listens and uses "I"-messages until he or she fully hears what the child's problems and needs are. Then student and teacher "put their heads together" until a solution can be found that is acceptable to both. Method III creates a "no-lose" result, and no power struggle is involved. Either the student or the teacher can suggest the solution, but the final agreement must be acceptable to both members involved in the conflict.

In our opening vignette, we saw Ms. Walker use these three methods of problem solving with Darrin. *"There are a number of ways we can handle this. One, I can call the assistant principal, Mr. Mack, and he will remove you from my classroom, which will only result in even more problems for you. (**Method #1: Teacher Wins**) Or, two, I can just ignore this name-calling and behavior (**Method #2: Student Wins**), but that is unacceptable to me as a teacher. There is a third way that we can handle this difficulty. If we can talk this out we might be able to find a 'no-lose' solution where you don't get into more trouble, and I can get the respect that I need as a teacher."* (**Method #3: No-Lose Problem Solving**)

Explaining these three methods to Darrin is not a threat, but simply a reality explanation to give Darrin a perspective on the use of power and an invitation by Ms. Walker to share her power and enter into an authentic relationship of shared problem solving.

Gordon also suggests that to create a **"no-lose"** climate, the teacher can introduce the **"scientific method,"** involving the following six steps as a process for **Method III** problem solving:

The Six Steps to Problem Solving

- *Step 1. Defining the Problem:* With the use of active listening and "I"-messages, the teacher helps a student or an entire class focus on a problem that affects them. During this defining step, the teacher should not attempt to provide a solution or make an evaluation, but instead simply attempts to get everyone involved, to clarify their needs.

- *Step 2. Generating Possible Solutions:* During this second step, the goal is to brainstorm many different solutions for the problem, again without attempting to make an evaluation of the ideas presented. Premature evaluation of solutions will limit creativity, and the teacher might need to use "I"-messages to keep the discussion guided toward brainstorming.

- *Steps 3 and 4. Evaluating and Deciding on Solution(s):* Having made a list of the possible solutions in Step 2, the teacher and student, or group, need to go over each solution to determine which ones can be agreed upon by all involved. If the teacher or student cannot live with the solution being considered, he or she can express this through "I"-messages. It is important that all solutions be considered fully. The teacher will have to use much active listening to achieve this end.

- *Steps 5 and 6. Implementing and Evaluating Solution(s):* During the final steps, a clear agreement must be established as to who will do what and when they will begin. At this time, those involved should set a time to meet again to reevaluate the results.[7]

In using the *Method III* ("no-lose") conflict-solving process, Gordon suggests that there are some problems outside the teacher's "area or spheres of freedom." He provides a chart that looks much like a target with a bull's-eye, and places the teacher in the center. This center area represents activities—such as classroom organization, rules, assignments, and so forth—that are within the teacher's "area of freedom." In turn, each circle moving out from the center is labeled "principal," "superintendent," "school board," and so on (see Figure 8.6). Each new circle represents a higher level of authority that can limit the teacher's freedom to make certain decisions. For example, the state law requires compul-

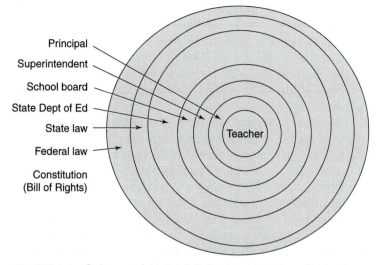

FIGURE 8.6 Spheres of Authority. Each outer sphere limits the teacher's authority to permit certain student behaviors or to make certain rules.

sory education for all students, so if by *Method III* the teacher and class were to decide that school attendance should be elective, there would be no way to implement their decision. This issue is simply outside their realm of decision making. In other words, there are certain social constraints within which both the student and teacher must live.

Although T.E.T. rejects the systematic use of *reinforcers,* which we will see described later, Gordon does acknowledge the need to create a classroom that is supportive of various activities. He suggests that the classroom environment can be modified in a systematic and creative way to alleviate student disruption. It can be changed to enrich the learning space and activities. In modifying the environment, time is another variable that relates to certain student problems. The effective teacher knows that at certain times in the day it is better to introduce difficult concepts to students, while at other times students tend to be irritable, which can make learning difficult. Time, within the T.E.T. model, is organized and viewed in three ways: (1) diffused time, (2) individual time, and (3) optimum time.[8]

When students are working closely with others in a busy classroom, they need to use a lot of energy for screening out stimuli in order to concentrate on such work as reading or working a math problem. *Diffused time* is the time period in which students work in close social contact. Students can effectively function only for a limited time in such a stimulating environment before becoming fatigued. It is necessary, therefore, for students to have some *individual time* when they can be by themselves for a short period (e.g., a "quiet corner" or an individual study carrel). The third classification, *optimum time,* is a period during the day when a student is able to meet individually with the teacher or a fellow student. If this time is not provided for, the child might attempt to fulfill his need for personal attention by being disruptive. This misbehavior forces the teacher to deal with the student and in turn gives the one-to-one contact that is desired. With these time classifications in mind, the teacher is encouraged to plan the day deliberately to create a balance of all three forms of time to maintain a teaching–learning environment that maximizes a "hassle-free" climate for child growth.

THREE SPHERES OF RELATIONSHIPS

Adults who are placed in charge of institutions (hospitals, prisons, or schools) or business sites (airline counter attendants or store check-out personnel) can begin to show *institutional behavior* when under day-in and day-out stress. They begin to deal with the public in a mechanical manner (inauthentic), showing curt speech, flat expressionless behavior, and an unthinking administration of the rules. They exhibit little consideration of the needs of the individuals with whom they are dealing and communicate no warmth. If we are not very careful, this same attitude begins to be seen in the behavior of teachers in the middle and high school classroom, especially if the classroom is imbalanced with regard to the number of students, insufficient supervisory teacher help (such as cafeteria or study hall supervisors), and lack of equipment and classroom materials.

The airline counter attendant is burned out because she has to manage too large a number of passengers. A snowstorm has grounded five flights, and she must deal with literally hundreds of angry passengers; the situation is obviously out of balance. Teachers working in an imbalanced classroom (too many kids, not enough materials) begin to become burned out and exhibit institutional behavior. Students spend many hours in school and classroom settings, and they must have a significant emotional investment by teachers. To go days, weeks, or months dealing with teachers or staff (including office personnel) who are "depressed" and "burned out" can have real and lasting destructive effects on students. Even a busy parent caring for a very small number of her own children, after a few busy weeks, suddenly stops and asks herself, "When is the last time I just stopped and totally listened to my child?" She feels guilty when she realizes that it has been many weeks or that she cannot remember how long it has been. We cannot permit this to occur in today's classrooms, and thus we use the *three spheres of relationship* construct to determine how we use our time with students.[9]

There are three basic spheres in a teacher's relationship with her students: Sphere 1, *one to one;* Sphere 2, *one to group;* and Sphere 3, *one to all* (see Figure 8.7). Viewed in reverse order, we see that the *one to all* sphere is a lecture format where the students must sit passively, refrain from communicating, and listen to the teacher speak. They feel no affection coming from the teacher and feel depersonalized—thus one teacher to all students.

One to One	A teacher interacts with one student (knee to knee).	The students receive near total emotional attention by the teacher and may dominate the conversation.
One to Group	A teacher interacts with a small group of four to eight students.	The student feels more emotional connection with the teacher and peers but needs to share conversation with peers.
One to All	A teacher speaks to or teaches the entire group of students (lecture style).	The student feels little emotional contact through spatial distance with the teacher and must generally inhibit the desire to talk rather than simply listen.

FIGURE 8.7 Spheres of Relationship

The *one to group* sphere occurs where the teacher is seated together with a group of six to eight students, and there is conversation among all members of the group. An example of this would be when the teacher is seated with students at lab or group work. There is much more warmth felt among this smaller group, but they do have to share the teacher's warmth and attention with their tablemates.

The *one to one* sphere is the time when the teacher and student are totally alone with one another, as with *knee-to-knee conferencing.* The student can receive total warmth and attention from the teacher and is free to dominate the conversation. Rogerian techniques, such as active listening, door openers, and acknowledgments, can be very helpful in communicating with the student during this *one to one* sphere of relationship, and to a lesser extent with a group of students in the *one to group* sphere.

We cannot leave it to chance and hope that every student will get sufficient personal time with a teacher. If we do this, the quiet and less assertive students will fall through the cracks. In staff meetings and during teacher planning time, we must use this three-sphere construct in planning the students' semester to assure that each student will have a relationship with the teacher in each of the three spheres. Some schools accomplish this through academic advisement groups. We can have a rich collection of materials and a well-designed classroom but still have teachers who are spending 100 percent of their time dealing with students in the third sphere of *one to all.* They are "lifeguarding," directing traffic and activities and dealing with the students in a custodial manner. In such a case, they are expressing cold, institutional behavior. We can test to see if this is occurring by asking, "What are the teachers doing during non-classroom time, such as in the cafeteria, during sporting events, etc.?" If no adult is seated with the students, then the teachers are merely playing "lifeguard."

Modeling

Although modeling is more systematically used in the Rules-Consequences models, such as behavior analysis, the *T.E.T.* model acknowledges its importance. For the teacher using *T.E.T.,* the rule of thumb is: Do it, don't talk about it. Practice, don't preach. In other words, the teacher, by her every action, is modeling to the students behaviors that reflect the teacher's values. Greater problems arise when the teacher attempts to "teach" students to behave in one way while she behaves in an opposite manner. The injunction to "do as I say, not as I do" produces a double standard that is easily recognized by students. Gordon would suggest that we as teachers look closely at our school and class rules and ask: Do the rules allow the adults to behave in one way while denying the same behavior to nonadults? Can teachers "paddle" students (corporal punishment), whereas acts of fighting among students are severely punished? Are teachers permitted to smoke in school, whereas students are not? Are students required to stand in the cafeteria line waiting, while teachers "cut" the line? A teacher's modeled behavior has a powerful effect on student behavior.

T.E.T. also addresses the modeling of behavior that a teacher uses while resolving a conflict with a student. Do we retreat to Method I power behavior that enables only the teacher to employ his authority to win? The Method III (no-lose) techniques of problem solving models the type of authentic behavior that helps relationships between the teacher and students. A youngster, having seen Method III techniques modeled by the teacher, may then begin to use similar techniques with adults and peers.

Action/Physical Intervention and Isolation

The use of physical intervention by the teacher, such as inhibiting a disruptive child by removing her from the classroom, is an extreme form of "roadblock" and would not be acceptable when using the *T.E.T.* methods—*except* when a student physically endangers himself or others.

SUMMARY

By using the Teacher Behavior Continuum (TBC) in Figure 8.8, we may now summarize and outline the "tools" that Gordon has provided to the teacher in his *T.E.T.: Teacher Effectiveness Training* model. This figure classifies (a) teacher actions that can be seen as the teacher interacts with the student and (b) guidelines, planning, or preparatory teacher actions. The teacher actions are those outward actions taken by the teacher that can clearly be observed: critical listening, acknowledgments, door openers, active listening, "I"-messages, Method III ("no-lose") problem solving, six steps to problem solving, and influencing statements. The guidelines, planning, or preparatory teacher actions are cause for teacher reflection on their daily actions, reorganizing classroom space, reorganizing time (diffused, individual, and optimum), and the three spheres of relationships.

Strengths and Limitations of the Model

The strength of this model is that it goes beyond the vague descriptions of being an accepting teacher to students and instead prescribes specific teacher actions and methods to attain that end. In this model students learn to solve their own problems, which they must own, thus developing responsibility. These practices are also seen as supporting the running of a democratic rule-setting classroom through appeal to the student's rational abilities, rather than as obedience to a controlling orientation. Techniques like "I"-messages, no-lose problem solving, and the prohibition of punishment are used in a manner that spare the students' feelings of guilt and related resentment. Well-meaning teachers whose motivation is to

Looking	Naming	Questioning	Commanding	Modeling	Reinforcment	Acting
1. Critical listening 2. Acknowledgment (gestures)	4. Active listening (mirroring feelings) "You're worried about...!" 5. "I"-messages (behavior-effect-feeling): "When I find tools left on the floor...!"	3. Door openers: "Do you want to talk more about it?"	8. Influencing "Watch your step!"	6. *Method III:* "no-lose" problem solving 7. Six Steps to Problem Solving 1. Defining 2. Generating 3. Evaluating 4. Deciding 5. Implementing 6. Evaluating	Reorganizing (a) Daily actions (b) space (c) time (diffused, individual, optimum) (d) Three spheres of relationship 1. One to one 2. One to group 3. One to all	

Numbers = *teacher actions*
Letters = *Guidelines, Planning, or Preparatory Teacher Actions*

FIGURE 8.8   Teacher Behavior Continuum (TBC): *T.E.T.*

work and help students are also given new guidance regarding "problem ownership."

T.E.T. can be seen by many teachers as a "powerless" model because of the lack of proposed punishments or consequences, but there are those who feel that this is the most powerful of all models because it is based on techniques used in therapy. The use of active listening and door openers encourages students to express deep structural emotional concern. But once the student verbalizes them, are teachers sufficiently trained to deal with such deep emotional concerns as physical and emotional abuse? In fact, sales personnel are taught these techniques for purposes of ingratiating themselves with customers. Those who are trained by Gordon are required to sign a consent statement stating that they will not abuse such power and methods.

Finally, secondary teachers dismiss *T.E.T.* as taking far too much time, but Gordon would counter with the position that misbehaving students are already eating up much of the teacher's time. Using T.E.T. early in the year and on a daily basis increases the likelihood that misbehaviors will not occur.

SUMMARY OF KEY VOCABULARY

acknowledgments	"I"-messages	reorganize space	Six Steps to Problem
active listening	influencing	reorganize time: diffused,	Solving
"areas of freedom"	Method III (no-lose)	individual, and	
critical listening	problem solving	optimal	
door openers	problem ownership		

CASE STUDIES

What actions would the *T.E.T.* teacher take using the five systems (limit setting, backup, incentive, encouragement, and management system) for the following discipline incidents?

1. **Andrew "Takes Over":** The students return to your classroom after being in the library-media center. The director of the center complains strongly about the poor behavior by your students, but gives you little details. Once the students are settled in their seats, you open a discussion with, "I want to talk to you about your behavior in the media center. (All heads drop.) Does anyone have anything to say?" Andrew is seated in the back of the room, slouched in his chair with his feet in the air propped over the top of the desk next to him. "Yea, I have something to say. Shut up! I hate that ugly bitch, and we aren't going back to the media center again." Most of the other class members respond, with "Yea! We're not going back there again!" Andrew seems to be respected and somewhat feared by the other students, and they often look to him for a signal as to whether they should comply with you as the teacher, and you often have the feeling that he can "take over" your class.

2. **Jake the Grenade:** Jake is like a walking grenade. One can never tell when he will explode. He passively seems to withdraw within himself, carrying a large "chip on his shoulder." If he is bumped or jostled accidentally by a fellow student, he will strike out. He has deliberately pulled a chair away from a fellow student just as she was seating herself and caused this student to fall to the floor, striking her head on the way down. He attempts to throw wet paper wads down the open blouse of one of the girls. He likes to draw monster-like cartoon characters on any surface that he can find, including the top of his desk. Today in chemistry class he got up and wandered about the room while the teacher was lecturing, and he opened all the gas jets at the chemistry tables at the back of the room—the smell of gas quickly filled the room.

3. **Linda the Passive:** Linda is a tall thin girl who is nearly always seen with her head down on her desk and her gangly long legs wrapped around the legs of her chair. She constantly has her first three fingers in her mouth, sucking them to the point that she has sucked off one fingernail. She

has a body odor that is noticeable to everyone and often looks as if she has not bathed for many days. It is November, and she has done no homework, answers no questions when called on, and when questioned by the teacher in one-to-one situations, grunts yes or no to all questions. Other children laugh at her, calling her a host of derogatory names. The parents do not have a phone number, and you have not been able to contact them for a conference. Other teachers have never seen the parents, but her address is near the railroad track where there are many trailers.

Limit-setting System

T.E.T. provides clear limit-setting actions (see Figure 8.8) for dealing with students like Mike: I-messages ("When I have my lectures disrupted by humorous actions, it breaks student concentration and focus, and I feel first frustrated and then angry.") followed by active listening, and possibly no-lose problem solving.

Backup System

Since isolation and similar forms of punishment are not used in T.E.T., there would be no backup system that would involve Mike.

Incentive System

(None found in or used in T.E.T.)

Encouragement System

The nonjudgmental, supportive communication process found in T.E.T. would be seen as the most authentic form of encouragement to students.

Management System

Gordon does spend much effort describing how certain student behaviors would be accepted in some contexts but not in others, for example, at a football games, but not in the classroom. The more and more controlling and teacher-centered the classroom is, the more certain students will break these formal rules. T.E.T. requires the teacher to reorganize the classroom space, materials, and equipment to grant the student maximum autonomy. Also, when classrooms are highly formal and teachers control the students, students like Mike feel that they are not getting attention in appropriate ways and thus "steal" the teacher attention through acting out. Gordon would suggest that the teacher reorganize his or her time to move out of "one to all" relationship with Mike and give him individual and optimum time. The change in relationship would now give Mike the special attention he wants, but in a productive manner.

Further Discussion

With Andrew's need to take over, how would T.E.T. approach him? How would Gordon view the motivation of Jake the grenade? According to Gordon, if Jake vented his anger in words, might his mean behavior stop? With Linda's passivity, getting her to open up (door openers) would be critical in using T.E.T. Is the teacher prepared to hear what is the root of Linda's helplessness?

NOTES

1. C. Moustakas, *The Authentic Teacher: Sensitivity and Awareness in the Classroom* (Cambridge, MA: Howard A. Doyle Publishing Company, 1966).
2. A. H. Maslow, *Towards a Psychology of Being,* 2nd ed. (New York: D. Van Nostrand, 1968), p. 3.
3. T. Gordon, *T.E.T.: Teacher Effectiveness Training* (New York: David McKay, 1974).
4. Ibid.
5. T. Gordon, *Teaching Children Self-Discipline: at Home and at School.* New York: Times Books, 1989), pp. 127–128.
6. Gordon, *T.E.T.*
7. Ibid.
8. Ibid.
9. Moustakas, *The Authentic Teacher.*

Books from Effectiveness Training International

Teaching Children Self-Discipline: At Home and at School by Dr. Thomas Gordon. Dr. Gordon's most recent book presents new strategies for parents and teachers to prevent self-destructive and antisocial behaviors of youth.

Parent Effectiveness Training (P.E.T.) by Dr. Thomas Gordon. Read the book that pioneered a new and more effective parenting method.

P.E.T. in Action by Dr. Thomas Gordon and Judy Gordon Sands. Parents tell how they transformed family life with P.E.T.

Effectiveness Training for Women (E.T.W.) by Linda Adams with Elinor Lenz. For women who want relationships that feel fair.

Be Your Best by Linda Adams with Elinor Lenz. Reach your personal goals and deepen all your relationships.

Leader Effectiveness Training (L.E.T.) by Dr. Thomas Gordon. One of the first books to identify the necessary skills to make "participative management" work.

Padres Eficaz y Tecnicamente Preparados by Dr. Thomas Gordon. The Spanish language version of the *P.E.T.* book.

DESIGNING ONE'S OWN MODEL OF DISCIPLINE

ALL THE techniques and methods in the seven models described in Sections I through III can now be compared with a matrix using the TBC as a power continuum. Each of the seven models is a *reactive* model; that is, it provides the teacher with practical actions for dealing with limit setting when a student breaks a rule, disrupts, or acts out. The teacher may choose to pick one of these models, believe in it totally, and implement it daily in his or her classroom. But teachers are often eclectic in their teaching actions, and the matrix in **Chapter 9** displaying all techniques permits teachers to build their own reactive discipline model that fits their philosophy for limit setting with students. The teacher is thus able to determine the degree of power needed to manage or deal with a specific classroom of students.

DISCIPLINE PREFERENCES: MATCHING PHILOSOPHY, VALUES, AND DISCIPLINE PRACTICE

Having gained an understanding of the various reactive discipline models and the techniques found in each of them with the use of the Teacher Behavior Continuum, you are now ready to consider what models or techniques you will accept and use. This decision will be based on a personality fit, possibly the grade level that the teacher will teach (see Figure 9.1, Teacher Preference by grade level), types of special needs of the children, the educational knowledge base, and, finally, experience regarding the development stages of teaching.

The developmental stages of teacher growth and changes may be viewed as four developmental levels (Katz, 1972): Level I: *Intuitive-Survival Teacher;* Level II, *Reflective-Confident Teacher;* Level III, *Prescriptive-Experienced Teacher;* and Level IV, *Analytical-Professional Teacher.*

LEVEL I: INTUITIVE-SURVIVAL TEACHER

The *intuitive-survival teacher* is the student in training to become a teacher or the beginning teacher who has only minimal experience. The immediate goal is to survive (Ryan, 1975) and to get through the day without major discipline disruptions to class activities. These teachers draw intuitively on the "child within themselves," disciplining others as they themselves were disciplined by their parents, teachers, or other significant adults. As they become more professional, they can move beyond this intuitive level of action to

Grade Level	Rules-Consequences	Confronting-Contracting	Relationship-Listening
Preschool/Kindergarten	2.5%	65%	32.5%
Elementary	18%	80%	12%
Middle and Secondary	87%	13%	0%

(The Beliefs about Discipline [BAD] inventory was taken by more than 1,000 teachers with these percentages of preferences demonstrated.)

FIGURE 9.1 Teacher Preference (BAD) by Grade Level

making professional decisions regarding the motivation of their students and ultimately what outcomes that they would like to obtain.

The intuitive-survival teacher will, when attempting to use discipline constructs, tend to identify strongly with one model or philosophy. All the techniques from many philosophies and models might be too overwhelming for the new teacher to master at this time in his or her development as a teacher. It would be advisable for this survival teacher to select one of the three approaches—Relationship-Listening, Confronting-Contracting, or Rules and Consequences *or* a *single* model—that best fits her personality or value system and learn to do it well. The *Beliefs about Discipline* (BAD) inventory at the end of Chapter 1 will help to clarify the teacher's beliefs for her. Readers may wish to stop and retake the inventory now that they have an understanding of the wide variety of techniques under each model and philosophy.

The Management System

For the beginning teacher, the establishment of good classroom management is critical and may make or break their internship, student teaching, or the first year of teaching. The management of the classroom furniture, equipment, the grouping of students, the ability to make transitions between activities, classroom rituals, and the making and teaching of classroom rules will be basic to preventing discipline problems from occurring and set the stage for dealing with problems when they do occur. Unknowingly we, in our misunderstanding of how to arrange classroom furniture, how to move students from place to place, or by simply not teaching or establishing rules, may be contributing to discipline difficulties. The beginning teacher may wish to read Chapters 14 and 15 on classroom management and clearly follow these principles to design an effectively managed classroom.

LEVEL II: REFLECTIVE-CONFIDENT TEACHER

The *reflective-confident teacher* is normally that teacher who has taught the same age youngster for a number of years. She has received feedback from her fellow teachers and administrators and the parents of those she teaches, as well as feedback from the students in her classroom, to tell her that she is respected, well liked, and viewed as an effective teacher. She has a repertoire of discipline techniques that she uses day-in and day-out, which enables her to have a smooth-working and well-disciplined classroom, and she is comfortable with her own values. The problem comes when she has a "time bomb" student, and no matter what discipline techniques work with other students, nothing seems to work with this one. Even though the teacher is *confident* about her own abilities as a successful teacher, she resents the amount of time this one child is "stealing" from other children. This difficult child can ruin an enjoyable year of teaching for the teacher.

The skill for this teacher is to be *reflective* about past discipline actions and realize that what she is doing is effective with most children, if not with the "walking time bomb" or the very difficult student. Simply doing more of the same with him or her will not help and can even make matters worse (Glasser, 1988). After reflection, this teacher must come to realize that she must expand her repertoire of techniques if she is to succeed with the difficult child. The *Reflective-Confident* teacher is ideally ready to make full use of the many models previously described.

Designing One's Own Discipline Model

Rarely do we find a practicing teacher who is a purist; that is, he or she uses only one model like *Assertive Discipline,* or only Glasser, and not other techniques suggested by these models. More likely we find the practicing teacher eclectically picking and choosing methods that best fit his or her personality and philosophy; the teacher in practice builds his or her own model. Figure 9.2 will provide help to enable the teacher to design this individual model, especially if that teacher is targeting the difficult-to-manage student. Firstly, looking closely at the matrix, one will see a display of all techniques from all models across the teacher behavior continuum (looking, naming, questioning, etc.), including a list of preplanning methods suggested by the models. This matrix has the benefit of viewing the techniques from the models with regard to the power and control inherent in their use. One can see that (1) an "I"-message of Thomas Gordon's model, placed under the Relationship-Listening techniques and the subheading of Naming as nondirective statement, is a much less cohesive action by the teacher than (2) the "what" questions of Glasser ("What are you doing? What is the rule?"), listed under Confronting-Contracting or (3) an assertive command by Canter, which is listed under Rules-Consequences.

The preschool, kindergarten, elementary school, or secondary school teacher faced with a student who is not attending, who is talking and disturbing others, and is disrupting your lesson, will need to determine whether to approach this student with an "I"-message, "what" questions, or an assertive command. That simple decision will be a projection of the teacher's need for power and control and the autonomy that he or she is willing to give to students when setting limits. Therefore, with this understanding and the matrix of all techniques from all models (Figure 9.2) the *reflective-confident teacher* might eclectically build his or her own model. How can this be done?

Step 1: Deselecting

Take the matrix in Figure 9.2, beginning at the bottom with "looking," and consider teacher techniques as you read across, making comparisons between techniques. You may wish to carry on a discussion with a fellow colleague whom you respect and debate these techniques: "Are they practical? Can I really do this?" If it is a technique that you can*not* see yourself using at any time, take a pencil and mark it out. Now move up the matrix with naming, questioning, and so on until you have eliminated all techniques from the matrix that are unacceptable to you.

Steps 2 and 3: Select and Design a Limit-setting System

Now that you have eliminated unacceptable techniques, the remaining techniques will stand out on your work copy. At this point, bring to mind one of those annoying but less confrontational discipline incidents that happen daily—let's say, "talking while I am lecturing." Of the remaining techniques on your work matrix, what would be the first action

Chapter 2 Behavior Analysis	Chapter 3 Tools for Teaching	Chapter 4 Assertive Discipline	Chapter 5 Cooperative Discipline	Chapter 7 Love and Logic/Glasser	Chapter 8 TET	TBC
Time out • nonseclusionary • contingent Observation • exclusionary • seclusionary	*(Part of backup system)* 1–2 "Quite time" 3. Large response: Staffing • principal • counselor • police	4.5 After 5th misbehavior: Consequence • go to office when necessary, call "who-squad" 6. Severity clause (send to principal)	As natural/logical consequence In times of danger	5. Classroom isolation (repeat 1–4) 6. Off to the office (administrator) (repeat 1–4) 7. Removal from school (repeat 1–4) 8. Referral to outside agency		Action (physical intervention/ isolation)
1. Extinction 2. Differential reinforcement 3. Response cost 4. Aversive stimuli (reinforcers: edible, sensory, tangible, PAP, social)	*Responsibility Training* (Stopwatch) 1. Bonuses • gift of time • hurry-up bonuses • automatic bonuses • bonus contest 2. Penalties 3. PAT *Omission Training* • remove from responsibility training • kitchen timer (increase time) • bonuses (group award)	4.2 After 2nd misbehavior: Consequence • check on board or tracking book • stay after class 4.3 After 3rd misbehavior: Consequence • check on board or tracking book • stay after class 4.4 After 4th misbehavior: Consequence • check on board or tracking book • stay after class 4.5 After 5th misbehavior: • call parents *Recognition Process* 1. Positive recognition • praise • note/call home • certificates/awards • tangible awards 2. Reminder for teacher • classwide recognition • use + behavior chart (or dropping marbles) • go to office for recognition/praise	6. Natural/ logical consequences 7. Encouragement 8. Social engineering • most wanted list	4. Reap the consequences of plan		Reinforcers

FIGURE 9.2 Teacher Behavior Continuum and Reactive Models

Chapter 2 Behavior Analysis	Chapter 3 Tools for Teaching	Chapter 4 Assertive Discipline	Chapter 5 Cooperative Discipline	Chapter 7 Love and Logic/Glasser	Chapter 8 TET	TBC
		(Teach the discipline plan) 1.2 show 1.3 check	5. Class meeting		6. No-lose problem solving 7. 6 steps to problem solving	Modeling
Behavioral Objectives: Identify • the learner • the ante- cedent condi- tions • target behavior • criteria for acceptable performance Teach prompts	*Backup System* (pri- vate/semiprivate 1.1 Small response: • ear warning • private meeting (a) think and talk (b) warn and deliver 2. Medium response: Class *Structure* • teach rules • say, show, check	Teach the discipline plan 1.1 say 2.3 Warning: "I"-state- ment, "I want you to stop ... now!" 4.1 Put student's name on board (or tracking book)	1. Hypothesize goal (atten- tion, etc.) 4. Make a plan (based on goal)	1. Confronting, "stop..." 3. Press for a plan	8. Influenc- ing	Commands
		(After 1st misbehavior) 2.2 Warning: As a question "What should you be doing?"	2. Confronting 3. Verifying goal (look for reflex)	2. "What" questions • doing • helping • rule • plan to change	3. Door openers	Questions
		2.1 Warning: Hints: "Class, we should be..."			4. Active lis- tening 5. "I"-mes- sages	Naming (non-direc- tive state- ment)
	1. Work the crowd 2. Limit setting Proximity far: 1. relaxing breaths 2. work the crowd 3. with-it-ness 4. terminate instruction 5. turn, look, and say Proximity near: 5. closing space 6. prompt 7. palms 8. camping out 9. moving out				1. Critical listening 2. Acknow- ledgments	Looking
					Steps 1–4 can be car- ried out in class meet- ings	

FIGURE 9.2 *(continued)*

(figure continues)

Chapter 2 Behavior Analysis	Chapter 3 Tools for Teaching	Chapter 4 Assertive Discipline	Chapter 5 Cooperative Discipline	Chapter 7 Love and Logic/Glasser	Chapter 8 TET	TBC
a. count and collect observation data b. determine and change reinforcement schedules	*Structure/Management* • determine and teach rules/structure • desk arrangement (interior loop) • work the crowd Principles: • discipline before instruction • keep it private • use little power	a. Establish/publish plan to: • students • principal • parents b. Post rules 1.4 positive repetition (teach 4 times first month)	a. observe/collect information b. ask yourself, "Do I feel annoyed, beaten, etc." c. recognition of verifying reflex	a. Observe • the student • the situations b. Assess • what am I doing? • what success is student having? c. Classroom reorganization and activities/instructional change	Changes a. daily actions b. space c. time (diffused, individual, optimum)	

FIGURE 9.2 *(continued)*

you would take? Give this much reflection while looking over all of your choices. Circle that action or technique and place a number 1 above it. Was your first action a response that was Relationship-Listening, Confronting-Contracting, or Rules-Consequences? Now assume that the action that you circled was not effective, and the student continued in his misbehavior. What would you do next? Circle this technique and place a number 2 above it—and continue in like manner, taking this to the extreme that the student might need to be removed from the classroom. What you have done is to create your own limit-setting pathway of techniques acceptable to you.

Take another sheet of paper and make rows with the general behavior of the TBC (looking, naming, etc.) on them. Now take the technique that you circled as #1 and write this on your limit-setting plan. Continue to add #2, #3, again in like manner until all of your chosen techniques are displayed for you—you have now designed you own limit-setting system.

Next, share this limit-setting system with a colleagues or an administrator, again using a typical and real-life discipline incident, and describe how you might see yourself progress thorough this limit-setting pathway. Feel free to go back to the working matrix, selecting more techniques or adding new ones from your discussions with another professional. See Figure 9.3 for an example of an eclectic limit-setting pathway. The TBC created by one teacher is a display of techniques that this teacher found acceptable and would be comfortable in using—thus, this may be viewed as a meta-model, picking and combining techniques from all models.

Step 4: Backup System

At the end of your limit-setting pathway, you may have included techniques that might involve isolation or time out or perhaps the involvement of parents or the school principal.

MINIMUM POWER				MAXIMUM POWER
Looking	**Naming**	**Questioning**	**Commanding**	**Acting**
• Low profile correction • Spatial proximity — far — near — intimate • Relaxing breaths • Acknowledgments • Individual conferences or class meeting	• Active listening • I-messages • Conferencing Six Steps to Problem Solving 1. Defining 2. Generating 3. Evaluating 4. Deciding 5. Implementing 6. Evaluating	Door opener 2. "What" questions — What did you do? — What is the rule? — What will you do to change? 3. Contracting — consequences 4. Isolation (relax chair) Repeat 1, 2, 3, 4 (do 3 cycles) 5. Notify parents 6. Staffing	1. "Stop it!" 1. Assertive command (name, gesture, touch, eyes) 2. Broken record 3. Promise a consequence	• Shaping strategy defined — establish (+,−) reinforcers (food, tokens, social, PATs) • Reinforcement schedules — one to one — ratio — random • Modeling rules — say — show — check • Prompting • Chaining • Saturation • Time out • Activity pairing • Encouragement • Logical consequences • Social engineering • Most wanted

FIGURE 9.3 Limit Setting (A Hypothetical Meta-Model)

If not, then you need to add this as a backup system. Will you use "off to the castle" to permit students to calm down and discuss their behavior, as Glasser would do, or will you use strong removal techniques, such as those of Assertive Discipline? You may also consider the Behavior Analysis suggestions of time out (nonseclusionary, contingency, exclusionary, etc.). If you teach for many years, you will have a student who is outside of your abilities to manage, and you will need help from others. Then a discipline plan must be developed that includes a backup system, the use of the principal, school counselor, or psychologist, and in very serious situations the school resource office or local police. You are now ready to try your limit setting and, if necessary, a backup process in a real classroom setting. It would be advisable to share it with the principal, possibly even parents, and to have the principal keep it on file in his office—especially if there are steps taken to remove the student from the classroom that will involve principal or parents. Include this backup system on your limit-setting pathway and put it writing.

Step 5: Incentive System

Writers like Alfie Kohn would say that if we have a democratically run, exciting educational program that is meeting the needs of our students, we would not need a discipline system, especially one based on incentives, which he characterizes as bribes. This is the time for the reflective teacher to take a position regarding reward, reinforcers, and an incentive system. If you do not believe in them, possibly because you are a Relationship-Listening teacher and do not like and cannot use incentives, you may move on to the next step. If you are a Rules-Consequences teacher, reinforcers as incentives will be central in your discipline-management system. Think them out beforehand! Are you going to use Assertive Discipline's group rewards, such as "dropping marbles" in a glass fish bowl until the students earn a popcorn party, or Jones's process of giving students free time and then taking it away if they misbehave? Or are you going to use well-thought-out behavior analyses procedures? Write your incentive system in such a manner that a substitute teacher could read it and carry it out.

Step 6 Encouragement System

An encouragement system will need to be done based on one of the three philosophical orientations or philosophies. If you are taking a Rules-Consequences approach, you may reward students with a defined method, such as "bonus" points (Jones's *Positive Discipline*), or use behavioral analysis to design a specialized reinforcement plan. If we were looking through the eyes of the Confronting-Contracting teacher, we would take direct actions to help the student find social acceptance (see Chapter 7 for many suggestions for such actions, including the use of class meetings). Finally, if you wish to encourage the very difficult student using Relationship-Listening, the key is to take the time to establish a nonjudgmental, accepting relationship with this student and to encourage him to talk out and share his needs.

LEVEL III: PRESCRIPTIVE-EXPERIENCED TEACHER

The *prescriptive-experienced* teacher is beyond simple survival and is so professionally secure that she has few or no questions about her own effectiveness. She is secure in admitting to difficulty in handling such students as the "walking time bomb," and she seeks the help of colleagues and other professionals, as a backup system, to assist her in prescribing a proactive intervention strategy for a very difficult student. She can collect data on this student, is comfortable in handling staffing with a team (see Figure 9.4), creates agreed-upon strategies, and writes individualized discipline plans (IDPs). She then finds time during the classroom day to carry out such interventions. Again, the confidence level of this teacher is never concerned with whether she is effective; instead, it tends toward, "I am an experienced teacher faced with a problem (an unmanageable student). How can I use the help of other professionals to learn new ways of becoming effective with this student?" How can this be done at the practical level?

Backup System (Staffing)

Once the classroom door is closed, the teacher enters a private world of intimate interaction with students that can be rewarding, dynamic, and exciting. This is teaching at its best! However, this relationship and interaction can also produce a hostile, frightening environment for the teacher and students, where little learning takes place. Teachers generally

Step	Topic	Speaker	Time (minutes)	Purpose
1.	Statement of the Problem	Teacher	2	To give general descriptions of student's behavior and state change desired.
	a. Background Information—teacher	Teacher	10	To present background information using the collected data from (Figure 9.5) form (no questions asked).
	b. Group	All members	15	To add information from others throughout the school day (Figure 9.5) to background form (no questions asked).
	c. Clarification of background information	All members	8	Questions and discussion for clarification is not addressed to any member.
2.	Generating Solutions	All members	3	Each member writes 3 to 5 actions that could be taken to help this student.
	a. In writing			
	b. Given verbally	All members	15	Each member reads his suggested actions with a master list made on chart in the room.
3.	Evaluate and Generate Suggestions	All members	15	To explore and evaluate all solutions and look for new ones out of the discussion.
4.	Decide on Actions	All members	10	To decide on a group plan with some members assigned responsibilities.
5.	Implementing a Commitment	All members	1	To have members make a commitment to plan by signing the written form (Figure 9.6).
6.	Reevaluation	All members	5	At a later data all members meet to discuss the success or lack of success of plan. If there is no success, the above steps are repeated.

FIGURE 9.4   Staffing Agenda

have been given the charge by parents, school administrators, and fellow teachers to be the "lion tamer" or to be an exponent of the "don't smile until Christmas" syndrome. The message is that you are given *this* number of students for *this* period of time, and for "heaven's sake," it is your responsibility to keep them under control. If she cannot do this, the teacher will eventually find her performance evaluations carrying such criticisms as "has difficulty with discipline," a phrase that seems to reflect the ultimate sin of being a teacher. This causes teachers to feel they have been branded with the scarlet letter *D* for discipline and to feel shunned by their colleagues who, in subtle ways, suggest to them that they are ineffectual and unworthy to be part of their profession.

Let us therefore suggest that teachers turn from the view of themselves as a "classroom island" to that of becoming part of a cooperative team effort involving some or all of the school staff. In having a variety of students, including special needs students who have been mainstreamed, a teacher will encounter a student whose behavior disrupts the class or the school as a whole. Ideally, the models of discipline previously presented may be applied not only individually, but also as a team effort called "staffing" as a supportive backup system.

Staffing, which may be called for by a teacher, especially the prescriptive-experienced teacher, involves a team of fellow teachers (who may have worked with this student the previous year), the student's current teacher, the principal, school counselors, or psychologist, and other school personnel meeting together to develop a plan of action regarding this particularly difficult student. The Staffing Agenda (Figure 9.4) provides guidelines for the steps and procedures to follow and the time needed to permit the meeting to move smoothly. The student Background Information form (Figure 9.5) would be completed by all members before the meeting, and the Individualized Educational (socialization) Plan (IEP) form (Figure 9.6) may be used to document the actions agreed upon and taken.

LEVEL IV: ANALYTICAL-PROFESSIONAL TEACHER

The highly mature *analytical-professional* teacher is one who can view the school program and, through her own analytical skill of reasoning, raise ethical issues, value questions, and philosophical questions as to what is best for the students. She can challenge the status quo. She is able to ask questions concerning what life is really like for students in the school and whether rules and procedures have been made for the betterment of the students or for the convenience of the teachers. The analytical-professional teacher may be ready to ask many of the questions and address the criticisms raised by Alfie Kohn's writing. These issues include:

- What do we want our students to become?
- Do our discipline methods lead to teaching students democratic skills?
- High-stakes testing
- The use of competition in schools
- Ethical questions regarding rewards and punishment
- School uniforms
- The teaching of values
- Methods of grading
- School and curriculum reforms
- ADHD label
- School choice and magnet schools (Kohn, 1998; 1999)

These *analytical-professional* teachers can be effective leaders for the teaching profession. They provide leadership in the school by becoming mentors for the *intuitive-survival* teacher, through involvement in professional teacher associations, and by lobbying school boards and governmental agencies for the purposes of making the school a better place for students. The many models in the following chapter involve human relationship skills and methods of dealing with others in conflict situations. Not only can the *analytical-professional* teacher use these techniques with children, but she can also use the techniques and skills with adults, including parents, fellow teachers, and administrators. The *analytical-professional* teacher uses the many techniques to become fully empowered as a professional.

Students _____ Date _____

Staff Members: _____ _____

                          _____ _____

                          _____ _____

Part I: Student's Misbehavior(s)

1. Describe misbehavior(s)

   a. _____

   b. _____

   c. _____

2. How frequent is each type of misbehavior?

3. What time of day does misbehavior occur?

4. In what physical surroundings?

5. With which peers or adults were the student involved when incidents occured?

6. What are the activities the student is engaged in before misbehavior occurred?

Part II: Teacher's Actions

1. What actions did you take when the student misbehaved?

2. How did the student respond to your actions?

3. When are your actions most successful?

4. When are your actions least successful?

Part III: Student Motivation

1. What responsibilities (assignments, tasks, or orders) does the student fulfill?

2. What types of reinforcement does the student receive?
   a. positive (and/or encouragement) _____
   b. negative (and/or logical consequences) _____
3. How does the student respond to reinforcement?
   a. positive (and/or encouragement) _____
   b. negative (and/or logical consequences) _____
4. How does student relate to the group? _____

Part IV: When Student Is *Not* Misbehaving

1. Describe positive behaviors, how frequent, time of day, in what physical surroundings, with what peers or adults, and during what kind of activities? _____

Part V: Additional Questions:

   1. What does the student enjoy doing (hobbies or subjects)? _____
   2. What does student do well? _____
   3. Are there any reasons to suspect health or physical disabilities? _____

FIGURE 9.5 Student Background Information Form

Student's Name _____   Summary of Present Behaviors: _____

Head (homeroom) Teacher _____

Date of Staffing _____

Long-term Behavioral Changes   1._____

Desired   _____

2. _____

3. _____

Short-term behavioral change wanted	Specific action	Person responsible	% of time	Approximate date of completion	Reevaluation date

Criteria for Evaluation Changes	Staff Members
	1.
	2.
	3.
	4.
	Date of Staffing
	Date of Reevaluation

FIGURE 9.6   Individualized Educational (Socialization) Plan (IEP)

SUMMARY

Teacher skills can be viewed as developing through four major states of maturity. The discipline models, methods, skills, and issues that a teacher understands and applies will vary depending on the stage of development and maturity of the teacher. The beginning teacher may make limited use of the many models found in the preceding chapters, while the maturing teacher gains greater confidence and moves from being concerned about herself to being concerned about what is best for the student. Finally, the teacher becomes a leader in the professional community, able and willing to provide guidance regarding improving the lives of students. Each of these stages requires the teacher to return to various models presented and to reread and reconsider them regarding his or her needs at each professional stage.

REFERENCES

Glasser, W. *Control Theory in the Classroom.* New York: Harper & Row, 1986.

Katz, L. G. "Developmental Stages of Preschool Teachers." *The Elementary School Journal,* 1972, pp. 50–54.

Kohn. A. *What to Look for in a Classroom ... and Other Essays.* San Francisco, CA: Jossey-Bass Publishers, 1999.

Ryan, K. *Don't Smile Until Christmas: Accounts of the First Year of Teaching.* Chicago: University of Chicago Press, 1970.

PROACTIVE OR PREVENTIVE MODELS OF DISCIPLINE

THE **REACTIVE** discipline models tell us what to do on Monday morning with the Walters who challenge us by their misbehavior and prevent us from teaching. There are other respected proactive models that do not help us on the spot with Walter, but take the position that a school and a teacher in the classroom must establish a process of educating students beforehand as to how to mediate potential conflict that might develop in a school setting, how to develop social skills, and to treat rule making and consequences in a humanistic manner based on our democratic judicious rights.

CHAPTER 10. The Peer Mediation Model, is a formal well-developed proactive program to have students run a mediation program whereby the student in conflict can bring a problem to a mediation process that would be run by a student facilitator, thus heading off a wide variety of school problems that might lead to aggression and discipline actions.

CHAPTER 11. The Judicious Discipline Model, is another proactive program or model that enlists teachers in accepting the manner in which school and classroom rules are democratically created, and encourages them to view their dealings with students who break rules in a manner congruent with judicious democratic ideals. Rules are built on the Bill of Rights and enforced with regard to due process; the students thus learn to live in a democratic society, and are not managed and controlled through an arbitrary authoritarian manner.

CHAPTER 12. Skillstreaming—Teaching Prosocial Skills, is another program that takes the position that the reason for many of the disruptive behaviors seen in schools today is because these students have never been taught prosocial skills that most people have picked up through incidental learning. Through direct instruction, the model teaches those prosocial skills, drawing from a list of 50 to 60 identified skills. The proactive teaching and training will then have the direct effect of less misbehavior in the classroom and in the wider society.

THE PEER MEDIATION MODEL

Writers/Theorists: Fred Schrumpf, Donna K. Crawford, and Richard J. Bodine

- *Peer Mediation: Conflict Resolution in Schools*
- *Creating the Peaceable School: A Comprehensive Program for Teaching Conflict Resolution*

OUTLINE OF THE PEER MEDIATION MODEL

Basic Assumptions about Motivation

- Students are growing up today not learning how to handle conflict and disagreements, therefore they respond with aggressive, hostile, or passive behaviors

- Schools are settings that need to teach not only academic skills but the social skills of mediation and mastering of conflict

- Students can be trained to mediate conflict between other students better than teachers

- Peer mediation is a proactive process that will produce more productive school behaviors among students

Teacher (Mediator) Behaviors

Although teachers and administrators set up and administer the peer mediation process, students carry out the follow mediation steps or behaviors:

- Step 1: Agree to Mediate

- Step 2: Gather Points of View

- Step 3: Focus on Interests

- Step 4: Create Win–Win Options

- Step 5: Evaluate Options

- Step 6: Create an Agreement

Guidelines, Planning, or Preparatory Teacher Actions

▓ Phase 1—A staff and student conflict resolution program team is created and trained. A program coordinator is designated, a needs assessment is conducted, and a faculty consensus is built for the program.

▓ Phase 2—This phase involves establishing a timeline for implementation, forming an advisory committee, developing policies, and identifying and developing funding sources to support the program.

▓ Phase 3—Student peer mediators are recruited through nominations, and then selected and trained.

▓ Phase 4—Workshops are held for staff, students, parents, and the community so that a critical mass of people within and outside of the school understands the mediation process.

▓ Phase 5—A promotional campaign is carried out through various communication sources, including the news media.

▓ Phase 6—The daily operation of the program is designed, including requests for mediation, scheduling of mediation and mediators, supervision of mediators, recording of data, provision of training and support, and finally evaluation of the program.

OVERVIEW

The scene is a small conference room where three middle-school students are seated around a square table. As we watch the interaction progress among these three students, we will see that Roger is the leader or mediator seated between the two other students James and Mike, the disputants, who have some conflict between them. We see that in attempting to mediate the dispute between his peers, Roger will follow a series of predetermined steps and procedures as he performs his role. We will see this process unfold and then later describe how the peer mediation model can contribute to good discipline in our schools and classrooms, whether in a middle-school setting (as in this illustration) or even with younger children.

Six Steps of Mediation

Step 1: Agree to Mediate

Opening the Session (introductions, setting ground rules, and agreeing to mediate)

MEDIATOR ROGER: I welcome both of you to this mediation session. I'm Roger and I'll be your mediator today. What's your name?

MIKE: Mike Zates.

ROGER: What is your name?

JAMES: James Allen.

MEDIATOR ROGER: The rule is that I won't take either of your sides and I will remain neutral. (Ground Rule 1: Mediator remains neutral) I'll keep our conversation private because what is said here should remain in this room and I'd like you to do the same! (Ground Rule 2: Confidentiality) Everyone gets to talk. When James is talking, Mike, you can't interrupt him, and when Mike is talking, James, you can't interrupt him. (Ground Rule 3: Take turns talking without interruptions) Will you accept these rules, and are you willing to work for an agreement?

JAMES: Yes.

MIKE: Yes.

Step 2: Gather Points of View (each side presents its view)

MEDIATOR ROGER: Mike, tell me your side of this problem.

MIKE: Well, for the last two weeks, James has constantly been putting me down, and today he grabbed my shirt, pushed me against the lockers, and threatened me. I can't understand it. He tells me to stay away from his girl and keeps accusing me of attempting to hit on her.

MEDIATOR ROGER: Is there more you can tell us?

MIKE: No, he just better get off my case!

(While Mike was talking, Mediator Roger faced him and stayed visually focused on him—Communication Skill: Attending)

MEDIATOR ROGER: So, James is accusing you of hitting on his girlfriend, putting you down, and getting physically rough today? (Communication Skill: Summarizing)

MIKE: Yes! But he's not so tough.

MEDIATOR ROGER: James, what is your side to this?

JAMES: Well, he is hitting on my woman, Carolyn. Natoya told me he had his arm around her in Health class, and he was hitting on her again in chemistry.

MIKE (interrupts): I ain't hitting on his girl!

MEDIATOR ROGER: Just a minute, Mike, it's James's turn to talk. Remember the rule: everyone gets to talk uninterrupted. You'll have a chance to talk later.

JAMES: And today I find him carrying her books and being in her locker.

MEDIATOR ROGER: Is there anything else?

JAMES: No. But, he is going down!

MEDIATOR ROGER: Well, James, you feel that you're hearing from others that Mike is showing too much attention to your friend Carolyn, and today he was in her locker. You are angry about this. Is that it? (Communication Skill: Summarizing)

JAMES: Yeah.

MEDIATOR ROGER: Is there anything else you want to tell us?

JAMES: No.

MEDIATOR ROGER: Your turn, Mike.

MIKE (Roger turns to face Mike—Communication skill: Attending): Well, in Heath class the teacher paired me up with Carolyn and we were practicing the Heimlich maneuver for helping people who are choking. Carolyn was my partner and I had to put my arms around her to practice the maneuver. James's friend ragged me when I did this. I didn't choose Carolyn; the teacher assigned us as a pair. Since both of our last names begin with "Z" we are at the end of the alphabet and when the teacher sits us in alphabetical order, I'm always at the end with Carolyn. It's the same way in Chemistry. All the "Z's" are seated at the same lab table and I'm next to Carolyn, and again she's my partner. I like Carolyn as a friend but I don't want to date her. In fact, she tells me she likes James and wants to go to the dances with him. Same thing with the lockers—they're assigned alphabetically, and Carolyn's is next to mine. She had to go to band practice, which is on the other side of the building, so she asked me to do her a favor and put her books in her locker. I'm not hitting on Carolyn.

MEDIATOR ROGER: So you're not interested in dating Carolyn and because of the letters of your last name being the same, you are placed together and paired up for activities. (Communication skill: Summarizing)

MIKE: That's it.

JAMES: Well, if she needs her books taken to the locker, I'll do it.

MEDIATOR ROGER: James, you see it as your role to help Carolyn. (Communication Skill: Clarifying)

JAMES: Yeah.

Step 3: Focus on Interests (identify common interest)

MEDIATOR ROGER: James, <u>what is it that you want</u>?

JAMES: I want Mike to stay away from my girl!

MEDIATOR ROGER: So, you want Mike to stay away from Carolyn, and Mike, <u>what is it that you want</u>?

MIKE: I want to be friends with Carolyn, but just friends, and be able to work with her in school without James getting jealous. I want to be able to feel safe and that he isn't gonna jump me, punch me, or push me against the locker. I don't want to be James's enemy, and also have his friends turn against me.

MEDIATOR ROGER: You want to be working friends with Carolyn and feel safe with James and his friends.

MIKE: Yes.

MEDIATOR ROGER: James and Mike, what do you think might happen if things continue this way and this isn't settled?

MIKE and JAMES (in unison): We'll get into a fight and get suspended.

MEDIATOR ROGER: Do you both want this? (Goal: Establish a common interest)

MIKE and JAMES: No.

MEDIATOR ROGER: Then it's in your best interest to find a solution to the difficulties between you. (Determine the interest of each disputant) I hear Mike saying that he has no interest in becoming Carolyn's boyfriend, but finds himself required to work closely with her, and he can't stay away from her all the time. And neither of you wants to fight and get into big trouble.

Step 4: Create Win–Win Options (no criticism, evaluation, or discussion)

MEDIATOR ROGER: We will now brainstorm some solutions, but we have a rule for brainstorming: we just say anything that comes into our mind and we will not criticize the ideas or discuss them. Just say any solution, no matter how silly and ridiculous it might sound, and let's come up with as many ideas as we can.

JAMES: Well, I could agree to meet Carolyn in the hall at end of fifth period, and get her books and take them to the locker for her.

(Mediator Roger writes down this and all other possible solutions.)

MIKE: I'm going to talk to Carolyn and tell her that James wants to carry her books. I could talk to Mrs. Herrington and get her to move me to a different lab table, but in Health class Carolyn and I have a cooperative learning activity. We're halfway done with it, and if we stop working together we'll lose too much.

JAMES: Well, I guess I can stop listening to rumors and things my friends tell me about Mike and Carolyn.

MIKE: I know that Carolyn's dad has given her four tickets to the rock concert, and I know she wants to take James. Maybe I could get a date and all four of us could go together. And, if he has an issue or problem with me, that he should talk to me about it instead of manhandling me—I need to feel safe.

Step 5: Evaluate Options

MEDIATOR ROGER: OK, here are some possible solutions. Let's evaluate them and decide on a solution. (Turn his notepad so both boys can read the solutions that have been proposed)

JAMES: I'd like to go to the rock concert with Carolyn, and double with Mike—but only if I drive. (Mike nods in agreement.) I could carry Carolyn's books on Monday through Wednesday, but I can't do it on Thursday because I have practice—maybe Mike could take her books to the locker on that day. And I could tell him if he's doing something that I don't like instead of pushing him.

MIKE: I could ask the teacher to change my lab partners.

JAMES: That's not necessary; Carolyn tells me that she needs your help on difficult problems.

MEDIATOR ROGER: OK, are these solutions fair? (Both nod yes.) Mike, will you now feel safe? (Mike states, "Yes.") James, do you still think Mike is hitting on Carolyn?

JAMES: "No, but I'll be watching."

Step 6: Create an Agreement

MEDIATOR ROGER: OK, now let's formalize this agreement by writing it down and signing a contract. The problem was that James thought Mike was hitting on his girlfriend; but Mike only wanted to be friends with her and had to work with her on many projects because the teachers put them together.

Now, James you agreed to do this: (a) talk to Mike if you have a problem with him, and (b) talk to Carolyn about working out carrying her books, with Mike helping on Thursdays. And, Mike, you'll talk with Carolyn about doubling for a date to the rock concert. Are you both in agreement with this contract? (both agree).

I'm going to sign this contract and I want each of you to do the same (both sign). Now, I'd like to thank you for letting me be your mediator and I want to shake your hands. Thanks, would you like to shake each other's hand? (They do so).

UNDERSTANDING PEER
MEDIATION AND DISCIPLINE

What you have seen is one incident in which a student mediator attempted to follow a predetermined structured procedure for getting two students to settle a dispute that, if it continued, could have gotten both boys suspended for fighting. The peer mediation model belongs among the collection of discipline models presented in this book and can be clearly classified as a Relationship-Listening model, since the mediator brings potentially hostile disputants together, stays neutral in the process, encourages each person to listen and communicate with each other, and then finds a solution that satisfies each. The mediator does not impose his or her own solution and does not take action involving any punishment.

Peer mediation is not a reactive tool, and delineation must be made between conflict resolution and a discipline program. Mediation is a proactive approach that helps set the school climate, so many of the self-destructive and violent behaviors requiring disciplinary action will not occur. It is not well suited to handling disputes after incidents have gotten out of hand or the misbehavior has occurred. But this mediation process can be used to mediate between students after everyone has calmed down and to lessen the likelihood that future incidents will occur.

The theorists and writers Fred Schrumpf, Donna K. Crawford, and Richard J. Bodine do not see peer mediation working with forms of discipline they call "obedience training," whereby students' behavior is maintained by teachers following the role of enforcer through coercion. The key to positive behavioral change is not to simply say, "Don't do that!" Instead, the key is for students to be educated in alternative ways to behave. Positive discipline as a program of behavior management relies on a program "dependent upon students' ability to evaluate their own behavior and generate alternatives behavioral choices, ones accepted in the system" (Schrumpf et al., 1997, p. 10); it is not involved in fault-finding and punishment for past behaviors.

Rationale for Peer Mediation

Today every child is affected by violence, whether or not physical harm is evidenced (Schrumpf, Crawford, and Bodine, 1997, p. 5). Acts of physical violence in school are seen repeatedly in the public media, and today's students increasingly find themselves overwhelmed by other students who are hostile, aggressive, violent, and disconnected. For many students, the only way they know to handle varying degrees of conflict is through violent actions. Many schools that take pride in the idea that they do not experience overt violent confrontations are unaware that their students may be experiencing passive psychological violence through intimidation. Peer mediation, as a proactive process, is seen to help discipline incidents as a "result of jealousies, rumors, misunderstandings, bullying, fights, misuse of personal property, and the ending of friendships."[1]

A peer mediation program is executed by training a cadre of peer mediators, as a third party, who can be called on to mediate disputes among students. Generally, the faculty helps administer the program, but teachers are not the mediators; the educator is thus taken out of the time-consuming role of arbitrating sanctions that rarely resolve the real conflict among students. Students are seen as more effective mediators because (1) they are able to connect with peers in a way that adults may not, (2) peer mediators can frame disputes in language that may be more understandable to peers, (3) students, using peer mediators will not feel that adult authority figures are judging them, (4) peer mediators are respected, (5) the process self-empowers youth, and (6) when students are in control they feel more committed to solutions.

The philosophical position of peer mediation is that

> *Schools must be places from which viable, positive future pathways for young people can be built. They must, above all, be places where youth can learn to live and get along with one another, as well as to become ready to assume their future roles as responsible citizens of a democracy, as parents, as community members and leaders, and as productive members of the work force. Many students have no other place from which to gain these experiences. Only schools can extend these possibilities equally to all students—this is the constitutional mandate to the schools.*[2]

UNDERSTANDING CONFLICT

The peer mediators are trained to understand conflict as a natural process of living. Conflict occurs when there is a discord between two individuals or between groups of people related to blocked needs—the need for belonging, for power, for freedom, or for fun.[3]

Responses to a conflict may be viewed as three different types: soft responses, hard responses, and principled responses. The *soft response* occurs when people attempt to avoid conflict by withdrawing from the situation, ignoring the problem, or denying that a conflict exists. When this occurs, one person adjusts to the position of the other and does not get his or her needs met or served within the relationship. This person's passive response will produce feelings of disillusionment, self-doubt, fear, and anxiety about the future, thus this soft response is not a healthy or productive response. The *hard response* is when one individual applies pressure to win a contest of will. Hostility, physical damage, and violence can often result from this type of response to a conflict, and it is destructive to cooperation. The *principled response* to conflict occurs when communication between disputants is established. Through this communication each person has the opportunity to create a resolution through which both parties get their needs met and blame is eliminated.

The soft response is a lose–lose approach in which both parties deny the existence of the conflict, and issues are not dealt with. The hard response produces a lose–win outcome in which one individual gets what he wants while the other does not. Finally, the principled response produces a win–win situation where both disputants get their needs met by focusing on the interests of both, bringing people to a gradual consensus reaching rather than emotionally destroying relationships.

PROGRAM ORGANIZATION AND OPERATIONS

The implementation, design, and operation of a peer mediation program involves a six-phase plan:

Phase 1: A staff and student conflict resolution program team is created and trained. A program coordinator is designated, a needs assessment is conducted, and a faculty consensus is built for the program.

Phase 2: This phase involves establishing a timeline for implementation, forming an advisory committee, developing policies, and identifying and developing funding sources to support the program.

Phase 3: Student peer mediators are recruited through nominations, and then selected and trained.

Phase 4: Workshops are held for staff, students, parents, and the community so that a critical mass of people within and outside of the school understand the mediation process.

Phase 5: A promotional campaign is carried out through various communication sources, including the news media.

Phase 6: The daily operation of the program is designed, including requests for mediation, scheduling of mediation and mediators, supervision of mediators, recording of data, provision of training and support, and finally, evaluation of the program.

The peer mediation text and student manual contain training procedures, forms, and all other necessary materials to carry out these six organizational phases.

STEPS AND PROCEDURES

The role of peer mediators is to follow a prescribed procedure of steps and guidelines to create an atmosphere that fosters cooperation and problem resolutions. A mediator must be impartial and empathetic and must be a good listener, respectful, trustworthy, and able to get peers to work together.

The mediator arranges the physical space, normally a private room with a square table and three chairs, with the disputants seated opposite each other with the peer mediator in the middle. The materials needed are the peer mediator request (filled out the by parties beforehand), a brainstorming worksheet, a peer mediation agreement form, a pencil or pen, and an easel pad and marker.

The steps for peer mediation are:

Step 1: Agree to Mediate

Step 2: Gather Points of View

Step 3: Focus on Interests

Step 4: Create Win–Win Options

Step 5: Evaluate Options

Step 6: Create an Agreement

See Figure 10.1 for a summary of these steps as they are placed on the Teacher Behavioral Continuum.

Step 1: Agree to Mediate

The peer mediator introduces himself or herself and each disputant, as mediators usually are assigned to disputants whom they do not know personally. The ground rules are stated:

Looking on	Nondirective statements	Questions	Directive Statements	Physical Intervention
	Communication Skills (a-2) Attending (looks at speaker) (a-3) Clarifying "So, I hear you saying. . . ." (a-4) Summarizing "These are your points and position . . . ."	Step 1: Agree to Mediate Open session (a) "What is your name?" Step 3: Focus on Interests "What is it that you want?" (a-1) Goal—establish a common interest "Do you both want . . .?"	(b) "Here are the rules" (neutral mediator, confidentiality, and no interruptions) Step 2: Gather points of view (a-1) "Tell me what happened." Step 4: Create Win–Win Options (no criticism, evaluation, or discussion) "Each of you tell me solutions." (write them down) Step 5: Evaluate Options "Let's evaluate these options." Step 6: Create an Agreement (write it down, and sign contract) "All shake hands."	

FIGURE 10.1   Teacher Behavioral Continuum—Peer Mediation Model

(1) the mediator remains neutral; (2) mediation is private; (3) the disputants must take turns talking and listening; and (4) the disputants must cooperate to solve the problem. The peer mediator gets a clear statement from the disputants that they will commit themselves to mediate the dispute and obey the ground rules. Now that we understand the components of an effective peer mediation program, let's look back on the earlier illustration:

MEDIATOR ROGER: I welcome both of you to this mediation session. I'm Roger and I'll be your mediator today. What's your name?

MIKE: Mike Zates.

ROGER: What is your name?

JAMES: James Allen.

MEDIATOR ROGER: The rule is that I won't take either of your sides and I will remain neutral. (Ground Rule 1: Mediator remains neutral) I'll keep our conversation private because what is said here should remain in this room and I'd like you to do the same! (Ground Rule 2: Confidentiality) Everyone gets to talk. When James is talking, Mike, you can't interrupt him, and when Mike is talking, James, you can't interrupt him. (Ground Rule 3: Take turns talking without interruptions) Will you accept these rules, and are you willing to work for an agreement?

JAMES: Yes.

MIKE: Yes.

Step 2: Gather Points of View

The peer mediator now asks each disputant (one at a time) to tell his or her point of view about the problem. The mediator listens to each disputant and summarizes after each statement. This is when the mediator uses his or her communication skills. The mediator does not interrupt, offer advice, judge, ridicule, criticize, distract, or bring up his or her own experiences. The peer mediator uses the communication skills of (1) attending (looking at and listening to the speaker with accompany nonverbal gestures to encourage the speaker to talk), (2) summarizing (active listening techniques, whereby the facts are restated and feelings are reflected, as previously presented in the T.E.T.[4] model), and (3) clarifying, through which the peer mediator deliberately asks open-ended questions to get additional information, such as, "How did you feel when this happened, do you have more to add, tell what happened next, or what do you think is keeping you from reaching an agreement?"

Again, returning to the dialogue from our example:

MEDIATOR ROGER: Mike, can you tell me your side of this problem—what's been happening?

MIKE: Well, for the last two weeks James has constantly been putting me down, and today he grabbed my shirt, pushed me against the lockers, and threatened me. I can't understand it. He tells me to stay away from his girl, and keeps accusing me of attempting to hit on her. (We may remember this process continuing in our opening example.)

Step 3: Focus on Interests

Next, the peer mediator attempts to get the disputants to find a common interest. The mediator may ask, "What do you want? Why do you want that?" The mediator will listen and summarize. To clarify, he or she may ask:

- What might happen if you don't reach an agreement?
- What would you think if you were in the other person's shoes?
- What do you really want?

Finally, the mediator summarizes with a statement that the defines this interest, such as, "Your interests are _____."

Again, returning to our introductory example, we may recall the interaction between Mediator Roger and Mike:

MEDIATOR ROGER: James, *what is it that you want?*

JAMES: I want Mike to stay away from my girl!

MEDIATOR ROGER: So, you want Mike to stay away from Carolyn; and Mike, *what is it that you want?*

MIKE: I want to be friends with Carolyn, but just friends, and be able to work with her in school without James getting jealous. I want to be able to feel safe and that he isn't gonna jump me, punch me, or push me against the locker. I don't want to be James's enemy and also have his friends turn against me. (Again, we may recall or return to read the interaction in our example.)

Step 4: Create Win–Win Options

When people are in dispute and angry, they tend to be in either an offensive or defensive position. The win–win options are created through a brainstorming process that encourages everyone to think creatively, without concern for judgments and criticism. The peer mediator explains the brainstorming rules:

- Say any ideas that come to mind
- Do not judge or discuss the idea
- Come up with as many ideas as possible
- Try to think of unusual ideas

The mediator writes these ideas down on a brainstorming worksheet, and may ask more questions to help generate even more ideas.

Step 5: Evaluate Options

The goal in this step is to have the disputants evaluate and improve on the ideas listed in Step 4. The mediator may ask each disputant to name the options or parts of options that they approve of, and these are circled on the brainstorming form. Then the peer mediator can go back over the circled items, asking such questions to the disputants as: "Is this fair? Can it be done? Do you think it will work?" and so on.

Step 6: Create an Agreement

After the discussion in Step 5, the mediator uses those options that have been agreed on and pushes for a plan that is satisfactory to both disputants and to which they will commit themselves—including a willingness to sign a contract. Once the agreement is written, the mediator will review the central points, have it signed by all parties, thank the disputants, and shake hands.

SUMMARY

In today's schools much of the misbehavior that leads to discipline incidents that must be dealt with by teachers or school authorities stems from conflict between individuals. This conflict is inevitable and is part of life's experiences, but many of today's students are growing up without the communication skills and abilities to deal with their blocked needs. They are left having to choose between responding in an aggressive hostile manner (hard resolution) or passively withdrawing into a shell of insecurity and feelings of not being safe (soft resolution). Peer mediation is not a reactive process, but is proactive, utilizing a schoolwide mediation program to foster an atmosphere that says that "Our school is a place where we can talk over our differences. We don't have to fight to get justice."

The peer mediation writers have presented a well-thought-out and designed process, along with procedures for preplanning and creating a schoolwide peer mediation process. This includes training a cadre of student mediators, and procedures for daily execution of the program.

Strengths and Limitations

Because of the violence that is seen in schools today, the public and school officials want to prevent such actions. Peer mediation appears to be one well-developed model for being proactive. Some still question the advisability of students being the mediators. Students in schools where this is used often report that the mediators do not keep the process and problems confidential. This can mean public humiliation for some students who are gossiped about and become objects of other students' laughter. The model's creators state clearly that peer mediation is to be used to create a climate of working together in a school and should be separate from discipline procedures. But students report that schools often use peer mediation after a school conflict as a choice. "You have been involved in a fight. You can either go to mediation or get three days' suspension." Most students, of course, will take the mediation; when they are asked if they are ready and will commit themselves to mediation, many will fake agreeing to commit just to avoid the suspension. The designers, of course, cannot be held responsible for the misuse of the program.

SUMMARY OF KEY CONCEPTS

attending	evaluation of options	peer mediation	summarizing
clarifying	hard response	principled response	win–lose
define interest	lose–lose	soft response	win–win

INSTRUCTIONAL MEDIA

Fred Schrumpf, Donna K. Crawford, and Richard J. Bodine. (1997) *Peer Mediation: Conflict Resolution in Schools-Program Guide* (rev. ed.) Champaign, IL: Research Press.

Fred Schrumpf, Donna K. Crawford, and Richard J. Bodine.

(1997) *Peer Mediation: Conflict Resolution in Schools-Student Manual* (rev. ed.) Champaign, IL: Research Press.

Richard, J. Bodine, Donna K. Crawford, and Fred Schrumpf. (1994) *Creating the Peaceable School: A Comprehensive*

Program for Teaching Conflict Resolution: Program Guide. Champaign, IL: Research Press.

Richard, J. Bodine, Donna K. Crawford, and Fred Schrumpf. (1994) *Creating the Peaceable School: A Comprehensive Program for Teaching Conflict Resolution: Student Manual.* Champaign, IL: Research Press.

Kathryn Girard and Susan J. Koch. (1996) *Conflict Resolution in the Schools: A Manual for Educators.* San Francisco, Ca: Jossey-Bass Publishers.

NOTES

1. R. Schrumpf, D. K. Crawford, and R. J. Bodine, *Peer Mediation: Conflict Resolution in Schools* (Champaign, Ill: Research Press, 1997).

2. Ibid., p. 13.

3. W. Glasser, *Control Theory* (New York: Dell, 1984).

4. Thomas Gordon, *T.E.T.: Teacher Effectiveness Training* (New York: David McKay, 1974).

CHAPTER 11

THE JUDICIOUS DISCIPLINE MODEL

Theorist/Writer: Forrest Gathercoal
- *Judicious Discipline*

Theorist/Writer: Barbara McEwan
- *Practicing Judicious Discipline: An Educator's Guide to a Democratic Classroom*

OUTLINE OF THE JUDICIOUS DISCIPLINE MODEL

Basic Assumptions about Motivation

- The concept of *in loco parentis* has been replaced by the position that students do not lose their constitutional rights in school.

- The traditional approach of giving schools nearly unchallenged authority (much like that held by parents) to make rules that fit the teacher's or the school's values is now seen as disserving the students.

- Judicious discipline suggests that the teaching of core amendments to the Constitution as a basis for establishing classroom and school rules helps the students mature morally and prepares them for citizenship.

- All discipline practices or sanctions must protect the student's due process rights, in varying degrees, based on the seriousness of the student's actions and the severity of the sanction.

- Traditional practices such as grading and homework may be viewed very differently when applying a test of liberty as it affects the student's future lifelong earnings potential.

Teacher Behaviors

- Teaching principles of individual rights

- Establish class rules based on three core amendments: First, Fourth, and Fourteenth Amendments directly

- Post and publish rules

- Use "compelling state interest" standard to justify withdrawal of personal rights

- Teach examples of judicious consequences

Guidelines, Planning, or Preparatory Teacher Actions
▓ Committing to running a democratic classroom

OVERVIEW

> *Sam is a large, muscular senior high school student with a consistent B average and*
> *no record of any discipline difficulties. His father currently is an unemployed aeronau-*
> *tics worker in his late 40s who is beginning to drink heavily. When intoxicated, the*
> *father begins a taunting harassment directed at Sam. Last evening the verbal conflict*
> *degenerated into an actual physical assault, with both Sam and his father exchanging*
> *blows. The father literally kicked Sam out of the house telling him, "Get out and stay*
> *out!" This occurred at 10:30 P.M. on a cold January evening, and Sam found himself*
> *on the street without money or adequate outer clothing. He walked to a public bus sta-*
> *tion, where he attempted to sleep most of the night. He arrived at school hungry and*
> *cold the next morning. It is now 12:45 P.M., and he is standing in the school cafeteria*
> *line, having borrowed lunch money from a friend. As Sam patiently waits for the line*
> *to advance, two other students cut the line directly in from him. He shouts at them and*
> *pushes them out of the line. A shoving match begins between Sam and one of these*
> *boys, escalating to the point that Sam strikes the schoolmate. Mrs. Adams, the super-*
> *visor of the cafeteria, attempts to stop the fight but is accidentally hit in the face by the*
> *back of Sam's hand, crushing her glasses into her face. Sam is taken to the assistant*
> *principal's office, where he is told that the school rule calls for a three-day suspension*
> *for fighting. Less than 15 minutes after the fight, Sam finds himself out of the school,*
> *wandering down one of the city's back streets on his way to the arcade and game*
> *room in a nearby mall. He has no idea where he will sleep that night.*

If we ask why Sam was suspended, we would be told that the school administration under-standably feels that fighting is one of the most serious discipline offenses. The school has a rule that has been approved by the school board, published in the student handbook, and widely publicized to all students: fighting results in a three-day suspension, clear and sim-ple. The administration feels that rules need to be fair, clear, and applied to all students evenly. Everyone who fights in the school is suspended, and making an exception for Sam would not be fair to other students—in short, a rule is a rule and must be enforced.

Was the school administration right in its action? Were all the students of this school well served by this discipline action? Was Sam well served by the action? What rights do we have as citizens, and what rights do students have in schools? Who will pay for Mrs. Adams's broken glasses and any medical needs? These are not easy questions to answer, but the discipline model *Judicious Discipline* written by Forrest Gathercoal may give the educator much help in answering these questions.

Before we can talk about rules and discipline, we must have a beginning understand-ing of the child's moral growth and understanding, a child's sense of right or wrong, as a developmental process. Why do we obey rules? If we do break rules, what is appropriate punishment? The questions apply at all ages, including adulthood. Suppose you are rush-ing home, driving your car down a busy street when the traffic light turns red, requiring you to stop. What is your reasoning if you see no one around and proceed through the light? What is it if you instead stop at the light and obey the law? If a police officer writes a citation for violating the traffic law, what is appropriate punishment?

MORAL GROWTH AS A DEVELOPMENTAL PROCESS

From a child development perspective, based on psychological theory, there are two basic motivators: Level 1: Fear of Authority, or Level 2: Feelings and Understanding of Social Responsibility. (If you haven't already done so, stop now and score yourself on the Authoritarian/Democratic Teaching Scale, Figure 11.1, so that you may gain a new perspective on

---

Place a check in column (a) for each statement from column (b) that you do in your classroom and fits with your beliefs.

(✓)   **Classroom practice or beliefs**

( ) 1. Rules are written with a specific punishment, incorporating the degrees and number of times a rule is broken.

( ) 2. When assignments are late, the student's grade is lowered or a set number of points are lost toward the final grade on that assignment.

( ) 3. I agree that some school-wide rules are necessary so that when certain behaviors occur every student breaking the same serious rule should be suspended.

( ) 4. Punishment has a very central role in teaching students responsible behavior.

( ) 5. I keep an open grade book, meaning that the students may ask at any time to see the data, comments, or grades I am keeping on them.

( ) 6. If a student were found cheating, I would have him retake another test or be tested by writing a paper or other alternative method.

( ) 7. If the student did not come to class with pencil, paper and appropriate books, he would miss out on the classroom activity and be graded down for failing to do the work.

( ) 8. I will not under most circumstances send a student out of my classroom because of misbehavior.

( ) 9. Passing notes among students is okay by me, but must be done in a manner that does not disturb others and follows our classroom rules.

( ) 10. I have rules that toys, such as squirt guns and similar items, are not permitted in my classroom, and if found I confiscate them and they are lost to the student forever.

( ) 11. As a general practice I would not search a student's locker.

( ) 12. Hats, message buttons, and similar items may be worn in my class.

( ) 13. If a student were discovered skipping school, I would permit that student to make up a test or work that he missed.

( ) 14. A good rule is to predetermine, so everyone knows ahead of time, that if a student comes x number of times late for my class he will receive y number of detention hours.

A   [   ]   In the space next to the letter "A" (for Authoritarian) place the number of checks you made next to items: 1,2,3,4,7,10,14.

Subtract [   ] In the space next to the letter "D" (for Democratic) place the number of all of checks you
D   made next to items: 5,6,8,9,11,12,13.

Total [   ]   Subtract "D" from "A" to obtain a total. Note this may be a negative number (i.e., –1, –2, –3, –4, –5, –6, –7).

Next, use this total (number) on the Authoritarian/Democratic scale and circle that same number on the scale below. From the descriptive words above the scale you may now determine to what degree you are a Highly Authoritarian, Somewhat Authoritarian, Somewhat Democratic, and Highly Democratic teacher.

Authoritarian/Democratic Scale

Authoritarian		Democratic	
Highly	Somewhat	Somewhat	Highly

–7	–6	–5	–4	–3	–2	–1	0	1	2	3	4	5	6	7

FIGURE 11.1   Scale of Authoritarian versus Democratic Teaching Style

your own teaching style to better understand the concepts that you will learn later in this chapter.)

Fear of Authority

When we as adults stop our cars at a traffic signal, is our reason a fear of being punished—ticketed and fined, arrested, perhaps even deprived of the opportunity to drive? Or in stopping the car do we recognize that in our society we are dependent on others and that rules are necessary to keep us safe so that life's activities may proceed in an orderly, safe, and productive manner?

Fear of authority is the first moral understanding of very young preschool age children (ages two to seven); they intellectually cannot understand how their actions can deprive others of their rights, and they simply obey parents' rules out of fear of losing their parents' love.[1] In this first childish moral position, what is right or wrong is not related to motive, but is tied to Mom and Dad's punishment or reprimand. As soon as children are out of the sight or supervision of the parent or other adult authority, they lose the ability to control themselves; when their wants and selfish needs are in conflict with the established rules, selfishness wins out and the rules are broken.

There are many students in elementary and secondary school, and even adults, who grow up but never grow out of this first moral position, fear of authority. They will obey rules only under the strict monitoring of a strong authority figure, and when out from under the close supervision of that authority they will quickly break society's rules (such as stealing or lying) and will take destructive actions to serve their selfish and self-centered needs. It is in the elementary, and middle-school years that children grow into an understanding of how their actions affect others in society and gradually, with the right educational experiences, they move to the second moral position: feelings and understanding of social responsibility and empathy for others.

Feelings and Understanding of Social Responsibility

It seems that in the natural order of human development, a growing child who learns a new developmental skill is nearly "drunk" with practicing it. Once the 12 month old can walk, he or she is "drunk" with movement, constantly preoccupied with walking. Near the age of seven, at the beginning of the elementary school years, the child has fully developed a conscience, as can be attested to by the kindergarten or first-grade teacher who hears a constant stream of tattling on the playground: "Teacher, Tommy did so-and-so!" The natural order of development permits the early elementary child to practice risk-free how to obey rules through his or her games and activities. This elementary-school-age child is "drunk" with wanting to play games with rules—sports such as baseball or football, board games like Candy Land, checkers, and Monopoly, or card games. This elementary-school-age child will constantly seek out peers and make demands of their parents to join them in these rule-governed games. While playing these games, which appear to be just using up spare time, the child of this age is really practicing the moral position Level 2: Feelings and Understanding of Social Responsibility. The child is learning how to obey rules, what happens when he breaks rules, and the social responsibility and joy of being a cooperative participant in rule-governed activities. The child is gaining an empathetic understanding of others. (See Figure 11.2, Moral Development.)

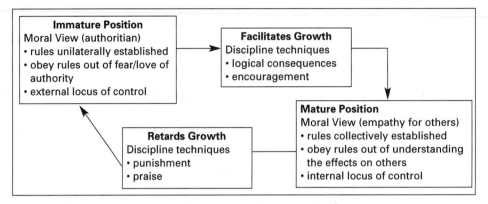

FIGURE 11.2 Moral Development (a concept of right and wrong)

From a child development perspective, it is our role to build our discipline plans on an understanding that students are still in transition from this immature **fear of authority** (first moral position), and are growing to a more mature **social responsibility** (second moral position). They are gaining empathy for others, and a social conscience to understand that their actions can endanger others and disrupt the social society in which they live. If our discipline actions are based on fear, power, and unilateral authority to simply bend the will of students and coerce them to perform under strict rules and severe punishment, we will retard the children's moral growth and development. Highly authoritarian school discipline procedures not only disserve the student but also disserve the democratic society in which the student will become an adult and assume responsibility as a citizen. A democratic society such as ours requires the student to develop to the second moral position of feelings and understanding of social responsibility. Children must develop the abilities to inhibit their self-centered approach of wanting it now, being first, and being childishly indulged. As they grow and mature, they must develop to an understanding of a moral view that holds that rules that are collectively established by citizens serve to give everyone an equal chance (equal rights), that these rules are for our safety and society's good (property loss or damage and health and safety), and they permit an opportunity for everyone to find a chance for their needs to be adequately met (obtain an education).

"Why do students obey rules?" We want our students, after their educational experience in our *judiciously* oriented schools, to answer this question with a second moral position answer reflecting an intellectual understanding of society's rules and feelings and understanding of social responsibility.

What Actions Should Be Taken When Rules Are Broken? When children as students break rules, the teacher, principal, and parents need to take actions, and the actions taken can be morally directive and controlling as **punishment** or educational and supportive as **logical consequences.**[2] A food fight among students occurs in the cafeteria. One possible set of sanctions includes a "paddling," two weeks of detention after school, or some similar deprivation. This is punishment and keeps the student in the first moral position of being **externally** controlled by fear of authority. Instead, the school authority could require the food-fighting students to lose their after-lunch recess period and clean up the cafeteria floor and tables for a three-week period—a logical consequence of their actions.

Punishment, then, is an authoritarian action requiring the educator to take a position that the students are "sinful" or are unworthy because of their misbehavior and therefore must suffer some degree of discomfort in the form of punishment action. A logical consequence, in contrast, is educational. It takes the position that the student is still immature and growing, and will make mistakes. The mistake, which appears as misbehavior by the student, is an educationally valuable *judicious "teachable moment"* for the school and parents. The actions that adults take toward that misbehaving student will serve to enable the student to gain a new perspective on his or her behavior and actions. Such students can learn how they may have taken away the rights of others, and they can become more aware of their social responsibility toward others.

The punishment response to the food fight, such as detention, only requires a passive response from the misbehaving student. He or she simply has to "grin and bear it," and soon the discomfort will be over. While the student is "suffering" the punishment, he or she can and will have strong feelings of resentment toward the educator and school, and might feel martyred for being treated "unfairly." Usually, punishment such as detention or "paddling" has no logical relationship to the child's previous misbehavior.

Logical consequences, as in the example of the food fight, require the student to be active and by this action make amends or "give back" to society or others for the negative behavior and actions (e.g., cleaning up the cafeteria for three weeks). Logical consequence as a sanction, in direct contrast to punishment, is directly and logically related to the misbehaving act of the student. The student, through his misbehavior, trashed the cafeteria; now, logically, as a consequence he must clean it up, and continue to clean it up for three weeks. Society—the school and the school cafeteria—has predictable and reasonable rules that make it safe and comfortable for people to eat in this space. The misbehaving student has broken the social contract, and thus loses his right to act in such a manner, and now must make amends or take actions to make things right again (clean up the cafeteria). Through suffering the logical consequences directly related to the misdeed, the student is educated as to the cause and effect of his misbehavior.

In many ways punishment, as an authoritarian procedure or process, is easy for the student and easy for the adult educator. When suffering a punishment, the student simply has to "grin and bear it" and it will soon pass. For the educator, punishment requires little or no thinking. The student did x (misbehaved) and therefore, based on the "rule book," must suffer y (two weeks of detention). This punishment stance by the educator eliminates any real thinking on the educator's part. The result of this punishment is resentment by the student toward the educator and the school, and little or no educational growth or benefit will occur.

But some adults might say, "Yes, but after that harsh punishment the student did not do it again." Normally, this is true only to the limits of this one narrow misdeed, but is not true at a deeper level because new behavior will result that is unseen by the adult. Punishment rarely educates and stops misbehavior, but simply causes the student to respond passively out of resentment. The student may become lethargic and passive at school, and at the first opportunity may drop out from what he considers a punishing environment (school). Or the student may become active by engaging in other misbehaviors to get even with the educator or school (such as putting inflated condoms on the teacher's car antenna, destroying school property, or becoming more sneaky or skilled at continuing the same misbehavior as before). A motorist who is fined for speeding on the interstate highway rarely stops speeding—he simply purchases a radar detector and becomes more skilled at breaking the law.

If we return to the opening vignette of Sam and the fight in the cafeteria line, we now see that the administration's arbitrary rule calling for punishment of a three-day suspension was representative of Level 1: Fear of Authority reasoning and practices. Putting Sam out into the street with a suspension is clearly punishment that bears no logical relationship to his action, and because of Sam's negative home situation it was quite illogical—the action was of no educational value to Sam and was also destructive to his well-being. Previously a good student, he may now feel resentment toward school as a place that has compounded his problem of lack of home security and his anxieties over how to handle a serious life problem. The school's action may be characterized as the "principle of the tyranny of fairness," which holds that the school must deny or punish everyone equally out of a warped sense of fairness. In a similar unilateral fashion, we see the same reasoning regarding rules and punishment when we have schools enforcing compulsory attendance requirements by telling students, "You'd better come to school or we will kick you out!"[3] The student is truant for one day, so we suspend him for three days; this punishment is not a logical consequence, and there are a host of similar rules and punishment events that do not follow the notion of a judicious school discipline program.

Our goal in school is to work with educators and parents to move to a school discipline plan that attempts to use, as far as possible, creative and imaginative thinking in the form of logical consequences and *judicious discipline* toward the students' misbehavior. Through education, we try to help the child develop maturity in moral reasoning and become an individual who has empathy for others and understands that rules are needed in a productive democratic society.

The model of *Judicious Discipline* would suggest, from a feelings and understanding of social responsibility position, that the question the school must ask is, "What is it that Sam must learn in this 'teachable moment'?" The answer is that he must learn that the school is not a knowledge "gas station" where he pulls in and fills up, with only a narrow selection of services available at one or two pumps. These pumps may or may not meet his needs, and if he has other needs, he is simply out of luck, because this educational filling station neither provides nor cares to provide that service. He must instead learn that, in a judicious school, he will be permitted to make mistakes and that this does not make him unworthy of the school's services and school membership. He must also learn that he will be given due process with empathetic educators who wish to help and counsel him in finding answers to his problems and needs, and that he should handle stress and tension in a nonviolent manner. If sanctions are needed, they will be ones that teach rather than punish.

CONSTITUTIONAL RIGHTS

For students and adults who have learned the skills and reasoning of the Level 2: Feelings and Understanding of Social Responsibility, the dilemma for true moral reasoning is the conflict between "the good of all" and "the rights of the individual." Sam's school administrators have the "good of all" in mind as they create their rules about fighting. But what are Sam's rights in such situations? Generally, our concept of democratic rights dictates that the majority rules. When we decide what game to play, what film to see, or what colors and mascot will represent our school, we vote on it and follow the majority's decision. But there is another, second aspect of democracy that is not easily understood or often taught, and that is *individual rights*. If Sam insists on having his hair a certain style or length, wearing certain nonstandard clothing, displaying highly unpopular political buttons, refusing to say the pledge to the flag, or choosing not to read certain school-assigned books because his church says they are sinful, laws should protect his individual rights from being taken away by the majority.

The standard for judging individual rights is a democratic country's constitution. In the United States, of course, the key provisions are contained within the Bill of Rights, particularly the First, Fourth and Fourteenth Amendments.

The First Amendment

Congress shall make no law respecting an establishment of religion, or prohibiting the free exercise thereof; or abridging the freedom of speech, or of the press; or the people peaceably to assemble, and to petition the Government for a redress of grievances.

In a school context, this amendment would raise such questions as:

- Does a student have a right to publish and distribute material on school premises (freedom of press)?
- Can a student refuse specific assigned reading based on religious practices and beliefs (freedom of religion)?
- Can the child wear clothing that is outside the school handbook rule but is an expression of his religious faith?
- Can the student be absent from school for religious practices and not lose the opportunity to learn the educational content and avoid being punished with regard to her grade for this absence?

The Fourth Amendment

The right of the people to be secure in their persons, houses, papers, and effects, against unreasonable searches and seizures, shall not be violated, and no Warrants shall issue, but upon probable cause, supported by Oath or affirmation, and particularly describing the place to be searched, and the persons or things to be seized.

This amendment would raise such questions as:

- Can a teacher or school official search a student's property, including lockers, purses, pockets, or vehicles in the parking lot?

The Fourteenth Amendment

All persons born or naturalized in the United States, and subject to the jurisdiction thereof, are citizens of the United States and of the State wherein they reside. No State shall make or enforce any law which shall abridge the privileges or immunities of citizens of the United States; nor shall any State deprive any person of life, liberty, or property, without due process of law; nor deny to any person within its jurisdiction the equal protection of the laws.

This lengthy amendment, parts of which are quoted here, contains the key due process and equal protection clauses, which would raise such questions as:

- Can a teacher, as a discipline action, put a student in a hall or isolated room, or suspend or expel the student, thereby depriving the student of the property right to be educated, without a due process hearing? May legal counsel be present to represent the student?

- Can the student's grade—described by Gathercoal as his "property"—be lowered or withheld because he is late to class or truant?

In Loco Parentis

Prior to 1969, these amendments were simply not applied to students in public schools. Before that date, teachers and school officials were considered to be *in loco parentis*. This meant that schools were granted the same legal authority over students as that of a parent. Gathercoal notes that minor children who live with parents or legal guardians enjoy no constitutional rights. For example, parents may search their daughter's bedroom without a search warrant and would not be violating her Fourth Amendment protections against unreasonable search or seizure. A son denied the keys to the car would have no Fourteenth Amendment right to appeal his parents' decision.[4] Because of *in loco parentis,* schools historically enjoyed the widest power and authority—just like parents—to impose their will on students, as long as it was not capricious, arbitrary, malicious, or in bad faith.

This changed in 1969 with the case of *Tinker v. Des Moines Independent School District* (393 U.S. 503), a landmark decision that has set the precedent for our present school practices, especially those related to discipline. In the *Tinker* case a high school student was suspended by his principal for wearing a black armband to school to protest U.S. involvement in Vietnam. The student won the right to express his political beliefs, with the U.S. Supreme Court holding that:

…First Amendment rights, applied in light of the special characteristics of the school environment, are available to teachers and students. It can hardly be argued that either students or teachers shed their constitutional rights to freedom of speech or expression at the schoolhouse gate. (emphasis added)

Parents today may still dictate to their children that they will obey certain rules because those rules represent the parents' values. Under *in loco parentis,* most schools previously acted in a similar fashion, unilaterally making rules that fit the values of the school, the teachers, and the administrators—a Level 1: Fear of Authority position. Now, in the wake of *Tinker,* courts have forced the school authorities to work in a Level 2: Feelings and Understanding of Social Responsibility system based on constitutional rights. As a result, school officials are faced with the moral dilemma of balancing "the good of all" against "the rights of one."

Due Process

…nor shall any State (the school) deprive any person (student) of life, liberty or property (an education), without the due process of law…

If we return to the case of Sam, we will see that the school—an extension of the state—deprived Sam of his education (property) by suspending him for three days. This is a serious matter because the state has deprived him of his rights. Was this legally done?

The state, in the form of the school, may deprive someone of established rights if the school can show a *compelling state interest.* To do this, the school must demonstrate that one of four interests is involved:

State Interest	Examples of Student Violation
Property loss or damage	• Putting graffiti on classroom walls
	• Destroying the property of others
	• Walking on the gym floor with cleated shoes
Legitimate educational purpose	• Failing to bring a textbook, pencil, and notebook paper to class
Heath and safety	• Failing to wear eye and ear protection while operating the drill press in the industrial arts class
	• Running down the "up" stairs
	• Failing to obtain a doctor's examination before playing school-sponsored sports
Serious disruption of the educational process	• Rough-house behavior that prevents other students from concentrating on their work
	• Setting off firecrackers down the stairwells
	• Food fights in the school cafeteria

If the student's behavior violates one of these four state interests, the school has a responsibility to prohibit the behavior because it affects the welfare of the school. Sam's behavior did violate a number of these state interests. He caused the loss and damage of property, endangered the safety and health of student and teacher, and seriously disrupted the educational process (the cafeteria). But where the school may have failed is in the *due process* steps.

The state, through the school, may not arbitrarily deprive the student of his property (education) without a number of procedural due process criteria being met:

- Adequate notice—an oral or written notice of the charges, such as a description of the rule the student violated.

- A fair and impartial hearing.

- Evidence—a summary of the evidence against the student, for example, the report of a teacher who witnessed the student's behavior.

- Defense—an opportunity for the student to be heard; the student has an opportunity to tell his or her side of the story.

- The right to appeal any decision.

The school clearly gave *adequate notice,* having previously published the rule and corresponding punishment in the student handbook as well as verbally notifying all students. However, it did not provide a *fair and impartial hearing* during which Sam would have been notified of the specific rules he broke, a witness—preferably a teacher—might describe the incident, and finally, Sam would be asked to tell his side of the story. All levels of state government have administrative offices above them in a chain of command, and Sam would have the right to appeal the principal's decision to the superintendent or school board, and eventually even to the state or federal courts. This is rarely done, but the right for Sam (or any other student) to do so remains in place.

These due process steps are required to give fairness to discipline actions as a sanction. The basic rule that fighting in school means a three-day suspension was wrongly stated and conceived from a Level 1: Fear of Authority position. Such rules as "if you do *x*, then you will suffer *y*" provide no judicious flexibility during the due process steps to enable sanctions to be fair. The school wrongly boxed itself in by establishing an arbitrary rule framed for punishment, Level 1: Fear of Authority, rather than for purposes of educating a student. Discipline incidents are never "cut and dry," but always involve extenuating circumstances. In Sam's case, the fact that he has no home to be sent to when suspended must be taken into consideration.

Gathercoal speaks clearly to this matter:

> *One of the problems educators often express when considering individualizing consequences is the fear that students will fault them as being unfair if others are treated differently. Those employing punishment models are forced to be consistent, as students are usually quick to remind educators their punishment was not the same as that which others received for the same offense. (The students are trained to also think in a Level 1: Fear of Authority position of reasoning.) On the other hand, judicious consequences by definition respect individual differences among students and allow more flexibility by styling consequences to meet the educational and self-esteem needs of all parties involved. When students perceive consequences as educational in nature, feel they make sense for them and are acting on their own volition, they should show little interest in comparing their situation to that of others. The variety of educational methods educators employ to remedy individual **learning problems** are seldom questioned by students. Why, therefore, should students object to educators employing different consequences as they work with the many different individual needs and attitudes their fellow student bring to **behavioral problems**?[5]*

The use of judicious discipline by Sam's school principal after the fighting incident would be guided by the following questions:

- What needs to be learned here?
- How would an educator manage the problem?
- Do I need more information about the student or the student's family?
- What strategies can be used to keep this student in school?
- How will the student perceive the consequence?
- How will it affect the school community?

And, in order for the important issues of the problem to unfold and for workable solutions to take form:

- How can I keep intact the mutual respect needed for a strong student/educator relationship through the life of the consequence?[6]

If these questions had been addressed, the discipline actions regarding Sam would have been resolved in a judicious and educational manner so that any action would have been taken to help Sam gain security and confidence in his future.

Let's take another discipline action—that of revising grades based on behavior—and think it through from the judicious perspective of Level 2: Feelings and Understanding of Social Responsibility. These ideas may surprise the large number of educators who still rely on established tradition despite *Tinker.*

GRADING

Historically, teachers have "docked" students' grades or subtracted points leading to grades because of tardiness, unexcused absences, late papers, insolence, and a host of deportment behaviors that are not acceptable to educators. In practice, educators have intertwined achievement with behavior, but courts have ruled that a grade is perceived by society as a summation of academic achievement.[7] The letter grade on a report card or transcript is perceived by employers or university admission officers as reflecting a level of skill and knowledge. A gifted student's English grade may be lowered because of unexcused absences, resulting in his rejection by a university with competitive admission standards. However, the gifted student may have read extensively and mastered the entire course content, as demonstrated on a standardized national English test. Many courts today are saying that the school's grade, which mixed behavior with achievement, was highly unfair. The authoritarian teacher who arbitrarily decides that a letter grade will be a mix of achievement and behavior assessment, in order to control students, is violating the students' rights. A grade is seen as property, as defined by the Fourteenth Amendment, and the students have earned this property by the mastery of academic skills and knowledge. Thus this property cannot be denied as a part of a discipline action to control behavior. This discipline action of lowering the grade may also deprive the student of the opportunity to get into a prestigious university that would ensure a higher income for the remainder of his life. This touches on the cherished phrase, *"nor shall any State deprive any person of life, liberty, or property."* This does not mean that there may not be consequences for misbehavior—merely that these consequences or punishments must be kept separate from the student's letter grade.

Teachers might be quite surprised to learn that proponents of *Judicious Discipline* suggest that homework should not be graded or reflected in the final letter grade. According to this thinking, students who come from homes with many resources—including money and parental guidance and time—will also show superior performance with homework compared to a child whose home situation is antithetical to homework. Thus, if we grade this homework, we are not grading the student's knowledge but rather the supportiveness of his home context. In such a case, the grading discriminates against the child based on a home situation he cannot control and violates his equal opportunity guarantees. Where homework is still used in the classroom today, the teacher and school must find creative ways for students to complete these assignments supported by the school structure and not solely dependent on parents. No matter how homework is used, according to this philosophy, the grading of the homework should not be mixed with more objective measurements of just what the child has learned.

Figures 11.3 to 11.10 provide a quick-reference summary of classroom and school practices that may be impacted when using judicious thinking similar to the previous grading example.

"You'd better come to school or we will kick you out"[10]			
Discipline Issue	**Moral 1** **Authoritarian Position**	**Moral 2** **Judicious**	**Judicious School Procedures**[a]
Unexcused absences or tardiness	The school provides students an education and if they fail to take advantage of what is provided by skipping class and showing academic deficiencies, bad attitude and offensive cultural values, the school and teacher have no further responsibilities to the student. By his/her actions, the student is less worthy and the school will not serve him/her. Law requires mandatory days of school attendance.	The gates will be open, a commitment to help all students will be given, and the school will place no walls to bar those "less worthy." The focus of mandatory school attendance should not be on days of attendance, but on whether the student has acquired the knowledge and skills needed to graduate and succeed in life.	Grades under no circumstances are lowered because of lateness or absences; alternative times, such as evenings and weekends, will be offered and special tutoring may be available to enable the student to learn the material.
Denying credit and dropping students from classes	After a specific number of absences, the student will be dropped from the class. This will apply to everyone.	The essential question is not the rule itself but the individual circumstances that serve as the substance of appeal. Each case must be looked at individually to determine whether the student is capable of completing satisfactory class work.	Students may be assigned to alternative education classes with tutors for the remaining grade period, and individualized instruction would be available. Students should not be punished for nonattendance, and should be given credit for the course if they demonstrate that they have obtained the knowledge by other means. Alternatives include a term paper covering the subject matter missed, a book review on the subject, or several pages outlining the chapters missed. Schools could also provide flexible schedules, including after-school and weekend programs, to alleviate overcrowding in alternative programs. If one student is ill and a second simply skipped class, should both be allowed to make up the work? Judiciously, the answer is yes, because both are still in need of an education regardless of the reason for nonattendance; each should have equal educational opportunity.[b]

FIGURE 11.3 Compulsory School Attendance

Discipline Issue	Moral 1 Authoritarian Position	Moral 2 Judicious	Judicious School Procedures[a]
Tardiness	The tardy student must be sent to the office for an excuse, and after three unexcused incidents of tardiness the student is suspended for one or two days. Problems: students losing more class time by going to the office; disruption for a second time; students playing games with rules by being tardy twice but never the third time (what if all 30 students in the class played this game); difficulty in judging and proving acceptable excuses; students learn more about following rules than about responsible behavior.	Each case must be handled individually, and the student who is tardy needs to be taught the skills of getting organized and being punctual. Tardiness should be approached as an educational instance and not as a moral judgment.	The teacher should be well prepared, start class promptly, and model behavior congruent with expectations of students. The teacher should have the responsibility of handling tardiness as an educational learning problem, with administrators becoming involved only in the most chronic cases.
Suspension A short-term denial of the student's right to the benefits of public education. Because of the brief duration the student would not suffer substantial loss of his/her educational opportunity.[c]	Rules are written, and breaking them will result in suspension. Judicious suspension. A Level 1 Authoritarian position is, "This will teach you a lesson."	The attitude of the educator is critical to a judicious suspension. The Level 2 Judicious position is, "We could both use time away from each other." The school would offer weekend and after-school tutoring to help the student make up missed content. A fostering of the student's self-esteem is critical, and the administrator calls the student during the suspension to offer encouragement, indicate that the student is wanted back, and maintain a student/educator relationship.	*Gross v. Lopez,* 419 US. 565, requires due process: — Notice: an oral or written notice of the charges (i.e., the rule the student violated). — Evidence: a summary of the evidence against the student (i.e., a teacher witnessed the student's misbehavior). — Defense: an opportunity for the student to be heard (i.e., the student has an opportunity to tell his or her side of the story).[d] An administrator does not have to comply with a student's request for an attorney or presence of a witness. (The courts have judged that this overburdens the school.)
Expulsions A longer duration than suspension, and usually results in the loss of grades and credit, thereby substantially depriving the student of educational opportunity.		As above, the administrator must attempt to project an attitude that maintains a student/educator relationship.	The school must provide substantive and procedural due process rights, offering charges, evidence, and a hearing to substantiate the reasons for its action. The student has the right to be represented by counsel, to receive a complete and accurate record of the proceedings, and to appeal the decision.

FIGURE 11.3   *(continued)*

Discipline Issue	Moral 1 Authoritarian Position	Moral 2 Judicious	Judicious School Procedures[a]
Handicapped student's suspension or expulsion			Handicapped students have additional rights that are not necessarily extended to the nonhandicapped. If the handicapped condition is the cause of the removal, other procedures legally come into play. Since these laws change quickly, up-to-date legal advice should be sought from an appropriate attorney.

[a] Gathercoal. p. 63.
[b] Gathercoal, pp. 65–66.
[c] Gathercoal, p. 67.
[d] Gathercoal, p. 67.

FIGURE 11.3 *(continued)*

Discipline Issue	Moral 1 Authoritarian Position	Moral 2 Judicious	Judicious School Procedures
Withholding privileges	Would be considered the teacher's right.	Participation in the graduation ceremony, for example, is a privilege and can be withheld. The student, however, does have a right to graduate; that right is not to be taken away as a consequence of unacceptable behavior.	Must be clearly in perspective with the gravity of the offense proportionate to the age and mental, emotional, or physical condition of the student. The school must give adequate notice, both written and taught. Judiciously considered an acceptable punishment.
Corporal punishment	Has long been used to punish students for unacceptable behavior and is still legal in many states. However, many new state child abuse laws are making principals and teachers subject to abuse charges because of corporal punishment.	Would be rejected as noneducational. However, reasonable physical force may be necessary at times to maintain order.	Follow these guidelines, with *Parent approval:* — A due process procedure with charges, evidence, and the student's right to be heard; — Reasonable administration with moderation, prudence, and consideration of the gravity of the offense, and physical condition and size of the student; — Privately administered, apart from the presence or hearing of other students; — Witnessed by a certified staff member; — Properly recorded and placed on file as a matter of record; — Notification to parents or legal guardian.[a]

FIGURE 11.4 Forms of Punishment

Discipline Issue	Moral 1 Authoritarian Position	Moral 2 Judicious	Judicious School Procedures
Punishing the group for the acts of one student	If no one admits to the "crime," the whole group suffers.	Not permitted	The judicious attitude is to take steps to prevent the action from occurring.
Punishing the student for the acts of his/her parents	The student may be disciplined because the parent brought him to school late.	The student is not responsible for the acts of people beyond his control, such as parents.	It is not permitted to punish the student for the actions of parents.
Sitting outside classroom doors, names on the blackboard	If the student fails to perform as required, this is the deserved punishment.	This type of punishment would do damage to the student's self-esteem.	May be considered holding the child up to ridicule by peers and may have detrimental psychological effects.
Keeping students after school	Often used as punishment; students will suffer public ridicule for unworthy actions.	Not educational; only serves to lower self-esteem.	Safety concerns about the child returning home in non-traditional time and manner.
Not permitting student to participate in class because of not having pencil/school supplies	"If you are unprepared, you may not participate."	Inconsistent with the child's right to equal educational opportunity	Have community equipment that may be "borrowed."
Detention rooms	"Doing time" is seen as an appropriate punishment.	Seen as a form of jail and may require due process criteria to be met; does not correct the behavior but causes resentment from the student; hurts the student/educator relationship.	Rename detention rooms to correction rooms or problem-solving rooms with tutors for learning.

[a] Gathercoal, p. 78.

FIGURE 11.4   *(continued)*

Discipline Issue	Moral 1 Authoritarian Position	Moral 2 Judicious	Judicious School Procedures
Destroying school property	The student must conform to behavior that will not do damage to school property, whether or not these expectations have been modeled in the student's home environment.	The judicious consequences must be proportionate to the severity of the loss incurred and the student's feeling of remorse.	Requires adequate notice; requires public service; parents are liable for damage done by their child. The school may use small claims court to recover costs.
Student's personal property loss		Efforts will be taken to help make personal property secure.	Inform parents and students of the risk involved in bringing objects from home. Educators and parents must explore alternative methods for securing items that must be brought. Parents of a student suffering property loss may take a classmate and his/her parents to small claims court to recover loss caused by that classmate.

FIGURE 11.5 Property Loss and Damage

RULES

Public schools may not create rules unilaterally just because a teacher or administrator values certain kinds of behavior and deportment. But fair rules <u>are</u> necessary and schools are often required to put a discipline statement and plan into writing; these are usually placed in student handbooks to provide a guideline and *prior notice criteria* for students and parents. (This does not necessarily pertain to private schools that receive no public money.) Substantive due process means a rule must: (1) have some rational basis or need for its adoption; (2) be as good in meeting this need as any alternative that a reasonable person might have developed; and (3) be supported by relevant and substantial evidence and findings of fact.[8] In other words, substantive due process means the rules and decisions must have a legal basis before the school may deny a student the opportunity to act in a specific manner.

Next, the judicious rules should be written with the justification that depriving the student and prohibiting their behavior is necessary because of the compelling state interest test of: (1) property loss or damage, (2) legitimate educational purpose, (3) health and safety, or (4) *serious* disruption of the educational process. The written rules, in a Level 1: Fear of Authority manner, establish a one-to-one relationship between a rule and a specific punishment or degree of punishment, thus boxing in the administrator or teacher and not permitting a judicious due process in determining a sanction or consequence. These rules

Discipline Issue	Moral 1 Authoritarian Position	Moral 2 Judicious	Judicious School Procedures
Dress and appearance	The school usually will provide a long list of specifics: no short shorts, frayed trousers, shirttails outside pants, bare midriffs, etc.	Have one broad rule covering the importance of dress in the educational environment; parents of the offending student would be notified that if the dress were patently vulgar or clearly inappropriate it would be prohibited.	First Amendment rights do protect a certain amount of self-expression. Students should be handled individually through educational means, and schools should enlist the help of parents; the educational means will serve as prior notice because of the vague broad rule.
Public displays of affection	Unacceptable in public.		Notify parents and enlist their help.
Student's refusal to say *Pledge of Allegiance*	Each student must state the pledge.	First Amendment guarantees the student a choice.	Protected by the Constitution; students may not be forced or punished.
Reading materials brought from home or pictures displayed in lockers			In the student's free time, the right is protected to read these materials as long as they are not patently vulgar.
Wearing robes for graduation; wearing shoes at all times; wearing protective gear for industrial arts, athletic activities, etc.			May be required as a legitimate educational purpose.
Insubordination and open diffidence; profane language; indecent gestures; bigoted statements.	Punishment would be administered.	The teacher would not be offended, but would confront the student and attempt to determine what is behind the verbal aggression in an educational way.	Rarely if ever is punished.
Free speech activities		Predetermine a place and location for such independent expression.	Place a bulletin board in hallways and classrooms for displaying free speech materials; "controlling the reasonable time, place, and manner of student expression"[a] or the distribution of expressive materials.

[a] Gathercoal, p. 86.

FIGURE 11.6 Speech and Expression

Discipline Issue	Moral 1 Authoritarian Position	Moral 2 Judicious	Judicious School Procedures
Searching lockers, purses, bags, or students' cars in the parking lot.	Teachers may open desks, bags, etc. on any occasion that they think they might find something that is not allowed.	Teachers must have "reasonable cause" to search; no search warrant is needed (for example, during the last week of class in an attempt to find missing school property).	Must have witnesses and, if possible, the student should be present and given prior notice.
Searching the body or conducting "strip searches"		Risky if the student fails to cooperate; avoid if possible. Reasonable cause must exist and be considered when determining legality of the search.	The school may wish the parent or police to perform such searches if the situation is serious.
Random searches		The searches are legal if a "compelling state interest" can be shown.	Not permitted unless there is prior notice or authorities are looking for misplaced school property or spoiled food that might cause health problems; bomb threats make such searches legal for safety reasons.
Seizure by school authorities of a student's property (toys, fad items and similar "brought from home" items) that disrupts the classroom or school environment	Student's property may be confiscated because students were warned not to bring such items. These items are lost to the student forever.	A teacher may confiscate disruptive items. These items shall be returned as quickly as possible.	A teacher may give a receipt for the items, showing respect for ownership.

FIGURE 11.7　Search and Seizure

Discipline Issue	Moral 1 Authoritarian Position	Moral 2 Judicious	Judicious School Procedures
Prior restraint Mandating in advance what someone may publish	The administration has the right to restrict content of students' speech.	Students only enjoy some substantive rights because of their age and impressionability, and the fact that they are not legally liable for what they publish.	Create a publication advisory board composed of a student editor, advisor, student-body representative, teacher, administrator, school board member, and possibly local newspaper editor. Review editorial problems within 48 hours. Write publication guidelines.
Passing notes	Passing notes is not acceptable.	May be viewed as a matter of civil rights if not disruptive to the educational process.	Teacher works with students to find an acceptable manner for note passing, showing the learning of responsible behavior.

FIGURE 11.8　Press

Discipline Issue	Moral 1 Authoritarian Position	Moral 2 Judicious	Judicious School Procedures
Religious celebration/ advocating religion; prayer at assemblies within school	The school has always done this, and large numbers of the public would complain if it stopped using prayers, religious symbols at Christmas, etc.	Advocating religion in a school context is clearly forbidden, but the study of religion as an academic study is permitted.	Religion and related activities are approached from an educational perspective.
Not participating in classes on religious grounds	All classes must be attended or the student fails the course.	If a student or his parent feels the class is contrary to his religious beliefs, he may be excused from attending the class without have his grade lowered.	Assigning alternative work is advisable to serve an educational purpose, not for punishment.
Wearing religious attire	School dress code must be observed.	This is clearly a student right, but a teacher may not wear religious dress if it appears to advocate a particular religious belief.	
Religious themes/ music	Christmas and other Christian holidays may be observed in school.	Religious music, etc., may be used in a secular manner. The attitude of the teacher and leadership is critical.	Students will have bulletin board space allocated to express religious preferences, and students are allowed freedom to express religious beliefs.
		Religious beliefs may be unacceptable to the minority, and therefore are not to be advocated by the school.	
Religious decorations	Christian holiday symbols have always been allowed, and to stop such practice would offend the majority.	Particular religious decorations are not advanced.	Not permitted as a wide distribution through the school, but may be allocated space for student expression.

FIGURE 11.9 Religion

Discipline Issue	Moral 1 Authoritarian Position	Moral 2 Judicious	Judicious School Procedures
Required payment for school supplies	All are required to pay; if one person were given an exemption, it would be unfair to the rest.	Make all efforts to eliminate such fees, because of possible discrimination against those students whose families may not be able to afford them.	When fees are needed, have other funds available for those who cannot afford to pay, and be very discrete in awarding this.
Access to the student's school records		Parents or the student (18 years or older) may not be denied an opportunity to review records.	Student/parents must be able to view, make copies at their own expense and challenge the content of the student's records.

FIGURE 11.10 School Fees and Records

should also reflect a Level 2: Feelings and Understanding of Social Responsibility (judicious) attitude by having them stated in positive terms rather than negative "thou shalt not" decrees. The student should be told what to do, rather than told not what to do. Level 1 negatively states the rule as, "Don't run in the hall!" or "Don't shout in the hallways!" or "Don't walk on the gym floor with street shoes!" These same rules can be positively stated, reflecting a Level 2 attitude, as, "Move in a safe manner through the halls" or "Keep your voice down so that others are not disturbed" or "Wear appropriate footwear when walking or playing on the gym floor." See Figure 11.11 for an example of a rule preamble statement that may appear in a student handbook written from a positive judicious perspective.

JUDICIOUS DISCIPLINE AND THE TEACHER BEHAVIOR CONTINUUM

Most discipline models provide the teacher with specific techniques to use in dealing with a student during and after an incident of misbehavior, while the teacher is feeling the "heat" and stress of the situation. Judicious discipline, however, basically is a reflective and teaching model requiring the teacher to cognitively think out her general approach and pass nearly all school practices through the filter of democratic rights. Once this is understood, the teacher will change rules, sanctions, grading, and host of other procedures to create a fairer, nonauthoritarian classroom. The judicious classroom will present a climate of acceptance whereby the teacher focuses on maintaining the student–teacher relationship. The teacher will also actively teach the class constitutional rights, either by having the students create their own judicious classroom rules or, if limited by short classroom periods, announcing rules founded on these same democratic amendments.

Judicious discipline is not a "stand-alone" discipline model, but must be used interactively with other more proscriptive discipline models. The author suggests that the ideas, techniques, and models of Dreikurs, Cooperative Discipline, Glasser, and, to a lesser extent, Gordon's *T.E.T.* philosophy, would add strength to these models. In the Dreikurs, Glasser, and other models, rules are necessary but the teacher must decide which rules are fair, necessary, and acceptable; clearly, judicious discipline answers these questions and makes a major contribution to an understanding of rules and democratic fairness.

Questions/Directive Statements

The primary elements used from the Teacher Behavior Continuum are questioning and directive statements. First, the teacher questions her own orientation to authoritarian and democratic procedures, and then reflects on the fairness of each set of procedures. When a discipline incident occurs or a rule is broken, the teacher asks questions to help ensure due process for the student while determining actions that will maintain a judicious attitude and healthy student–teacher relationship. (Visually looking on and nondirective statements are not used in the judicious discipline's TBC.)

Judicious discipline is not a discipline model that prescribes a formula or specific procedures of handling discipline incidents in our classroom. Rather it is a preventive

---

Student Handbook Preamble

Kent High School is a learning community where students feel accepted, and the teachers value each child's abilities and rights. Members of this community of learners are interdependent and must work to show others that they are respected for their distinct and unique differences. Every member must strive to make this school a community that is healthy and safe for all, and a place where everyone can learn. As a student-citizen of this community-school, each person will be guaranteed the right to know the reason for rule and actions that personally affect him or her, and will have the responsibility to contribute and participate in procedures ensuring these rights. The student will respect the rights of all members and the school will take actions to stop students who willfully attempt to take away others' rights by their behavior.

The major goal of Kent High School is to educate students as citizens who understand and can contribute to a democratic way of governance and living. The school as a democratic laboratory will teach academic and social skills that will serve its students as mature citizens.

Signed: Written by the 1994 faculty and administration of KHS

School Rules:
Act in a Safe and Healthy Way.
(Use furniture appropriately, walk when inside the building, etc. Compelling State Interest: Safety) Treat all Property with Respect.
(Take care of textbooks, library books, school materials and equipment, etc. Compelling State Interest: Property) Respect the Rights and Needs of Others.
(Show courtesy, cooperate, use appropriate language, etc. Compelling State Interest: Serious Disruption of the Educational Process)
Take Responsibility for Learning
(Work hard, come prepared, be on time, etc. Compelling State Interest: Legitimate Educational Purpose)[a]

---

[a] Gathercoal, pp. 36–37.

FIGURE 11.11   Rule Preamble Statement

guide and a teaching model that uses our legal rights and laws to give a democratic perspective to the framework for creating rules. ("Do the rules meet our nation's legal standards?") It also gives the teacher steps and procedures, called "due process," for dealing with the student after a discipline incident. The following is a step-by-step process that attempts to make this model clear for the user. Again, the Teacher Behavior Continuum is used (see Figure 11.12).

> *Step 1 Teacher commitment.* The teacher must question her own procedures and behaviors and commit herself to running a democratic classroom by teaching principles of constitutional amendments, due process procedures, and the difficulties of group versus individual rights. The teacher would change a host of general practices in order to advance democratic practices.

> *Step 2 Teach democratic principles.* (*Note:* Step 2 is for the teacher who is not confined to a 50-minute period with students and has time to teach this inductively through activities and discussion. The teacher who has limited time should skip Step 2 and go to Step 3.) The teacher asks the class to list what rights they have in their country. She then asks the class to list what rights they have in school as students. These two lists are compared by placing them both on the board, with the teacher asking questions.

Looking on	Nondirective Statements	Questions	Directive Statements	Modeling	Reinforcement (Judicious consequences)	Physical Intervention/ Isolation
Step 1. Teacher Commitment to Democratic Classroom		Step 2. Teach Principles Students list their individual rights: • "What rights do you have in this country?" • "What rights do you have in this school?" Compare two lists (on board) "Are these rights the same?" (Skip to step 3 for teacher with limited class time)			Step 7. Teach/examples of Judicious Consequences, apology, conference with parents, etc.	
			Step 3. Teach 1st, 4th, and 14th amendments directly (property loss/damage, legitimate educa-tional purpose, health/safety serious disruption of educational process)			Consequences: — Time out — Loss of privilege — Suspension — Expulsion — Others
		Step 4. Establish Class Rules related to the three amendments "Which of our rules are justified by the amendments?"				
		Step 5. Teach "compelling state interest" Teacher: "When can society take away individual rights?" compelling state interest • Property loss/damage • Legitimate educational purpose • Health and safety • Serious disruption of educational process	Write, post, sign rules.	Step 6. Give examples of group vs. individual rights.		

FIGURE 11.12   Teacher Behavior Continuum (TBC): Judicious Discipline

Step 3 The teacher teaches the First, Fourth, and Fourteenth Amendments through directive teaching (directive statements).

Step 4 Establish class rules. Through questioning, the class now compares the amendments and democratic rights with the previously established rules (Step 2) (*Note:* The deductive teacher will announce and explain predetermined rules based on judicious guidelines.) The class then discusses and reflects until the students can agree on all the salient rules needed to guide them in their class-room activities and social interactions. The rules are posted, signed by each student, placed in the student handbook, and sent home to parents (due process: prior notice).

Step 5 Teach "compelling state interest" (property loss/damage, legitimate educational purpose, health and safety, and serious disruption of educational process)

Physical Intervention

Step 6 Teach rules of the group versus individual rights. The teacher provides examples of students' rights that cannot be taken away (i.e., speech, how to wear hair and clothing, etc.). The students will learn at what point the teacher and school administration will prohibit and intervene [physical intervention] by taking away the individual's rights in order to stop inappropriate behaviors or when needed to protect a compelling state interest.

Reinforcement

Step 7 Teach/explain judicious consequences and attitude. With the use of Figure 11.13, the teacher will describe the types of consequences a student might experience (loss of privileges, required apology, restitution, suspension, expulsion, and others) if the student's behavior takes away others' rights. Just as important is to show that the teacher will always work to maintain a student–teacher relationship and will attempt to provide educational consequences when rules are broken. The teacher explains that in applying judicious consequences not all children will get the same consequence for breaking the same rule; rather, the response will be individualized.

Modeling

The teacher must use her manner of establishing rules and awarding sanctions to model a Level 2: Feelings and Understanding of Social Responsibility approach. This also means that the teacher cannot allow herself special privileges (cutting in line in the school cafeteria when there is a rule against cutting by students, smoking when students may not, or failing to wear safety glasses in the industrial shop when students are required to do so). The teacher must take a "do as I do" approach, rather than just one of "do as I say."

Property Loss and Damage	Legitimate Educational Purpose	Health and Safety	Serious Disruption of the Educational Process
apology	apology	apology	apology
clean it up	redo the assignment or take	complete a research	private conference
give it back	another test	report	mutual agreements
restitution	complete an alternative	community service	time out
mutual agreements	assignment	project	problem-solving room
community service	study with a tutor	private conference	counseling
project	private conference	mutual agreements	mediation
counseling	mutual agreement	counseling	conference with parents
conference with parents	counseling	conference with parents	reassignment
reassignment	conference with parents	reassignment	community service
loss of privileges	reassignment	loss of privileges	loss of privileges
suspension	loss of privilege	suspension	suspension
expulsion	suspension	expulsion	expulsion
	expulsion		

FIGURE 11.13 Examples of Consequences Suggested by *Judicious Discipline*

SUMMARY

When a teacher or administrator is faced with a situation in which the student has broken a rule and has to be prohibited from acting in a manner that impinges on state interests or the rights of others, the attitude utilized is critical. It is important to teach constitutional rights, rules, compelling state interest, and due process, but the cement that holds all of this together to build a solid and democratic classroom or school is the attitude of Level 2: Feelings and Understanding of Social Responsibility. It is critical for the educator to take the time, when about to discipline a student, to utilize due process and ask:

- What needs to be learned here?
- How would an educator manage the problem?
- Do I need more information about the student or the student's family?
- What strategies can be used to keep this student in school?
- How will the student perceive the consequence?
- How will it affect the school community?
- How can I maintain the student–teacher relationship?[9]

Sam, with his fight in the school cafeteria, would have been better served if he had had a more judicious school that did not have as its rule a punishment statement that boxed the educators into a unilateral authoritarian position. The previous questions would have permitted the school administration to understand Sam's family situation. This in turn would have enabled them to take actions that might work to improve the father–son relationship, strengthen Sam's ability to handle his own behavior under stress, and maintain a relationship with him through which he would feel that he is not in a "them versus me" relationship. This would allow him to feel that school is a place that cares about him and his needs and that really wishes to help him become a more complete, better educated person during these adolescent years.

Strengths and Limitations of the Model

Models of discipline have been included in this text because they present to the teacher concrete and specific techniques on what to do with a misbehaving student when the misbehavior occurs. Judicious discipline is not a model that provides help for the teacher on daily limit setting, but does present a framework for possible prevention of discipline difficulties. In addition, it shows how to use a legal framework to create a climate, attitude, and set of procedures for running a democratic classroom based on the principles of the Bill of Rights. Students, families, schools, and society in general are changing, and teachers have lost their former *in loco parentis* position of simply creating rules and sanctions based on their own values and for their own convenience.

The seasoned teacher sees that judicial actions and court cases have expanded into playing a significant role in today's daily classroom procedures. Modern teachers must rethink previous *in loco parentis* practices for two key reasons: (1) they do not want to find themselves in court as a result of their discipline actions, and more important, (2) schools and classrooms play an essential role in preparing students for the democratic society in which they live and will fully join as adults. The establishment of rules, and due process procedures to be employed by teachers or school authorities provides a practical model for teaching students democratic ways of living. Especially challenging, difficult, and sometimes contradictory is the tension of individual rights versus the rights of the group. Historically, most school practices were created to serve the good of all, with only limited if any concern for individual rights.

Again, many seasoned teachers will be surprised to discover that such practices as lowering a student's grade because of repeated absences might be challenged from a legal perspective. But the suggestions made by judicious discipline for teaching the Bill of Rights, and attempting to use them as a construct for assessing fairness and the justification for various rules, might provide experiences that lead these students to a high moral understanding of society's complex interactions.

SUMMARY OF KEY CONCEPTS

adequate notice	feelings and understanding	judicious consequence	substantive due
compelling state	of social responsibility	liberty	process
interest	*in loco parentis*	moral growth	teachable moment
due process	individual rights	student/educator	
fear of authority	judicious	relationship	

EXERCISES

The four examples of Mike, Andrew, Jake, and Linda, described in preceding chapters, do not give the teacher help with limit setting, encouragement, and management system, but do provide some help regarding backup responses. The teacher and school officials would need a clear understanding of group versus individual rights if students such as Jake the Grenade are removed from the classroom or school. Because such actions as turning on the gas jets in the chemistry laboratory would endanger the lives of others, this issue would become one of compelling state interest. The teacher and school officials would need a clear understanding of group versus individual rights if Jake is removed from school because of compelling state interest in (a) health and safety and (b) serious disruption of the education process. If Jake were removed, due process procedures would need to be followed.

Here are other school discipline problems more connected to the judicious discipline constructs.

1. The editor of the yearbook has taken one senior female student picture and morphed it into a sexually provocative body. Instead of labeling her as "best dancer," "most popular," or "most likely to succeed," he labeled her as "most easiest to make," suggesting that she is promiscuous. This has slipped by the school officials, and the yearbooks have been sent to all students. The parents are very unhappy and threatening to sue the school. As a discipline action, the principal has refused to permit the yearbook editor to participate in the graduation ceremony. Can he do this? Can the school withhold his diploma?

2. The high school has an underground newspaper not sanctioned by the school that historically has contained humorously written articles about the faculty and students. This year an article appears on the Internet version, but in print, that makes racial and violent proposals regarding one African-American teacher. Can the school officials take any discipline actions toward these students? Would such incidents be turned over to local legal authorities? Is material published on the Internet protected by freedom of speech?

3. A middle-school student wishes join the school wrestling team, and he is required to take a physical examination, including an AIDS test. One student, because of his religious convictions, refuses to take the test. Could this student be refused the opportunity to be on the school wrestling team?

4. A kindergartner has had a chronic case of head lice. Finally, after many notices to the parents, school officials refuse to permit the student to come to school. Can the school do this? Why or why not? How would Gathercoal handle this incident?

5. An extreme form of shoes with dramatically oversized heels has become a fad, and many students begin to wear them to school. While at school one student tripped, causing a serious sprained ankle, and another student fell down the school stairs. The school has banned these shoes from school. The students claim that this is not in the school dress code and that the school has no right to do this. What would the judicious discipline position be regarding this ban?

NOTES

1. J. Piaget, *Moral Judgment of the Child,* trans. Marjorie Gabain (New York: Free Press, 1965).
2. R. Dreikurs, *Psychology in the Classroom: A Manual for Teachers,* 2nd ed. (New York: Harper & Row, 1968).
3. F. Gathercoal, *Judicious Discipline* (Davis, CA: Caddo Gap Press, 1991).
4. Ibid.
5. Ibid., p. 44.
6. Ibid., p. 42.
7. Ibid.
8. Ibid.
9. Ibid.

REFERENCES

Dreikurs, R. *Psychology in the Classroom: A Manual for Teachers.* 2nd ed. New York: Harper & Row, 1968.

Editors of Deskbook Encyclopedia of American School Law. Information Research Systems, P.O. Box 409, Rosemount, MN 55068 (yearly).

Gathercoal, F. *Judicious Discipline.* Davis, CA: Caddo Gap Press, 1991.

Kern, A., and Alexander, M. D. *The Law of Schools, Students and Teachers in a Nutshell.* Los Angeles: West Publishing Co., 1984.

Kirp, D. L. and Jensen, D. N. *School Days, Rule Days.* New York: Falmer Press, 1986.

McEwan, B. *Practicing Judicious Discipline: An Educator's Guide to a Democratic Classroom.* Davis, CA: Caddo Gap Press, 1991.

Piaget, J. *Moral Judgment of the Child.* trans. Marjorie Gabain. New York: Free Press, 1965.

Yudolf, M. G., Kirp, D. L., Geel, T. V., and Levin, B. *Educational Policy and Law.* McCutchan Publishing, Co., 1982.

CHAPTER 12

SKILLSTREAMING—TEACHING PROSOCIAL SKILLS

Theorist/Writers: Goldstein and McGinnis

- McGinnis, Ellen, and Arnold P. Goldstein. *Skillstreaming the Elementary School Child.*
- McGinnis, Ellen, and Arnold P. Goldstein. *Skillstreaming in Early Childhood: Teaching Prosocial Skills to the Preschool and Kindergarten Child.*
- Goldstein, Arnold P., Robert P. Sprafkin, N. Jane Gershaw, and Paul Klein. *Skill-streaming the Adolescent: A Structured Learning Approach to Teaching Prosocial Skills.*

OUTLINE OF THE SKILLSTREAMING MODEL

Basic Assumptions about Motivation

- Many students today who are disruptive or ineffective in classroom have failed to acquire basic social skills.
- These social skills can be identified at the early childhood, elementary, and secondary levels.
- Students can be assessed as to their mastery or lack of social skills.
- Social skills can be taught through direct instruction based on behavioral analysis constructs.

Teacher Behaviors (steps in direct instruction)

1. Define the skill
2. Model the skill
3. Establish student skill need
4. Select role-players
5. Set up the role-play
6. Conduct the role-play
7. Provide performance feedback

8. Assign skill homework

9. Select next role-player

Guidelines, Planning, or Preparatory Teacher Actions

1. Select group leaders (teachers).

2. Select students who have difficulties with interpersonal relations, aggression management, and related problems.

3. Evaluate these students through direct observation or a skills checklist, based on the prosocial skills.

4. Place the students together, based on similar skill needs, for teaching purposes as a group for periods of 25 to 40 minutes three to five times a week.

5. The set-aside space may contain a chalkboard or easel pad, chairs, and a few selective props related to the theme of the role-play.

OVERVIEW

A young teacher-in-training sees her favorite teacher from high school at the local mall and approaches to reintroduce herself as a past student and to tell her that she, too, is now becoming a teacher. The veteran high school teacher responds unenthusiastically with, "Oh, well! I retired last year, thank goodness. Students today are not what they used to be, and I am very glad to have gotten out of the classroom." The writers and designers of skill-streaming suggest that we, as teachers, are hearing and seeing this attitude more and more often from today's seasoned and experienced teachers. We hear about students' noncompliance, confrontations with one another, their failure to work and show interest in their studies, the decline in their joining and supporting activities, and a host of other complaints. In addition to this list is also the new concern about violent and aggressive students and passive introverted students who are socially isolated with little sense of belonging.

> John is a student who constantly interrupts the teacher's instruction and directs put-down remarks to other students when they are talking. He is disliked by his peers and is unwanted for classroom cooperative groups. The teacher's overtures and discussions with John are met with claims that "You're picking on me."
>
> Kate cannot focus and stay in her seat long enough to do her work. Her body— especially her arms and legs—is constantly in motion, and when she is free to interact with her peers, she pushes and takes similar physical actions that produce fights with others. At the same time, the teacher knows that Kate is bright and academically capable but her work does not show it.
>
> Mario is an introverted boy who sits passively slumped down into his chair behind his desk. He tends to be bored and complies with the teacher's requests only grudgingly. Other students are fearful of him; on one occasion, when a fellow student accidentally jostled him, he threatened the student with severe violence.

These are some examples of misbehaving or problem children who are in our classrooms today. Discipline models in other chapters of this book provide different theoretical positions of how to view these children and their behavior; they differ dramatically on how to intervene or deal with such children. Skillstreaming makes a clear claim on being able to help teachers have an impact on such children to improve their preschool, kindergarten, and secondary classrooms. Skillstreaming is a psychoeducational intervention program that draws on both psychology (primarily behavior analysis) and education (mainly direct instruction).

Defining Skillstreaming

To describe it in abbreviated form, skillstreaming is a skill-deficit model. Designers view the misbehaving student as lacking the necessary social skills, which they call prosocial, to function well with peers and adults. This lack of skills in handling potentially stressful social interactions and conflicts leaves these children with the stereotypic responses of passivity, isolation, or violent actions toward others.

The skillstreaming designers developed a list of 60 necessary prosocial skills that they believe most students absorb through incidental learning. They believe that students today—in significantly greater numbers than in the past—are not acquiring these social skills. Thus, skillstreaming attempts to teach these skills directly.
These skills are

- Classroom survival skills (asking for help, saying thank you, asking questions, etc.)
- Friendship-making skills (introducing yourself)
- Beginning a conversation (joining in, etc.)
- Dealing with feelings (expressing your feelings)
- Recognizing another's feelings (dealing with anger, etc.),
- Finding alternatives to aggression (maintaining self-control, responding to teasing, avoiding trouble, staying out of fights, etc.).
- Dealing with stress (dealing with boredom, reacting to failure, saying no, accepting no, etc.).

Figure 12.1 lists these skills and allows the reader to compare them in categories at the early childhood, elementary, and adolescent levels. The prosocial skills are structurally taught by selecting students, through pretesting, in need of these skills and enrolling them in group training session three to five times a week. Two adult leaders use modeling and role-playing with the help of skill cards, performance feedback, and homework activities in an attempt to transfer the training to real-life situations for these students' daily living. The instructional principle is based on behavior analysis, so rewards and incentive systems are used; therefore we can classify this model as Rules and Consequences, along with the 60 prosocial skills.

Skillstreaming and Discipline

Skillstreaming was first used with special needs children who had to be taught social skills to be able to leave protective care as adults and live in independent self-care homes and situations. With the national trend toward more and more violence, and with increasing

	In Early Childhood[a] (ages three to seven)	With the Elementary School Child[b] (first to fifth grades)	With the Adolescent[c] (Middle and Secondary School)
Group	I: Beginning Social Skills	I: Classroom Survival Skills	I: Beginning Social Skills
	Listening Using nice talk Using brave talk Saying thank you Rewarding yourself Asking for help Asking a favor Ignoring	Listening Asking for help Saying thank you Bringing materials to class Following instructions Completing assignments Contributing to discussions Offering help to an adult Asking a question Ignoring distractions Making corrections Deciding on something to do Setting a goal	Listening Starting a conversation Having a conversation Asking a question Saying thank you Introducing yourself Interrupting other people Giving a compliment
Group	II: School-related Skills		II: Advanced Social Skills
	Asking a question Following directions Trying when it's hard Interrupting		Asking for help Joining in Giving instructions Following instructions Apologizing Convincing others
Group	III: Friendship-making Skills	II: Friendship-making skills	III. Planning Skills
	Greeting others Reading to others Joining in Waiting your turn Sharing Offering help Asking someone to play Playing a game	Introducing yourself Beginning a conversation Ending a conversation Joining in Playing a game Asking a favor Offering help to a classmate Giving a compliment Suggesting an activity Sharing Apologizing	Deciding on something to do Deciding what caused a problem Setting a goal Deciding on your abilities Gathering information Arranging problems by importance Making a decision Concentrating on a task

(Figure continues)

FIGURE 12.1 A Comparison of Prosocial Skills—Early Childhood, Elementary Years, and During Adolescence

Group	IV: Dealing with Feelings	III: Dealing with Feelings	IV: Dealing with Feelings
	Knowing your feelings Feeling left out Asking to talk Dealing with fear Deciding how someone feels Showing affection	Knowing your feelings Expressing your feelings Recognizing another's feelings Showing understanding of another's feelings Expressing concern for another Dealing with your anger Dealing with another's anger Expressing affection Dealing with fear Rewarding yourself	Knowing your feelings Expressing your feelings Understanding the feelings of others Dealing with someone else's anger Expressing affection Dealing with fear Rewarding yourself
Group	V: Alternatives to Aggression	IV: Alternatives to Aggression	V: Alternatives to Aggression
	Dealing with teasing Dealing with feeling mad Deciding if it's fair Solving a problem Accepting consequences	Using sel-fcontrol Asking permission Responding to teasing Avoiding trouble Staying out of fights Problem solving Accepting consequences Dealing with an accusation Negotiating	Asking permission Sharing something Helping others Negotiating Using self-control Standing up for your rights Responding to teasing Avoiding trouble with others Keeping out of fights
Group	VI: Dealing with Stress	V: Dealing with Stress	VI: Dealing with Stress
	Relaxing Dealing with mistakes Being honest Knowing when to tell Dealing with losing Wanting to be first Saying no Accepting no Deciding what to do	Dealing with boredom Deciding what caused a problem Making a complaint Answering a complaint Dealing with losing Being a good sport Dealing with being left out Dealing with embarrassment Reacting to failure Accepting no Saying no Relaxing Dealing with group pressure Dealing with wanting something that isn't yours Making a decision Being honest	Making a complaint Answering a complaint Showing sportsmanship after a game Dealing with embarrassment Dealing with being left out Standing up for a friend Responding to persuasion Responding to failure Dealing with contradictory messages Dealing with an accusation Getting ready for a difficult conversation Dealing with group pressure

[a] McGinnis, Ellen, and Arnold P. Goldstein. *Skillstreaming in Early Childhood: Teaching Prosocial Skills to the Preschool and Kindergarten Child.* Champaign, IL: Research Press Company, 1990.
[b] McGinnis, Ellen, and Arnold P. Goldsein. *Skillstreaming the Elementary School Child: New Strategies and Perspectives for Teaching Prosocial Skills.* Champaign, IL: Research Press Company, 1997.
[c] Goldstein, Arnold P., Robert P. Sprafkin, N. Jane Gershaw, and Paul Klein. *Skillstreaming the Adolescent: A Structured Learning Approach to Teaching Prosocial Skills.* Champaign, IL: Research Press Company, 1980.

FIGURE 12.1 *(continued)*

numbers of very difficult children requiring excessive disciplining by teachers in regular classrooms, the designers have reshaped it and created direct instructional programs appropriate for normal functioning children, as well as the special needs students being mainstreamed in public school classrooms who have not yet acquired many of the most basic and simple social skills.

Skillstreaming is a proactive model, not a reactive one. Such discipline models as Glasser, Albert/Dreikurs, and Assertive Discipline do provide direct and concrete actions for the teacher to use in reacting to a classroom situation of a misbehaving student. Skill-streaming is a program that is initiated with students <u>before</u> the misbehavior would occur, enabling students to acquire the prosocial skills that can help them become more effective. As a result, the students would not be getting into or causing trouble, not only at school but also at home and in the wider society.

How Is the Skillstreaming Model Implemented?

Getting Ready for Skillstreaming   First, group leaders are selected. When possible, the leaders are either two experienced teachers or a teacher and another adult paraprofessional. The selection process requires an understanding of cultural diversity and methods of motivating students through behavior analysis constructs and actions. The program suggests methods of selecting students who have difficulties with inter-personal relations, aggression management, and related problems. These students are evaluated, through direct observation or a skills checklist, based on the prosocial skills mentioned previously to determine their level of proficiency regarding the needed skills. The students with similar skills needs are then placed together and taught as a group for periods of 25 to 40 minutes three to five times a week, in a set-aside space that may contain a chalkboard or easel pad, chairs, and a few selective props related to the theme of the role-play. The program with a particular student may last as little as two days or as long as three years, and will be based on the individual student's progress. The instructional system uses skill cards, which cue the role-playing student in practicing the skills. For example, for the skill "Listening" the card will require the student to:

1. Look at the person who is talking

2. Sit quietly

3. Think about what is being said

4. Say yes and nod the head

5 Ask a question about the topic to find out more

The program also utilizes two booklets: a Skillstreaming Student Manual that introduces skillstreaming to the student along with the procedures of modeling, role-playing, per-formance feedback, and transfer training (homework); and a Program Form booklet that provides essential program forms, checklists, and charts that may be reproduced.

Skillstreaming Teaching Procedures   In order to carry out the program's teaching principles of modeling, role-playing, performance feedback, and transfer, the teacher as group leader follows an orderly nine-step program (see Figure 12.2).

```
1. Define the skill.
2. Model the skill.
3. Establish student skill need.
4. Select role-players.
5. Set up the role-play.
6. Conduct the role-play.
7. Provide performance feedback.
8. Assign skill homework.
9. Select next role-player.
```

FIGURE 12.2 Skillstreaming Teaching Steps

Step 1: Define the Skill (Show Skill Card)

The group training session begins with the teacher defining the skill, stating why it is needed, and getting the students to engage in some discussion about the skill.

Step 2: Model the Skill

Once the skill is defined and introduced, the teacher moves to modeling the skill. Modeling is simply defined as learning through imitation. The modeling permits the student to learn new behaviors (observational learning) by imitating others. Peers who model aggressive behaviors and see this behavior go unpunished during routine daily living will learn to become aggressive as well. On the other hand, modeling of altruism and care by peers under the training of skillstreaming can help inhibit these same negative aggressive behaviors. Through this modeling, a child who deals with a confrontational peer in a positive effective manner may enable the classmate to approach future confrontations in a similar positive manner.

The teacher-leader of the training group understands and uses the various modeling stages of attention, retention, and reproduction. The teacher minimizes distractions and keeps the students focused and alert so their attention is on the model. The retention—that is, remembering the behaviors after the modeling stops—is done through *covert rehearsal.* This is accomplished by having the student perform activities under the questioning and guidance of the teacher in a way that requires the student to verbally retell the actions he saw or role-play the behaviors themselves. Finally, reproduction is the process of arranging reinforcing rewards to get the student to show not just that he knows the skill, but also that he can use it in a real-life social situation.

The guidelines are:

- Do two examples for each skill demonstrated

- Select themes and situations related to the real life of the student

- Have a modeling student or adult leader resemble the real-life antagonist as much as possible

- Model positive outcomes and reinforce them
- Use modeling that follows and depicts the list of actions on the skills cards
- Use modeling that depicts one skill at a time

Step 3: Establish Student Skill Need

The student is asked to describe where, when, and with whom he will need this skill in the future. (Write the student's name with future person and theme.) Relevance must be established for the use of this skill in real life.

Step 4: Select the Role-player (everyone role-plays each skill, reluctant student goes last)

Generally, every member of the group gets to role-play the skill. (The writers offer guidelines and techniques for dealing with the reluctant student.)

Step 5: Set up the Role-play

Once the need for the skill is established in Step 3, a main actor in the role-play is appointed, and a second person (co-player) with characteristics of the real-life person is chosen. The teacher-leader then questions the main actor to set the scene and context for the situation. The leader requests additional information to set the stage and describe the physical setting, events immediately preceding the situation, and the mood or manner of those being portrayed.

Step 6: Conduct the Role-play

The role-play now begins and the main actor is asked to follow the behavioral steps on feedback cards, as the second teacher-leader near the chalkboard points to various behaviors on the cards to cue the actor. The audience is also assigned a role to observe the skills and describes them later. An unusual technique of "think aloud" is requested of the main actor: Rather than thinking internally about what is happening, the actors are asked to speak their thoughts out loud for all to hear.

The actors are coached to stay in their roles, and prompts are given if needed. Each member gets to role-play, and the actors' roles may be reversed or the group leader may play a role. For performance feedback reasons and to reinforce actions after the role-playing, the "production" may be videotaped.

Step 7: Provide Performance Feedback

After the role-play is completed and as part of the performance feedback, the students are asked to react to how the (1) co-actors, (2) assigned observers, and (3) group leaders followed the skill steps. The leaders will use praise, approval, and encouragement statements. After hearing what has been said, the main actor may comment on the feedback he or she has received. Finally, it may be helpful to have the actors repeat their roles after hearing the feedback.

Step 8: Assign Skill Homework

After the successful role-play, the students are given the homework assignment of using that skill at some future date in a real-life situation. Through questioning and coaching by the leaders, the students decide when, how, and with whom they will use the skill in a future context. "Oh, I will use this with my older sister, after diner when we normally argue about clean-up duties!"

The homework, as the transfer training activity, is viewed at three levels, depending on the age and capabilities of the student. It assumes a level of increased difficulty as the levels progress.

Homework Level 1: Preparation   The teacher helps the student fill out a homework report form, which requires the student to name the person with whom he will attempt to practice this skill in the future. On the form the student indicates the date, skill, and steps he will take in performing this practice. After completing this homework assignment, the student is asked to indicate on the form what happened and how well he did, using the criteria of "good," "okay," or "not so good." Since these activities can be done at the preschool/kindergarten, elementary, and adolescent levels, these forms vary in the amount of writing required of the student. For example, the evaluation done at the preschool/kindergarten level requires the student to evaluate how he did by circling one of three "smiley faces": one with a smile, the middle with a mouth as a straight line, and a third with a downturned mouth. Finally, the teacher would talk it over with the student to see why he evaluated his actions as he did.

Homework Level 2: Use Homework Report Form 2 Independently
The student at level two has achieved mastery of a particular skill and is now ready to document his homework independently. The Homework Form 2 requires the student to record short documentation of "When did I practice?" Note that at this level the child uses the skill many times, but always just the same one skill. The student turns this homework in to the leader, who writes comments on the report and returns it to the student.

Homework Level 3: More Than One Skill Listed on a 3 × 5-inch Index Card   Finally, at level three, the child documents his practice as homework by writing not just one but all skills practiced that week, making tally marks for each time a skill is used. Each new training session begins with a homework report, with the leader reinforcing the student's performance positively or negatively. The teacher also uses a Group Self-Report Chart (the student places a "sticker" or indicator when the skill was used) listing all the students' names as a continued reinforcer and reminder. Skill contracts, self-recording forms, and skill awards are also included and described in the booklets.

The written materials also provide guidelines and procedures for handling student behavioral problems while teachers are conducting the training sessions. These actions are based on behavior analysis principles, which may be seen in the chapter on behavior analysis in this book.

Step 9: Select the Next Role-player

The next student is selected to become the main role-player and the previous steps are repeated.

SUMMARY

Skillstreaming is a structured approach based on behavior analysis. It works by teaching prosocial skills directly to students at all age levels through modeling, role-playing, performance feedback, and transfer (homework). The teacher will follow step-by-step procedures (see Figure 12.3). The philosophical position is that the misbehaving student has a skill deficit and if he is taught these skills, he will be able to transfer this training to his school and daily

Looking	Naming	Questioning	Commanding	Modeling	Reinforcement	Acting (physical intervention)
		Step 1-*Define the skill.* Step 3: *Establish student skill need.* Student describes where, when, and with whom they will need this skill in the future. (Write the student's name with future person and theme.)		Step 2: *Model the skill.* Step 4: *Select role-players.* -Everyone role-plays each skill; the reluctant student goes last. Step 5: *Set up the role-play.* -Actor chooses second person (co-player) with characteristic of real-life person -Request additional information to set the stage. -Describe the physical setting. -Describe events immediately preceding the situation. -Describe mood or manner of those being portrayed. Step 6: *Conduct the role-play.* -Follows behavioral steps on feedback cards. -"Thinks aloud." -All others are instructed to watch for behavioral steps (may assign a step to be observed to an audience member). -Coach actors to stay in roles. -One group leader points to behavioral steps on chalkboard as they are enacted. -Repeat with other group members. -Do two of each skill each session. Actors' role may be reversed or group leader plays role.	Step 7: *Provide performance feedback.* -React to role-play (1) co-actors, (2) assigned observers, (3) group leaders (using praise, approval, and encouragement) of following skill steps. -Main actor comments on feedback received. -Actors may repeat role after criticism. Step 8: *Assign Skill Homework.* -Decide when, how, and with whom the student will use the skill in future context. -Use Homework Level in order of difficulty; Level 1: Preparation: fill out homework report form (name, date, skill, steps, who?, when?). After completed: What happened? How did I do? (evaluation: good, OK, or bad). Why did I evaluate as such? Level 2: Documentation: Uses Homework Report Form 2 independently, turns in to leader who writes comments and returns it. Level 3: All skills: Listed on 3X5 index card, tallies each time a skill is used. (Each session begins with homework report, with leader reinforcing positive or negatively.) -Teacher uses Group Self-Report Chart (students place "sticker" or indicator when skill was used). -Continued reinforcers and reminders: skill contracts, self-recording forms, skill awards.	

FIGURE 12.3 Teacher Behavior Continuum (TBC) Skillstreaming

life, thus becoming a socially skilled and well-behaved productive person. The books and other written documents, including training videos, demonstrate to teachers how they may carry out such training in their schools.

Strengths and Limitation of the Model

If one accepts the behavior construct of behavior analysis and the classic experimental studies, skillstreaming provides an adequate review of the research, data, and theories that support and define the use of modeling, role-playing, performance feedback, and homework that are a major strength for this model.

Practicing teachers will quickly criticize this model for the amount of time required to pull out groups of stu-

dent for such specialized training. Skillstreaming would counter that attitude and say that by spending "pennies" of time up front, you can save "dollars" of time in the future. By this we mean that such skillstreaming activities would be very time consuming in the course of the school day, but if we identify the students in need of these skills and train then beforehand, being proactive, we will eliminate the need for reactive discipline actions that are very time consuming to the teacher, administrators, and the school system in general. The prosocial skills may be as important or even more important for some children as "reading, writing, and arithmetic" because as well-functioning children with these skills they will have greater life successes.

SUMMARY OF KEY CONCEPTS

attention
covert rehearsal
homework
modeling
observational learning

observers
performance feedback
practice
prosocial skills
reinforcement

reproduction
retention
role-playing
self-recording
self-report

skill award
skill constructs
skillstreaming
themes
"thinking out loud"

CASE STUDIES

Since skillstreaming is a preventive program to teach positive or prosocial skills as a precursor to any future misbehavior by the student, this model does not give the teacher any concrete techniques for limit setting, incentive, or management or backup systems with the exception that in some schools when a student is isolated outside the classroom (backup), this time is used for carrying out skillstreaming instruction, rather than simply letting the student sit passively in time out or detention.

Skillstreaming can clearly be seen as the most meaningful encouragement system. A single student or a small group who lacks the social skill can be targeted for direct instruction. Thus, skillstreaming, more than any other models presented in this book, can be considered the most developed encouragement system for students in need of excessive attention, such as the "class clown," the power child who "takes over," and others in the vignettes at the end of the various chapters.

REFERENCES

McGinnis, Ellen, and Arnold P. Goldstein. *Skillstreaming the Elementary School Child.* Champaign, IL: Research Press, 1997.

McGinnis, Ellen, and Arnold P. Goldstein. *Skillstreaming in Early Childhood: Teaching Prosocial Skills to the Preschool and Kindergarten Child.* Champaign, IL: Research Press, 1990.

Goldstein, Arnold P., Robert P. Sprafkin, N. Jane Gershaw, and Paul Klein. *Skillstreaming the Adolescent: A Structured Learning Approach to Teaching Prosocial Skills.* Champaign, IL: Research Press, 1980.

Print Components

Preschool/Kindergarten Level

Program Text

Skillstreaming in Early Childhood: Teaching Prosocial Skills to the Preschool and Kindergarten Child by Ellen McGinnis and Dr. Arnold P. Goldstein, 1990 (ISBN 0-87822-320-7).

Program Forms

Skillstreaming the Elementary School Child: Teaching Prosocial Skills to the Preschool and Kindergarten Child—Program Forms (rev.ed.) by Dr. Ellen McGinnis and Dr. Arnold P. Goldstein, 1990 (ISBN 0-87822-321-5).

Elementary Level

Program Forms

Skillstreaming the Elementary School Child: New Strategies and Perspectives for Teaching Prosocial Skills—Program Forms (rev. ed.) by Dr. Ellen McGinnis and Dr. Arnold P. Goldstein, 1997 (ISBN 0-87822-374-6).

Student Manual

Skillstreaming the Elementary School Child—Student Manual by Dr. Ellen McGinnis and Dr. Arnold P. Goldstein, 1997 (ISBN 0-87822-373-8).

Skill Cards

Skillstreaming the Elementary School Child—Skill Cards by Dr. Ellen McGinnis and Dr. Arnold P. Goldstein, 1997 (480 cards in all).

Student Video

People Skills: Doing 'em Right! (Elementary Level) by Dr. Ellen McGinnis and Dr. Arnold P. Goldstein, 1997 (17 min-utes). (Shows an elementary-level skillstreaming group in progress and teaches the group members what is expected of them.)

Adolescent Level

Program Text

Skillstreaming the Adolescent: New Strategies and Perspectives for Teaching Prosocial Skills (rev. ed.) by Dr. Arnold P. Goldstein and Ellen McGinnis, 1997 (ISBN 0-87822-369-X).

Program Forms

Skillstreaming the Adolescent: New Strategies and Perspectives for Teaching Prosocial Skills (rev. ed.) by Dr. Arnold P. Goldstein and Ellen McGinnis, 1997 (ISBN 0-87822-371-1).

Student Manual

Skillstreaming the Adolescent—Student Manual by Dr. Arnold P. Goldstein and Ellen McGinnis, 1997 (ISBN 0-87822-371-1).

Student Video

People Skills: Doing 'em Right! (Adolescent Level), by Dr. Ellen McGinnis and Dr. Arnold P. Goldstein, 1997 (17 min-utes). (Shows an adolescent-level skillstreaming group in progress and teaches the group members what is expected of them.)

Skill Cards

Skillstreaming the Adolescent—Skill Cards by Dr. Arnold P. Goldstein and Ellen McGinnis, 1997

Professional Training

The Skillstreaming Video: How to Teach Students Prosocial Skills by Dr. Arnold P. Goldstein and Dr. Ellen McGinnis, 1988 (26 minutes) (Shows teachers how to perform the skill-streaming steps of modeling, role-playing, performance feedback, and transfer learning.)

VIOLENCE, GANGS, AND LEGAL ACTIONS

TOO OFTEN the front page in our newspapers or the lead story on the evening news shows a shocking incident involving raw violence in our schools, with fights between students, attacks on teachers, shootings, and negative gang activity. Nationally, teachers are quietly being trained on how to deal with a potentially violent student or situation, and to learn to use methods to keep themselves safe while the acting-out-student is restrained or transported to a safe location. **Chapter 13,** Managing Student Violent Assaults and Breaking Up Student Fights, introduces the teacher to these ideas and methods, but hands-on, physically engaging workshops will be needed to implement these safety processes.

MANAGING STUDENT VIOLENT ASSAULTS AND BREAKING UP STUDENT FIGHTS

Regrettably, today's schools increasingly are the scenes of worsening violence. Assaults occur with greater frequency and ferocity than ever before, posing a serious threat to teachers and the students whose lives they hope to improve. This unhappy trend creates a new set of difficult challenges for today's classroom teacher.

Revengeful, assaultive, and violent students are simply "reflex" beings, their negative behavior automatically triggered by external stimuli or situations and internal fears. To help such students requires strong intrusion and controlling techniques that demand that the teacher first be assertive, and then plan a systematic shaping behavioral process to help the students gain self-control and a reawakening sense of trust. If necessary, in order to keep the student and others safe from the student's violent and raw aggressive actions, the teacher will need to nonaggressively restrain the student. Let us see an example of such a student and the teacher's response with the use of Rules and Consequences techniques.

Crisis Level 1: Potential Crisis[1]

Mrs. Monroe is supervising the campus area near the school cafeteria when she comes upon James, standing before the school wall and bouncing a golf ball off the bricks. Each time the ball hits the wall it makes a white circle on the bricks and is coming dangerously close to nearby windows.

TEACHER: "James **(name)**, stop!" She points to James's hand holding the ball **(gesture)**, and moves face-to-face **(eye contact).** "The ball is causing damage and may break a window. Put the ball in your pocket or I will need to take it."

JAMES: (Stands still, holding the golf ball tightly with both hands, glares directly at the teacher, and then looks down at the wall and throws and catches again.)

TEACHER: "James **(name)**, stop!" (points to James's ball **[gesture]**, moves face-to-face **[eye contact]**, and places herself between James and the wall.) "Put the ball in your pocket or give it to me." **(broken record)**

Crisis Level 2: Developing Crisis—Ventilation and Defiance

JAMES: (screams) "You bitch! You bitch! Keep your bitch hands off me! Keep your bitch hands off me! No, let me go—don't touch me!"

TEACHER: (lets 45 seconds pass) "James **(name),** stop! Put the ball in your pocket or in my hand! **(broken record)** If you cannot, then I will need to take the ball from you." **(preparatory)** (Moves toward James)

Crisis Level 3: Imminent Crisis—Assault

(James turns and with both hands—including the one still holding the ball—forcefully pushes the teacher at shoulder level, causing her to fall back three full steps; the teacher quickly catches her balance.)

TEACHER: "James **(name),** stop! Put the ball in my hand or your pocket." **(broken record)**

JAMES: "No—f——k off, old lady!" (James screams at full volume, and again attempts to push the teacher with both hands; the teacher grasps both his arms at the wrist to prevent him from throwing the ball again. He drops the ball and attempts to butt her with his head. He now lashes out with his right leg in three quick kicking motions, one of which strikes the teacher squarely on the shin, causing her definite discomfort.)[2]

(She now releases him to see if he will quiet down; instead, he runs to the door to the band room. The teacher physically prevents him from leaving by holding the second door. He kicks the door, to his discomfort, and runs his arm across a storage shelf holding musical instruments, knocking most of the instruments to the floor with a great crashing noise. He now moves to the window and violently strikes it with a fist; it cracks, but the window pane stays intact. This action carries the real potential for James to injure himself, but before a second blow lands, the teacher again grasps his wrists and pulls him away from the window. He now runs out the open door and into the arms of Mr. Harrison, a male teacher significantly bigger than James.)

Mr. Harrison puts his arms around James, grasping his right wrist with his left hand and left wrist with his right hand, and pulling toward him in a way that causes James's arms to cross over the front of his body. (See Figure 13.12.) Mr. Harrison moves his body sideways to the student, at a 45-degree angle. This places James's back or hip on Mr. Harrison's right thigh, and he then pulls his arms back toward him and lightly lifts up. This causes James's heels to come slightly off the floor, forcing him to stand on his tiptoes with his weight supported by the teacher's thigh, thus preventing him from kicking, biting, or struggling free.

While holding James in this *basket restraining hold,*[3] Mr. Harrison parallels his physical action with accompanying verbal explanation and reassurance to James.

MR. HARRISON: (now whispers) "James, I am not going to hurt you, and I am not going to let you hurt me. You are safe—I will keep you safe, I will not hurt you!" **(broken record)** I am the teacher, I keep students safe; I will not hurt you! James, I am holding you with my hands to keep you safe. See my hands, they are holding you, but they are not hurting you. **(broken record)** (James attempts to struggle free but Mr. Harrison holds him firmly.) See my hands, they are holding you, but they are not hurting you. **(broken record)** I need to hold you until you can relax. I am holding you, but I am not hurting you!"

James attempts to bite Mr. Harrison, but the teacher moves to prevent this; James screams a list of profanities at the teacher, but Mr. Harrison continues to speak to him in a whisper: "I am not going to let you hurt me, and I am not going to hurt you. I am not hurting you. These are helping hands that do not hurt students! You are safe, I am going to keep you safe. I am the teacher, I am the boss and I can keep students safe. I am going to keep you safe!" (James now begins to cry and slowly stops struggling.)

Crisis Level 4: Reestablishing Equilibrium

Mr. Harrison: "James, I can see by your face that you are very angry. But look, here are my hands and they are holding you to keep you safe. I will not hurt you—you are safe now."

(James's body goes limp in Mr. Harrison's arms. He permits James to be released and to be seated on a nearby chair.)

We have just witnessed one of the most demanding teacher–student interactions, one that involves a clear assault on the teacher and a danger to the student. As a teacher dealing with such a student, our heart is pounding and the adrenaline is rushing through our body, pushing us to a state of hyperalertness and creating a defensive stance for our own protection and the student's safety. Out of our own understandable fright, we ourselves may emotionally flood, thus causing us real difficulty in thinking correctly and acting constructively as these sudden and quick actions unfold.

Experts who have studied such violent actions by students recognize a general level-by-level progression in the child's behavior and actions. If we as the teacher understand these levels of crisis progress, then when these rapid developments do occur, as we saw previously, they can be better understood and thus be less frightening. Previous *thought rehearsal* will permit us to respond constructively.

There are generally four levels of crisis development leading to possible violent acts by the student : Level 1: Potential Crisis; Level 2: Developing Crisis—Ventilation and Defiance; Level 3: Imminent Crisis—Assault; and finally, Level 4: Reestablishing Equilibrium. (These levels parallel the construct explained in Figure 13.1.)[4]

CRISIS LEVEL 1: POTENTIAL CRISIS

As a result of some source of frustration, in Level 1: Potential Crisis the student appears as if he is a tightly wound spring ready to snap. Inner emotional energy and tension are mounting; his hands may be clenched into a fist with white knuckles, and he may drop his eyes or glare intently, his gaze either focusing sharply on a peer or teacher or, instead, alternately focusing on his subject and then darting away. He may become physically restrictive, pulling inside of himself and turning away, or actively pacing like a caged cat and exhibiting nervous tics. His actions clearly attract the **attention** of peers and observant adults. Students will ask, "Why is James acting funny?" while adults will say, "It looks like James is going to have one of his bad mornings." The student, if caught quickly, is still rational enough to respond to the teacher's use of language. Our goal is to take this built-up internal energy and have the student ventilate it externally in one of two ways: through the use of language (talk it out) or through the use of physical activity (play it out).

Crisis Level	Student Behavior Characteristics	Teacher Goals and Techniques
1: Potential Crisis—attention getting	As a result of some frustration, the student appears as if he is a tightly wound spring ready to snap. His hands may be clenched into a fist with white knuckles, and he may drop his eyes or glare intently, with his gaze either focusing sharply on a peer or teacher or, instead, alternately focusing on his subject and then darting away. He may become physically restrictive, pulling inside of himself and turning away, or become active—pacing like a caged cat and exhibiting nervous tics. His actions clearly attract the **attention** of peers and observant adults.	The student, if caught quickly, is still rational enough to respond to the teacher's language. Have the student ventilate representationally through language (talk it out). Redirect the student away from social interaction, giving him his "personal space." If possible make few or no demands. With the use of the teacher's language, employ Relationship-Listening techniques.
2: Developing Crisis—power, ventilation, and defiance	In order to maintain his **power** over a teacher or peer, the student now screams or shouts verbal aggression in the form of swearing, name calling, and similar verbal outbursts that appear as a release or ventilation of stored-up tension. This may quickly escalate to threats against peers and teachers and/or definite defiance of the teacher.	The teacher positions herself in an alert *supportive stance* and permits the child's ventilation through verbal aggression. If the verbal aggression turns to defiance, the teacher moves to provide an *assertive command* (assuring the student of potential consequences) and promises of safety. Give the student time and space to ventilate, and do not physically intervene if possible.
3: Imminent Crisis—assault	The student now becomes totally **revengeful** and nonrational, and cannot control his own actions. He physically strikes out in a direct assault toward a peer or teacher by choking, biting, or hitting/throwing.	In response to the assault, the teacher defends herself with *restraining techniques* (head down, basket hold), and accompanies her physical actions with an *assertive command* sending two messages: an order to desist action in a way the teacher desires, and verbal reassurance through a *promise of safety* and nonaggression toward the student.
4: Reestablishing Equilibrium	After the violent action the student is deflated and becomes passive with little energy. He has feelings of guilt and feels **helpless** as to how others might respond to him.	Help cognitively recapitulate the happenings for the student, first by having him verbally talk about it with the teacher using Relationship-Listening techniques, and then, if unsuccessful, advancing to Confronting-Contracting techniques. Reestablish the relationship verbally and by touch.

FIGURE 13.1 Levels of Crisis, Student Behavior, and Teacher Techniques

"Talk It Out" (Verbal)

If possible, we bring into use all the Relationship-Listening techniques we have learned. We use *door openers:* "James, I can see that you are very unhappy this morning. Tell me what is bothering you." If the student does speak, we use *acknowledgments* and *active listening,* and encourage the student to externalize or ventilate these strong pent-up feelings through language and words, keeping in mind that some of these words may be aggressive and hostile. If this "talking it out" is effective and we begin to hear the student tell us the root cause of his heightened emotional condition ("Coach Michaels cut me from the team!"), we might use the *Six Steps to Problem Solving* to help him resolve his problem or dilemma.

Let's repeat our earlier teacher–student example. Remember that the first time we encountered Mrs. Monroe and James, she immediately directed him to stop bouncing the ball against the school or she would take it from him.

TEACHER: (nondirective statements) "James, the golf ball is doing damage to the school building. That is fun and exciting for you, but part of my job as a teacher is to keep school property safe."

JAMES: "God damn it!"

TEACHER: "You're angry?" *(active listening)*

JAMES: "That bastard!"

TEACHER: "You are very angry with someone?"

JAMES: "Yeah, I'm one of the best players, and he let Robert play first string and cut me!"

TEACHER: "You're angry because you were cut from the team." *(active listening)*

JAMES: "Yeah, it ain't fair. I'm better than Robert. And I was only late three times."

Mrs. Monroe's efforts to determine the cause of James's aggressive throwing of the golf ball has exposed a deeper problem that James is facing, and she can begin dealing with him from a new perspective.

Six Steps to Problem Solving

TEACHER: "Ah, you have a problem, and that problem is, you were late to practice three times and were cut from the team. How can you deal with this? *(Step 1—Defining the Problem)* Let's think together of ways that you might solve this problem. What are your ideas?" *(Step 2—Generating Possible Solutions)*

JAMES: "I could have my old man talk to the coach."

TEACHER: "That may work, but let's think of a lot of other ways, too."

JAMES: "The 'Y' is putting together a team and I could play over there. Or I could apologize to Coach Michaels and tell him I won't be late again."

TEACHER: "There are other teams to play on, or apologizing might get you back on the team." *(active listening)*

JAMES: "Maybe, but the 'Y' team has a bunch of losers."

TEACHER: "Which one of your ideas is best?" *(Step 3—Evaluating the Solutions)*

JAMES: "I think I'll keep my father out of this, he might screw things up and make it worse between Coach and me. But I have a hard time talking to Coach, he makes me nervous and I can't speak." *(Step 4—Deciding Which Solution Is Best)*

TEACHER: "OK, you have decided that is not a good solution. What actions will you take?"

JAMES: "I will go by the 'Y' after school and see who's on their team, and maybe write Coach a note, apologizing and asking for a second chance."

The next day Mrs. Monroe watches James, who appears less tense. *(Step 5—Implementing the Solution)* After lunch she talks to James.

TEACHER: "Was your solution to your problem a good one?" *(Step 6—Evaluation the Solution)*

JAMES: "Yes, it was <u>great,</u> there are some good players on the 'Y' team and they said I could play on their team. Coach also accepted my apology and said I could come back next week. Now I have to decide between two teams!"

With quick and early intervention, the teacher has headed off an aggressive situation with James by having him talk it out through language, with the teacher using Relationship-Listening techniques.

If the root of the student's stress is beyond the immediate and manageable confines of the classroom setting, such as having been punished by a parent that morning, we would not be able to turn to the *Six Steps to Problem Solving,* but would instead continue with *active listening* and allow verbal ventilation for the student.

If we are <u>un</u>successful at resolving the problem in Level 1: Potential Crisis because we caught it too late or the intensity of the student's emotional flooding was excessive, most likely the student will regress to a more severe Level 2: Developing Crisis, with its two substages of ventilation and defiance.

CRISIS LEVEL 2: DEVELOPING CRISIS—VENTILATION AND DEFIANCE

In order to maintain his **power** over a teacher or peer, the student enters Level 2: Developing Crisis. He uses ventilation, screaming or shouting verbal aggression in the form of swearing, name-calling, and similar verbal outbursts, which appear as a release or ventilation of stored-up tension. This verbal aggression, no matter how it frightens us and classmates, is a good release or ventilation. We <u>do nothing,</u> we <u>do not</u> challenge his display of power as the student screams, shouts, and swears, because after many minutes of doing so the student will have no anger energies left for a more physical assault. So the longer the student ventilates by being verbally aggressive the better, because he is simply wearing himself out and dispersing his stored-up tension. Don't be frightened by the verbal aggression, but do be cautious. This verbal aggression may quickly escalate into threats to peers and teachers and/or definite defiance toward the teacher.

JAMES: (screams) "You bitch! You bitch! Keep your bitch hands off me! Keep your bitch hands off me! No, let me go—don't touch me!" **(ventilation)**

"No, it's my golf ball! I'm going to break your face!" (**defiance**)

In this Level 2: Developing Crisis situation, the student is not rational, but a defensive reflex has set in and he is not capable of controlling his own behavior. While in this state of hypertension the student will have much difficulty in hearing our words, but will depend visually and auditorily in assessing our nonverbal actions for any hint of action toward him, which he will interpret as hostile and aggressive. Once the defiance and threats are heard, the teacher should signal to a fellow adult or send another student to get the principal, any security personnel, the teacher across the hall—in short, ***get help.*** This second or third adult is helpful both in restraining the assaulting student and as a later witness to any actions that may occur in the event of any administrative evaluation. Also, the teacher should take actions to remove onlookers by either having the other students moved to another room, sectioning the area off from the view of other students, or, if possible, moving the student to another room. Witnessing an outburst by the revengeful, flooded student can be very frightening for classmates, and may cause the assaultive student not to back down because he would feel he is losing face among his peers. Later in this chapter we will describe how to explain the assaulting student's behavior and our restraining actions to onlooking students through a *problem-solving class meeting.*

When the Level 2: Developing Crisis event does occur, we have two ways of responding: assertive demand with its parallel assertive stance, and supportive demand with its parallel supportive stance.

Assertive and Supportive Demand

The *assertive demand,* as a part of the assertive discipline techniques, and assertive stance should be used with students whose behavior is a problem because of their need for attention (see Figure 13.2). The *supportive demand* and stance are used with flooded power-seeking and revengeful students who may pose a danger to themselves or others or to objects. Both the *assertive* and *supportive* commands are made up of two parts: our verbal *directive statement,* and a follow-up *preparatory command* if the student does not desist. We add one more important verbal statement said repetitively as a broken record, a *promise of safety:*

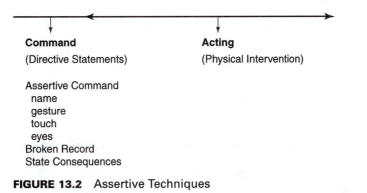

FIGURE 13.2 Assertive Techniques

"James, I am not going to hurt you, and I am not going to let you hurt me. You are safe—I will keep you safe, I will not hurt you and I will not let others hurt you. I want to help you be safe!" *(promise of safety)*

The nonverbal actions that are a part of the assertive and supportive stances differ dramatically, but the manner in which we deliver our verbal commands should have certain common characteristics. While issuing an assertive or supportive command, the teacher uses a well-modulated voice (controlled tone, volume, and cadence)—neither too fast nor slow, neither too loud nor soft. In the most normal voice possible, we tell the student the *motor actions* or behaviors that we want performed. Remember, we do not tell the student what <u>not</u> to do. Assertive demand can be seen as:

TEACHER: "James **(name),** stop!" (points to the ball James is holding—**gesture;** moves face-to-face—**eye contact;** and places herself between James and the wall) "Put the ball in your pocket or give it to me." **(broken record)**

FIGURE 13.3 The Supportive Stance

The parallel nonverbal behavior, or assertive stance, of the teacher to accompany the assertive verbal command is to gesture with our hands and fingers, move squarely in front of the student and make fixed eye contact, and touch the student. When accompanying the verbal assertive demand, these actions are extremely confrontational. By these actions, the teacher challenges the child's power directly. This assertive demand, with its accompanying stance, may be used effectively with the student motivated by attention-getting who may be having a *difficult moment*. However, this approach will be disastrous with the power and revengeful student who is flooded and has taken this general life-stance position toward his world. We do not use an assertive demand with a flooded, revengeful student at Level 2: Developing Crisis because the challenge will set him off and he will assault us, especially if we violate his *personal space*.

The teacher technique that we do use with these students at this level of crisis is the *supportive demand,* with the verbal technique previously described and its accompanying stance. The nonverbal behavior, or stance, that we use for the *supportive demand* includes:

1. We stand still and do not get closer than three feet from the student, nor do we touch the student, for this would be considered an invasion of his private space, or "bubble." A circle of space exists around all individuals, a hypothetical "bubble" in which they feel safe until others close in. When others do invade this space it is typically for purposes of expressing intimate affection (cuddling) or aggression. The hyperalert Level 2: Developing Crisis student will clearly interpret closing space as an aggressive act, which will arouse his aggressive instincts. This is why we beckon the student in Level 1: Potential Crisis to come to us ("walk to me and give me the golf ball").

2. The teacher turns her body at an angle, with her preferred foot pointed toward the student (see Figure 13.3) and the other foot at a 45-degree angle. The teacher should not put herself squared shoulder-to-shoulder with the student. This angled stance toward the flooded student is interpreted as nonhostile, while a squared shoulder is a position one would choose for confrontation and fighting. The foot pointed toward the student may be raised to deflect or block the kicking action of a youth's foot. The other, angled foot can be used for temporary balance; a stance with parallel feet leaves the teacher flat-footed and prone to being knocked off balance by any minor assault.

3. Eye contact by the teacher should not be fixed or glaring.

4. The teacher should place her hands behind her back but be ready to use them to block an assault (do not gesture or make any threatening moves with the hands, such as pointing). If assault appears imminent, the teacher should hold both hands open, one at stomach level and the other in front of her chin, with the palms open and showing the flat face of her hands to the student. The teacher also does not put her hands on her hips, clench her fists, or point.

While employing the supportive stance we state a *supportive verbal command* and repeat it two or three times *(broken record),* attempting to have the student hear us. If we do not get a change in the student's behavior, we clearly state a *preparatory* directive statement for possible consequences followed by a *promise of safety:*

"James, lower your voice, put the ball in your pocket, and go to the cafeteria (**supportive command;** teacher is also in a supportive stance). Lower your voice, put the ball in your pocket, and go to the cafeteria (**broken record).** If you do not, I will need to (teacher chooses one): call your mother and father and tell them of your behavior/have you go to the principal's office/have another teacher remove you from the campus to the office. James, I am not going to hurt you, and I am not going to let you hurt me. You are safe—I will keep you safe, I will not hurt you and I will not let others hurt you. I want to help you be safe!"

The standoff between the flooded Level 2: Developing Crisis student and the teacher's supportive demand and stance should not be rushed. Do not be in a hurry; what we are trying to do is prevent an assault by the student. We may permit many minutes to go by in hopes that the student will desist, back down, and comply. If he does not and instead regresses further, the next action is likely to be physical flooding and an assault.

Also, at this level we will hear verbal defiance.

JAMES: (screams) "You bitch! You bitch! Keep your bitch hands off me! Keep your bitch hands off me! No, let me go—don't touch me!"

Although these words are unpleasant to hear, they indicate ventilation, and the "pouring off" of stored-up anger. Allow this to occur, because the student can only do this so long until all of his energy is used up.

CRISIS LEVEL 3: IMMINENT CRISIS—ASSAULT

If the incident escalates further, the student now becomes totally **power-revengeful** and nonrational, and cannot control his own actions. He physically strikes out in a direct assault against a peer or teacher by choking, biting, kicking, grabbing, or hitting/throwing. In response to this assault, the teacher should defend herself with the following *restraining techniques* (using the help of a second or third adult if one is nearby). The teacher should accompany her physical actions with an *assertive command,* sending two messages: a directive to desist the unwanted action, and a promise of safety and nonaggression toward the student.

Assault by Choking[5]

When a student assaults us by a front choking—placing his hands around our throat and squeezing—we respond by standing erect, thrusting both arms above our head, stepping back one step to put the student off balance, and turning suddenly to the right or left so the child's hands will be pulled. We do not try to grab the child's hands and pull them off our throat; this will simply be inefficient or ineffective, and the student might dig his fingernails into our throat (see Figures 13.4 and 13.5).

Assault by Biting

If the student has caught us off guard and has sunk his teeth into us (most likely an arm), we can get ourselves free from the biting hold by putting the edge of a flat free hand under the child's nose and against his upper lip and quickly vibrating our hand up and down with sufficient force to free ourselves without injuring the student. Do not pull away from the bite but lean into it, as your pulling can cause more damage than the bite itself. If the student has turned in such a manner that we cannot immediately get to his lip-nose area, we

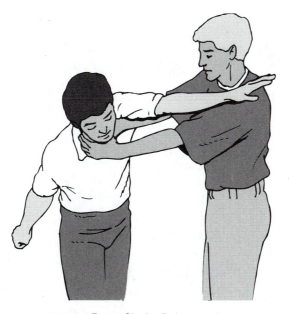

FIGURE 13.4   Front Choke Release

FIGURE 13.5   Rear Choke Release

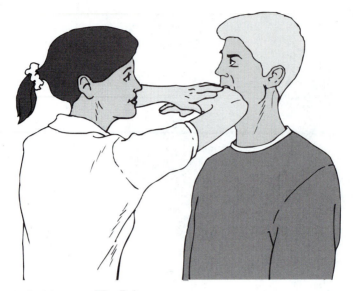

FIGURE 13.6   Bite Release

take the fingertips of a flat free hand and push them firmly into his cheek, finding the teeth between the upper and lower jaw and again vibrating our hand in an up-and-down motion to free ourselves (see Figure 13.6).

Assault by Kicking

From a supportive stance with our feet at a 45-degree angle, we are able to lift the foot pointing toward the student while balancing on the other foot. While holding up our foot as a barrier, we attempt to block the kick with the back of our foot or shoe. When we have a strength advantage over the student, we can remove his shoes and he will desist or else feel the natural consequences of his action (pain). If this kicking continues, a restraining hold might be required (see Figure 13.7).

Assault by Grabbing

The assault by grabbing will usually involve the student doing a one- or two-handed grab of either our arms or hair.

One- and Two-arm Grabbing Release   When the student uses either one or two hands to grab our arm, there is a weak link in the grab between the child's thumb and forefinger. Simply take your free hand, lock the fingers of your two hands, and pull in the direction that the child's thumb is pointing, normally up (see Figures 13.8 and 13.9).

One- and Two-hand Hair Pulling Release   If the student grabs our hair, either with one hand or two, we should clasp his hand and push it into or against our head, while

FIGURE 13.7   Kick Block

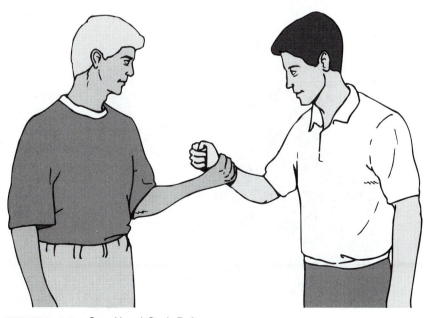

FIGURE 13.8   One-Hand Grab Release

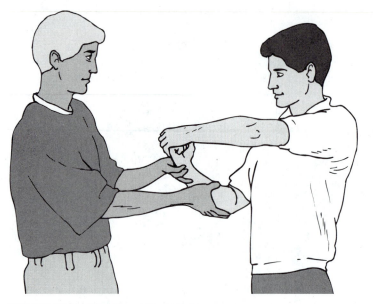

FIGURE 13.9   Two-Hand Grab Release

at the same time turning toward the student and bending our upper body down in a 45-degree angle. The child's wrist is bent backwards, causing a loss of strength in his hands and enabling us to break free. Then physically move away (see Figures 13.10 and 13.11).

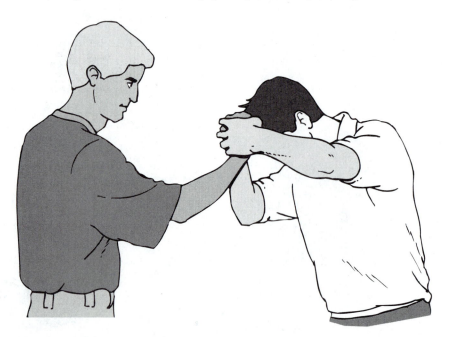

FIGURE 13.10   One-Hand Hair Grab Release

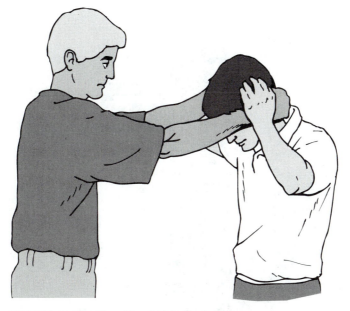

FIGURE 13.11   Two-Hand Hair Grab Release

Assault by Hitting and Throwing

When the student is hitting or throwing, there are two ways of handling an object moving toward us that has the potential of doing us bodily harm. We either can move out of its path and dodge, or we can block and deflect. If we have time and the student is strong enough to do us serious harm, we may pick up an object—such as a book or small chair much like a "lion tamer"—and use it to block and deflect the blow or object thrown. The three-foot spacing in the *supportive stance* may give us the room to use such an object. If the student catches us off guard and has closed in on us, striking with his right fist, we would block and deflect this blow with the edge of our right arm by holding it across our body (the reverse would occur with a left-hand blow).

If, after an incident of choking, biting, kicking, grabbing, or hitting/throwing, the student retreats and moves to a protective corner or space out of the way of classroom activities, presenting no danger to himself or others, we simply leave him alone. We consider him to have moved to Level 4: Reestablishing Equilibrium, and we use the following techniques. However, if the student still is endangering others, property, or himself, we must now use nonviolent restraining techniques on him.

Nonviolent Restraining

Basket-weave Hold Restraint[6]   If the student is small enough and we have the advantage of strength, we may choose to use the basket-weave hold. This hold is accomplished by getting behind the assaulting student and putting our arms around him, grasping his right wrist with our left hand and left wrist with our right hand, and pulling toward us in a way that causes the child's arms to cross over the front of his body (see Figure 13.12). As we

FIGURE 13.12   Basket-Weave Restraint

stand, we move our body sideways to the student, with our feet at a 45-degree angle. This places the child's back on our right hip, and we then pull his arms back toward us and lift up. This causes the child's heels to come slightly off the floor, forcing him to stand on his tiptoes with his weight supported by our thigh. We also may hold or restrain the student in a seated position. Remember to use only the minimum amount of force needed, so that no injury is done to the student. *Note:* The basket-weave restraint is the most powerful hold suggested for a small student when the teacher has a substantial physical strength advantage. If the child is too big and strong for us, we may be required to use a wrist-shoulder hold.

Wrist-shoulder Hold Restraint   Once a full blow has been thrown by the assaulting student, we quickly step behind the student and grasp his right wrist with our right hand, with the thumb side of our hand facing in. At the same time we take our open left hand and place it on the child's right shoulder from behind. The thumb of our left hand should be positioned in the "V" formed by the child's arm and rib cage (see Figure 13.13). We now push down with our left hand on the child's shoulder, while we turn the child's wrist clockwise with our right hand. Be careful to apply only the needed pressure because we would not want to hurt the child—these are to be nonviolent restraining techniques. The child is pushed head-down until his head is below his waistline; from this position it is impossible for him to pick up his feet to kick. If his head is not down far enough, he can

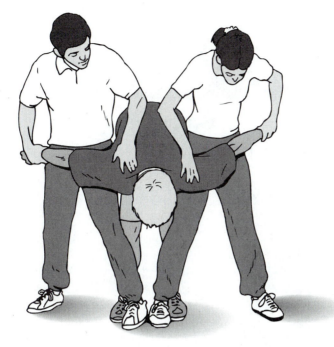

FIGURE 13.13   Wrist-Shoulder Pull-Down Restraint

take his free left hand and move it across himself with a blow that can strike us in the face. We also take our left foot and place it in front of the child's body and between his two feet, thus preventing the child from walking out of the restraining hold.

Team (Two Adults) Wrist-shoulder Hold Restraint   With the very strong assaultive child, if a second teacher or adult is available, the wrist-shoulder hold is more safely accomplished. The helping team member takes the child's free arm and does parallel wrist turning and shoulder pushing. Both adults must face the same direction as the student, and both place their inside leg in front of the student (see Figure 13.13).

Transporting Techniques

Keep the child in the wrist-shoulder restraint position until he has stopped struggling. Permit the child to rise very slowly, watching for any signs of renewed struggle, including the possibility that the free hand might strike you in the face. If struggling occurs again, push the child's head below the waist and reestablish the original restraint. Never try to transport a struggling child.

If the child does stop struggling and you now have him in an upright position, quickly take the hand previously holding the child's shoulder and move it under his arm. Being careful not to release the child's wrist, use your free hand to grasp the inside of the elbow of the child's other arm (see Figure 13.14). Now walk quickly, bringing the child with you at the fastest manageable pace.

FIGURE 13.14 Single Transport

This transporting might be done with a team helper, a second adult who holds the child's free arm in a similar manner. A third helper can get behind the child placing both hands on the student's shoulder blades and pushing (see Figure 13.15). If at any time during the transporting process the child excessively struggles to get free, simply reapply the wrist-shoulder down hold.

Important: We accompany our physical restraining with parallel language of *supportive command, preparatory directive statement,* and *promise of safety.*

"James, I want you to stop hitting and relax **(supportive command),** and when you do so, I will let you go **(preparatory).** You are safe, I am not going to hurt you and I will not let you hurt me." **(promise of safety)**

Also, repeat the entire verbal sequence over and over as a **broken record** to attempt to get the student to hear you from within his state of flooding.

Some teachers state that when they are hit, kicked, or bitten by a student they hit, kick, and bite back, so that the student "knows how it feels."

WARNING: Do not <u>ever,</u> under any circumstances, hit, kick, or bite a student who has done this to you. This could rightly be defined as child abuse, and you could properly

FIGURE 13.15   Two-Person Transport

be charged under the law. When a student is flooded and carries out an assault, he is no longer rational and capable of stopping himself; returning his aggression does not teach him "how it feels," but simply confirms his unreasonable concern that you are a person to fear. When we use *nonviolent restraining techniques* and parallel *supportive demands* and *promise of safety* and we do not return the student's aggression, the student gradually learns to trust us and give up his aggression and fears. Remember that during each of these levels of crisis—and especially during the assault action—the student is terribly frightened. He actually scares himself when he is out of control.

Again, if the student becomes passive after an assault, retreats to a protective corner or space out of the way of the classroom activities, and now presents no danger to himself or others, we simply leave him alone and consider him to have moved to Level 4: Reestablishing Equilibrium.

CRISIS LEVEL 4: REESTABLISHING EQUILIBRIUM

After the violent act, the student is deflated and becomes passive, with little energy. He has feelings of guilt and feels **helpless** as to how others might respond to him. Some students will retreat so far back into passivity that they fall asleep or begin self-abusive activities such as pulling out their hair, biting themselves, or some similar act of physical abuse on themselves. We will intervene if the student retreats too deeply into passivity by sleeping or beginning physically self-abusive activities.

Since the student is now rational, we wish to help him cognitively recall what has happened, for he may not actually remember what started the flooding incident or what occurred once it began. We will primarily use the Confronting-Contracting techniques.

JAMES: (Slouches down into the chair, drops his eyes, pouts with a frowning face for a period of four to six minutes, and then begins to sit up in the chair watching other students.)

TEACHER: (approaches) "I need to talk to you about what occurred. What did you do?" **(Step #2—Confronting: "What" question)**

JAMES: "I don't know." (or the student might say, "I was angry and hit!")

TEACHER: "Well, I saw what you did, and you were using the golf ball and throwing it against the wall causing damage, and you could have hit one of the school windows with the ball. What is the rule? **(Step #2—Confronting: "What" question** requesting a verbal statement of the rule) You got so angry that you wanted to hit and bite, but I stopped you and kept you safe."

JAMES: (eyes drop) "A-a-h, keep school property safe."

TEACHER: "Yes, when balls are bounced they need to be bounced on the pavement where they will do no damage. Also the rule is that hitting and biting are not allowed, and when someone is angry they need to use words to tell the other person. When you got angry and did hit and bite, I needed Mr. Harrison to help hold you tightly to keep you safe. We did not hurt you and I didn't let anyone hurt you. Mr. Harrison kept us both safe. These are helping hands, not hurting hands, and these hands keep students safe.[7] (Teacher restates the rule so it is very clear.) Now you and I must work this out. **(Step #3—Contracting)** We must have an agreement. (Teacher moves to James, takes him gently by the hands, makes eye contact) What will you do to change?" **(Step #2—Confronting: "What" question,** requesting change)

JAMES: "Bounce the ball on the pavement and learn to not hit."

TEACHER: "Yes. Do we have an agreement on this? Can I depend on your remembering the rule?" **(Step #3—Contracting: verbal agreement)**

JAMES: "Yes." (looks up and makes eye contact with the teacher)

TEACHER: "What will you do when someone makes you angry?"

JAMES: "Words."

TEACHER: "Yes. Do we have an agreement on this? Can I depend on your remembering the rule?" **(Step #3—Contracting: verbal agreement)**

JAMES: "Yes." (looks up and makes eye contact with the teacher)

TEACHER: "Good, we now have an agreement. If you agree, I want to shake hands to show a special agreement between us." (The teacher holds out her hand to James and smiles warmly) **(Step #3—Contracting)**

JAMES: (returns the teacher's smile and shakes her hand)

TEACHER: "Good, we now have an agreement! You can now remember rules regarding the care of school property. But if you forget the rules, your behavior will say that you do not know how to use the outdoor campus and you will not be able to go outside after lunch. **(Step #3—Consequence)** Now, you may feel free to come back to class and work with us, when you feel that you are ready." **(handling isolation)**

It is recommended that during Level 4: Reestablishing Equilibrium the student and teacher be eye-to-eye in a very close, intimate space. This can be done by seating the student on an adult chair, with the teacher sitting on a small student-size chair.

To summarize, during this level it is important that the student be able to cognitively state—or for the teacher to describe—the events that have occurred in a way that imparts no guilt, and for the relationship between the teacher and student to reach a new emotional equilibrium free of hostility. Both the student and the teacher need this reunion.

We would caution against the teacher forcing a verbal apology that requires the student to say, "I'm sorry." The verbal statement may be something that the teacher needs, but, if forced, the student will begin to have feelings of guilt. Students, if the equilibration goes well, will have feelings of remorse and wish to apologize, but they may express it to us in nonverbal form. The student meets the teacher's eyes, saying nothing but smiling affectionately. We as teachers must also learn during the interaction to nonverbally express our "forgiveness" back to the student through similar smiling, but we must also do it in the form of verbal expression as a statement of *promise of safety*.

Classmates as Onlookers to the Assault

It has been previously suggested that steps should be taken to remove onlookers by either having other students move to another room, sectioning the area off from the view of other students, or, if possible, moving the student to another room. Witnessing the revengeful, flooded student is very frightening for classmates, or they may "get a kick" out of it, and seeing our restraining actions on the assaulting student may appear as if we are hurting this student. "Mr. Harrison was hurting James!"

It is quite important to deal with the classmates who were onlookers to an assault by the revengeful student. Witnessing such aggression can cause an individual student or an entire group of students to move to Level 1: Potential Crisis, whereby they become highly anxious with accompanying behavior that might escalate through these crisis levels. We may deal with this by doing the ventilating techniques previously suggested in working with Level 1: Potential Crisis students. We now view the entire class, if the incident occurred in our classroom, after these violent incidents as being in Level 1: Potential Crisis, so we want them to "talk it out." This involves holding one or more class problem-solving meetings, as suggested and described by Glasser, using the Relationship-Listening techniques.

Class Meetings (Verbal Ventilation)

The entire class is seated on student-sized chairs along a line. The assaulting student is included in the meeting. Just as the Confronting-Contracting techniques were used for Level 4: Reestablishing Equilibrium to enable the teacher to establish an emotional equilibrium with the previously assaulting student, this equilibrium will also need to be reestablished with the child's classmates. They have seen or heard the frightening event, and have identified themselves as a part of the action. Through verbal ventilating in the class meeting, we attempt to reach the point where the teacher and students have gotten rid of any feelings of hostility. If we do not do this, the classmates—out of their fear of the acting-out student—will begin to make him the *outside aggressor.*

Let us watch the meeting unfold. Notice that the process begins with the teacher wearing a Relationship-Listening face with its accompanying techniques, and then moves to Confronting-Contracting:

TEACHER: (opens the meeting) "Friends, I'd like to talk about some upsetting and frightening things that happened this morning. (**Door opener**)

STUDENTS: (no one speaks for a few minutes, but then a discussion begins)

FIRST CLASSMATE (HARRIET): "James was a mean dude—he really lost it!"

SECOND CLASSMATE (PAUL): "Man, he tried to deck the teacher. Definitely uncool."

TEACHER: "James was very angry. And when he gets angry, he explodes." (**Active listening**)

DIANA: "He frightens me when he gets like that—you never know what he's gonna do next!"

TEACHER: "When people hit, it can be hard to like them or feel safe around them."

JOHN: "What bothered me was that Mr. Harrison hurt James's arm."

TEACHER: "When he held James, you thought he was hurting him." (**Active listening**)

PAUL: "Mr. Harrison didn't hit James."

TEACHER: "What else did you see and feel?" (**Door opener**)

NANCY: "I saw James hit you and bite Mr. Harrison. He cried, screamed, and cussed."

(This verbal ventilation may continue for five to ten minutes with the teacher maintaining a Relationship-Listening face and techniques. Now the teacher moves to Confronting-Contracting and does not hesitate to deal with the realities of the situation and explain misinformation.)

TEACHER: "What happened first ... Harriet?" (**Confronting: "What" questions**)

HARRIET: "James was throwing the ball against the school."

TEACHER: "What happened next?" (**Confronting: "What" questions**)

JOHN: "You told James to stop. He pushed you and ran into the music room."

TEACHER: "What happened next?" (**Confronting: "What" questions**)

DIANA: "James screamed, knocked over the musical instruments, and tried to break a window."

TEACHER: "What happened next?" (**Confronting: "What" questions**)

JOHN: "Mr. Harrison hurt James's arm."

TEACHER: "No, because James got so mad that he could hurt me, he could hurt others, and he could hurt himself, I needed to have Mr. Harrison hold him tightly to keep him safe. Being the teacher puts me in charge, but I don't hurt students. I am a friend, but sometimes when students get very angry I need to hold them tight to keep them safe." (**A reality explanation and** *promise of safety*)

JOHN: "Well, it sure looked like he hurt James's arm."

TEACHER: "No, John, Mr. Harrison was holding his arm and hands tightly so that his hands would not hurt me. He did <u>not</u> hurt James; he was keeping him safe. Come up here, John." (John stands before the teacher) "Let me show you how safely he was holding James." (The teacher now demonstrates the basket-weave restraint on John and two other students. John chuckles as if it is a game, and now a number of other students want a chance to see how their classmate was held.)

TEACHER: "When people get very angry, they sometimes try to hurt other people. But I am a teacher, and no matter how angry a student may get I will not hit them, I will not hurt them, I will not kick them, and I will not bite them. We teachers will hold students to keep them and others safe." (**Reality explanation and** *promise of safety*) Now we need to have an agreement. What should we do when others make us angry?"

Various members of the class volunteer: "We need to talk it out."

TEACHER: "Right. When others make us angry, we need to talk it over, and you can come to a teacher to get help. But <u>don't</u> try to straighten things out by hitting, biting, kicking, or spitting—this will only make things worse. Use your head to come up with a solution instead. Can we all agree to that?"

Almost in unison, the class members nod their heads in agreement.

TEACHER: "Great, now we all have an agreement. We are going to deal with these kinds of problems with our heads, using language to resolve things." (**Contracting**)

This vignette, of course, is for purposes of modeling teacher techniques, and is certainly somewhat artificial. This ventilation process and the confronting and contracting might take many minutes, or even many meetings, and may need to occur throughout the year if aggression is high in our classroom. But the techniques to be used, and the general attitude and processes to be employed, should develop in a direction much as the one demonstrated in the vignette.

This class meeting will serve a number of purposes: (1) it ventilates any pent-up anxiety and feelings that any student might have after witnessing such aggression; (2) it helps both for James and his classmates to reestablish an emotional equilibrium, potentially preventing him from becoming the *outside aggressor;* (3) it helps students understand that if they, too, should become angry (and they will), the teacher will not aggress against them but instead will help; and (4) it dispels any misinformation and misperceptions the students might have ("Mr. Harrison was hurting James's arm.").

VERBAL AGGRESSION

Verbal aggression is defined as any vocalization, such as crying to get one's own way, shouting, whining, swearing, name calling, verbal threats, and similar actions. We can decide what action we should take toward such verbal aggression by asking the question, "What is the motivation of the student for such verbal aggression?" The answer will be one of the following: attention getting, power, or revenge.

When dealing with students who are swearing, we can apply the Three Faces of Discipline in the following way:

Relationship-Listening

"Harold, when that swear word is said, I am afraid that other students will begin to say those words, and those are not school words that I can permit students to use in our classroom." Before delivering such an *"I"-message,* we take Harold by the hand and move him out of the hearing and possibly the vision of the other students.

Confronting-Contracting

If the "I"-message fails to work, we may move to confronting-contracting techniques. "Harold, come with me (take him out of the hearing of classmates), I need to talk to you about these harsh and aggressive words. What are you doing? Well, I think what you are doing is trying to get other students to see you when you use those words so you can have everyone look at you **(attention getting),** or these words can make you the boss **(power)** and feel strong. The rule is that they are not school words and they will not be permitted."

Rules and Consequences

We approach the attention-getting or power-seeking student who is swearing, take him off to the side out of the hearing of others, and deliver an *assertive demand.* "Harold **(name),** stop (holds Harold's hand—**touch**), this is not a school word **(eye contact).** If this word is said again, I will need to call your mother and I will send you to *time out* **(preparatory)."**

In the alternative, we may take a *behavioral analysis* response to Harold's swearing. If the student is motivated by attention getting or power seeking, he may use the "F" word or similar swearing so that others will see him and respond in a way that makes him the center of attention. In such an instance, we may behaviorally deal with this by <u>not</u> giving attention and acting as if we do not hear it. We refuse to give our attention **(extinction** by withdrawing **social reinforcement),** thus the student has no payoff. When we do withdraw our attention, a number of actions will occur. The attention-getting and power-seeking student will intensify the action, since his motivational payoff is to get attention, and experiencing the opposite prompts him to escalate the swearing action. We may be able to "tough it out" by refusing to respond to the swearing, and after it gets worse it will dissipate **(extinction).**

At times, we as teachers might observe unwanted reinforcement and attention for the swearing student from classmates who might giggle and begin saying the same word. This provides the swearing student with a very powerful social reinforcement. We then isolate the student **(time out)** in such a space that classmates will not socially reinforce him. We enforce this isolation each and every time the attention-getting student acts out through swearing. The power-seeking student will refuse to stay in this isolation, and it might require us to restrain him in the isolated, screened-off space; it certainly will require that we remain with him in this space. When we are restraining in time out, we do not speak to the student or give him any other form of verbal or nonverbal acknowledgment. It is helpful to set an egg timer for 5 to 15 minutes, and once it goes off the student is permitted to return to classroom activities. (See Chapter 2 on Behavioral Analysis and the guidelines for the use of time out.)

Swearing is a very different matter for the revengeful student regressing through the levels of crisis. When such students are flooded emotionally in Level 2: Developing Crisis, their verbal aggression in the form of swearing, threats, and other hostile verbal actions is considered ventilating. As odd as it might seem, the more verbal aggression the better, because it means that the child's internal anger, anxiety, and related energy are being ventilated.

Crying to Get One's Own Way/Whining

Crying to get your own way, sometimes called "water power," and whining are both auditorily abrasive expressions that grate on our nerves to such a point that we give in to the student's demand just to get these sounds to stop. To deal with such behavior, we again may follow the escalation of power techniques of the Three Faces of Discipline continuum.

Relationship-Listening

The "I"-message contained in the Relationship-Listening face is a particularly helpful technique to use both for "water power" crying and whining.

CRYING: "When I hear crying, I cannot understand what the person wants, and crying hurts my ears."

WHINING: "When I hear a squeaky little voice, it hurts my ears, and I have a very difficult time listening to what the squeaky voice wants. People who want me to hear them must use an adult voice for me to hear." We do not give the student what he wants while he is crying, nor shortly after, and the behavior will soon dissipate.

Confronting-Contracting

TEACHER: "What are you doing? What is the rule?" (use words to tell your needs; possibly apply a logical consequence) "That 'squeaky voice' hurts our ears and we are not able to be comfortable at the work table. If that 'squeaky' voice is used again, it is showing us that you do not know the rules for being with us, and I will need to ask you to work at a table by yourself where that 'voice' will not hurt others' ears."

Rules and Consequences

"CAROL (name and gestures), stop (eye contact, touches), move now to choose a new table, and begin." The teacher may choose to reinforce another student who is not crying or whining, use extinction to attempt to withdraw reinforcement given to these acts, or use forms of time out.

BREAKING UP A FIGHT

The National Crisis Prevention Institute, which conducts training on the restraining techniques previously described and prepares educators to deal with aggressive students, states that in general a fight occurs between students for one of the following reasons:

Saving Face

People will commonly risk their personal well-being to maintain their dignity.[8] This is, of course, especially true for the adolescent child who has peers looking on.

Defending Property or Territory

Concern for material objects of real or imagined value will occasionally cause people to sacrifice their safety or even their lives.[9]

Fear (Fight or Flight)

The emotional physiological response of fear can be great enough to impair rational thought. In peak fear response, the body can switch to a self-defense mode that demands fleeing or fighting.[10]

Testing the Pecking Order

One person may become jealous over the status of another and respond by picking a fight or generally looking for trouble.[11]

One of the best ways of dealing with fights is to attempt to stop them before they start. This can be done by:

- Responding to early warning signs
- Getting assistance (call principal/other teachers)
- Removing peers (order students out of the area)
- Approaching calmly and confidently (don't rush in)
- Using a supportive stance (see earlier)
- Using distraction (blink or shut off lights, make a loud distracting noise)
- Using firm nonverbals and paraverbals (control your voice and actions, and use assertive commands)
- Setting and enforcing reasonable limits (use assertive command)
- Separating, if necessary (move the students so they cannot see each other to let them calm down)[12]

When a fight between students is in progress, the teacher's first critical response is to get help. He or she may send a student to bring the principal or neighboring teachers to assist you in dealing with this disruption. If possible, remove any obstacles and weapons that are manageable by the teacher, and quickly order peers as onlookers to move out of the area. Next, start with verbal intervention by using the supportive demand.

The teachers would not step into the middle of a fight unless they are absolutely certain that they can manage the size and strengths of all participants—never intervene alone. If two students are fighting, their behavior will change over time, being either combative or defensive. Try to identify which position each is taking as the fight is progressing. It will be easier to physically restrain the students if they both have a defensive stance because this will signal that they really want to stop.

Also, energy levels will fluctuate between highs and lows. Never grab to restrain a student at the maximum energy upswing; wait until a lull. Team restraining actions by teachers should only occur as a last resort. The teachers will now use verbal commands in the form of assertive demands, grabbing at each student and putting them into a team (two adults) wrist-shoulder hold restraint, keeping the students' heads down until they cease struggling and agree to stop their fight. Move the students to different rooms and out of visual sight of each other by using the transporting techniques. Once control is established, permit the students to cool down and then, by talking to them individually, move to Level 4: Reestablishing Equilibrium through Relationship-Listening and Confronting-Contracting techniques. Then bring both students together, normally with a table between them, and counsel them with the Confronting-Contracting techniques for the purpose of attempting to reestablish a positive working relationship between the two students. The meeting should end with a contract or agreement. If hostilities remain, more discussion should occur permitting ventilation of issues, or both students may be kept in isolation until they are ready to work it out.

SUMMARY

At times we are faced with a student who is so "flooded" that he or she acts out in an assaultive and violent manner that endangers himself and others. We are required to understand the level of crises through which the student will move, and first make attempts to get the student to ventilate inner tensions through language.

We will also be required to mediate for classmates who have witnessed violent behavior through the use of classroom meetings. We can use any of the techniques previously learned in all of the Three Faces of Discipline to deal with many other forms of verbal aggression, including swearing, whining, and crying.

Instructional Media and Training

Name	Time	Format	Address of Distributor
The Nonviolent Crisis Intervention Instructor Certification Program	24 hrs (6 hours per day)	Video and Role-play	National Crisis Prevention Institute 3315-K North 124 Street Brookfield, Wisconsin 53005 1-800-558-8976 Fax: 1-262-783-5906 Email: info@crisisprevention.com

The first phase of the Instructor's Program has you participating in the 12-hour training program just like the staff you will eventually be training. This section is designed to teach you the basic skills and techniques of nonviolent crisis intervention. The next phase focuses on facilitating dynamics. Your professional instructor will train you in teaching techniques that have proven extremely effective throughout the years. Using CPI materials most effectively, facilitating role-play, class size, teaching physical techniques, answering difficult questions from participants, and dealing with staff resistance will be major topics. Phase three, instructor practicum, gives you the opportunity to do a presentation of these skills.
Four Videos are available for purchase: Volume I—The Disruptive Child; Volume II—The Disruptive Adolescent; Volume III—The Assaultive Student; and Breaking Up Fights—How to Safely Defuse Explosive Conflicts
Volume III The Assaultive Student also, Breaking Up Fights—How to Safely Defuse Explosive Conflicts

NOTES

1. T. McMurrain, *Intervention in Human Crisis* (Atlanta: Humanics Press, 1975).

2. After reading the full explanation that follows we will see that the teacher in our example made a number of mistakes in handling this incident and dealing with a revengeful child. She should have used *supportive demand and stance* rather than *assertive demand and stance* (soon to be explained). But if the teacher has had little past experience and does not know the history of this child, she might judge his actions as an attempt to grab attention or power, and then might find herself handling the revengeful incident as best she can once it begins.

3. *Nonviolent Crisis Intervention for the Educator: Volume III The Assaultive Student* (Brookfield, WI: National Crisis Prevention Institute, Inc.)

4. This is also a reconceptualization of the Crisis Development Behavior Levels as developed by the National Crisis Prevention Institute. Their training videos and workshops are highly recommended; more detail on them may be found on page 289.

5. National Crisis Prevention Institute, Inc.

6. National Crisis Prevention Institute, Inc.

7. Often it is adult hands that do hurt children and create great fear in them.

8. D. Rekoske and G. T. Wyka, *Breaking Up Fights—How to Safely Defuse Explosive Conflicts* (Brookfield, WI: National Crisis Prevention Institute, 1990), p. 3.

9. Ibid.

10. Ibid.

11. Ibid.

12. Ibid., pp. 3 and 4.

Related Readings

Freud, A. *Normality and Pathology in Childhood: Assessments of Development.* New York: International University Press, 1968.

McMurrain, T. *Intervention in Human Crisis.* Atlanta: Humanics Press, 1975.

Nonviolent Crisis Intervention for the Educator: Volume III, The Assaultive Student. Brookfield, WI: National Crisis Prevention Institute, Inc.

Wolfgang, C., and M. E. Wolfgang. *School for Young Children: Developmentally Appropriate Practices.* Boston: Allyn and Bacon, 1992.

Wolfgang, C. H. *Helping Aggressive and Passive Preschoolers through Play.* Columbus, OH: Charles Merrill Publishing, 1977.

CLASSROOM MANAGEMENT

THE **ARRANGEMENT** of furniture in our classroom, the grouping and movement of students, the creation of rules, and other examples of daily management activities have shown us that when these management activities are done poorly, they are actually instrumental in causing disruptive behaviors requiring discipline actions.

CHAPTER 14 summarizes the classic research and writings of Kounin, Evertson, and Emmer regarding classroom management for the elementary and secondary levels.

CLASSROOM MANAGEMENT: A DISCIPLINE PREVENTIVE PROCESS

Writers/Theorists:

▨ Carolyn M. Evertson and Edmund T. Emmer, *Preventive Classroom Management*

▨ Jacob Kounin, *Discipline and Group Management in Classrooms*

OVERVIEW

Nearly everyone has sat in a classroom with a teacher who walks up and down the aisles passing out a handout one at a time to each student, wasting valuable time while all students sit idle. Before the teacher completes the process, most of the class is bored and busy chatting with each other and much time has been lost—this is not effective classroom management. Another example may be a kindergarten classroom with four boys at table with Magic Markers, scissors, and construction paper, all ready to begin a project of cutting out a paper Thanksgiving turkey. One marker rolls off the end of the table and two children go under the table to retrieve it. A third student sees that they are not returning, decides that there is something interesting occurring, and joins them under the table. The child left behind stands to collect the scissors from the center of the table and mistakenly tramps on the finger of one of the students "down below" who screams and punches at the standing student's leg to get him off of his fingers. When the screams start, a second child stands too quickly and bumps his head on the underside of the table and begins to cry. To say the least, we have a management problem and possibly a discipline problem in this kindergarten classroom.

In passing out the papers the teacher could have counted out groups equal to the number in each row, handed that pile to the first person in the row to pass back, and then proceeded to his or her lesson immediately, thus saving time and not being required to get the class's attention back. The kindergarten teacher could have taken the Magic Markers, turned them upside down, and placed the caps in plaster in a small cup before letting them harden. When student were finished using the marker they would place it back into its cap, thus it would not roll off or dry out—good classroom management in practice.

Many discipline problems occur because of poor practices of classroom management and they happen during transitions between activities or changes in space. Classroom management can be defined as the arrangement of students (grouping), materials (pencils, paper, etc.), and furniture (desk and chairs, etc.), and the movement of these over time (moving from large group lecture to small cooperative groups or lab tables). We have three major writers and researchers who help give us insights and advice on good classroom management—Kounin, Evertson, and Emmer.

KOUNIN'S WITH-IT-NESS AND OVERLAPPING

Jacob Kounin has conducted research with several colleagues of kindergarten, elementary, secondary, and college classrooms. His most important findings have come from videotaping 15 first- and second-grade classrooms and 15 third- and fifth-grade classrooms. They were videotaped on half days for two months. Kounin followed with another study of 50 primary classrooms videotaped for a full day. For each classroom, he recorded the behavior of eight students chosen at random and one emotionally disturbed child. His concern was with finding teacher practices related to student work involvement and low student misbehavior. Kounin isolated the teacher practices and procedures of "with-it-ness," "overlapping," "smoothness and momentum," and "group alerting" as parts of classroom-management success. Teachers who were aware of what was going on throughout the class in terms of student behavior and student work and who showed their awareness to students had high student work involvement and low student misbehavior. Kounin calls this awareness "with-it-ness." In other words, the teacher would pick up that several students did not understand their seat work, that a student was not listening, or a student was reading a comic book, and then would show awareness by such actions as moving over to the student, giving a quick reprimand, or asking the student a question. The teacher action showed the entire class that he or she was on top of what everyone was doing. On the other hand, if a teacher was not aware of such occurrences, then confused students would give up on their assignment and become agitated; students not listening to the lesson would tend to draw other students away from the lesson; students reading comic books or passing notes would be seen by other students as getting away with inattentiveness; and other students would begin to turn to nonacademic behavior of their own. The students knew which of their number were not paying attention, "goofing off," or being disruptive, and unless the teacher dealt with those students, their misbehavior spread to others. Additionally, if a teacher blatantly showed his or her lack of awareness by reprimanding the wrong student for talking or the last person in a chain of students who had picked up comic books, or commanding one student to pay attention while other students were even more "off-task," then the class became further convinced that the teacher was not in tune with what was going on and that they could feel safe in continuing to be uninvolved in school work.

Kounin also found that teacher "overlapping" was a complementary practice with the "with-it-ness" of successful classroom managers—attending to two events at the same time. A teacher who could instruct a group of students while responding to student concerns from outside of the group could keep an entire classroom working smoothly. On the other hand, a teacher who was in the habit of attending exclusively to students in the instructional group would lose the work involvement and increase the misbehavior of students outside of the group. For example, let's consider the case of a teacher with a reading group that has students recite; another student comes up to the reading group with a question about a seat assignment. If the teacher turns away from the reading group and focuses entirely on the student asking the question, misbehavior and off-task behavior will increase in the reading group. On the other hand, if the teacher ignores the student and the student goes back and sits down without direction, and the teacher continues to direct his or her attention to the reading group, then the questioning student is left without anything productive to do. He or she then starts talking with other students or exhibits other misbehavior that gets the attention of students who were working productively. The result of the teacher's ignoring one segment of the class is compounding misbehavior. We're reminded of a recent airport experience in which an airline agent showed overlapping behavior. The agent, the only one on duty, issued tickets, placed labels on baggage, and at the same time conversed on the phone with a distressed ticket holder. The line of twelve persons could easily have started grumbling, demanding, and complaining if the agent had ignored their needs to be checked through the line and instead talked on the phone. Similarly, the phone caller could have been upset if the agent had attended only to the waiting passengers. Instead, both were accommodated. The passengers reached their plane on time and the confused caller was rerouted to a more desirable flight. The same type of simultaneous accommodations holds true for a classroom teacher who must juggle the competing demands of students and not just play to one student or one group.

Let's look at the classrooms of Ms. Wedgeworth and Mr. Wadsworth to understand how Kounin's categories of with-it-ness and overlapping explain Ms. Wedgeworth's preventive management and Mr. Wadsworth's compounding discipline problems. Ms. Wedgeworth is "with it." She is engaging all students in an activity of tracing the Mormon route. The seated students are trying to chart the part of their maps while Fred is doing the work in front of the class. Ms. Wedgeworth is helping Fred while at the same time scanning the room and listening to what the other students are doing. She shows the class that she knows what is going on by immediately picking up on a new noise and telling Samantha to stop talking. On the other hand, Mr. Wadsworth shows the class his lack of being "with it" by not being aware of note passing; a disruption occurs when he finally shouted at the victim, Jim, rather than at the students who are causing the misbehavior. Mr. Wadsworth's error confirms to the misbehaving students that they could continue to misbehave.

We can also understand how Ms. Wedgeworth keeps students on task by using her "overlapping" abilities while Mr. Wadsworth aggravates the situation by putting total emphasis on the misbehaving student (the wrong student at that); this distracts those remaining students who are still doing the learning activity. Ms. Wedgeworth corrects Samantha and in the same breath asks the class to hold up their maps. She shows the class that she could attend to two events together. Mr. Wadsworth stops the lesson entirely to confront Jim. The class has nothing else to do now but stop and watch the confrontation. When Mr. Wadsworth decides to return to the lesson, the students have to refocus their attention and begin all over again.

Besides with-it-ness and overlapping, Kounin found some other classroom practices related to successful classroom management—smoothness, momentum, and group alerting. Smoothness is shown by the teacher continuing with the learning activity without going on a tangent, being distracted by some unplanned event, interrupting students from working, leaving a learning activity in midstream, or reversing direction. Smoothness is staying with the logical organization of a lesson. Those teachers who get easily distracted by such examples as beginning a mathematics lesson, showing the class how to do a calculation, and then saying such things as, "Did I pass back your homework? Oh well, then let's put away our books for a moment. Here's your homework, your scores mean…" or when students are quiet and working on seat work and the teacher says, "Oh, I forgot to take lunch money—will those who are getting milk please come up here." Teachers who stray and break up the continuity of the lesson will have a higher incidence of student misbehavior and lower student attention than those teachers who organize their time so as not to interfere with the goal of the lesson.

Momentum is another critical factor in successful classroom management that relates to the organization and delivery of the lesson. Momentum is a concern for the pacing of instruction. The lack of momentum or a slowing down occurs when the teacher continues to elaborate on a point that students already understand. For example, the teacher gives a writing assignment and says, "Before you begin, make sure your margins are one inch on both sides. In this classroom I want you to all be in the habit of keeping the margins to one inch. Look at this paper I am holding up. Now I measure one inch on this side, and one inch on this side. We must have good writing habits. Margins are important." By this time, the students who were ready to begin writing are impatiently waiting for the teacher to be quiet. Waiting students are prone to take up other non-instructional matters. Another example of lack of momentum is a teacher drawing out procedures by passing out papers, materials, and books one at a time via one person; instructional time is lost. Nagging students can be another loss of momentum (i.e., "Why is it that when I leave you alone, this class is so noisy? If you are going to be a grown-up, you need to act like grown-ups. In this country, we give adults a lot of responsibilities. Part of growing up is knowing when to behave. When I was a student…" A final type of slowdown is when a teacher keeps students waiting on other students for something insignificant. Examples would be, "I want to meet with reading group C now. You are to come to the group one at a time, but only when I call your name. Sit with your heads down until you are called. OK, Fred, you come and sit down. Sara…" or "Now it's time for group projects. First put your math books away and look up when they are all in your desks. Jerry, don't put your papers away yet until everyone has put their math books away. OK, now that everyone has put their math books away, let's put your papers away. Now, I didn't say anything about taking out your projects yet!" A teacher with momentum might instead say, "Reading Group C, come quietly up here with your materials in hand" and "Now it's time for group projects. I'll give you a minute to clear your math materials, get out projects, and start thinking about what your group should be doing today." A teacher without momentum loses instructional time and causes student restlessness. A teacher with momentum capitalizes on transition periods as short flowing times into the next activity.

Kounin found *group alerting* as another teacher practice highly related to effective classroom management. These are behaviors used to keep students in suspense and others "on their toes" as to whether or when they will be asked to demonstrate their knowledge. Students are called upon at random and often asked to recite as a total group. If a student tunes out from the lesson or does not keep up on the work, she or he can't avoid the high likelihood of being called on. Nonalerting practices are those that protect a student from being accountable. A predetermined pattern of calling students, such as singling out only those with their hands up (or down) or in a clockwise manner, is a example of a nonalerting practice. Kounin found that teachers who keep children alerted and on their toes are more successful in inducing work involvement and preventing deviancy than teachers who do not.[1]

To summarize Kounin's important work on classroom management, a teacher can minimize misbehavior by:

1. *With-it-ness:*

   - Keep constantly alert to sights and sounds around the classroom.
   - Arrange students to be within sight at all times.
   - Scan the classroom whenever attending to an individual or small group of students.
   - At the first detection of misbehavior, use a brief acknowledgment to let the class know that you are aware of the misbehavior (i.e., "Felina, would you please get back to work?").

2. *Overlapping*

   - Attend to two events at the same time whenever necessary so as not to leave students waiting.
   - When instructing one group, acknowledge difficulties that students outside the group may be having, but keep group instruction moving (i.e., "Marsha, keep explaining that logarithm out loud to us while I check on Petunia's problem. Now, Petunia, where do you need help—I see. Martha, check your logarithm with the rest of the group; then all of you do exercise B. Petunia, you're forgetting to invert the ratio…" Correct misbehavior but keep instruction moving (i.e., "Tom, it's your turn to read (teacher turns head to class in seats). There's too much noise. I can't hear Tom read. Tom, sound that word out by syllables: for, tu, nate. Good. Sam, get back to your seat. If you need help come over here. Sandra (who sits two seats from Tom in the reading group), please pronounce the same word Tom just had…"

3. *Smoothness*

   - Preplan the lesson so that extraneous matters are taken care of beforehand (i.e., "Now that today's schedule and assignments are handed out, have we forgotten any other items? If not, let's give our full attention to Gothic design. Let's look on page 13, the picture of the Cathedral of Chartres. No, Sally, I'll pass back the homework at the end of the class. What do you notice about this cathedral that is different from Notre Dame? Bruce?")
   - Once students are absorbed in their work, do not distract them. Leave them alone to work and assist them individually.

4. *Momentum*

   - Keep the lesson moving briskly.
   - Do not overdwell on a minor or already understood part of the lesson.
   - Correct students quickly without nagging and return to the lesson.
   - Have students move from one activity to the next without having to wait for each other on each subpart of the transition (i.e., avoid saying, "First everyone put your pencils away").

5. *Group alerting*

   - Call on students at random.

- Raise group interest by interspersing suspense between questions by saying, "This is a tough one coming up." "Can you figure this one out?" "You haven't heard of this before." "I want you all to think hard before responding."
- Have the entire group or class respond in unison.
- Physically move around the room and ask students to show what they have done.
- While asking one student to respond, look at other students.

Kounin found that with-it-ness, overlapping, smoothness, momentum, and group alerting were the teacher practices most highly related to management success. With-it-ness, overlapping, and group alerting are focused teacher behaviors, verbal and nonverbal, in scanning and responding to students. Smoothness and momentum are focused on the organization of the lesson, presentation of instruction, and transitions between work activities. Next we will discuss the more recent work of Evertson, Emmer, and their colleagues that concurs with much of Kounin's work and also adds some critical elements to successful classroom management.[2]

Evertson and Emmer[3] after collecting observations of 27 self-contained third-grade classrooms (from 25 hours of observation during the first three weeks) and 51 junior high school mathematics and English teachers (14 one-half-hour observations) were able to find significant differences between practices of good and poor classroom managers as measured by student achievement, student on-task behavior, and the amount of disruptive student behavior. With third-grade classrooms, they found that effective teachers at the beginning of the school year:

- *Broke down* their classroom tasks into specific rules and procedures for students to understand and follow.
- *Taught the rules* and procedures as an important classroom lesson consisting of presentation, examples, practice, and feedback.
- *Predicted* procedures where students would have the greatest confusion and emphasized the teaching of those procedures.
- *Monitored* and handled problems directly and immediately.

The study of junior high school effective and ineffective teachers found differentiating practices similar to the elementary teachers. The findings were that effective managers

- *Instructed* students in specific rules about appropriate behavior.
- *Monitored* student compliance by consistently enforcing acceptable behavior.
- *Made an accounting of student work* through precise record keeping of students' work accomplishment.
- *Broke down rules* from general "holisms" to specific do's and don'ts.
- *Organized* time so most classroom time was devoted to instruction (as with Kounin's terms *smoothness* and *momentum*).

What echoes throughout the Evertson and Emmer studies is that teachers break down the areas of expected student behaviors into specific classroom rules and procedures and then instruct their students in how to follow them.

Evertson and Emmer recorded the expectations and procedures of successful classroom managers. The reader who teaches in preschool or elementary school may wish to review Table 14.1. The reader who teaches in junior/middle or secondary school may wish to review Table 14.2.

After reading through these tables and considering Kounin's work, the teacher may think of some immediate classroom-management changes to make. Since the purpose of this book is to help teachers solve the discipline problems of individual students, the vast amount of literature and research on classroom management can only be briefly explored. Instead, this discourse on management is to suggest that if a teacher finds discipline problems pervasive throughout the classroom, then further study and a change in management techniques may be needed before looking at ways of dealing with individual students. A reader who wishes to pursue classroom management further can find excellent readings listed at the end of the chapter.

TABLE 14.1   Expectations and Procedures for the Elementary School Classroom

Area of Behavior	A Common Expectation or Procedure
A. Student use of classroom space and facilities	
1. Desks or tables and student storage space	Students are usually expected to keep these areas clean and neat. Some teachers set aside a particular period of time each week for students to clean out desks. Alternatively, straightening out materials could be a good end-of-day routine.
2. Learning centers/stations	Appropriate behavior at the center, access to the center, care of materials, and procedures for coming and going should be considered.
3. Shared materials, bookshelves, drawers, and cabinets.	Access and use should be spelled out.
4. Teacher's desk and storage areas	Frequently, these are off limits to students, except when the teacher's permission is given.
5. Drinking fountain, sink, pencil sharpener, and bathroom	Decide when and how these can be used. Most teachers prefer not to have lines waiting at any of these locations.
B. Procedures concerning other areas of the school	
1. Out-of-class bathrooms, drinking fountains, office, library, resource rooms	Appropriate student behavior needs to be identified. Procedures for students coming to and going from these areas should be decided upon.
2. Coming and going from classroom	Student needs to learn how to line up properly and how to pass through the halls correctly. Consider such things as the condition of the room before lining up and whether talking is allowed.
3. Playground	Expectations need to be identified for coming from and going to the playground, safety and maintenance rules, and ways to get students' attention for lining up or listening. Some teachers use a coach's whistle.
4. Lunchroom	Expectations for table manners, behavior, and noise level should be identified.
C. Procedures during whole-class activities	
1. Student participation in class discussions	Many teachers require students to raise their hands to be called on before speaking during whole-class activities.
2. Student involvement and attention	Students are expected to listen to the person who is talking.
3. Assignments	Many teachers require assignments on a chalkboard or elsewhere or have students copy the assignments in notebooks.

(continues)

TABLE 14.1 *(continued)*

Area of Behavior	A Common Expectation or Procedure
4. Talk among students during seat work	Some teachers require silence; others allow quiet talk (very soft whispering). Also, teachers sometimes use a cue or signal to let students know when the noise level is unacceptable. For example, a bell rung once means no more talking. Also needed are procedures for students working together, if this is to be allowed, and some procedure to enable students to contact the teacher if they need help. Typical procedures involve students raising hands when help is needed or, if the teacher is involved with other students or in-group work, the use of classroom monitors.
5. Passing out books and supplies	Supplies that are frequently used can be passed out by a monitor. Students need to know what to do while they wait for their materials.
6. Students turning in work	Teachers frequently have a set of shelves or an area where students turn in assignments when they are finished. Alternatively, a special folder for each student may be kept.
7. Handing back assignments to students	Prompt return of corrected papers is desirable. Many teachers establish a set time of the day to do this. Students need to know what to do with the material when they receive it (place it in a notebook, or folder, or take it home).
8. Make-up work	Procedures are needed for helping students who have been absent as well as for communicating assignments that must be made up.
9. Out-of-seat policies	Students need to know when it is acceptable to be out of seats and when permission is needed.
10. What to do when seat work is finished	Some teachers use extra credit assignments, enrichment activities, free reading, etc.
D. Procedures during reading groups or other small-group work	
1. Student movement into and out of group	These transitions should be brief, quiet, and nondisruptive to other students. Many teachers use a bell to signal movement from seatwork to small group. This works when there is a preset order that students know.
2. Bringing materials to the group	Students need to know what they are to bring with them to the group. One way to communicate this is to include a list of the materials along with posted assignments.
3. Expected behavior of students in the small group	Just as in whole-group activities, students need clear expectations about what behaviors are appropriate in small-group work.
4. Expected behavior of students not in the small group	Students out of the group also need clear expectations about desirable behavior. Important areas include noise level, student talk, access to the teacher, and what to do when the seatwork assignment or other activities are completed. Effective managers avoid problems by giving very clear instructions for activities of students out of group. Checking briefly between groups also helps prevent problems from continuing as well as allowing monitoring. Student helpers may also be identified.
E. Other procedures that must be decided upon	
1. Beginning the school day	Establishing a consistent routine, such as saying the Pledge of Allegiance, the current date, birthdays, an overview of the morning's activities, or passing back graded papers helps start the day while still giving time for later arrivals and for administrative matters to be accomplished.

TABLE 14.1 *(continued)*

Area of Behavior	A Common Expectation or Procedure
2. Administrative matters	Such details as attendance reporting, collecting lunch money, and other record keeping must be done while students are in the room. Teachers can set aside a specific time of the day for performing these tasks during which the students are expected to engage in some activity. For example, 10 minutes of quiet reading fills the time constructively while allowing the teacher to handle administrative tasks with little interruption.
3. End of school day	Routines can be planned for concluding each day. Straightening desks, gathering materials, singing a song, or reviewing activities and things learned during the day provide some structure for this major transition time.
4. Student conduct during interruptions and delays	Interruptions are inevitable and sometimes frequent. Students can be taught to continue working if interrupted, or to sit patiently and quietly otherwise.
5. Fire drills, and other precautionary measures	School procedures need to be identified and carefully taught to the children.
6. Housekeeping and student helpers	Most children love to help, and the teacher needs only to identify specific tasks. These are also a good way to help some children learn responsibility. Some possibilities: feeding classroom pets, watering plants, erasing chalkboards, acting as line leader, messenger, etc. A procedure for choosing and rotating responsibilities among students needs to be established.

Source: Evertson, Carolyn M., and Emmer, Edmund T. "Preventive Classroom Management." In *Helping Teachers Manage Classrooms,* Daniel L. Duke, ed. Alexandria, VA: ASCD, 1982.

TABLE 14.2 Expectations and Procedures for Junior High School/Middle School Classrooms

Area of Behavior	A Common Expectation or Procedure
A. Procedures for beginning class	
1. Administrative matters	The teacher needs procedures to handle reporting absences and tardiness. Students need to know what behaviors are expected of them while the teacher is completing administrative procedures. Some teachers begin the period with a brief warm-up activity such as a few problems or a brief assignment. Others expect the students to sit quietly and wait for the teacher to complete the routine.
2. Student behavior before and at the beginning of the period.	Procedures should be established for what students are expected to do when the tardy bell rings (be in seats, stop talking), behavior during PA announcements (no talking, no interruptions of the teacher), what materials are expected to be brought to class each day, and how materials to be used during the period will be distributed.
B. Procedures during whole-class instructional activities 1. Student talk	Many teachers require that students raise their hands in order to receive permission to speak. Sometimes teachers allow chorus responses (everybody answers at once) without hand raising, but the teacher then needs to identify and use some signal to students that lets them know when such responding is appropriate.

(continues)

TABLE 14.2 *(continued)*

Area of Behavior	A Common Expectation or Procedure
2. Use of the room by students	Students should know when it is appropriate to use the pencil sharpener, to obtain materials from shelves or bookcases, and if and when it is appropriate to leave their seats to seek help from the teacher or other students. Unclear expectations in this area result in some students spending time wandering about the room.
3. Leaving the room	Some procedure needs to be established for allowing students to use the bathroom, go to the library or school office, etc. Usually the school will have some specified system. We have noted that teachers who are free with hall passes frequently have large numbers of requests to leave the room.
4. Signals for attention	Frequently teachers use a verbal signal or a cue such as moving to a specific area of the room, ringing a bell, or turning on an overhead projector to signal to students. Such a signal, if used consistently, can be an effective device for making a transition between the activities or for obtaining student attention.
5. Student behavior during seatwork	Expectations need to be established for what kind of talk, if any, may occur during seatwork; how students can get help; when out-of-seat behavior is or is not permitted; how to gain access to materials; and what to do if seatwork assignments are completed early.
6. Procedures for laboratory work or individual projects	A system for distributing materials when these are used is essential. Also, safety routines or rules are vital. Expectations regarding appropriate behavior should be established for students working individually or in groups, and when extensive movement around the room or coming and going is required. Finally, routines for cleaning up are suggested.
C. Expectations regarding student responsibility for work	
1. Policy regarding the form of work	Procedures can be established for the placement of headings on the paper, for the use of pen or pencil, and for neatness.
2. Policy regarding completion of assignments	The teacher will have to decide whether incomplete or late work is acceptable, under what conditions, and whether a penalty will be imposed. In addition, some procedure for informing students of due dates for assignments should be established, along with procedures for make-up work for students who were absent.
3. Communicating assignments to students	An effective procedure for communicating assignments is to keep a list of each period's work assignments during a two- or three-week period of time. Posting this list allows students who were absent to easily identify necessary make-up work. Another useful procedure is to record the assignment for the day on an overhead projector transparency or on the front chalkboard, and require students to copy the assignment onto a piece of paper or into a notebook. Students who do not complete assignments in class will then have a record of what is expected when they return to the assignment at home or during a study period.
4. Checking procedures	Work that is to be checked by students in class can save the teacher time and provide quick feedback to students. Procedures should be established for exchanging papers, noting errors, returning papers, and passing them in to the teacher.
5. Grading policy	Students should know what components will be included in determining report card grades and the weight (percent) of each component.

TABLE 14.2 *(continued)*

Area of Behavior	A Common Expectation or Procedure
D. Other procedures	
1. Student use of teacher desk or storage areas	Generally these are kept off-limits to students, except when the teacher gives special permission.
2. Fire and disaster drills	Students should be informed early in the year about what they are to do during such emergencies. Typically, the school will have a master plan and will conduct school-wide drills.
3. Procedures for ending the class	Expectations regarding straightening up the room, returning to seats, keeping a tolerable noise level, and signaling for dismissal may be established. When cleanup requires more than a few seconds, teachers usually set aside the necessary time at the end of the period to complete the task before the bell rings.
4. Interruptions	Students need to know what is expected during interruptions (continue working or sit quietly).

Source: Evertson and Emmer, op. cit.

SUMMARY

Classroom management has been discussed as a preventive process for many discipline problems. Research by Jacob Kounin on "with-it-ness," "overlapping," "smoothness," "momentum," and "group alerting" and the research by Evertson and Emmer on rules and monitoring provide insights to help teachers organize their classroom practice. It is our belief that management will reduce, but not eliminate, all discipline problems. Therefore, a teacher needs strategies and behaviors for both.

Alfie Kohn's Criticism of Kounin, Evertson, and Emmer

Kohn's criticism is that Kounin, Evertson, and Emmer all begin with the wrong premise: they were looking at student compliance with teacher-controlled classrooms.

"With-it-ness." This term meant the teacher not only was attentive to what students were doing, but let them know she knew what was going on; she developed a reputation for having, as it were, eyes in the back of her head. Such teachers were shown to be more effective than their without-it colleagues. But what does it mean in this context to be "effective"? To Kounin, it meant getting "conformity and obedience" (p. 65); it meant students didn't do whatever was defined as "deviant" and kept

busy at "the assigned work" (p. 77). Now, if a good classroom is one where students simply do what they're told, we shouldn't be surprised that a teacher is more likely to have such a classroom when students are aware that she can quickly spot noncompliance. After all, if a good society was defined as where citizens obey every governmental decree, then scholars might be able to adduce scientific evidence that a good leader is one who resembles Orwell's Big Brother. (Kohn, 1996, p. 55)

In fact, researchers since Kounin have found that classroom management was more effective "when long periods of student talk (recitations) were avoided. In other words, the teacher retained control over pacing." For that matter, the effective teachers retained control over just about everything, closely directing and monitoring students and providing tasks that were "very highly structured" (Emmer and Evertson, 1981, pp. 345, 343). Again, these results are perfectly logical if we accept the premises; the techniques follow naturally from the objective. The objective is not to promote depth of understanding, or continuing motivation to learn, or concern for others. It is to maximize time on task and obedience to authority. (Kohn, 1996, p. 55)

Would she nevertheless have to start the year by securing control of the classroom in order to reach these goals? Absolutely not. In fact, to do so would make it far more difficult to be successful later on.

You may be familiar with the hoary educational adage that teachers should not smile until Christmas (or even Easter)—that is, that they should be severe and controlling for months and only then relent a bit, displaying a bit of kindness and revealing themselves to be actual human beings. I don't know who came up with that appalling saying, but I can only hope that he or she is no longer in a position to do harm to children. It is difficult to imagine an approach more out of step with everything we know about child development and learning. Even construed narrowly, that advice makes no sense: the available research "clearly demon-

strates that nice teachers are highly effective ... [and refutes] the myth that students learn more from cold, stern, distant teachers" (Andersen 1987, pp. 57–57)—except, of course, that they may learn to be cold, stern, and distant themselves. (Kohn, 1996, p. 65)

Further Questions

1. Should a teacher begin her first day by stating the rules to the class, or is it better to have a class meeting and have the students come up with rules for managing the classroom?
2. How much "with-it-ness" is needed by the teacher? Does this seem like overcontrol as Kohn would state?
3. Take a position regarding Kohn's Orwellian Big Brother criticism as a form of overcontrol through monitoring the students' behavior.

NOTES

1. Jacob Kounin, *Discipline and Group Management in Classrooms* (New York: Holt, Rinehart, and Winston, 1970), p. 123.
2. Please see the following references for the many contributions to research and writing on classroom management.
3. Carolyn M. Evertson and Edmund T. Emmer, *Preventive Classroom Management* (Boston: Allyn & Bacon, 1990), p. 17.

REFERENCES

Anderson, L., Evertson, C., and Emmer, E. "Dimensions in Classroom Management Derived from Recent Research," *Journal of Curriculum Studies, 12* (1980): 343–356.

Brophy, Jere, and Evertson, Carolyn, "Context Variables in Teaching," *Educational Psychologist, 12* (1978): 310–316.

Brophy, Jere, and Evertson, Carolyn, *Learning from Teaching: A Developmental Perspective.* Boston: Allyn and Bacon, 1976.

Emmer, E., Evertson, C., and Anderson, L. "Effective Classroom Management at the Beginning of the School Year," *Elementary School Journal* (1980): 219–231.

Emmer, E. T., Evertson, C. M., Sanford, J. P., Clements, B. S., and Worsham, M. E. *Classroom Management for Secondary Teachers.* Englewood Cliffs, NJ: Prentice-Hall, 1984.

Evertson, C., and Anderson, L. (1980) "Effective Classroom Management at the Beginning of the School Year," *Elemen-tary School Journal* (1980). Chicago: University of Chicago Press.

Evertson, C., Emmer, C., Clements, B., Sanford, J., and Worsham, M. *Classroom Management for Elementary Teachers.* Englewood Cliffs, NJ: Prentice-Hall, 1989.

Evertson, C., Sanford, J., and Emmer, E. "Effects of Class Heterogeneity in Junior High School," *American Educational Research Journal, 18* (1981): 219–232.

Good, T. L. "Teacher Effectiveness in the Elementary School: What We Know About It Now," *Journal of Teacher Education, 30* (1979): 32–64.

Kounin, J. D. *Discipline and Group Management in Classrooms.* New York: Holt, Rinehart, and Winston, 1970.

Stanford, J., and Evertson, C. "Classroom Management in a Low SES Junior High: Three Case Studies," *Journal of Teacher Education, 32* (1981): 34–38.

WORKING WITH PARENTS

TEACHERS READING earlier editions of this book requested help in dealing with parents. In a long-term relationship with a challenging student that is disruptive, there comes a point when parents or guardians become involved in this process. Sometimes, support and help come from these student's parents, but often this is not the case. Some parents become defensive, hostile, or threatening to the teacher and school officials. By their own actions, they may become a part of the problem or perhaps the cause of it.

CHAPTER 15. Parents: Difficulties, Problems, and the Teacher's Methods of Responding, provides a construct for looking at the behavior of parents, viewing this behavior regarding their or their child's blocked need, evaluating the seriousness of the situation, and then applying human relationship skills (or discipline skills) learned in Chapters 2 to 12. These constructs will give orderliness to parent behavior, helping us to know how to respond.

CHAPTER 15

PARENTS: DIFFICULTIES, PROBLEMS, AND THE TEACHER'S METHODS OF RESPONDING

The day-to-day life of the teacher is almost never free of questions or problems stemming from relationships with the parents of some students. The overwhelming majority of parents love their children deeply and want nothing but the best for them and value us as educators. Even some of these devoted parents, however, can conduct themselves—and their relationships with their children—in ways that adversely affect the children's behavior in school. Parents' statements, questions, and behaviors—sometimes even destructive behaviors—are signals that alert us to their needs and those of their children. How can we make sense of this continuous parental input, prioritizing needs and making reasonable responses? On what basis would you make a decision to take action as a teacher in the following situations?

Situation 1: "The hole in the doughnut"

Holly's parents are what would be called yuppies. They want to do only the best for their daughter. Holly's father is personable, greets you warmly, and is always ready to question you about the latest "how-to" parent book, public television program on children, or an article on "how to raise your child smarter" that he found in an in-flight magazine. His attitude is described by one teacher, with some frustration, as, "He always sees the hole in the doughnut!"—in other words, he focuses on what is missing rather than appreciates what is there.

He wants the school to provide him with a parallel home curriculum through which he and his daughter would have specific hours set aside for instruction at home. Holly's mother is a volunteer for a host of social activities in the city, and is first to respond when parental help is called for. She is well liked by teachers, but periodically brings questions from her husband: "Tom wants to know..." There is always an urgency and intensity to their demands, though they are grateful and positive toward teacher observations and suggestions. After a school pageant they were very displeased that their daughter did not have a more central part to play.

Situation 2: New Role Demands and Family Separation

Jason, a new kindergarten student, has an eight-year-old brother who attends a private school. His father has opened a new business located near Jason's school, and his mother has just returned to a full-time job on the opposite side of town. The father's new responsibilities include getting the boys up, making their breakfast and lunch, and dropping the boys off at their schools. He is at the school gate to Jason's school 15 to 30 minutes before the school playground is officially opened and leaves him for a period of time unsupervised. When teachers arrive early to make preparations, he requests that Jason be allowed to enter early, so he can drop off his other son and get to his business. Usually, Jason enters the school carrying a bag containing an Egg McMuffin and orange juice. When Jason is found on the playground before opening hours he has, on a number of occasions, lacked an appropriate warm coat for very cool morning hours.

During the first three weeks of school, Dad forgot Jason's health forms, lunch money, and a series of other school requests. Because of the father's morning haste, there is no time to talk to him; when the mother is informed her response is, "That's Jim's responsibility. Tell him about it, not me." Jason is a personable child who greets you with a warm smile much like that of his salesman father, a smile that makes you feel special. However, at times—especially when he is asked to do a task—Jason's expression becomes flat and emotionless. He usually responds to a new activity, no matter how simple, with, "No, I can't do it." During these times, when he seems to pull inside of himself, he also pulls at his hair on one side of his head, until now he has a number of bald spots.

Situation 3: Aggressive Behavior

Brandon is the only son of a rugged, athletic, intense chain-smoking father and an attractive primary school teacher mother. Because of recent moves, he has been in and out of a number of schools. He is a thin-featured, pale-complexioned (to the point of looking anemic), tense child who appears as tightly coiled as a spring. He cannot look a teacher directly in the eyes and usually turns away when invited to join activities. At lunch, he seats himself with the more excitable boys and uses bathroom talk in a whispered, covert manner, whipping the boys into a giggling frenzy that usually ends with their throwing food at each other. When the teacher approaches to stop this behavior, Brandon puts his head down, smiles slightly, and acts as if he is totally innocent.

His most productive behavior is during storytime, when for the first time his eyes are focused on the teacher and the book. It is rare that the teacher finds a book to read to the group that Brandon's parents have not already read to him. His answers to questions after story reading are insightful and animated and show understanding as well as enjoyment of books (remember that his mother is a primary teacher).

During open activities he is like a caged tiger, normally crouched in a protective corner in the room or playground, wanting to use the materials but not feeling free to do so. His attitude stems from his fear that if he starts a project, someone will destroy it. This almost totally frightened and untrusting view of his peers causes him to lash out with sharp fingernails, sometimes directly at the other children's eyes, and to repeatedly bite peers for the most minor contact. After an aggressive act he tells the teacher that the other child was hostile to him, but, upon investigation, it usually turns out that the other child merely bumped him accidentally or inadvertently stepped on one of his toys. During conferences, his mother refuses to discuss this behavior, changing the topic to his performance in the more academic curriculum.

Last week the mother and father separated, and when school closed on Friday there was no parent to pick him up. The home and emergency numbers provided at registration time were called with no results. Brandon was taken home by the classroom teacher, who made repeated telephone calls during the weekend without success, and Brandon spent the entire weekend at the teacher's house. Late Sunday night, when the mother responded to the teacher's telephone call, it was discovered that neither parent was aware that the child had to be cared for by the teacher, in her home, for the entire weekend. When told of this, both mother and father blamed the opposite parent, claiming that it was the other's responsibility.

Situation 4: Sexual Actions and Apparent Injuries

Carol's mother's new boyfriend brings Carol to school, not using the school bus provided, normally an hour to two late each morning. The student appears wearing black leotards, a tank top, and, on one occasion, a red lacy garter belt. The mother's boyfriend does not come into the school, but leaves Carol at the school gate with a kiss that appears passionate and adult-like. Carol is a beautiful child with long black hair and large round eyes, but a nervous smile. She often drops her eyes when spoken to by the teacher and turns away looking over her shoulder in a coy manner. She is not defiant, but simply passive and noncompliant toward teachers. One day Carol came to school walking as if in pain, and was found to be bruised and bleeding in her anal area.

In considering the cases of Carol and the other children, most teachers will realize that some of these parental situations are clearly not serious, while others might call for consulting or legal action. However, each situation does demand some degree of teacher or school intervention; each requires educators to make a reasoned decision. To respond effectively to these situations, we must determine what degree of power would be appropriately used in our intervention. Various incidents might call for simply a Relationship-Listening response from the teacher, while others might warrant a Confronting-Contracting response, possibly a Rules and Consequences response, or even a legalistic-coercive approach that goes beyond the teacher's and school's authority. The following construct may be useful in determining appropriate teacher responses to particular parental situations.

NEEDS OF STUDENTS

Our four examples concerned Holly's parents (with their competitiveness and "hole-in-the-doughnut" questions), Jason's father (new role demands and family separation), Brandon (aggressive behavior and parental difficulty in handling him), and Carol (excessive sexual actions and apparent injuries). Obviously, each situation is related to a need of the parent or child. An analysis of this need can be made by using a construct such as Maslow's[1] hierarchy of needs (see Figure 15.1) to give order to what might appear to be unrelated behaviors of parents and children.

From a Maslowian position, before parents or children can gain self-fulfillment, their lower needs must be met. One must first meet the **physiological** needs of food, water, and basic physical health care (see situation 4, where Carol was physically injured). Once these physiological needs are attained, **security** can become a focus for a parent's or student's

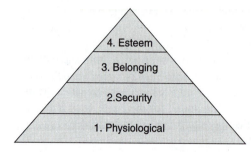

FIGURE 15.1 Maslow's Needs Hierarchy

energies. The teacher can attempt to help establish these feelings of security. (Brandon, in situation 3, exemplified a child with fears of others' aggression.) The next hierarchical need is **belonging** (a situation that is absent in Jason's withdrawal into himself in situation 2). Last is **esteem,** the need to attain a degree of respect from one's peers and those to whom one is related (situation 1, Holly's parents' competitiveness).

Within the context of Maslow's theory, it is suggested that a teacher can analyze the behavior of the parent-related problems or challenges and identify which of the child's needs are being blocked and where this would fall in the Maslowian hierarchy. The teacher is then ready to evaluate the degree of severity of these problems.

DEGREES OF CRISIS

When looking at the human needs underlying some of the problems portrayed in these situations, it is apparent that the degree of seriousness of the situation may vary from life- or psychologically threatening (sexual abuse, physical injury) to limited seriousness (social competitiveness). As we move through Maslow's needs hierarchy, we see a classification of crises: (a) imminent crisis, (b) developing crisis, and (c) potential crisis.[2]

Imminent Crisis

An *imminent crisis* would be a situation in which the Level 1 **physiological** needs are involved, and there is a life-threatening situation. If Carol's injuries are not immediately treated with medical care, irreversible damage *will* occur and may already have caused psychological damage. Time is of the utmost importance with this incident.

Developing Crisis

The *developing crisis* is generally related to the blocked needs of Level 2 **security.** The consequences are serious, but there appears to be more time to head off the event. Brandon's loss of his home stability constitutes a *developing crisis.* If changes do not occur, his behavior may continue to regress, with the potential of becoming an *imminent crisis.* In the situation of Jason and his busy parents, another blocked need is **belonging,** which also suggests a *developing level of crisis.*

Potential Crisis

With the desire of Holly's parents for their child to always be special, the need level is **esteem,** and there is a *potential crisis.* The situation might be strongly felt by the parent, but the seriousness is related to a blow to self-esteem.

THE TEACHER'S HELPING BEHAVIOR

With the understanding of these two correlated constructs—Maslow's levels of need and the levels of crisis—we come to the question of what responding actions the teacher or school should take. The answer is found in the continuum of human relationship (discipline) models: Relationship-Listening, Confronting-Contracting, and Rules and Consequences. Although it is not one of these "models," another point along this continuum is Coercive-Legalistic, a process through which the teacher follows prescribed procedures to implement actions required by law. The degree of power used for the teacher's intervention would escalate or de-escalate relative to the level of needs and the severity of the crisis (see Figure 15.2).

In the case of Holly's parents, with their social competitiveness, the need level is esteem, and we have a potential level of crisis. The helping techniques for the teacher are found in Relationship-Listening. The Relationship-Listening mode of *T.E.T.,* described in Chapter 8, discusses techniques that may be used with Holly's parents such as door openers, verbal encoding as active listening, "I"-messages, the Six Steps to Problem Solving, acknowledgments, conferencing, and problem ownership. Just as we may have used the Teacher Behavior Continuum (first presented in Chapter 8 as Figure 8.8) with children, we may now employ these similar techniques with the parent at needs Level 4 **esteem.** Such Relationship-Listening techniques permit us to be active in dealing with Holly's parents, but in an accepting relationship to help the parents gain some emotional control and do

Needs Level	Crisis	Model (method of responding)
Level 4 Esteem	P O E N T	Relationship-Listening
Level 3 Belonging	D E V E L I A L O	Confronting-Contracting
Level 2 Security	I M M I N E P I N G	Rules and Consequences
Level 1 Physiological	N T	Coercive-Legalistic

FIGURE 15.2 Needs, Crises, and Relationship Methods

Minimum Power

Looking	Naming	Questioning
	• Active listening ———————▶	Door Opener
	• "I"-messages	
Acknowledgments ◀—————	• Conferencing	
	Six Steps to Problem Solving	
	1. Defining	
	2. Generating	
	3. Evaluating	
	4. Deciding	
	5. Implementing	
	6. Evaluating	

FIGURE 15.3   TBC: Relationship-Listening

some problem solving to meet their needs and the teacher's needs in a cooperative, shared manner.

SCENE: Parent–Teacher Conference

PARTICIPANTS: Holly's parents and the head teacher

CRISIS LEVEL: Potential

MODEL: Relationship-Listening (see Chapter 8 for a display of the TBC methods; also see Figure 15.3)

TEACHER: "You were not pleased that Holly did not have the lead part in the school pageant." (active listening) Would you like to talk about it?" (door opener)

FATHER: "Yeah, she never gets picked for 'good' things!"

TEACHER: nods head (acknowledgment)

FATHER: "She did have a part in the last two pageants and she is a better speaker than all the other children in that class."

TEACHER: "You're not quite satisfied with the experiences that Holly is receiving at this school." (active listening)

FATHER: "Well, maybe you should learn to pick the best child for your pageants!"

MOTHER: "Holly had three paintings on display at the art show."

TEACHER: "Seeing Holly's products pleases you very much." (active listing)

FATHER: "How do we know that Holly is going to be ready for kindergarten? We taught her all her colors and letters of the alphabet, and she can count to 100!"

TEACHER: "Helping Holly with academics is very important to you." (active listening)

FATHER: "Yes, we are concerned whether she will get into medical school. It's very competitive. Can you guarantee that Holly will be reading before she leaves your classroom this year? We would be glad to help with any homework at home. And is Holly doing A, B, or C work—what grades should she be getting?"

TEACHER: "If we were to give grades (behavior) and create competition, this would violate our concepts of how your children need to be educated at this age (effect) and would make us feel guilty (feeling) for contradicting our views." ("I"-message)

"Let's see if we can identify your needs or problems and then see if we can work on these needs together. (Six Steps to Problem Solving—Step 1: Define the Problem) Which problem is most important to you?"

MOTHER: "I think my husband would like to have some help on doing activities with Holly at home that would help her learn."

FATHER: "Yes."

TEACHER: "Okay, helping Dad with activities that he can do with Holly. (define the problem) Let's try to do this together—we are studying the farm and farm animals. What ideas can we think up to supplement our unit of study?" (Step 2: Generating Possible Solutions)

FATHER: "You're studying farm animals; well, I saw in the children's section of the newspaper that there is a petting zoo at the Highland Mall."

TEACHER: "What other ideas?" (door opener)

MOTHER: "We could buy some books on farm animals for Holly."

TEACHER: "Book reading sounds good. Are there other sources of books?"

FATHER: "I might take Holly to the public library and get some animal books."

TEACHER: "Here is a school activity book for parents on good parent activities with children's literature. You may wish to borrow it for two weeks. Okay, let's see some of the solutions we have designed:

1. Check the newspaper children's section for activities.

2. Go to the petting zoo.

3. Borrow the school's activity book.

Which of these will you choose to do?" (Step 3: Evaluating Solutions)

PARENTS: (in unison) "We could do all of them!"

TEACHER: "Who will do what?"

FATHER: "My wife can take Holly to the petting zoo, I will take her to the library on Saturday morning, and we can get the book from you."

TEACHER: "Let's check back at the end of the month and see if this has all worked out." (Step 6: Reevaluation)

The teacher has used the Relationship-Listening methods with parents who are motivated by **esteem** needs. We have seen that the teacher did not "own" the problem, but first encouraged the parents to talk out any negative feelings or problems. She then defined a manageable problem and guided the parents through the Six Steps to Problem Solving process, permitting the parents to come up with their own solutions. This, of course, may possibly empower them to do that for themselves the next time. If the parents' request was not acceptable to the teacher—such as the suggestion of giving grades—the teacher responded with an "I"-message. Thus, the teacher and school were not defensive about the parents' criticism, but actually encouraged more criticism to get it all "out on the table." Once the problem was understood, the problem-solving process could begin.

In the case of Jason's parents with their busy schedules, the blocked need is **belonging** and suggests a *developing crisis*. The techniques of Confronting-Contracting described in detail in Section II would be most useful for the teacher in dealing with such a situation. These techniques place a high value on getting needs met in a social context, and give clear suggestions as to how to accomplish a positive sense of belonging (see Figure 15.4).

SCENE: Parent–Teacher Conference

PARTICIPANTS: Jason's parents and the teacher

CRISIS LEVEL: Developing

MODELS: Confronting-Contracting (see Chapters 5–7 or Chapter 9 for TBC display of methods)

Jason has been showing behaviors that indicate he is feeling more and more stress these days, and it is obvious since last month that roles at home have changed. Things are not working, and this needs to stop for Jason's benefit. (Confronting Step 1: Stop it) The teacher seeks to determine what is happening here. (Step 2: "What" questions)

MOTHER: "It is his father's responsibility to get him here in the morning."

FATHER: "Sometimes Jason is too difficult in the morning. He refuses to let me dress him, and then in all the confusion I have periodically forgotten his school papers."

TEACHER: "Things are not working for you at home, things are not working for Jason, and because Jason comes to us like a bull in a china shop, things are not working with us here at school. Things must change for all of us. We will be glad to help— we must work this out! How can we make things change?" (Step 2: What will you do to change?)

MOTHER: "This is not my problem, I leave for work at 6:30 A.M. and I can't do anything!"

Minimum Power			Maximum Power
		Command	Acting
Naming	Questioning	(directive statements)	(physical Intervention)
		1. "Stop" statements	
		2. "What" questions	
		"What did you do?"	
		"What is the rule?"	
		"What will you do to change?"	
		3. Contracting	
		Consequences ⟶	• Encouragement
		4. Isolation (relax chair)	• Logical Consequences
		Repeat 1, 2, 3, 4 (do three cycles)	• Social Engineering
		5. Notify parents	• Most Wanted

FIGURE 15.4   TBC: Confronting-Contracting

FATHER: (drops eyes and gives no response; neither parent appears willing to speak)

TEACHER: "I see that there is no willingness to work together here. We need to work this out. We can take many actions to help Jason do well when he gets here. But if he goes through home interaction that causes him to 'flood' and he comes into us out of control, we must have one teacher deal with him all morning, and our program is disrupted. We need to work this out. What are your suggestions for change?"

PARENTS: (drop eyes, with mother appearing angry and father looking helpless)

TEACHER: "Well, since there appears to be no willingness to negotiate and contract for change here, I need to tell you the logical consequences of not working together. (Step 3: Consequences) Jason will not be permitted to return to our school until we—you as mother and father and me as teacher—have an agreement." (*preparatory command* and a promise of *isolation* or *logical consequence*)

MOTHER: "Are you throwing us out of your school?"

TEACHER: "No, I am saying that we need to work this out. The school is a stable environment for Jason and he needs to be with us and we love him dearly. Things are not going well at home, and this is having a negative impact on Jason and then a negative impact on us and our school. We are willing to work with you—but we need a contract for change to occur. How will you change?" *(broken record)*

PARENTS: (no response; four minutes pass)

TEACHER: "Well, we can work this out now, or meet in the morning before school starts, giving you some time to talk this over tonight, or you can call me later in the week when you're ready to work this out and wish Jason to return." (follow through to isolation and logical consequence)

FATHER: "Well, what do you want us to do?"

TEACHER: "We, together, need to come up with ideas so that things can get worked out. I have heard one problem regarding forgetting lunches and school papers, so let me make this suggestion. We need you to remember to bring Jason's lunch, but on the rare occasions when you forget, let us take the pressure off you to need to find a lunch later that morning. We will take care of Jason's lunches on those rare mornings. We have snack food, such as fruit, cheese, bread, and milk, and we will make Jason a healthy lunch on the day that you forget. Please don't feel guilty for this. It really will be no big problem for us and it will relieve pressure from you on this one problem. Now, I think bringing lunch is just one minor problem, and there are a host of others. What are they, and how will you work this out?"

FATHER: "Well, I have just opened an auto-body painting business. I have a great deal of pressure on me to make this business work or we could go bankrupt. It opens at 6:00 A.M., when most customers drop off their cars, but your school doesn't open until 7:30, and I am not able to be there to see how things are working out at my business."

MOTHER: "Well, I have started a new job as a high school teacher on the opposite side of town, and I am not going to drop Jason off. It's much too far and dangerous for me to travel each morning through all the traffic. This is Jim's responsibility—after all, his business is just two blocks away!"

TEACHER: "Well, it seems that dropping Jason off is inconvenient for both of you. How will you solve this?"

MOTHER: (after much thought) "I know that Amy Gibson's mother and father live in our neighborhood and they wait at the bus stop each morning. I wonder if they would mind…?"

TEACHER: "I know that Mrs. Gibson is having some difficulty in meeting Amy at the end of the day when the bus arrives at 3:25 on Tuesdays and Thursdays."

MOTHER: "Well, I don't have any trouble getting home in the afternoons. Maybe I should call Mrs. Gibson about swapping … No, that is Jim's job. It is his responsibility to handle the boys in the morning. Jim, you call."

FATHER: "I really don't know the lady, and I hesitate to call. Could you arrange that, Mrs. Walker (the teacher)?"

TEACHER: "No, my job is to teach the children and to serve as a leader in this meeting."

FATHER: "Oh, all right, I'll call."

TEACHER: "Are there any other problems we should discuss?"

PARENTS: "This has really helped. If we can take care of the drop-off getting to school problem, that will take a lot of stress out of our life!"

TEACHER: "Good, then we have a contract. Jim will call Mrs. Gibson to take care of the morning drop-off problem and Jim will make an effort to have Jason off to school with his lunch. But on the rare occasion that the lunch is forgotten, the cafeteria will make him lunch here and relieve you of that concern. Do we have an agreement and a contract? (teacher reaches out and shakes both parents' hands)

PARENTS: "Yes." (they shake hands with the teacher and smile)

Notice that in the use of the Confronting-Contracting methods, the teacher and school express a willingness to bend their own procedures (making lunch on rare occasions for Jason). But they did not assume the parent's responsibilities. The locus of control for solving problems is always with the child or parent when dealing with disciplining a child, or with the parent when we are in a confronting conference. The teacher and school must be clear as to what logical consequences they have within their power, and is it wise to use this power if the parents fail to contract. This kind of meeting by its nature is confrontational and requires the use of some degree of power. The Teacher Behavior Continuum, with its escalation and deescalation of power, has been a central construct to provide an advanced organizer of teacher behavior and actions. When dealing with parents, the teacher and school must be clear as to the power given to them by law and governing authorities (including licensing authorities, departments of education, or school boards). In the example of Jason and his parents, the school had the power to refuse service (a form of isolation and logical consequences), and was willing to use it. In some public schools this option might not be available; other consequences must be clearly identified. If the school has not identified its power and the available logical consequences, or it is not willing to use that power for the betterment of the child under its care, the Confronting-Contracting methods will be toothless when used with parents and will be ineffective if the parents refuse to contract. If a developing crisis is not dealt with constructively, it will escalate into an imminent crisis, which could ultimately require the school to call on child abuse or neg-

Maximum Power

Command (directive statements)	Acting (physical intervention)	

	Modeling	Reinforcement

• Assertive Command
  1. Name
  2. Gesture
  3. Touch
  4. Eyes

• Contingency contracting
• Positive reinforcement or
  negative reinforcement
• Event recording

• Broken Record
• State Consequences
• Isolation
• Professional Team Staffing
  1. Defining
  2. Generating
  3. Evaluating
  4. Deciding
  5. Implementing
  6. Evaluating

> Write an individualized
> discipline plan

FIGURE 15.5   TBC: Rules and Consequences

lect authorities or juvenile legal authorities if the actions are extremely serious. But the *methods* of the teacher and school are to encourage the parents to work actively with the school to find solutions to their problems, with the teacher and school being a partner in the contracting. The example involving Jason's parents was resolved ideally, but more likely a great deal more time will be spent and fewer positive results will be attained in "real-life" situations with parents involved in a Level 3 developing crisis. The Jason example could have resulted in the parents getting family counseling or other social services to help them over this difficult period. Other options might include their church or relatives, depending on the type of problems faced by the parents in a Level 3 developing crisis. Some other parent difficulties that could result in a developing crisis are divorce, the father's loss of his job, or the destruction of the home by fire or other disaster.

SCENE: Parent-teacher conference

PARTICIPANTS: Brandon's parents and his teacher

CRISIS LEVEL: Developing to Imminent

METHODS: Rules and Consequences (see Chapters 2–4 or chapter 9 for TBC display of methods; see also Figure 15.5)

In the case of Brandon, with his aggressive behavior and the family's marital difficulties, the need is Level 2 **Security** and the level of crisis can be considered as *developing to imminent*. The teacher in this instance may choose techniques from the Rules and Consequences

Methods and Coercive-Legalistic approach. This means that in dealing with Brandon's parents, the teacher would first specify actions to be carried out by the parents. If they carry out these actions, every effort will be made by the teacher to be positively reinforcing; if they do not, then negative actions—including moving to Coercive-Legalistic—might be necessary. The Coercive-Legalistic option for the teacher and school might include using a social service agency to provide family counseling or turning the case over to child abuse or neglect authorities (see Figure 15.5).

TEACHER: (Makes eye contact with parents, gestures, touches, and uses names) "Carol and Michael, I want you to obtain the services of a child and family counselor, for Brandon's sake, to help you as a family and Brandon individually to handle the problems related to your home difficulties." *(assertive command)*

FATHER: "We are sorry about failing to pick up Brandon last Friday. It won't happen again."

TEACHER: "We care for Brandon, and we are an intimate and central part of his life at school. Brandon is suffering emotionally and socially at this time, and he and you need professional help. I want you to obtain the services of a child and family counselor, for Brandon's sake, to help you as a family and Brandon individually to handle the problems related to your home difficulties." *(broken record)*

FATHER: "I can't afford that. We won't forget to pick him up again. I don't want any counselor."

TEACHER: "We have a commitment to Brandon and you, and we wish to work with both of you during this difficult time for you and especially for Brandon. I want you to obtain the services of a child and family counselor, for Brandon's sake, to help you as a family and Brandon individually to handle the difficulties related to your marital situation. *(broken record)* We have a list of private counselors or publicly available ones if you cannot afford the cost. We would like to meet, as a team, with you, a counselor of your choice, and our staff and do some solid problem solving to set up guidelines for us here at the school and you at home so that we may best help Brandon."

FATHER: "No way. This is none of your business."

TEACHER: "We have a commitment to Brandon and you, and we wish to work with both of you during this difficult time for you and especially for Brandon. I want you to obtain the services of a child and family counselor, for Brandon's sake, to help you as a family and Brandon individually to handle the difficulties related to your marital situation." *(broken record)*

FATHER: "No way! I am going to remove him from this school."

MOTHER: "Where will he go, Michael?"

TEACHER: "If you remove him from our school, or will not work with us to change things for Brandon, then your past actions would suggest the possibility of child neglect, and I will be ethically obligated to report this to the child abuse and neglect authorities."

FATHER: "What child abuse and neglect?" (See Figure 15.6.)

TEACHER: (opens a folder containing a written anecdotal record and event recordings on Brandon and his parents collected over the past two months) "Our data collected over the last two months would suggest neglect for the following reasons:

	Physical Indicators	**Behavioral Indicators**
Physical Abuse	Unexplained bruises and welts: • on face, lips, mouth • on torso, back, buttocks, thighs • in various stages of healing • reflecting shape of articles used to inflict injury (extension cord, belt buckle, etc.) • on several different surfaces areas • regularly appear after absence, weekend, or vacation Unexplained burns: • cigar, cigarette burns, especially on soles, palms, back, or buttocks • immersion burns (sock-like, glove-like, doughnut shaped on buttocks or genitalia) • patterned like electric burner, iron, etc., rope burns on arms, legs, neck, or torso Unexplained lacerations or abrasions • to mouth, lips, gums, eyes, external genitalia	Wary of adult contacts Apprehensive when other children cry Behavioral extremes: • aggressiveness • withdrawal Frightened of parents Afraid to go home Reports injury by parents
Physical Neglect	Consistent hunger, poor hygiene, inappropriate dress Consistent lack of supervision, especially in dangerous activities Unattended physical problems or medical problems Abandonment	Begging, stealing food Extended stays at school (early arrival and late departure) Constant fatigue, listlessness, or falling asleep in class Alcohol or drug abuse Delinquency (e.g., thefts) States there is no caretaker
Sexual Abuse	Difficulty in walking/sitting Consistent touching of genitals Torn, shredded, or bloody underclothing Bruises or bleeding in external genitalia, vaginal, or anal areas Venereal diseases, especially in preteens Genital warts Pregnancy	Unwilling to change for gym or participate in physical education classes Withdrawal, fantasy, or infantile behavior Bizarre, sophisticated, or unusual sexual behavior or knowledge Poor peer relationships Delinquency or runaway Reports sexual assault by caretaker

(continues)

FIGURE 15.6 Physical and Behavioral Indicators of Child Abuse and Neglect (Children are normally defined as persons under 18 years of age)

	Physical Indicators	**Behavioral Indicators**
Emotional Maltreatment	Speech disorders Lags in physical development Failure to thrive	Habit disorders (sucking, biting, rocking, etc.) Conduct disorders (antisocial, destructive, etc.) Neurotic traits (sleep disorders, inhibition of play) Psychoneurotic reactions (hysteria, obsession, compulsion, phobias) Behavior extremes: compliant, passive; aggressive, demanding Overly adaptive behavior: inappropriate adult or infant Developmental lags (mental, emotional) Attempted suicide

FIGURE 15.6 *(continued)*

1. There were six occasions when Brandon wore the same soiled clothing for a period of over five days.
2. On 15 occasions Brandon's lunch contained a coke and two slices of bread. His ferocious appetite suggests he is not being properly fed.
3. There was the complete failure to pick him up or be at home last Friday.
4. Brandon has reported nine occasions when no one was at home with him for long periods of time.
5. Our recording shows that Brandon has been physically aggressive 30 to 35 times per day over the last three weeks.

Please, be assured that I find it difficult to say these things to you. We have a commitment to Brandon and you, and we wish to work with both of you during this difficult time for you and especially for Brandon. I want you to obtain the services of a child and family counselor, for Brandon's sake, to help you as a family and Brandon individually to handle the difficulties related to your marital situation." *(broken record)*

MOTHER: "Michael, this school has been so good to Brandon. He likes it here."

FATHER: "It's Carol's job to give him a bath and make his lunch. (silence) You mean that Brandon is doing all those things?"

TEACHER: "Yes, Brandon is having a very difficult time right now."

FATHER: "You mean we wouldn't have to pay for a counselor? What would he do?"

TEACHER: "I can give you a list of publicly supported social service counselors, and you would call and meet with him or her. We would have a team meeting with you, Carol, and our staff to set up a program (IESP) for you working at home and us here at school. (The teacher defines a *behavioral objective* for the parents.) Michael *(identify the person),* you will use my phone to call now and set an appointment to meet with a counselor *(identify the target behavior)* within the next 24 hours *(identify the conditions).* I will call the counselor two days from now to see if you have made your appointment *(identify the conditions).* If you have made your appointment with the counselor, I will take no actions to call in outside authorities *(negative reinforcement).* If you fail to make and attend the appointment, I will call the authorities" *(punishment).* (This may also be considered contingency contracting.)

In viewing the interaction of the teacher using the Rules and Consequences Methods, one might consider her insensitive, cold, and unforgiving in dealing with these parents. But we must realize that past actions by the parents have placed Brandon in a psychologically damaging situation; the teacher or school is one of the few people and organization who sees this occurring, and they would have a moral obligation to take actions to safeguard this child's rights and well-being.

While using the Rules and Consequences Methods, we do not do *listening* to the parents, nor are we *contracting.* Instead, based on the serious nature of the previous actions, we take a position concerned with the immediate actions we want the parents to take to help Brandon, and then go about assertively taking actions toward the parents to obtain compliance. If cooperation does not come in the form of behavioral change by the parents, we would not hesitate to escalate to the next level of Coercive-Legalistic and call social service abuse and neglect authorities. We have a Developing to Imminent Crisis situation that calls for immediate action.

CAROL'S PARENT AND BOYFRIEND

NEED: LEVEL 2: PHYSIOLOGICAL

CRISIS: Imminent

METHODS: COERCIVE-LEGALISTIC

How to Report Suspected Abuse or Neglect

The Law A report must be made to the state child protection service. Most states require anyone who knows of or has reasonable cause to suspect child abuse or neglect to report that abuse or neglect. Any person failing to report, knowingly preventing another from doing so, or making a false report generally is guilty of a criminal offense and may be prosecuted. Normally, state laws specifically mention the requirement of the school teacher or other school officials to make reports. Many state laws protect those teachers reporting child abuse in two ways: immunity from liability, and confidentiality. Anyone making a report "in good faith" is specifically immune from any civil or criminal charges that might result. The name of the person making the report will not be released to anyone other than the protective investigating agency or prosecutors without written consent of the person reporting. The reporting individual is not required to give his or her name, although all persons are encouraged to do so to facilitate the investigation (based on one state—Florida).

Though child protection service systems vary from state to state, normally there is a toll-free abuse registry line operating 24 hours per day. Reports should include the following:

- Names and addresses of child, parent(s), guardian(s) or other persons responsible for the child's welfare.

- Child's age, race, sex, and sibling's name(s).

- Nature and extent of alleged abuse or neglect.

- Identity of abuser, if known.

- Reporting person's name, address, and telephone number if desired (normally this is not required).

- Direction to the child's location at the time of the report.

In the case of Carol, the injured student, the need level is **physiological** and the crisis is *imminent*. This life- and psychologically threatening situation calls for very powerful intervention, which we call Coercive-Legalistic. When time is of utmost importance, the teacher's goal is to get immediate help and legal protection for the child. It is no longer necessary—and perhaps not even advisable—to discuss the situation further with Carol's mother. In most serious cases where sexual abuse is suspected, the steps required of the teacher are clearly set by law. The teacher would be ethically bound, and possibly legally bound, to take coercive action for the student's welfare. To clarify, Coercive-Legalistic is not a method, but is instead a process through which the teacher uses assertive techniques to carry out actions required by law. In its simplest form, the teacher calls child abuse authorities and turns over all records of data gathered to support the charge.

SUMMARY

What is suggested is that the teacher, possibly with school officials, as a problem solver dealing with parent–child situations, can reexamine his or her own "personal wisdom response" in the broader perspective of the constructs described here. For our discussion, direct parallels were made between *situations, needs, and methods; in reality this division presented here might be less clear-cut, and actions would have to be adjusted accordingly, with the teacher making a professional judgment as to their seriousness.*

SUMMARY OF KEY CONCEPTS

belonging	esteem	needs	security
crisis	methods	physiological	

NOTES

1. A. H. Maslow, *Toward a Psychology of Being,* 2nd. ed. (New York: D. Van Nostrand, 1968).

2. T. McMurrian, *Intervention in Human Crisis* (Atlanta: Humanitis Press, 1975).

CLASSROOM DISCIPLINE SITUATIONS

The following situations can be used to consider the applications of the models, techniques, or an eclectically designed discipline model to deal with each of these discipline problems. Consider how you would set limits, possibly using a backup system, an encouragement system, or incentives. What classroom management activity could you have used beforehand to prevent this from happening, or what could you do now by preplanning to prevent this from occurring again?

VIGNETTE 1

A student who had been retained was much larger than his fellow classmates. He was domineering, bullied other children, and hurt them. He developed behaviors of yelling out and threatening others with scissors. He had wild tantrums, throwing chairs and other objects. Most of his peers were quite afraid of him.

VIGNETTE 2

Mario is an extremely active boy who loves to be the center of attention. He always has to be in charge and choose the game to be played. He yells out answers before others have time to reflect on the question, and even when he was in time out he would yell across the room and dominate the learning time. When given some free time to move about, he annoyed others, cut one child's hair, poured glue on another's papers, and colored with Magic Markers on his own body. He was constantly in motion, seeming to enjoy both negative and positive forms of attention.

VIGNETTE 3

This young child came from a large family where everyone used each other's things and there wasn't any ownership even of such personal items as clothing. In the classroom, this student would just take an item belonging to someone else when he needed something: money, desk items, clothing, and so on.

VIGNETTE 4

Twin five-year-old boys who were constantly in motion would not follow rules. They refused to sit in a group and would run from adults who tried to work one-on-one with them. They loved to see if they could get an adult to chase them, jumping on tables, running out of the classroom, climbing on top of shelves, and so on. Trying to engage them in learning activities was only successful if it was an activity that they wanted to do. Their parents were supportive of the teacher; however, they were at a loss as to what to do.

VIGNETTE 5

A six-year-old boy whose mother had been a drug addict (crack) had to eat every two hours and always wore his outdoor coat even in very hot weather. He avoided touch and would run from anyone who tried to touch him. His learning abilities were difficult to establish due to his constant movement and his aversion to touching items such as pencils, markers, or paper.

VIGNETTE 6

Craig is a small, stocky boy with excellent intellectual and athletic abilities. He sees himself as a "man's man" and when injured in sliding to home plate during a softball game, he showed no emotion. He finds women teachers "inhibiting" and "controlling," while he blushes and becomes obviously nervous when required to work with female class members. There is no report of him disrupting any of his male teachers' classes, but his two female teachers find him very annoying and disruptive. He is seated at the first desk at the side of the classroom, and just as the teachers are attempting to make a final point in a lecture, he shouts out a comment that causes the class to laugh loudly and destroys the point of the lesson. The female teachers feel "snipered" day in and day out by his ability to verbally disrupt their lessons. He is well liked by fellow students, and the comments he makes are actually quite funny and insightful, but done at the wrong time in the judgment of the female teachers.

VIGNETTE 7

Juan is the son of a school board member who was motivated to run for a school board office because of Juan's older sister's difficulties in school. He is an overweight, nonathletic child who plays mostly with the girls on the playground. He constantly responds to all of the teacher's requests with "I can't!" or "I don't understand!" and does nothing. When the teacher insists that he participate in certain activities, he says, "My father told me that I don't have to do that!"

VIGNETTE 8

It is the third week of school, and the fourth-grade teacher is giving the first major test. During the test we see Jason not working and holding his stomach. When the teacher asks him what is wrong, he bends over "as if in severe pain" and says that his stomach aches—this is so dramatic that the teacher suspects the possibility of appendicitis. The teacher immediately telephones the student's mother at work and reports the incident. The mother responds in an angry tone to the teacher, instructing her not to call like this again. The mother states that the teacher should have been made aware by Jason's teacher from last year that he always does this during a test and that she should ignore it. Jason's teacher is still concerned that he may be having some major physical difficulty. The school principal is not in the school this day, and the school nurse is visiting another school that day and cannot be contacted.

VIGNETTE 9

This high school teacher lives in the school community and drives a small economy-size European car. A group of strong boys can literally pick up his car, and over the last three weeks they have picked it up outside his house and placed it in various locations, making it nearly impossible to drive out of the spot without help from others. Today, when he departs from school he discovers that someone has blown up a condom into a three-foot balloon and has tied it to the radio antenna. Two of the girls in the second-period class who did not find this incident amusing told him the names of the six boys who are responsible for the pranks.

VIGNETTE 10

During second-period class a sheet of paper is sent to each teacher listing all students who are absent that day. As soon as this paper arrives, five boys push to the teacher desk to get a hold of this paper and begin to count the number of students absent. After three or four incidents such as this, the teacher figures that many of the students in the school have started a gambling pool—someone is "bookmaking." They pay a dollar to one student and get to pick a number. If their number is the same as the number of students absent, they get the entire pool of money. Since no one has "hit the pool" for a while, the total amount is now over $600. Mr. Bailey is the only homeroom teacher who is aware of the pool.

VIGNETTE 11

Robb is the star football player and on the high school team that is in the final playoff game for the championship. There are strict school rules that anyone participating in extracurricular activities must pass all courses and make a grade standard in all required classes. Robb has handed in a paper for the final requirement in English class. This paper will determine whether he will pass or fail the course because of his poor grades on tests and other projects. The topic and writing seem especially well done and far beyond any previous writing that Robb has produced. At the end of the reference section of the paper was an Internet site address in small and nearly undetectable size lettering. When Mr. Markowitz brings up this sight, he discovers it is a "paper mill" that sells term papers to students and the title of Robb's paper is one that is listed as available. When questioned about this paper, Robb admits that he purchased it over the Internet.

VIGNETTE 12

Because of high-profile school shootings in another school within this rural state, the school board has passed a rule that if any student brings a weapon to school, he or she will be permanently expelled. A sign regarding weapons is posted at the entrance to all schools in the county and the regulation is printed in the student handbook and as well as being covered in the local newspaper. Most of the income in this county is dependent on the fishing and hunting industry, and most pickup trucks have a gun rack in their window, which normally holds a gun during deer hunting season. Today, in clear view of everyone, there is a red pickup truck in the student parking lot at the high school with a high-powered deer rifle on the gun rack in the back window. When the student is questioned about bringing a gun to school, he first denies it and appears surprised when shown the truck. He states that his car would not start that morning and that he drove his father's truck to school. He says he was totally unaware of the gun because it was quite dark in the morning. This student is well behaved and in the National Honor Society, making nearly straight A's with the likelihood that he will receive a scholarship to attend a prestigious university. The rule is, "bring a gun to school and you're suspended—zero tolerance!"

VIGNETTE 13

Jennifer is a well-liked B student who has just broken up with her boyfriend three days before the prom, for which her parents the previous weekend had purchased her an expensive dress. She now doesn't have a date to the prom and is passive and expressionless in class. Her teacher sees her change of behavior and, unaware of her problem, tries to joke and tease her gently as she has done on previous occasions. In front of the entire class, Jane looks straight at the teacher in a hostile, defiant manner and states, "Shut up b—ch!"

VIGNETTE 14

Angelo is discovered in the boy's room spray painting gang signals and names on the walls. When questioned about this he said he had to do it as a part of a gang initiation. Angelo is also wearing the gang clothing or uniform. During the last month a number of boys have appeared in class in such clothing, and other students have expressed a fear of this gang and for their safety.

GLOSSARY

Academic (Glasser). In-depth discussion of the topic involved in school subjects.

Acknowledgments (Gordon's T.E.T.). A modality of behavior, such as making eye contact or nodding one's head, to indicate that the teacher is listening and understanding when the student is talking.

Action dimension (Dignity). Actions, such as creating a social contract related to rules, that can be done to prevent potential or future misbehavior.

Active listening (Gordon's T.E.T.). The process of "mirroring" back to a student his emotional feelings and the problem being expressed, to the extent the teacher can understand it.

Adequate notice (Judicious Discipline). Students need to be informed or warned about a rule before they can be punished for breaking it.

Adrenaline "bleed" (Jones's Positive Discipline). A condition in which the teacher is tense, thus producing a slow release of nervous adrenaline into the teacher's bloodstream.

Adrenaline dump (Jones's Positive Discipline). Sudden incident that fills the teacher's body with adrenaline, producing a nervous condition.

Anecdotal reports (Behavior Analysis). Written summary of classroom incidents.

Antecedent condition (Behavior Analysis). Conditions preceding a behavior.

Assertiveness (Assertive Discipline). Being able to express one's wants and needs and to take actions to increase the likelihood of getting what is wanted.

Attention getting (Dreikurs/Adlerian). One of the goals students want when they are misbehaving—the teacher feels annoyed.

Aversive stimulus (Behavior Analysis). Harsh action that insults the senses.

Back talk (Jones's Positive Discipline). Any verbal response to the teacher to attempt to evade a teacher command.

Baseline data (Behavior Analysis). First step in data measurement preceding intervention.

Behavior (Behavior Analysis). Observable acts.

Behavioral objective (Behavior Analysis). Statement that identifies the learner, conditions, target behavior, and acceptable performance.

Bloom's Questioning Taxonomy (Love and Logic). A construct for looking at teacher questions, which suggests that as one moves up the list the student needs to do higher level thinking to answer the question.

Body telegraphing (Jones's Positive Discipline). Nonverbal actions that signal or prompt the student of our wanted actions.

Broken record (Assertive Discipline). A command that is repeated over and over until the student complies.

Camouflage (Jones's Positive Discipline). Giving a command to an off-task student in such a manner that other students are not aware that this occurred.

Camping out (Jones's Positive Discipline). Staying in close proximity to a student for whatever period of time it takes to get the student's compliance.

Check-it-out (Jones's Positive Discipline). When focusing on one student, periodic breaks whereby the teacher stops and scans the room for off-task behavior.

Class meeting (Glasser). Bringing a group of students together for discussions.

Classroom plan (Assertive Discipline). A teacher-designed action plan of what to do if students break the rules.

Closing space (Jones's Positive Discipline). Physically moving slowly toward a student while maintaining eye contact.

Comfort bubble (Jones's Positive Discipline). The three-foot circle around a student that is his private space; when others intrude into this area, the student becomes uncomfortable.

Commands (Assertive Discipline). Tell a student what actions you want through eye contact, naming the student, gesturing, and touching when appropriate.

Compelling state interest (Judicious Discipline). Individual rights may be taken away if there is a justification of state interest, such as safety or health needs.

Comprehensive social contract (Dignity). A social contract that is made with the student, parents, administrators involved, and the teacher.

Conditioned reinforcer (Behavior Analysis). A stimuli that through learned association produces a behavior.

Consequences (Glasser). Actions that may be required of a student if he breaks a contract.

Contingency (Behavior Analysis). A prerequisite behavior needed in order to obtain a desired action.

Convergent questions (Love and Logic). The second level of questioning in Bloom's taxonomy that requires the student to describe cause and effect.

Daily student rating card (Dignity). A feedback process of scoring or checking on a student action at home that can be monitored by the parent and teacher.

Defending Property or Territory (Crisis Prevention). A concern for material objects of real or imagined value will occasionally cause people to sacrifice their safety or even their lives in a conflict situation.

Demands (Assertive Discipline). A clear statement of the student actions wanted.

Deprivation state (Behavior Analysis). A lack of basic need.

Differential reinforcement (Behavior Analysis). Reinforcing a desired behavior different from the unwanted behavior the student is currently performing.

Divergent questions (Love and Logic). The third level of questioning in Bloom's taxonomy that requires the student to creatively go beyond the facts given to answer the question.

Door openers (Gordon's T.E.T.). When a student is having difficulty expressing something that is troubling him, the teacher uses a question as an "I"-message. This technique expresses to a student that a behavior is having a negative effect on the teacher. This statement must contain three elements: the student's <u>behavior</u>, its <u>effect,</u> and the teacher's <u>feeling</u> as a result of the behavior.

Due process (Judicious Discipline). Step to be taken to permit a student to present his side of the story when accused of misbehavior.

Duration recording (Behavior Analysis). Measuring the time between when the student begins the behavior until completion.

Encouragement (Dreikurs/Adlerian). A statement to the student that enables him to reflect on how he is being successful.

Evaluative Questions (Love and Logic). The fourth and highest level of questioning in Bloom's taxonomy that requires the student make an evaluative answer between potentially conflicting facts.

Event recording (Behavior Analysis). Counting or measuring a behavior each time it occurs during a predetermined time period.

Exclusionary time out (Behavior Analysis). Withholding reinforcement of a behavior by removing the student from the activity.

Extinction (Behavior Analysis). Withholding reinforcement of a behavior that was unknowingly previously receiving reinforcement.

Eye contact (Jones's Positive Discipline). Unbroken eye contact with a student.

Facts questions (Love and Logic). The first and lowest level of questioning in Bloom's taxonomy that requires the student to give names or labels as an answer.

Failure (Glasser). All attempts should be made so that the student will not experience failure in the classroom, especially as it is related to the use of grades.

Fairness (Love and Logic). The concept that often-identical treatment as a consequence to misbehavior is not always fair.

Fear of authority (Judicious Discipline). The developmental moral position of the young child for obeying.

Fear—fight or flight (Crisis Prevention). The emotional physiological response of fear can be great enough to impair rational thought with the person fleeing (flight) or fighting.

Feelings and understanding of social responsibility (Judicious Discipline). The more mature stage in moral development whereby the student obeys rules for the good of society as a whole.

Fight or flight (Jones's Positive Discipline). When in conflict, our nervous animal response is to run (flight) or fight.

Fighting words versus thinking words. (Love and Logic). When commands are used, fighting words are not advisable because students can refuse our request, but questions, as thinking words, give students choices and power to respond in a manner comfortable for them.

Fixed-interval schedule (Behavior Analysis). Awarding a reinforcer dependent on the occurrence of a behavior based on a specific interval.

Fixed-ratio schedule (Behavior Analysis). A schedule of rewarding a reinforcer based on a predetermined number of times the behavior needs to occur.

Fredisms (Jones's Positive Discipline). Specially coined words by the author to characterize behavior used in the Fred Jones model (see "high roller").

Frequency (Behavior Analysis). Number of times a behavior occurs during a fixed period of time.

Functional relationship (Behavior Analysis). A cause-and-effect relationship.

Going brain stemmed (Jones's Positive Discipline). An emotional automatic unthinking physical response to a misbehaving student, which is usually ineffective.

Gone chemical (Jones's Positive Discipline). Becoming so emotional that the teacher is no longer thinking and rational.

Group alerting (Kounin). Prompts to give to students to get them back on task.

Hard response (Peer Mediation). This occurs when one individual applies pressure to win a contest of will.

Helplessness. One of the goals students have when they are misbehaving. The teacher feels inadequate to help.

Heterogeneous grouping (Glasser). A classroom of students with various abilities and backgrounds, versus one where people are grouped by teachers based on one characteristic (i.e., IQ).

Hidden motivations (Dreikurs/Adlerian). One of the four mistaken goals of a misbehaving student.

High roller (Jones's Positive Discipline). Those one or two students who attempt to break the rules to see if they can get away with it (a "Fredism").

Hints (Assertive Discipline). Verbal prompts that signal the class that they are off-task.

Identity (Glasser). Feeling of worthiness and belonging.

In loco parentis **(Judicious Discipline).** School officials and teacher were given the same rights as parents to monitor and discipline students.

Incentive system (Jones' Positive Discipline). A reward for performing wanted actions.

Individual rights (Judicious Discipline). The individual has rights that cannot be taken away by the majority.

Insubordination rule (Dignity). Actions by the student so serious that administrators and others need to become involved.

Intense counseling (Glasser). One-to-one discussions and problem solving with the student.

Interval recording (Behavior Analysis). A period of time.

Involvement (Glasser). Students must find a place for themselves in the classroom and the curriculum.

I-statements (Dignity). A statement by the teacher to compliment the student, which contains three parts: student positive behavior, the teacher's feelings, and reasons.

Judicious consequence (Judicious Discipline). Rules and misbehavior based on the U.S. Bill of Rights.

Latency recording (Behavior Analysis). Measurement of time between when the stimuli is applied and the student acts.

Liberty (Judicious Discipline). Freedom.

Limit-setting system (Jones's Positive Discipline). Getting a student to desist off-task behavior and return to work.

Logical consequences (Dreikurs/Adlerian). A sanction required of the student who has broken a social contract. Requires the student to make things right again and is cognitively connected to misbehavior.

Lose-lose (Peer Mediation). This occurs when both disputants in a conflict do not get their needs met.

Low roller (Jones' Positive Discipline). A student who will stop off-task behavior after minimum prompting.

"Magic" people (Love and Logic). People whom the student loves and will do anything to please them.

Magic words and phrases (Love and Logic). Questions that give the students power and choices.

Mediation (Dignity). When teacher and student are in such a conflict that an administrator or another person comes in to mediate the situation.

Mental rehearsal (Assertive Discipline). In a private, quiet area, the teacher mentally thinks through an example of misbehavior and then "sees" herself taking action with her discipline plan.

Modality cueing (Gordon's T.E.T.). The first, minimum power level on the Teacher Behavior Continuum, through which the teacher—using the modalities of sight, touch, or sound—signals students to become aware of their actions.

Modeling (Behavior Analysis). Showing actions that one wishes the student to imitate.

Momentum (Kounin). Getting class started on time and maintaining a rhythm without break or stoppage in the lesson.

Moral growth (Judicious Discipline). A child's concepts of right and wrong go through developmental stages.

Natural consequences (Dreikurs/Adlerian). Everyday happenings that teachers use, because of negative consequences, as examples of unacceptable behavior (i.e., touching a hot stove).

Negative practice (Behavior Analysis). Exaggerated required behavior of students that will fatigue them and cause them to not want to repeat the behavior.

Negative reinforcement (Behavior Analysis). Contingency removal of aversive stimuli.

Neocortex (Jones's Positive Discipline). The thinking part of the brain.

Nonjudgmental view (Glasser). Using no guilt or value judgments regarding students or their actions.

Nonseclusionary time out (Behavior Analysis). The student is not permitted to participate in the activity, but is not removed.

Open-ended (Glasser). Any topics may be discussed.

Overcorrecting (Behavior Analysis). To eliminate an inappropriate behavior, the student is required to perform the desired action over and over until it becomes habitual.

Overlapping (Behavior Analysis). Being able to deal with one student while being aware what other students are doing at the same time.

Pairing (Behavior Analysis). Simultaneously presenting primary reinforcer (eatable treat) and secondary reinforcer (sound of a whistle) to condition the secondary one.

Paleocortex (Jones's Positive Discipline). The reflexive part of the brain—at times called the "horsey-doggy brain."

Palms (Jones's Positive Discipline). Placing your hand on a student's desk to show that you will not depart until you get him back on task.

Park the body (Jones's Positive Discipline). Placing the body in the classroom so that your back is not to the students and you can see what is occurring.

Part of the loaf (Jones's Positive Discipline). A student who gives only partial compliance actions that the teacher wants.

Pencil posturing (Jones's Positive Discipline). Pretending to work as if you are writing with a pencil.

Permanent product recording (Behavior Analysis). Scoring or measuring the concrete results of a student's actions (i.e., academic work).

Ph.D. in the teacher game (Jones's Positive Discipline). A Fredism meaning that the students are wise to the ways of teacher behavior and how to "push her buttons."

Pheasant posturing (Jones's Positive Discipline). When a teacher loses control and acts threatening toward a student in such a manner that the student knows there will be no carry through.

Pinpointing (Behavior Analysis). A targeted behavior for change.

Positive reinforcement (Behavior Analysis). A stimuli following an event that causes this event to occur again or speed up.

Power and control (Dreikurs/Adlerian). One of the goals students have when they are misbehaving. The teacher feels beaten.

Prevention dimension (Dignity). All the actions that a teacher can take beforehand to prevent misunderstanding and discipline problems.

Primary reinforcer (Behavior Analysis). A stimulus connected to a biological need.

Principled response (Peer Mediation). This occurs when communication between disputants is established, and with each person's needs being met.

Prompt (Behavior Analysis). A stimulus that will most likely bring a desired behavior.

Prompt (Jones's Positive Discipline). Signals a students that you want behavior changes on their part.

Proximity (Jones's Positive Discipline). The physical distance between teacher and student.

Pseudocompliance (Jones's Positive Discipline). The student pretends to be on-task when he is attempting to fool the teacher.

Punishment (Behavior Analysis). A consequence following a behavior that decreases the likelihood of the behavior's occurring again.

Reality therapy (Glasser). A form of counseling with students based on the realities of their behavior rather than psychoanalyzing them.

Recognition reflex (Dreikurs/Adlerian). When misbehaving students are confronted with questions about their hidden goals, they respond with a smile or some action that shows that we are correct about our assumptions.

Reinforcer (Behavior Analysis). A stimulus that increases or maintains the possibility of the behavior's occurring again or speeding up.

Relaxing breaths (Jones's Positive Discipline). When becoming nervous, the teacher stops to take three slow, controlled breaths to calm herself before acting.

Relevance (Glasser). Curriculum should be connected to the students' everyday lives.

Reptilian brain (Jones's Positive Discipline). The reflexive brain that works automatically when frightened.

Resolutions dimension (Dignity). The actions that the teacher can take with or toward an "out-of-control" or chronic rule-breaking student.

Response-cost (Behavior Analysis). Reducing the amount of a pleasurable stimulus each time an unwanted behavior occurs.

Responsibility (Glasser). In confronting students, the teacher challenges them to commit themselves to new ways of behaving.

Responsibility training (Jones's Positive Discipline). Teaches students behavior that is wanted in the classroom.

Revenge (Dreikurs/Adlerian). One of the goals students have when they are misbehaving. The teacher feels hurt.

Rewards (Assertive Discipline). Treasured activities or treats that students will get for good behavior.

Satiation (Behavior Analysis). A state whereby the student's basic need has been fully satisfied.

Saving Face (Crisis Prevention). People, including students, will commonly risk their personal well being to maintain their dignity in a fight situation.

Schedules of reinforcement (Behavior Analysis). A pattern of time to award a reinforcer.

Seclusionary time out (Behavior Analysis). Removal of the student from the educational situation.

Secondary reinforcers (Behavior Analysis). Stimuli that were first neutral but have been conditioned to become reinforcers.

Shaping (Behavior Analysis). Teaching new behavior by reinforcers, gradually approximating the target behavior.

Show time (Jones's Positive Discipline). When a teacher loses self-control and the students are amused by her behavior.

Signed statements (Glasser). Contracts and agreements between teacher and student that both people sign as a signal of agreement and commitment.

Silly talk (Jones's Positive Discipline). A teacher's language when she has lost control and begins to threaten or berate students.

Six steps to problem solving (Gordon's T.E.T.). A structure or "recipe" for carrying out a problem-solving conference between the teacher and student or group of students. The steps are: (1) define the problem, (2) generate possible solutions, (3) evaluate, (4) decide, (5) implement, and (6) reevaluate later.

Slack jaw (Jones's Positive Discipline). Washing out the teacher's facial expression while in confrontation with a student by keeping the lips closed and opening the mouth.

Smiley face (Jones's Positive Discipline). When a student wants to be appealing to the teacher to get her to move away, he gives her a "heartwarming" smile.

Smoothness (Kounin). Moving from one part of a lesson to another without breaks and bridging the lessons so that they are understood to be related.

Social contract (Dignity). The rules and consequences established at the start of a new class through a class meeting involving the teacher and students.

Social reinforcers (Behavior Analysis). A secondary reinforcer that has been conditioned to some form of human interaction.

Soft response (Peer Mediation). The response when people attempt to avoid conflict by withdrawing from the situation, by ignoring the problem, or by denying that a conflict exists.

Squaring off (Jones's Positive Discipline). Facing the student shoulder to shoulder and face to face.

Structure (Jones's Positive Discipline). The preplanning task done in the room to create routines and rules so that the desired behavior would most likely occur.

Student/educator relationship (Judicious Discipline). The relationship during discipline situations should be one of "what can be learned here?"

Substantive due process (Judicious Discipline). Legal representation may be permitted when dealing with a major discipline situation in which the student may be losing his right to attend school.

Systems approach versus principled approach (Love and Logic). The rejection of prescribed discipline models, such as the rules and consequences models, that give the teacher no or little choice in responding, in contrast to the teacher's responding to the student based on principles.

Target behavior (Behavior Analysis). Behavior that is the desired end of a shaping or reinforcement process.

Testing the Pecking Order (Crisis Prevention). One person may become jealous over the status of another and respond by picking a fight or generally looking for trouble.

Teachable moment (Judicious Discipline). Discipline incidents are good times for teaching problem solving and judicial understanding.

Teacher enthusiasm (Kounin). Positive energy expressed by the teacher during a lesson.

Teacher rights (Assertive Discipline). Teachers are free to choose what conditions they want and need to be able to teach.

Thinking versus memorization (Glasser). All curriculum should require real thinking by the student rather than memorizing isolated facts.

Thinning (Behavior Analysis). Making the stimulus or reinforcer occur less often while the behavior continues.

Three-step lesson (Jones's Positive Discipline). A process for teaching rules that involves (1) say, (2) show, and (3) check.

Tight circle (Glasser). Moving chairs together in a circle for a class meeting.

Time out (Behavior Analysis). Reducing undesirable behavior by removing the student spatially to a location where he is denied reinforcement.

Triune brain (Jones's Positive Discipline). The concept of the three parts of the brain: neocortex, paleocortex, and reptilian brain.

Tyranny of fairness (Judicious Discipline). Justification often given for denying someone a need based on fairness to others ("If I give this to you, I must give it to everyone").

Unconditioned aversive stimulus (Behavior Analysis). Stimulus that results in a physical pain or discomfort to a student.

Uniform standards (Assertive Discipline). Rules and follow-up actions should be the same for all students.

Variable-interval schedule (Behavior Analysis). Random awarding of the time given for a reinforcer based on a specific time period.

Variety (Kounin). Changing the delivery mode of the lecture or learning activity to keep the interest of the students.

Verbal encoding (Gordon's T.E.T.). Labeling the student's emotions and feelings, both positive and negative, though the use of the teacher's words.

Who-squad (Assertive Discipline). A team of school staff that arrives to physically remove the student from the classroom.

Win-lose (Peer Mediation). This occurs when in dispute where one individual wins out over another.

Win-win (Peer Mediation). This occurs when both disputants get their needs met through mediation.

With-it-ness (Kounin). Being aware at all times of what is going on in all parts of the classroom ("eyes in the back of the head").

Working the crowd (Jones's positive Discipline). Teacher moves about the classroom instead of being seated.

INDEX